NATURE AND MIND

NATURE AND MIND

SELECTED ESSAYS OF

FREDERICK J. E. WOODBRIDGE

PRESENTED TO HIM ON THE OCCASION
OF HIS SEVENTIETH BIRTHDAY
BY
AMHERST COLLEGE
THE UNIVERSITY OF MINNESOTA
COLUMBIA UNIVERSITY

WITH A BIBLIOGRAPHY
OF HIS WRITINGS

NEW YORK / RUSSELL & RUSSELL
1965

REISSUED, 1966, BY RUSSELL & RUSSELL
BY ARRANGEMENT WITH COLUMBIA UNIVERSITY PRESS
L.C. CATALOG CARD NO: 65—18839
PRINTED IN THE UNITED STATES OF AMERICA

FOREWORD

FREDERICK J. E. WOODBRIDGE was graduated from Amherst College in 1889. He taught in the University of Minnesota from 1894 to 1902 when he entered upon his teaching at Columbia University. These three institutions are celebrating the seventieth birthday of their son and intellectual leader by publishing and presenting to him this collection of his essays.

These essays and addresses, some of them hidden away in publications difficult of access, have been selected from a wide range covering a period from 1894 when he addressed a Church Congress at Boston to 1936 when he contributed to the Thirty-third volume of the *Journal of Philosophy*. Brought together in this volume, they show the changes and developments in a philosophy essentially constant, and probably make more available a unified view of the author's constructive ideas and metaphysical position than any single one of his published writings.

They have been selected by a small group of his former students who in this work merely represent the whole company of those who have enjoyed his teaching and who have long wished to publish and to own his essays. On this happy occasion they add their greetings and their good wishes to those of the institutions which Professor Woodbridge has served these many years.

THE EDITORIAL COMMITTEE

March 26, 1937

ACKNOWLEDGMENTS

THE editors appreciate the courtesy of the publishers who have given their permission to reprint the essays included in this volume. Special acknowledgment is due to The Macmillan Company for permission to reprint the essay entitled "Confessions" from *Contemporary American Philosophy*; to Charles Scribner's Sons for "Natural Teleology" from *Essays in Modern Theology and Related Subjects*; to Houghton Mifflin Company for "The Problem of Consciousness" from *Studies in Philosophy and Psychology*; to Longmans, Green & Company for "Perception and Epistemology" from *Essays in Honor of William James*; to *The Yale Review* for "The Preface to Morals"; to *The Atlantic Monthly* for "Creation"; to *The Hibbert Journal* for "Naturalism and Humanism."

To Miss Shirley M. Carson acknowledgment is made for editing the manuscript, reading the proof, and preparing the bibliography. In the preparation of the bibliography the help of Professor Sterling P. Lamprecht and Mr. Edwin N. Garlan is also appreciated.

CONTENTS

CONTENTS

CONFESSIONS

CONFESSIONS*

As I review the course of my philosophical studies and attempt to express the conclusions to which they have led, I am conscious of special indebtedness to Aristotle, Spinoza, and Locke among the dead and to Santayana among the living. It is to them that I repeatedly turn both for refreshment and discipline. They represent, I may say, a selection or survival from the forces that have influenced me rather than a sequence which my own thinking has followed. I can not name a date when they were first recognized as controlling. I know, however, that when I began teaching at Columbia University in 1902, Aristotle, Spinoza, and Locke had already become the philosophers in whom I was most interested, and Santayana appeared to me as a brilliant and provoking writer. After reading his *Life of Reason*, which I reviewed for the New York *Evening Post*, I felt that I had found in it a matchless commentary on our human thinking. Since the contributions to this volume of essays are admittedly personal and egotistic, I may as well say now that the *Life of Reason* is a book I wish I could have written myself. I do not ask Santayana to take this as a compliment, for it is a doubtful one. I make the confession to indicate that his book is the kind of book which appeals to me as genuinely philosophical. For as I understand the *Life of Reason*, it makes no attempt to explain why the life of man should be intellectual. It attempts, rather, simply to tell the truth about that life. And telling the truth about the life of reason and trying to discover what that truth implies seem to me to be the business of philosophy. I had reached this conviction before I read the *Life of Reason*, but after reading it the conviction had received a force and an illumination which it had not had before.

* In *Contemporary American Philosophy,* New York, Macmillan, 1930, pp. 415-438.

And more than this; my understanding of the history of philosophy seemed to be enhanced. I felt that I could enter into the thoughts of others with a keener and more sympathetic appreciation. Indeed, if I may use a chemical figure, the reading of Santayana has acted upon my own thoughts like a catalyzing agent, dissolving them and recombining them in ways better suited to my own satisfaction at least. Two examples may serve as illustrative. When I read, "With Aristotle the conception of human life is perfectly sound, for with him everything ideal has a natural basis and everything natural an ideal fulfilment"—when I read this, not only did the disorderly writings of the Stagerite combine together to produce one impressive effect, but what I myself had been clumsily feeling for received a clarified and satisfactory expression. In that one sentence was revealed what certainly seems to be one of the major tasks of philosophy: to exhibit the passage from the natural to the ideal; from common sense to reason; from animal love to ideal love; from gregarious association to free society; from practice and invention to liberal art; from mythology to enlightened religion; and from crude cosmologies to that impersonal objectivity found in science. In that one sentence, too, I found an acceptable standard of criticism, for it seemed to me that ideals are significant as they round out and complete some natural function, and that the natural, when cut off from the ideal, must not be looked upon as affording by itself any standard of conduct or reason for its existence; it is brutally impersonal. And when I read, "Knowledge is not eating and we can not be expected to devour what we mean," I found the vanities of epistemology exposed more conclusively than any laboured exposition of my own had exposed them. I could have insisted that "knowing a world" and "having a world to know" are never the same condition, but I could see it better with the metaphor to help. To these illustrations I may add that reading and re-reading the *Dialogues in Limbo* has become a prized experience in the clarification of my own ideas. I must rate that book very high in the philosophical literature I have read.

I have dwelt on my indebtedness to Santayana first because of its especial character. The basic ideas of "my philosophy"

—I use the phrase conscious of the egotistical privileges of this essay—were laid before I read him. Perhaps it would be more modest and even more truthful to say that I think they were. The thing, however, of which I am acutely conscious is, that through reading him I seem to have won for myself greater freedom and clarity in the handling of my ideas. I think I know better what I am about. The scheme which was forming itself in my own mind through the study of Aristotle, Spinoza, and Locke in particular, became more definite, and it became easier, for myself at least, to formulate the chief conviction to which that study had led. A synthesis of Aristotle and Spinoza, tempered by the uncompromising, yet compromised, empiricism of Locke, became something which I thought I clearly conceived and which I believed to be useful in removing some of the confusion for which modern philosophy seemed to be clearly responsible. Aristotle's thoroughgoing naturalism and his conception of productivity, Spinoza's rigid insistence on structure, and Locke's doctrine of the acquisition of ideas through experience, seemed to afford, when taken together, a means of backing up the philosophical enterprise with a metaphysics which would be analytical instead of controversial. If effective ideas are really acquired through experience, an analysis of these ideas should reveal something about the world in which that experience occurs; and the chief revelations seem to be a limiting structure or structures for all events and a genuinely productive activity within these limits. The structure determines what is possible and the activity determines what exists. But this result should not be taken as an absurd dualism which starts with two gods and then produces a world through their co-operation. Structure and activity are things implied by the fact that the world is known and controlled by getting ideas through experience. They are arrived at analytically and are not invoked as demiurges to account for the world we live in. The development of a germ into thoughtful consideration of its habitat and of the manner and incidents of its development is the basal fact for every philosopher. He can never get behind it. He can only tell the truth about it and try to find out what that truth implies. He may explore his world and control it in some measure, but he can never find originals which brought it into being.

All this at the age of sixty seems to me to be so simple as to need no elaboration. One's familiarity with one's own line of thought begets this illusion. I have to confess—like every other worker in these mazes of thought—that I have entertained in the past, with entire conviction, opinions which I can hold no longer. This, if nothing else, should make me recognize that what now seems so clear to me may not seem clear at all to others, and that I myself may be among those others at a later date. Yet I venture to think, even if so thinking savours of contradiction and dialectic, that the principle of hesitation which I have just expressed is an essential part of the position to which I have been led. Hesitation, doubt, perplexity, uncertainty, the sense of incompleteness and of more to be done, the prospect and probability that one will change one's mind—all these things are as real as anything else. The doubtful man is as much a product of nature as the confident. Indeed, nothing that happens can be convicted of impossibility. There must, consequently, be room in one's metaphysics for anything that may happen. This I take to be a very solid principle. We may condemn philosophies as false, but we can not impugn their existence. It is easy to claim that men ought not to think in certain ways and forget that they do think in those ways. Their thinking may be improper, but it is clearly not improper from the point of view of its existence or as an illustration of nature's productivity. From the point of view of existence one might as well accuse the diversified flora and fauna of the earth of impropriety. The principle, therefore, that there must be room in one's metaphysics for whatever may happen or that nothing that happens can be convicted of impossibility seems clearly to imply that our distinctions are distinctions within one common field and not between two fields which the distinctions make incompatible. Rather clumsily expressed, they are distinctions "within" and not distinctions between "within and without." Appearance and reality, truth and error, good and evil, beautiful and ugly, are all correlative. An existence which did not own them would not be our existence. A metaphysics which abolished them would not be a true metaphysics, but it would demonstrate them. Even in being false it would have a claim on existence. I could boast that my metaphysics recognizes this, making it a cardinal principle. Rather than boast, however, I would make this the first step in metaphysics—the recognition that existence is primarily what it is and can neither be explained nor explained away. The most that can be done is to find out what it implies. And the great error of metaphysicians is the supposition that the implications of existence are its causes and lead us to something more fundamental than existence, or prior to it, or in itself irrelevant to it.

I have, consequently, often called myself a realist, and one of a very naïve sort. But calling names seems to have parallel consequences, whether oneself or others be the object. One is not always comfortable with one's associates. The linking name is not a marriage ring symbolizing community of bed and board. Yet I confess a sympathy with all realists of whatever stripe, even the mediaeval and the literary. They are evidently trying to see things as they are, even when what they see is selected. Novelists often tell us what real life is by telling us about some unfamiliar life, and philosophers also often discern real existence in the unfamiliar. The realism I would urge is one of principle rather than one of selection. As a principle it does not dichotomize existence. There is, for example, an ancient question, whether a rose is red when it is not seen. The answer always has seemed to me to be: a red rose is. The colours of roses are not like guesses in Blind Man's Buff, and many a rose is born to blush unseen. I can attach no meaning to the question: *Is* the colour of a rose what it is? I am too sensible of the fact that I have bought bushes of a nurseryman who—nor I—has not as yet seen the roses they will bear. Such experiences may drive us back on the general fact of colour and lead us to ask: Do colours exist when they are not perceived? It is hard for me to attach a meaning even to this question. A dark room may exclude all colours save black when the eyes are open, and a similar effect may be produced by binding the eyes in a lighted room. And this simple experiment forces me to conclude that colour is as much something with the existence of which I have nothing to do as it is something with the existence of which I have something to do. When I try to find out how much I have to do with it, I find that much very little—no more than the fact that if I did not exist, I would never ask such curious questions. I would not ask any questions at all. And I can not possibly conceive what a world is like about which no questions whatever are asked. Furthermore, it seems monstrous to me to conclude that *the* world is only *my* world, for "my" world means nothing unless distinguished from a world not mine. I may distinguish such a world just as I distinguish houses which are not mine. A metaphysical distinction, if made at all, must be of a similar kind, or it is meaningless. This is what I mean by a realism of principle rather than of selection. As I am fond of saying, the only universe relevant to inquiry, the only universe that exists for purposes of observation, experiment, and ratiocination, is the universe of discourse. Any other universe is meaningless. If I am challenged to prove this, I point out such obvious facts as this: we do not proceed originally from the implications of colour to colour, but from colour to its implications. The subject-matter of inquiry can not be called in question. Individual existences may be related to one another and compared, but "the whole of existence" can be related to nothing or compared with nothing.

This is the basic dogma of metaphysics. I can not remember when it first gained possession of me. I am tempted to think that I always thought that way. I remember quite distinctly that when I first read Berkeley, which was in my college days at Amherst, I was troubled over the conflict between the incredibility of his doctrine and the obvious truth of its foundation. Looking back now at the experience, I can formulate it as I could not have formulated it then: I was conscious that he converted a definition of subject-matter into the cause of its existence. He saw clearly enough that existence implies mind in some objective sense, but he made mind the creator of what exists. In those same days, I had a similar experience with Kant, but it was many years before I could say that this synthetic philosophy was anything more than a definition of subject-matter converted into a wholly incredible explanation of experience. And the little I had then of Hegel—getting his ideas, not through reading but through the fascinating exposition of Professor Garman—fired my imagination as a little of Hegel did that of many of my contemporaries. Glimpses of the organic unity of experience were inspiring for minds distracted by an associationist psychology on the one hand and the artificiality of the "critical philosophy" on the other. We read no Aristotle in those days, and it was only later that I saw that Hegel had done little more than turn Aristotle upside down and done it clumsily. I am conscious of such early experiences and such later formulations, but conscious of them as a pretty steady and natural development of my thinking unmarked by a sense of violent conversion. This development seems to be a line along which I have been led rather than a program ever deliberately adopted. This seeming may be one of the illusions which I egotistically cherish, but I set it down with the frankness which confessions like these inspire.

I could cite other things more casual, perhaps, than those already mentioned. A remark in a cherished copy of Jevons' *Lessons in Logic* stands pencilled with a question mark: "We can not suppose, and there is no reason to suppose, that by the constitution of the mind we are obliged to think of things differently from the manner in which they are." There is a note to the remark: "Discuss light, colour, sound, etc." The book is a heritage from college days and carries the name of a classmate. I must have purloined it. The question mark and the note were put there when I taught logic at the University of Minnesota. I was very conscious of the hopelessness of an obligation to think of things differently from the manner in which they are, and ended a contribution to the *Essays Philosophical and Psychological in Honor of William James* with the remark of Jevons. When I read, shamelessly, as youth is wont to do, the *Essays* of Matthew Arnold while Professor Shedd lectured on Dogmatic Theology at the Union Theological Seminary, there was tucked away in my memory one of Arnold's favourite quotations: "Things are what they are and the consequences of them will be what they will be; why then should we wish to be deceived?" So I take the principle of realism as something pretty well ingrained and constitutional in me. Like everybody else, I pride myself on a sense of fact.

I have tried to support this pride by teaching and by the little I have written. The principle of realism seems so important to me for metaphysics and philosophy that I have been more busy with championing it than with developing it. Yet to keep insisting on it seems worth while. It helps me not to wish to be deceived. If this world were *explained* as so many of us philosophers try to explain it, it wouldn't be this world at all. It may cry for an explanation, but a metaphysician in his wish not to be deceived will set that down as one interesting fact about it. He will see poetry and religion, and art and society, and morals and science and philosophy even, as responses to that cry and be glad and not contemptuous of them. He will recognize them *as* responses, confident that when they cease to be such, there will be no more world. The cry is essential to what existence is. Nature has generated and supports it. With Aristotle we may make it the evocation of God's bare presence and rest content with that, for God is a rather final explanation of things. But if we do not wish to be deceived we will not make him the creator of the world, responsible for microbes and men, or try to deduce from his nature the way of a man with a maid. We may insist with theology that he must be incarnated, born of a virgin, even, to be as effective with men as he is with the stars, but we will recognize in that insistence a supreme illustration of the cry. The appeal of existence will not have ceased. First and fundamentally it is an appeal.

To find it first and fundamentally something else is to acknowledge oneself a selective realist rather than a realist in principle and to have chosen one instance of the natural kinesis instead of the character of them all. Matter, atoms, space and time, ions, electrical charges, the stable bodies and rhythmic motions of the physical world, the microscope's revelations of the mutations of the seeds and carriers of subsequent developments, and the natural evolution of living organisms, must bulk large in one's thinking. They make an imposing spectacle, suited to arouse both the admiration of a poet and the curiosity of a scientist. It is trivial to ask which treats them the more adequately unless one specifies the purpose for which they are treated. The heavens declare both the glory of God and an opportunity for astronomers. They declare neither exclusively. If we look for an exclusive declaration, it is found, not by selecting one from a number, calling the one real and the others illusion; it is found rather in the steady recognition of the fact that something is declared. This is but saying again that existence *is* what it reveals itself to be to a seeker, without addition or subtraction. And this may be turned around. It is the seeking of what existence reveals that defines the unity in existence and discovers the manifoldness of its revelations. This shows again how metaphysics is realistic in principle. At the risk of seeming to talk nonsense, I may say that the question, What is existence? is an existing question, one thrown up in the operations of nature, an event in the world fully as much as an eclipse of the sun, but more conspicuous than the latter. Familiarity with it may breed contempt. It is not, however, to be set aside and neglected. For man does not stand outside of nature and ask her questions. He stands inside. His questions well up within him, form on his lips as naturally as his smiles, and are as much a revelation of existence as his answers are. They are more. They are the final revelation of existence, declaring it to be—for metaphysics at least—first and foremost a question. When this is seen, the metaphysician need not hesitate to see a question answered in the growth of an acorn into an oak or the revolution of a planet about the sun. He may even go so far, running the risk of being laughed at as a poet or lover of metaphors, and say that acorn and planet have asked questions and found answers. At any rate, existence seeking will be for him a more impressive fact than existence found. That is why he will not put the inquisitive mind outside of nature and suppose that it is obliged to think of things different from the manner in which they are. He will keep it inside as the sure indication of what natural processes are, and if he finds an atom, he will not let the little thing drive mind out of nature and make of mind a problem never to be solved. He will gladly be something of an Hegelian and more of an Aristotelian to avoid that disaster.

All this, as I have said, seems very simple to me. I have been told that it is too obvious, too much bare matter of fact, and that a philosopher, if he accepted it, would have nothing left to do. He would lose his profession. I might answer that, if this were true, humanity might profit by the loss. But I do not believe it to be true. There is something still left for the philosopher. He can at least keep on asking questions and seeking their answers, and do this with the added consciousness of knowing what he is about. His questions may be less foolish than they were. He may find that he has to give up many cherished problems, like that of the red rose, the doubled moon, the vanished star, the bent stick, the presence of evil, the ubiquity of error, the clash of freedom and necessity, the reconciliation of mechanism and teleology, the possibility of knowledge, and the relation of soul to body, but he ought to thank God for it. He ought to be glad to be rid of appendages, sloughing them off, as nature seems to do, when they become useless or a hindrance. Even then he will have plenty to do in making confession to the world and, by his teaching, warning others from a sad employment of their time, using the history of philosophy as a text. And then, if he has sympathy, he may do some good.

These remarks are a further confession of my own thoughts. I have never been interested in the "problems" of philosophy. That is, perhaps, not strictly true. Yet I can not remember ever having been seriously worried about them. This fact, rather than the problems, has often worried me, for it convicts me, even to myself, of a lack of sympathy and stimulates my natural egotism unduly. These problems have been very important things in history and have had serious consequences. To be cold to them is not to be wholly comfortable in the society of others or in the quiet reading in one's study. I have known souls desperate in the clutches of necessity and I have read about Erasmus and Luther. The cry for a just God in a naughty world I have heard. But it all seems to me, speaking quite frankly, unfortunate and absurd, and sometimes abominable. I know, of course, that these worries are quite real and very important. I have had enough practical experience, enough of that sort of dealing with others which acutely exposes the conflicts which go on in men's souls, to know how real these things are, to be stirred with deep concern and to be prompted to be resolute in action. Yet

I could never translate the practical conflicts of life into problems which philosophy must solve in order that these conflicts may be reduced. This may be in me what is often called temperamental, or it may be a consequence of my father's influence on my education. He was one of the justest and fairest men I have ever known, unselfishly solicitous about others, but he never worried about the world. Its make-up and that distribution of good and evil which marks the life of man were never problems crying for a theoretical solution. He was a devout Christian and a devoted Churchman, but he never worried over any doctrine. I was early heretical and brought back Herbert Spencer from college. His serenity was undisturbed. He was serene. I can think of no better adjective. To borrow Matthew Arnold's words about Wordsworth—the cloud of mortal destiny he put by. His constant prayer was: "We know not what a day may bring forth; we only know that the hour for serving Thee is always present." We were intimate companions. And it may well be that living from childhood in the shadow of his unruffled confidence, I early grew to be indifferent to much that otherwise might have disturbed me. There have been times when the evident indifference of the order of nature to human concerns has been emotionally shocking and the sense of estrangement acute, but it is rare indeed that I have felt that such experiences implied a theoretical problem to be solved. In this sense, I was early, without knowing it, something of a pragmatist, asking myself what difference does it make tomorrow whether I am fated or free. And in my student days in Berlin, in 1893, I wrote a never-published and now-lost paper to prove that it made no difference. I wish I could read it now to see how well reminiscence is confirmed.

Yet I have been and am interested in the problems of philosophy as excursions of the human mind. The history of ideas is one of the most absorbing and fascinating subjects in which I have ever engaged. Of all the great philosophers, Leibniz is the only one I could willingly eliminate. Here I confess to a prejudice. I know its origin. When I heard Ebbinghaus lecture on Leibniz in Berlin, he remarked: "Leibniz went about introducing himself to prominent people as a promising young man." That remark stuck. I always see Leibniz that way first and, consequently, come at his ideas with amusement. Yet, as I forget this, I can enjoy some enthusiasm in seeing how the differential calculus and the doctrine of pre-established harmony admirably work together, the monads reflecting the function of one equation, each with its own little differential. It is, generally, such congruences in ideas that I find more fascinating than any concern about their validity. Here I confess a greater debt to Ebbinghaus than amusement over Leibniz. He had the habit, every now and then, of brushing aside his notes, which followed a rather stupid method of classification, and running his fingers through his hair, exclaiming: "Aber nun, meine Herren, müssen wir ein bisschen interpretieren. Was *will* der Mensch?" Then, there was a lecture indeed. Yes; what would a man have? How does he go about having it? Whither is he led? Into the grip of what ideas does he fall? Where does he arrive, with or against his will?—like Hobbes sending Christian souls to martyrdom in a heathen state as the only allowable escape from the absolute sovereignty of a king who orders them to renounce their faith. There is an inevitability to which ideas bow. They are gotten of experience, as Locke so abundantly shows, but once gotten, they lead experience instead of following it. And that to which they lead may send them back to clarify or mock their source. It is so with the problems of philosophy. They are born of ideas which experience generates. Once born, they run their course and then come back to clear or muddy their origin. They exercise a function rather than lead to a solution. The exercise of that function seems to me to be better displayed in the thinking of the great than it is displayed in introductions to philosophy, like Paulsen's for example, where the problems are systematically detached and rendered as the outgivings of a universal experience which no man ever had. *Was der Mensch will* is then entirely forgotten, although it is always what some man would, what he would in his day and generation, moved by the forces that played upon him, which has generated these problems with vitality. Deprived of individual and social backing, they are little more than formal exercises, good for discipline in ratiocination, but poor substitutes for the vitality of Plato or of Hume.

While I have been writing, a rather cryptic saying of Professor Garman's has been claiming attention: "A man never *thinks* wrong; his danger lies in *not* thinking." It was a perplexing utterance and mixed up, as I remember, with some Hegelianism. Errors of thought seemed to be all too frequent and familiar things to be swept aside with an aphorism. The maxim did pedagogical service in his classroom. I will not say that he made us think right, but he made us think fatally. I well remember a classmate, one of the best students in the college, who, after a thrice-repeated perfect analysis of Hume on causation, was made to swallow the doctrine much against his will, because he found no fault with it besides his own dislike. I can not say what "Garman's philosophy" was. He certainly left me with no system of philosophy and no consciousness of one. He did leave me with an immense respect for the thinking mind. Its wanderings and where it would go next became more alluring than stopping at some comfortable inn along the way. And I remember another classmate, a partner of the Berlin days, who asked me what system of philosophy I had decided on to teach when I returned to America. The question struck me as preposterous. I was diffident about admitting that I had no system, but I had heard the phrase "the Odyssey of the spirit," and was more interested in what that phrase implied than in indoctrinating youth with any system, whether borrowed or egotistically thought to be original. I fear I may have changed in this respect, although I still boast of a contempt of discipleship. These things are said, however, not to praise my character but rather to illustrate my education and its bearing on my attitude toward the problems of philosophy and the history of ideas. The mind, like the body, has its excursions. The profit of them is the traveller's profit.

I have already hinted that the travelling has a consequence. With me it has become a major one. Ideas, as Locke urged, are born of experience, of the body's contact with the body's world. He thought that God could—although he believed that God did not—have made the body think without the addition of a soul to help it. There was a beautiful courage in that honest Englishman who, like some other philosophers, came near to being a clergyman. Yet he seems to have been a little afraid of the soul, a little afraid of "ideas" and used the term abominably. They ran away with him at times, as is well illustrated in his chapter on "Solidity." In this chapter Locke makes two statements which deserve critical attention: "That which hinders the approach of two bodies when they are moved one towards another, I call solidity"; and "If anyone asks me what this solidity is, I send him to his senses to inform him." Who will forbid the sending? But who can deny that the effect of it is a definition? Solidity turns out to be more than something at the tips of our fingers; it turns out to be something characteristic of the system of things in which our fingers move. Going to the senses opens the door to definable relationships. A man thereby enters a realm of being in which ideas enlarge and fructuate and from which he may return to his senses with a different touch. He is on his way to knowledge. This is not a matter of comparing our ideas to see whether they agree or differ as one might compare a sound and a colour. It is not a matter of compounding them as one might compound the tastes of water, sugar, and lemons and get the taste of lemonade. Locke's illustration is "gold," but his examples of knowledge are pitiful. When he is through with knowledge, he throws most of it over in favour of what he calls judgment, leaving the remnant as a foretaste of future bliss. It can all be made very ridiculous. Yet he was fundamentally sound. We must go to our senses, not our souls, if we are ever to enter the realm of mind. Far less acute than Descartes and far less subtle than Hume or Kant, he was far more solid than any of them. We enter the realm of mind through our senses, but it is a realm we enter. There a different authority rules than the porter who let us in. There one travels among ideas which are forced to acknowledge a controlling fate.

And so, to continue this apology for my life, I have leaned on Locke as on a sure support. I have ridiculed before my classes what has seemed to me to be ridiculous in him, and I have forced him to exhibit the fate to which his own ideas were committed. If, however, I am at all sane, I thank him from the bottom of my heart, I thank him for sending me to my senses to find the mind rather than to Descartes to find it in doubt. For this "sending to the senses" when thoroughly worked out, reveals that what the senses define is not a discrete series of isolated contacts on which some synthesis must be superimposed. Locke so supposed, and his working out of the supposition amply demonstrates its futility. He was forced to define *real knowledge* as something no man could ever attain and make it, consequently, a conception of no use whatever in this mortal life. He should have paid more attention to what he had left, to those sciences he would free from the dictation of philosophers. We can never *know* whether our ideas agree with things, but we have to *proceed* as if they did! But if we can not know the former, what possible sense is there in saying the latter? What is the sense of saying that we must proceed on the basis of something we know nothing about? What is the sense of trying to reduce knowledge to psychology, when psychology must be a branch of knowledge or not worth the paper on which it is written? Is psychology, too, the taking of ideas to agree with something without any knowledge whether they do or what that something is? Is the "science of knowledge" the same sort of thing? I must protest. The doctrine of the "association of ideas" in some form or other has remarkable vitality. The reason is, I suppose, that they *are* associated. When, however, we turn the fact of their association into an explanation of knowledge, we have to make a number of assumptions for which association cannot account. Chief of these is the great assumption which Locke himself made: that there is, to begin with, an order in things to which the mind tries to conform, sometimes succeeding, perhaps, but more often failing. This makes "the order in things" the crucial thing for the whole doctrine. If there is no such order, it is senseless to suppose that the association of ideas conforms to it or reveals it. If there is such an order, and if it is helpful to explain the association of ideas, then the association of ideas does not explain it or our knowledge of it. If we try to escape these alternatives by concluding that we have *only* an association of *ideas* to deal with, we may, perhaps, understand what we mean by "association" in this conclusion, but we ask in vain for an answer to the question, What do "only" and "ideas" distinguish? What are "ideas" contrasted with and what does "only" exclude? The conclusion excludes an answer, and is, therefore, meaningless. It is much better to go to one's senses, to go to what even Locke too much neglected, to the enterprises in which men are engaged in discovering order and not in supposing it exists or in trying to account for its existence—to the hope of getting knowledge, not to the hopelessness of explaining it. Then order imposes itself upon us. It is found to be, not an assumption which we make, but a discovery which we welcome and fear. On it our happiness and misery depend. The better we know it, the more we can modify our destiny; and we are in its hands as in the hands of fate. We go to touch for solidity to discover it to be that which keeps bodies apart, something more than an isolated sense datum, something in an order of things.

So I once wrote an article on "Structure" and, later, the *Realm of Mind*. The principle of realism, carried out, seems to me to lead repeatedly to at least the implication of structure. I have frequently hinted at this in what I have here written. Even the attempt to write something like one's philosophical biography, calling the past to remembrance and probably distorting it for effect, involves the attempt to find a framework into which events, readings, and reflections fit and thereby own some relation to one another. Whatever our account may be of, it is an account with some order or structure that is aimed at and expected. Without it the account cannot be understood; we call it unintelligible. If it is of the world or of nature that we would give an account, the same implication holds; we must discover or invent an order or structure. We are often deceived by invented orders when they are brilliant and tightly knit. They may impose on mankind for centuries. Even when we reject them, we admire them, and we more readily believe a man who tells us lies in an orderly fashion than one who tells us the truth in disorder. The reason for this is not our credulity. Invented orders are rarely pure inventions or wholly arbitrary. I doubt if they ever are. One lie forces a man to tell another, but this other must be a supporting lie, one which fits into a structure, the structure which the first implies, so that with the first lie a man is doomed to go on inevitably, if he goes on at all in its support. Even Fairyland and Nowhere soon rob their explorers of freedom. Premises freely or conventionally accepted lead to conclusions which their acceptance never suspected. Mathematics is the crowning example. Counting by tens is a convention, but Kant made a good deal of the fact that $7 + 5 = 12$ is not. He belaboured the fact with astute phraseology which ought not, however, because of a dislike of words, to obscure the leaning of the proposition on an order and not on its subject. Mathematics *is* the crowning example, and with its many applications is powerful enough to prove that order is not a human bias or an imposition on reluctant material. It is an implication of all existence, something to be set down as metaphysical, something which we creatures of a day never made—for if we did, why do we rebel against it, cry over it, and yet seek it with our whole heart in the belief that it is the final answer to every question that we ask? It, and not our minds, is responsible for the intelligibility of the world, and we have minds because our bodies are in contact with other bodies which jointly with it are in an order enmeshed. That is why I wrote the *Realm of Mind*.

And that is why I have joined Spinoza to Locke in my affections. Few philosophers have had the sense of order as supremely as Spinoza had it. It overpowered him and set him all atremble. Ostracized by society and ill with consumption, he could rest in it as in the embrace of God's love. The beauty of it in him for a modern reader lies in his freedom from epistemology and the confusions of subjectivism. He is astonishingly free from empiricism also. This, I find, is a matter of offence with students. It is difficult to get them to put, with him, the empirical world aside or take it for granted as something acknowledged but not allowed to interfere with the fatality of thought. They expect him to show why, as a consequence of God's nature, the seasons change and the clouds drop down their dew. That he is wise about men and has a profound knowledge of human nature seems clear from many a penetrating remark, but to affirm that whatever is—even in this matter of human nature—is in God and without God can neither be nor be conceived, is a queer sort of psychology.

They often look at him as a juggler, who presents to them an apparently empty hat in the shape of definitions and axioms and then proceeds to draw out of it astonishing things. They rarely fail in the end to be impressed by an inevitability, august, sublime, and possibly tender. The empirical world is somehow caught in it and illustrates it just as *this* circle is caught in and illustrates *the* circle. The question why, if *the* circle exists, *this* circle should also exist, remains unanswered, but it tends to become unimportant, for there seems to be some sense, even if an obscure and baffling sense, in saying that without *the* circle, *this* circle could neither be nor be conceived. Quite possibly, Spinoza, like the rest of us, was a man who thought he proved more than he did. There is abundant evidence of it; and his method of exhibiting his thoughts leaves much to be desired. He was a very interesting person and a baffling one. People found him that. They thought he had said something important which they did not understand and which seemed to violate cherished beliefs and obvious facts, and when they asked him about it, he had the habit of telling them that they did not understand, that they knew nothing of God and the human mind. A psychoanalyst can readily find in him an inferiority complex and a defensive mechanism. It may be ungrudgingly admitted that he had both, and fled to God because the world rejected him or because he was too weak to accommodate himself to the world. The fact of him, however, and what he did are more important than any analysis of his personality. The *Ethics* is a book which, like Euclid, should be read with no curiosity about its author. It is a book in which personal opinions and prejudices should not be allowed to count. They are as irrelevant to the reader as Euclid, the man, is irrelevant to the boy studying geometry. For it is a geometrical effect one comes away with. In the light of this effect, the language can be discounted. The mediaeval terminology, all the apparent jugglery with essence, existence, idea, and power, is an instrument to impress upon the reader an overwhelming sense of the fact of order and structure. He must get *substance* before he gets anything else. He must begin philosophy with God and not with Locke. Unless he begins in this way, he can never understand anything; he may go to touch for solidity, but if he stops there he can never understand what he is saying when he says: By solidity, I mean this or that. For knowledge is not eating and we can not be expected to devour what we mean.

And so I lean on Spinoza as well as on Locke. To touch the world or experience it is very far from knowing it. Experience and knowledge seem to me to be very different things. I quote Santayana again, from memory: "I have often wondered at those philosophers who have said that all our ideas are derived from experience. They could never have been poets and must have forgotten that they were ever children; for the great problem of education is how to get experience out of ideas." It is the great problem of life and science: how to fit oneself into an order, how to get out of the idea of relativity white marks on a photographic plate. Doing these things is knowledge. Bumping one's head against a wall is experience and a poor substitute. There is joy in going to the senses—to experience—if one does not stay there. They open the door to the realm of mind, to order, to structure, to the inevitable, to freedom, to substance, to God—if God is that in view of which our destinies are shaped.

It is with one of those unreasonable enthusiasms which we often have that I turn to Aristotle. He has said everything that I have ever said or shall ever say. He tells me that that is continuous which, when cut, has common boundaries, and I find it unnecessary to go to Dedekind. This is quite stupid, I know, but I may as well confess it. He tells me that A is the cause of B, and B the cause of C, and so on forever, but that B is not the cause of C because A is the cause of B; and the weight of an infinite series is lifted from my mind forever. Everything begins when it does, and there is no need to search the past for a first cause or origin of things. Existence begins now fully as much as it ever began. A road begins at this end, but it also begins at the other end, even if it began at this end before it began at the other; for nothing ever begins before or after it does begin. I admire this cool insistence on such simple and obvious things—taking the beginning of a road as a first illustration of "principle" and then going to the keel of a ship, the axioms of geometry and the rules of a city. The principle of a thing is found where the thing begins, and we must never forget that in searching for principles. The tenses of the verb are the carriers of time. One thing may begin before or after another or may so have begun. Things may be and are arranged that way. But to arrange principles themselves in temporal order is to forget that we are always dealing with a dynamic world. Form, matter, efficacy, and end (purpose) are just as much now as they have ever been, but this particular case of them—this man, this house, this stone—never was or is, or will be again. It is this particular case which is interesting and important and the object of our questions. What is it? Out of what did it come? What effected its coming out? What purpose does it serve? A complete answer to these questions would tell us everything about the case. It would help us to the formulation of conditions which are "catholic," which hold good "on the whole" or for the most part, and so help us to arrange our knowledge in bodies of knowledge appropriate to this or that particular subject-matter. While we must always remember that we are dealing with a dynamic world and recognize that it is only some particular, individual case, not something in general, that raises the question of the "four causes," we may address ourselves to this very fact and discover that particular field of inquiry which was later called metaphysics. What we must remember and recognize and what questions we ask when dealing with a stone or a house or a man, ought to give some indication of what it is *to be,* whether it is a stone, a house, or a man—or even a god—that *is*. The implications of being something are the implications of being anything, if "things will not be governed ill"—τά δε ὄντα οὐ βούλεται πολιτεύεσθαι κακῶς.

I owe to Aristotle my conception of metaphysics and the love of it. His errors and omissions—I can point them out as confidently as the next man. I know how history has distorted him and what a tyrant he became over the minds of men. That was because few really read and studied him, or because they read and studied him with a mental set previously determined by their own language and ideas. I had to tell a very brilliant student once that the word "cause" never occurs in Aristotle, before I could make him see that his contention that Aristotle was not justified in the use of the term was amusing rather than critical. Students who go to his text often forget that his writings are not translations of English. Even so, he has a gripping power and, when read attentively, is still the great intellectual force he has always been. Compared with that, his errors, omissions, and tyranny are now trivial. From him I learned that metaphysics is a special interest and not a superscience which should dictate to others and criticize them. They can get on without it, although it can not get on very well without them. Yet it admits no servile dependence. It does not wait on their permission or advice any more than they wait upon its. It would share with them mutually in the interests of the mind. But it frequently has to protest against the substitution of them in its place. It dares to be as egotistical as they are and be thankful. If Aristotle could try to keep them all together in happy companionship, why not keep on trying? For metaphysics would never aim at usurping their place. It would not boast, even if it boasted perfection, that it could solve a single problem in physics, chemistry, or biology, and it would not expect them to do its own work of analysis. Yet it would claim to be a very human enterprise without which a man may be easily intellectually warped and deficient in sympathy with the great episodes of human life. Aristotle, with all his errors, is immune to that.

And, more technically, I have learned from him that metaphysics is analytic. It produces nothing out of a juggler's hat, and certainly not God and the world. It takes things as they are, in all their obvious plurality, and never supposes that they can be reduced to ultimates from which they sprang by miracle or evolution. It leaves the history of existence to historians and its evolution to evolutionists. Its interest is in what it is to be a history and what it is to be an evolution. That there are space and time, and matter and energy, and life and death and thought—a world to know and minds to know it—it admits beyond question. Faced with these things, it has no interest in why they are as they are—why the body has a mind or the mind a body. It does not try to justify the ways of God or matter. Since nature produces many things, it is content to take her productivity as a fact without asking for a reason for it, knowing that the only possible reason would be "something that produces." But metaphysics would analyze productivity to see what it implies, without supposing that the results of its analysis disclose factors which once, in some far-away time, conspired together to make a world.

One further debt I must acknowledge to Aristotle—an appreciation of language which I never had until I studied him. I was early impressed with his use of the verb "to say" and his insistence that truth is not a matter of things but of propositions. Knowledge, with him, is largely a matter of *saying* what things are. This gives a dominant *logical* note to all his writings, noticeable even in his descriptions and illustrations. It would seem, at times, as if a coherent system of sayings in a given field was of more importance to him than its subject-matter. He points out how certain common uses and turns of speech vary as they are used in varying connections. τὸ ὄν λέγεται πολλαχῶς. The principle is generalized almost to the roots of being. What is said is relevant to the occasions of saying it, so that the same expression may exercise quite different functions in different connections. He made common words and phrases do unexpected service. He made, one might say, the Greek language conscious of itself as an instrument rather than as a language different from that of barbarians. And although truth is not a matter of nature, the *saying* of things is. When Socrates is said to be a man, something has happened to him of which he may be unaware, but he has proved conversation fully as much as he provoked the resentment of Athens. Existence is provocative. Its being so is one instance of its kinetic character, for speech is a motion fully as much as the movements of the spheres. What a saying effects is consequently more important than the way of saying it, although a scrupulous nicety about expression is to be commended highly. From all this I hope I have learned a respect for language and been made aware that alarmingly different expressions in the same language and in different languages may convey the same idea. I have often told my classes that when Jonathan Edwards called his sweetheart "a handmaid of the Lord" he was not very far removed from the modern youth, who might call his "a damn fine girl." The different expressions connote a different culture and different proprieties, but should a metaphysician quarrel with either of them? The maid was provocative. I should not be surprised, therefore, if I found out that Thomas Aquinas and Immanuel Kant were saying the same thing; or John Calvin and Charles Darwin—the many are called and the few chosen. It is again "Was *will* der Mensch"; and, perhaps, when a man thinks, he does not think wrong. The language he speaks may be unintelligible or sound absurd, but there is at least the suspicion that it is humanly vernacular. We all live in the same world of sunrise and sunset, but talk about it in languages which are diverse; and what our differing utterances are relevant to is more important than their relevances to one another. Since they are relevant to something, I have been led to consider language as an instance of that give and take in nature which discovers ideas.

And so I end, conscious that I have left unsaid things that might have been said and not as sure as I should like to be that I have fulfilled the purpose of this volume. I have taken the opportunity to be one which permits and encourages a freedom of expression and intimacy which one ordinarily might prefer to avoid. Confession is said to be good for the soul. I think I have had some good of it. Receivers of confessions—one leaves the priest a little worried about what has been told. I think of David Hume: "I can not say there is no vanity in making this funeral oration of myself, but I hope it is not a misplaced one; and this is a matter of fact which is easily sensed and ascertained."

METAPHYSICS AND LOGIC

THE ARGUMENT FROM DESIGN AS AFFECTED BY THE THEORY OF EVOLUTION*

IT IS usual to urge the argument from design in the interest either of theology or of ethics. When so urged, it is beset by numerous logical difficulties which render even its apologetic value questionable. Logic has seen in the argument a splendid example of some of the more subtle fallacies; but it has not usually seen one of its fundamental postulates. Accustomed to attack the argument, logic would not be likely to seek its support. But I think that any thoroughgoing conception of evolution, in fact any thoroughgoing theory of nature, raises certain questions which logic can meet by taking refuge only in something very much akin to design—not in the argument from design, in its usual theological form, but in what we may call the essential belief which that argument expresses. I shall, therefore, attempt to show the effect upon logic, or the significance for logic, of the argument from design, especially when logic is confronted by certain considerations drawn from evolution.

It is necessary, at the outset, to have some clear conception both of the argument and of the theory. The essence of the argument from design I take to be the belief in the superiority of intelligence to all else in the universe. What is precisely meant by the term "superiority" I propose to let the sequel explain. It is enough for the present to say that the essence of the argument from design consists in the belief that intelligence is, in some way, superior to all else in the universe. There is, in this connection, another point that requires some notice. It will be clear to anyone who attends to the matter that all analysis of the objective world reveals nothing but

* In *Papers, Addresses, and Discussions at the Sixteenth Church Congress in the United States,* New York, Thomas Whittaker, 1894, pp. 193-197.

sequence, continuity, action, and reaction—in other words, simply natural law which expresses the relations of parts of that world to each other. That is true even in the life of his fellow man. He finds there, too, nothing that does not come under the forms of natural law. Just as the astronomer, after watching the heavens with his telescope, exclaimed, "I can find no God there," so all of us, after a disappointing analysis of the world of our experience, must exclaim that, apart from our own intelligence, we find no intelligence there. The fact that analysis of this sort reveals no intelligence has often been regarded as sufficient to overthrow the argument from design in its usual theological form—namely, that from the evidence of design in nature we must infer a designer. To such an argument, it has always seemed a sufficient answer to say that nature evinces no design. If, therefore, we are to retain any vitality for our argument, let us deny for it a place in scientific analysis, and assert it in the sphere of rational belief. With this explanation, I trust it is clear what is meant in the main by the statement that the essence of the argument from design consists in the belief in the superiority of intelligence to all else in the universe.

We now turn to determine our conception of evolution. It is clear that it is with the broad generalizations of this theory that we are concerned. I know no better exposition of the theory than is given in C. M. Williams's *Evolutional Ethics.*[1] I think the theory of evolution there presented will be found most thoroughgoing and scientific. In fact, anyone inclined to accept evolution at all will find it exceeding difficult to escape from the generalizations there given. I give these generalizations in the words of the book itself, because I can not improve upon their clearness and conciseness. After a careful analysis of our experience we reach these conclusions:

We have found in nature only variables, no constant and invariable factor, no independent one according to which the others vary; we have found no cause that was not also an effect; that is, we have discovered nothing but a chain of phenomena bearing constant relations to each other, no causes except in this sense. We have no precedent or data

[1] *A Review of the System of Ethics Founded on the Theory of Evolution,* by C. M. Williams, New York, The Macmillan Company, 1893.

from which to assert that chemical combinations could not have resulted in protoplasm and in living protoplasm, no data from which to assert that mere evolution could not have produced consciousness. As a matter of fact, however, we find the relations of consciousness and physiological process as constant as those of the different forms of material force, and while discovering no grounds upon which to pronounce either consciousness or physiological process more essential, find none, either, for pronouncing the one, more than the other, independent of what we call natural law. The logic of all our experience leads us to believe that neither protoplasm, nor the earth, nor any of the parts of the universe, could have originated otherwise than under natural law, that is, as the result of preceding natural conditions which must have contained all the factors united in the result, and would thus explain to us, if we knew them, in as far as any process is explained by analysis, the results arising from them. We know matter and motion only as united; we know no state of absolute rest, and we have no grounds for supposing any initial state of such absolute rest, or any in which motion not previously existent in the universe entered. On the other hand, we have no proof of the absence of consciousness outside of animal life, and no proof of the non-existence of transcendental causes, though likewise no proof of their existence. (Page 339.)

We have seen that any explanation of facts from analysis, except as we assume some transcendental intuition, is impossible.

Our mathematical habit of selecting some one side of natural process as independent, in order to trace, by its variation, the variation of the others, leads us to regard the one side, phase, or portion, of phenomena as actually thus independent, although we forget, in this assumption, that we may select any phase for our mathematical independent, and are not confined to any particular one. The organism is itself a part of the environment regarded as conditioning, when we consider the development of other organisms, or change of inorganic matter with which it is in contact. (Page 351.)

So much in general. And now for a particular generalization regarding design:

Our analysis of the development of thought, feeling, and will has an important bearing on the teleological argument. If all habit comes, in time, to be pleasurable, if pleasure merely follows the line of exercise of function, *whatever that line may be*, and ends are thus mere matters of habit, and habit, exercise, is a matter of the action and reaction of all conditions, then it is evident that the force of the teleological argument is at once destroyed. We cannot pass beyond nature, by this route, to the inference of a transcendental cause. Man's action being a part of nature and the result of all conditions as much as is the motion of the wind or of the waves, the results he produces, like theirs, only change and never creation, the only inference we could make from his will to other will must be an inference to will that is a part of nature, a result if also a condition, a link in the chain of nature, its ends coordinate with habit but not the cause of it, and no more determining than determined. (Page 381.)

From these generalizations we see that nature is to be regarded as one great process, no part of which is independent, but all parts inter-dependent. Analysis reveals no superiority of intelligence over all else in the universe. It reveals intelligence simply as one factor in the process, no more dependent or no more independent than any other factor. It is but one link in the chain, held on and holding on, but no better, no worse, no more important, no less important than any other link. Clearly on such a basis there can be no teleology, no design. But it will be replied that our conception of the matter frees us from this conclusion. We regarded the essence of the argument from design as a belief which added to analysis. But what it added, analysis itself does not reveal. True, so we regarded it, but the theory has its answer—that all addition, all belief is itself but one factor in the process of evolution. It is no more cause than it is effect. It is but one link in the chain, held on and holding on, no more determining than determined. It does not escape analysis, but the analysis reveals it as a factor, just as it reveals natural selection as a factor.

Is this the end of the matter? Perhaps a metaphysician who is not satisfied with the statement that the only explanation we can have is analysis may have a few questions to ask. First, he would probably ask a very old one. If analysis is the method of explanation who or what does the analyzing? If one factor in the process of evolution does it, then that one factor, the intelligence within you, must submit and subject all the parts of the universe to itself. The analysis does not reveal that, for it is the prerequisite of any analysis whatsoever. So we might say to the evolutionist, "Your analysis is excellent, but it grants all we ask—it grants the superiority of the analyzing intelligence to all else in the universe." But we are not out of the difficulties of the theory with such ease and rapidity. The evolutionist replies: "If that is the conclusion you draw you have mistaken my whole argument—that the analyzing intelligence, itself submitting and subjecting for the time being all the parts of the universe to itself, is itself but a factor in one great process, no more conditioning than conditioned." This answer is somewhat bewildering, and it is at this point where the combatants usually take refuge in abusive language. Let us avoid this difficulty by coming at the matter in another way. Let us start with a Cartesian axiom. If we can prove any theory of ours to be a delusion only by somewhere assuming its reality, we must give up the hypothesis of delusion. With this axiom well in mind, let us proceed to ask what becomes of our opinions of truth and error, confronted by this information from evolution. Centuries ago, as the result of the preceding natural conditions, to use the words of the theory, there appeared the Platonic theory of the universe. In our own century, as the result of preceding natural conditions, there appeared the evolutionary theory of the universe. Now which of these theories is true? The only difference evolution can show between them is simply this—that evolution appeared farther on in the line of development. But if "farther on in the line of development" is to be taken as the test of truth, what truth difference is there between conflicting theories of the universe held today by different people simply as the result of preceding natural conditions?

Let us get the state of the matter as clearly as possible before us. If all our judgments of truth and error are simply phenomena in nature, like the flight of a bird or the roll of thunder, then those judgments are no better, and no worse, than any other natural phenomena. Truth and error are delusions, because truth and error have no meaning when applied to phenomena. But note this—that "truth and error are delusions" is a judgment. Is it a true judgment? Now it is plain as the day that we can never answer that question, if judgments are simply phenomena. And if we answer it either by "yes" or "no," we must admit that in one case at least, judgment is not a phenomenon—that intelligence, in one case at least, is superior to all else in the universe. Hence our conclusion. We must admit the fundamental belief of the argument from design, if we are to admit any judgment whatsoever as valid.

Perhaps enough has been said to show that the theory of evolution, like any other theory about nature, needs as its supplement the argument for design, and that it needs it the more the more thoroughgoing we make our theory. The more complete we make our physics, the more urgent becomes our demand for metaphysics. Perhaps enough has been said; but I should like to add another consideration in the hope of removing a possible objection. It may appear from the conclusion that we have reached that we should infer that intelligence is lawless—that it is an undetermined thing. Such a conclusion is enough to make a man who believes in order suspicious. It will be said, not only by the evolutionist, but by many others, you must admit, that whatever a man thinks, says, or does is absolutely determined by the sum total of the conditions operating at the time of the action. That is a proposition which no one who thoroughly understands it will ever dispute. Now the sum total of conditions operating at the time of action includes the man as acting. It is clear that laws can be formulated to cover only completed series of events. A series of events which has no beginning and no end can not come within the formula of law, and that is why all physics courts confusion when it talks about beginnings and ends. Any series of events which includes intelligence as a factor can be formulated under law when we assume that intelligence is present in a certain way. In that sense intelligence is not lawless. But if we mean by law simply the determination of certain phenomena by other phenomena—if we define law in terms of mere phenomena—then intelligence is not a phenomenon, and then it is not law in the sense defined—it is lawless. The moment we make clear to ourselves that natural laws are simply expressions in their lowest terms of what takes place in a completed series of events, just that moment we will make clear that freedom, God, necessity, have absolutely nothing to do with law, but they are simply metaphysical concepts of the purest type. Nature herself evinces no freedom, no necessity, no cause, no effect, no truth, no error, no good, no bad, no design. Only when the logical intelligence, in its conscious superiority to nature, reads into nature these purely metaphysical conceptions, do they win the first shadow of meaning. Now if this is true—if, while intelligence may be part of nature, and may be dependent upon nature for its material, but not for the judgment of the material—then it is clear that we owe to intelligence the only intelligible conception we can frame from nature. What we want to know is, What is the meaning of nature, and above all, what is its ideal meaning; and the moment we raise that question, we demand an answer that includes design of some sort. We are striving to interpret nature, and to interpret it without design is an impossibility.

So much of the effect upon logic of the argument from design when confronted by the theory of evolution. It is necessary to stop here, though questions crowd in upon us. Have we really modified that conception of intelligence which the theory affirmed? I think we have modified it profoundly. If the attitude of intelligence toward nature is ideal, it can not be termed natural without a considerable extension of meaning. If by natural we mean "determined by the laws of phenomena," then the attitude of intelligence is not natural —it is ideal, and here is where the importance of the matter comes to a full head. Not only is the attitude of intelligence found to be ideal, but if we were to pursue the matter further, we should find that the attitude of feeling and that of will are also ideal. What we are after is not the fact of thought, feeling, and will, but their significance. What we are after is to find out how we can make this world what we feel and think it ought to be. Here we are in ethics, and we want to realize what we think and feel this world ought to be—the fullness of an order which is greater than we, and before which we bow in reverence. Here we are in theology, but here it will be necessary for us to stop. Bringing together the salient points that have been urged, they may be expressed in this way: Since truth and error, freedom and necessity, good and bad, are conceptions which we do not find in nature, but which, by virtue of our intelligence, we read into nature, then the question becomes, not, Can we find design in nature, and so infer a designer? but, What is the most lofty conception we can frame of beneficence in design in order adequately to explain the terribly earnest life of man in the world which he strives to explain, to enjoy, and to master?

THE PROBLEM OF METAPHYSICS*

Many tendencies in recent thought indicate a revivified interest in the problem of metaphysics. While philosophers for the last few decades have never wholly neglected the problem, their treatment has been, until very recently, largely historical. Old theories have been restated in the light of renewed study, but the statements have usually followed traditional lines which had become fixed. There have been few instances of attempts to state and solve the metaphysical problem as an immediate problem of human experience. But the recent work in logic and epistemology, with its return to the immediate facts of life for its subject matter, has tended to turn our attention to the same source for the study of metaphysics. The work of science in criticizing its fundamental conceptions has been largely metaphysical in its character, even when writers like Mach and Brooks repudiate, with feeling, the imputation. *Energy* begins to take its place along with *matter* and *spirit* as a metaphysical concept indicative of the nature of reality. These newer tendencies have something of scorn for traditional and historical philosophy. With a boast, akin to that of Descartes, they would claim to be without presupposition, without hypothesis, and without substantial dependence on the past. But this is an idle boast. These newer tendencies are what they are because of the history of thought which has preceded them. They get their freshness because much of the work of the past has won general recognition, and it is, consequently, possible to proceed without the preliminary critical discussions which have characterized the historical method. It is this fact which gives to the outlook for metaphysics its encouraging character. The study of history has taught us much, and we

* In the *Philosophical Review,* Vol. XII (1903), pp. 367-385. Read as the Presidential Address at the third annual meeting of the Western Philosophical Association, April 10, 1903.

begin to find ourselves in a position where, with this knowledge as a basal possession, we can restate the problem of metaphysics with immediacy and directness. These considerations have led me to attempt the suggestion of this restatement in the light of the lessons we have learned from the historical treatment of the problem.

The history of philosophy has, in the main, been dominated by two ideas, those of evolution and classification. The great systems have been presented in their mutual antagonisms, dependencies, and supplementations, as moments in an historical development; and they have been classified in accordance with a nomenclature traditionally accepted and rendered almost classic by treatises on the introduction to philosophy. But we have at last begun to be suspicious of the result. Aristotle reads so much like a modern that we can conceive his writing after Hegel with no great change in his system. And we look in vain for the thoroughgoing materialist, spiritualist, pantheist, and the rest, of traditional phraseology. The great men refuse to be classified in this ready way, and persistently present us with conceptions which the evolutionist has told us could not possibly have been entertained in their time. The recognition of these things is bringing us freedom, so that we no longer find it necessary to regard our work as merely the next evolution out of the unfolding process, or to classify ourselves under some department of the traditional scheme. We would drink deep of the past, and, so invigorated, proceed to our task with the independence and originality of which we may be capable. But we proceed with the experience of the past behind us, and with the lessons of its history.

We have learned not only that the great systems of the past refuse to be classified in accordance with the traditional characterizations, but also that these characterizations can not stand for us for any adequate description of ultimate positions. The types of metaphysics, made classic by our terminology, seem to render reality, as Professor James is fond of pointing out, implicitly or explicitly an accomplished fact at one stroke. They thus do violence to experience, in that they leave no room for its movement, its novelty, its variability. Just for this reason they have never won the unqualified approval of anybody. They have gained their absoluteness of statement only by insisting on our ignorance of the very conditions on which such absoluteness is made to depend. They have insisted that they would be satisfactory if only we had the knowledge to make them so. If we only knew enough about the nature of matter or spirit, we should then see how everything is somehow their result. But we have become at last bold enough to say, that just because we do not know that much, and apparently can never know it, we will not let our ignorance determine the character of our metaphysics. We desire firmer ground to stand on, and shrink no more aghast before objections and arguments that rest on unverifiable hypotheses. We will take raw experience as ultimate, before we will bow to any theory which radically changes its evident character. So we have learned that the classification of metaphysical systems, such as Paulsen has laid down in his *Introduction,* for instance, does not indicate the lines we must follow, or the names by which we must be called.

We have learned also that the gulf set between appearance and reality, and between the subjective and the objective, has resulted in our stultification rather than in our enlightenment. The meaning of the reduction of everything we know to the phenomenal or the subjective has at last dawned upon us. It is, indeed, a revelation, but not the revelation it was supposed to be. Instead of turning out to be an ultimate characterization of what we know, it has turned out to be a recognition that we have returned to our point of departure. For the reduction of everything to one character whose opposite has been so shut out from us that we can neither know nor formulate it, makes of that opposite something which we do not need and can not value; and it gives to what we do have its old primary interest and its old need of metaphysical handling. The assertion that we can have no metaphysics, no insight into the nature of reality, is only the recommendation to begin metaphysical inquiry anew along lines which will not lead to this stultifying result. Absolute phenomenalism, subjectivism, and solipsism are to be rejected, not because they are false, but because they are meaningless and barren of all enlightenment. To be of value, the distinction between appearance and reality, the subjective and the objective, the single ego and its other, must be so understood as to render the implied opposition clear and illuminating. So we have learned that the reduction of everything to a character which has no intelligible opposite is not metaphysics.

We have learned also the desirability and necessity of having a metaphysics which rests on its own foundation, in as complete independence as possible. Here the reversal of history is interesting and instructive. There was a time when science and religion had to fight long and hard for their independence of metaphysics. Now, we have to contemplate the struggle of metaphysics to free itself from science on the one hand and from religion on the other. We have, in my opinion, looked with a too jealous glance on science and its achievements. We have coveted a name which has won distinguished glory apart from our participation and aid. We have blushed at the imputation of not being scientific in our work. We have sought to make metaphysics a result of science, an outgrowth from it, a rounding out of it, a sort of sum total and unity of all scientific knowledge. We have done these things, but we are beginning to realize, and the great systems of metaphysics have taught us this, that we have a claim of our own to recognition quite independent of the revelations of science, a birthright by no means to be despised. It may be unfortunate that so useful and general a term as *science* should have come to have its present restricted meaning. Yet, on the whole, I am inclined to think that the distinction has been a gain, and, for my own part, would plead for a fuller recognition of it. I modestly shrink from a calling that imposes upon me the necessity of completing the fragmentary work of the physicist, the chemist, and the biologist, or of instructing these men in the basal principles of their respective sciences. My work lies in a totally different sphere, deals with totally different problems, and can be pursued in independence of them as much as they pursue their work in independence of me. There is scientific knowledge and there is metaphysical knowledge, and these two are widely different. They involve different tasks and different problems. Science asks for the laws of existence and discovers them by experiment. Metaphysics asks for the nature of reality and discovers it by definition.

The recognition of this difference is a great gain. It points at once to a need of method on our part. But a method, as Professor Ormond has pointed out, "is not defined fundamentally when we say that it is either deductive or inductive, synthetic or analytic. The real nature of a method is determined only when we bring to light the underlying concepts and presuppositions on which its procedure rests." We need for definition a method which will do just that; and that method, in proportion to its perfection, will distinguish still more clearly science from metaphysics. A definition of reality is that at which metaphysics aims, and the introduction to the attainment of that end is the method or logic of definition. The recognition of this is to secure for metaphysics something of that independence which it deserves. To be sure, the different departments of knowledge can not proceed in absolute independence of each other and succeed. But there is a relative independence for each specific branch growing out of consideration of the concepts and underlying presuppositions on which that branch rests. This is the independence which metaphysics should have, and I think we may call that day happy when the metaphysician recognizes that his work lies in a restricted field. He will glory then in a distinction of his own without sighing for that other glory which is the scientist's pride.

Metaphysics needs to be equally independent of religion. Kant did us a world of harm by his renewed insistence that the three things with which metaphysics has fundamentally to do, are God, freedom, and immortality. These may turn out to be legitimate subjects of metaphysical inquiry, but to admit them as the sole and basal subjects, is to prejudice the definition of reality at the outset. The suspicion and the hope that metaphysicians are really poets or theologians in disguise should both be dispelled. And to that end, the emotional atmosphere should not be that in which the philosopher does his work. That work may turn out to have emotional value of the highest kind, but such value is not his aim. His definition of reality may show what the reality of God must be, but of itself that may imply no more than the exhibition of what the reality of the yet unrealized future must be. It is doubtless an excellent thing that philosophers busy themselves so much about the meaning and content of religion, but in doing this they are only doing their duty as men, not their duty as metaphysicians. The motive which leads to metaphysical inquiry is as purely theoretical as that which leads to scientific inquiry. Ultimately both must react upon human life for its perfecting. Yet in the pursuit of knowledge we must recognize the relative independence in aim and method.

We have learned also that metaphysical knowledge is, in large measure, non-explanatory in character. Of course, all knowledge aims at some sort of explanation; but there is a very wide difference between explanation by definition, and explanation by laws of connection. The phenomena of existence in all their manifold interdependence may be left untouched by metaphysics. The definition of reality may leave unformulated and unknown the general and specific laws of the occurrence of events. That is quite true historically. The method of metaphysics has not given us the laws of any of the sciences. But metaphysical inquiry is not thereby rendered useless. Let the "soul" or the "will" be a metaphysical concept, and we can not say that the clarification of that concept has given us a single law of the connection of mental processes. The concept of purpose occurs repeatedly in much of our thinking, but it does not explain how the spider spins its web. The history of science has been, in one of its aspects, the history of the rejection of concepts that do not explain by leading to the formulation of laws. But these concepts may turn out to be the ones most important for a definition of reality. Indeed, they may reveal a truth of the greatest significance, namely, that metaphysics is non-explanatory in the sense in which these concepts are such. They may free us from the besetting prejudice of metaphysicians, that a knowledge of reality is itself quite sufficient for all the uses of man, both speculative and practical. And not only that: they may also reveal their own use as concepts which we still must retain in order to preserve sanity in our thinking, to keep it from being absolutely detached and meaningless. One of the most significant illustrations of this is the concept of purpose. We may deny design in nature, we may reject final causes as explanations of existence; but we can not define a single problem, isolate a single field of inquiry, determine the requisites of the solution of a single question, without this concept as the determining factor. So deep seated in all our thinking does it disclose itself, that we are tempted to say it defines the nature of reality in at least one of its essential characters. It has, therefore, that much use. If this use is for a moment thought to have only speculative validity, that need not abash us, for speculative validity has everywhere high importance in the realm of science, no less than in that of metaphysics. But it has also the greatest practical importance. It validates the purposeful life of man. It fills nature with a content of surpassing value. It makes human history worth the reading. Admit that it does not explain, but admit also that it does define. This admission may tentatively carry with it that of the general proposition, that much of metaphysical knowledge, just because it is knowledge by definition, is non-explanatory in the sense in which laws explain.

Once more: we have learned that the distinction between epistemology and metaphysics is apt to be quite valueless, even if it has proved to be methodically useful. The history of this distinction and its bearing on metaphysical inquiry is full of suggestiveness. The great work of Kant can not be too highly valued. He has done more to clarify our view of philosophical problems than any other philosopher. In his attempt to determine and define precisely what it is to know, we find a field for the most important logical inquiry. But Kant's metaphysical conclusion does not appear to follow necessarily from his critical analysis. For the discovery that knowledge can be defined in independence of its object, that so defined it is not representative, but synthetic, constitutive, and regulative in character, does not enlighten us at all as to the metaphysical bearing of this discovery. When once knowledge is defined from an analysis of its own nature, there still remains the question, Does knowledge apply with success to any concrete content? If this question is not raised, the results of epistemology are without great significance. Knowledge may be a regulative and constitutive synthesis in time and space, in the categories, in apperception, and in reason; but if things-in-themselves will submit to such a synthesis, they can not be so shut out from our experience as Kant would make them. We know, at least, that they are adaptable to knowledge; and I can not see how the fact that this conviction rests on the experience of success, renders it invalid. Indeed, even if things-in-themselves should somehow refuse to admit of the synthesis of knowledge, we should know at least that much about them. To recognize the general truth here involved is, indeed, to find oneself in possession of a pretty intimate acquaintance with things-in-themselves. They admit of spatial and temporal construction, they admit of causal arrangement and necessary connection, they infinitely surpass any finite comprehension of them in a completed system. The absolute separation of knowledge from its object can have, therefore, no metaphysical significance.

That is the lesson we have learned from the futility of such a separation. We can in no sense define reality in a way which makes it unrelated to knowledge, but this does not make a definition of reality impossible. It shows us rather that the conception of reality thus unrelated is quite meaningless. Knowledge is thus disclosed to be a real relation between things, a form of connection which has ontological significance in the general determination of reality's definition. Whatever may be the nature of reality, it is, in a measure at least, held together in a degree of continuity by the knowing process, and to that extent definitively characterized. And it must be further recognized, that, because reality is so characterized, it admits of numberless changes and transformations. For knowledge breaks forth into action, and reality becomes modified as the result. Reality thus not only allows knowledge to synthesize it, but it allows those transformations within it which such knowledge makes possible. And so the breaking down of the barrier between knowledge and reality, which had been set there because knowledge was found to be non-representative, reveals anew the possibilities of metaphysics.

These, then, are some of the lessons that we have learned from the historical method of handling the problem of metaphysics: the weaknesses in the evolutionary conception and in traditional terminology, the futility of the distinction between appearance and reality, the necessity of an independent metaphysics, the need of a logic of definition, the non-explanatory character of much of metaphysical knowledge, with a recognition of the value of such knowledge, the metaphysical failure of the distinction between epistemology and metaphysics. We have doubtless learned others of importance, but these have appeared to me to be among the most important. The recognition of them ought to serve us in determining in a positive way the general nature of the problem of metaphysics.

This problem is naturally the nature or character of reality. What is reality? How is it to be defined? is the metaphysical question. But such a question has its own meaning apart from any answer which may be given to it. For a search for the concrete characterization of reality implies the abstract form which is to receive the concrete content. The problem of metaphysics involves, thus, first of all, its detailed formal statement. We have to ask in most general terms. What does the solution demand in principle, under the conditions which we may discover as determining it logically? Here we come at once upon one of the most significant positive results of our previous discussion. It is this: reality can not be defined intelligibly as a system absolutely external to the one who formulates it, nor a system in which the one who formulates it is a mere incident, or of which he is a mere product. That is the positive contribution made by the weakness discovered in the traditional types of metaphysics, in the breach between reality and appearance, in all thoroughgoing evolutionary conceptions, and especially the weakness in the distinction between epistemology and metaphysics. The moment the definition of reality makes of reality an explicitly or implicitly complete system over against the metaphysician, or makes of him a merely incidental occurrence in its otherwise independent operations, reality has been put beyond any intelligible grasp of it. Reality absolutely external to the metaphysician will give him nothing besides himself. And reality, become momentarily conscious in the metaphysician, will give him no more than his moment of consciousness. Here, as I have said, we are back once more at our point of departure, with the metaphysical curiosity still unsatisfied. The failure results from the destruction of the only point of view from which anything can be defined, namely, the point of view which allows an independent position over against the matter to which it is directed. Destroy such independent positions, and the possibility of definition is destroyed. This fact is, of course, practically recognized. From some point of view, as independent, we define an object which from that point can be viewed and defined. But we should give to this epistemological principle its metaphysical significance, and recognize that the definition of reality involves numberless points of departure from which reality may be grasped, and that each of these points, in its relation to what is thereby defined, is an absolute and undivided individual.

Thus we may claim that the problem of metaphysics is fundamentally the problem of individuality, the definition of reality is primarily the definition of the individual. But individuality can not be defined away or argued out of existence. Its definition must give to it the fullest ontological recognition. No metaphysics must be allowed to vitiate the basal proposition about reality, namely, that it consists of that which can be defined and grasped solely from points of departure absolutely individual in character. If reality is a system, it is a system of individuals. If it is not a system, individuality is one of its essential characters. Whatever it is, individuals enter somehow into its constitution. If one should claim that thought immediately demands that we should transcend individuality, we can answer that the attempt to transcend it is to reinstate it. Thus it is that individuality can not be defined or argued out of existence. It is there to stay.

The definition of individuality is thus the first problem of metaphysics. From the nature of the case, this definition must be non-explanatory in the sense indicated in our previous discussion. If individuals are ultimate, we can never hope to show how they originate or what the laws of their occurrence are. We can define them, so to speak, only denotatively. We can exhibit in many ways their presence. We can show how they are repeatedly involved. We can employ other terms and conceptions to make them more palpable. Here such categories as *activity, change,* and *the transient* may be found to be of use. They exhibit that to which the term individuality is applied in its concrete bearings. The whole of the logical doctrine of universals and predication may serve in the desired determination. But our concern here is one of method and not of content. We may therefore leave the general consideration of the problem with these suggestions, since the definition of individuality has been pointed out as the primary problem of metaphysics, and the methodical character of this definition has been noted.

It is to be observed, however, that the attempt to carry over the idea of individuality into the realm of concrete determination, and, indeed, the attempt to construe what we mean when we say that reality has somehow individuals as its primary ingredients, involve new questions in the general determination of the problem of metaphysics. For we wish to know more of these individuals, their number, their kind, their order, and in this attempt we find ourselves involved in new problems. Then, too, that indefinite term *somehow,* which has been used to indicate the way in which individuals enter into the constitution of reality, demands determination. As these things are reflected on, the second basal problem of metaphysics arises, that of continuity. Individuality and continuity are bound together in all our thinking. Indeed, the assertion that thought demands that individuality be transcended is really the demand for continuity as a supplementary conception. Again, we should give to these epistemological principles their metaphysical significance. If we are bound to recognize that individuality enters into the constitution of reality, we are equally bound to recognize that continuity enters also. But before concrete significance is attached to this fact, we should concern ourselves with the problem of method.

It is to be noted that, while individuality and continuity are supplementary and correlative, they are radically opposite in nature. Continuity is not itself individual, but is the denial of individuality in the realm where it applies. We may dismiss at once, therefore, all attempts to derive individuals from a continuum, or to construct a continuum out of any number of individuals. The two facts may go together, may even imply each other, yet the one may not, therefore, be deduced from the other. This is, in fact, but another way of asserting that the concept of continuity, like that of individuality, is non-explanatory in character. It may be admitted that the character of the continuity may be determined by reference to the character of the individuals, as I shall attempt to show later, but the fact of its presence in reality may not be so explained or determined. The logical universal may serve here as a passing illustration. Any number of individuals may exist in a general class. The fact of class can not be deduced from that of individuality, nor the latter fact from the former. But the character of the class may be determined by the character of the individuals. So it may turn out that the continuity of reality gets its character from the individuals, or from one individual, as Aristotle maintained; but such a result would not militate against the recognition of the distinctness of the two conceptions. As I return to the consideration of this question later, I submit at present no further discussion of it.

Individuality and continuity are supplementary, but essentially different in nature. It is quite possible, therefore, that the continuity may also have a character essentially different from that of individuals. One such character, at least, is readily recognized, that of infinite divisibility. This can not be ascribed to individuals, but it appears to be of the very nature of a continuum. But as individuals can not be deduced from a continuum, they can not be arrived at by a process of infinite division. Again, the points determined in any way we please by intersecting directions in a continuum are not true individuals. But such points may involve individuality in their determination. A continuum can not determine itself or make its own directions intersect. Such a determination must come ultimately from outside the continuum, from an exterior point of departure. And when once this determination has originated, the continuum will present necessary relations between the points defined and all that beauty of a causal nexus which is so much admired. The impossibility of deducing necessary connection from individuals was the classic contribution of Hume to metaphysics, and it can hardly be claimed that Kant successfully supplanted it. But it may be recognized that necessary connection is the nature of a continuum determined in any direction. Such a consideration suggests quite different metaphysical conclusions to be drawn from the famous antinomies. Instead of indicating an inevitable dialectic of reason with itself, they point to a radical diversity in the constitution of reality.

Any attempt to grasp individuals in a continuity involves permanent acquisitions or relations for knowledge, at least. Of course, it is abstractly conceivable that individuals, even in a continuity, should be of such a character that every attempt to relate them would be futile. Yet this is not true as a matter of experience. Whatever the nature of our individuals and their continuity may be, the fact of their supplementation does involve successive changes which result in permanent acquisitions. The processes of reality are conservative. Individuals exist in continuity in such a way that the result is cumulative. Each individual, if it alters in any way, alters thereby the continuum in such a way that the alteration is not wholly lost. The continuum takes it up and preserves it. We can express this fact in no other way than by saying that the existence of individuals in continuity gives to such an existence the character of purpose. Thus the problem of purpose appears to be another fundamental problem of metaphysics.

It is by no means necessary to the conception of purpose that it be defined as something superimposed upon the individuals or existing prior to them, either temporally or logically. All that we need to embody in our definition is the recognition that the alterations in individuals are cumulative in effect. Such a recognition provides for the constant approach of this accumulation toward definite issues through the elimination of useless factors. Thus far the definition of purpose involves no explanatory elements. It is rather descriptive and definitive of the nature of reality. But we may inquire after the character of this purpose. This inquiry may reveal an explanation of the character of purpose through its reference to the character of the individuals or of their continuum. Here we return to the general problem of which further discussion was promised. Our attempt to define reality may show that there must enter into this definition three basal facts, individuality, continuity, and purpose. We may recognize that the nature of reality is such that these facts do not admit of deduction from each other or from any original, and consequently that they are non-explanatory in character. But we can not hold these facts in such isolation that there will result between them no unity of any sort. This desired unity, no matter what may be its origination, will be, in one aspect at least, a unity of character, that is, the three facts will present the same aspect in certain directions. We may ask, then, Whence does this unity of character arise?

It has been suggested already that the continuum may get its character from the individuals or from one individual. An illustration of this may be seen in the character of a people's history arising from its individuals and great men. But the converse of the general proposition does not appear to be true, namely, that the individuals get their character from the continuum. For such a supposition reduces continuity to individuality. It not only distinguishes continuity from individuality, but isolates it, and we should require a further continuum to bring our individuals and the first continuity thus isolated together. We should find ourselves here on the well-travelled road to no conclusion. We must recognize, therefore, that the continuity gets its character from the individuals. This is, indeed, but another way of saying that the continuity is progressive, cumulative, purposeful. And so our further question is answered, and we recognize that ultimately purpose gets its character from the individuals.

We are thus in a position to ask whether the character of continuity and purpose alike is to be derived from all the individuals, or from a restricted number? The answer to this question carries us into the material side of metaphysics, which it was the purpose of this address to avoid as far as possible. But the following suggestions are offered. We may recognize at once that all individuals must enter into the determination of the character as a whole. The question can refer only to the dominating characteristics. If these are to be ascribed to a single individual, this individual must be regarded as holding a unique and dominating position. Again, if knowledge, as indicated above, is a real connection between the elements of reality, and if we are entitled, therefore, to regard knowledge as in any sense the dominating character of the continuum, we may conclude that the individuals who can know are the essentially determining factors. Such a conclusion would involve a recognition that a unique individual, if insisted on, would very likely have a character akin to these factors. Even if the argument should not be pursued in this particular way, its general line of procedure has been indicated.

Purpose involves, as we have seen, that the alterations which may take place in the world of individuals are accumulated and conserved. We may admit that the bare conception of individuality does not oblige us to think of individuals altering in any way. But however *a priori* our conceptions may appear on analysis, they are never given apart from certain determinations of experience. We are obliged, therefore, when we view individuals in their existence, to recognize that they alter. Indeed, as noted above, *alteration, change, movement,* are concepts well calculated to assist in a fuller determination of the definition of individuality. Since individuals do alter, we find another problem of prime importance for metaphysics, namely the problem of potentiality. This problem is bound up not only with the fact of individuality, but with that of purpose also. For the fact of accumulation and the narrowing of this accumulation down to definite results to the exclusion of others, forbids our entertaining the supposition that the future is wholly without determination. We may admit that a given event may never occur, but if it should occur, we are forced to recognize that it will occur within certain restrictions which it calls into being. The acorn may never become an oak, but should it become one, there exist already in some shape the conditions which are to determine that result. This fact is the fact of potentiality. In all the determinations of our knowledge, few concepts are of greater value. We constantly ascribe to the elements with which we deal certain potentialities which allow us to formulate the possible results. Instead of recognizing this practice as an epistemological infirmity, we should recognize its ontological significance, and conclude that the potential is itself an element in reality's constitution.

We should have thus a fourth factor in our general definition of the metaphysical problem.

The fact that it seems impossible to formulate the potential with any exactness before it loses its character leads us easily to reject its validity. But it was pointed out as long ago as Aristotle that this rejection drives us to the alternative of affirming the whole realm of being to be in a state of changeless actuality. Violence is thus done to the facts of life. Alteration is driven out of the realm of the real. Such a result cannot dominate us long. Change and motion still persist, no matter with what amount of unreality we may designate them. We must give some status to the bare potential, even if the task appears most difficult. We may recognize at once that the bare potential contains within itself no elements which can lead to its own realization. To be more than a mere possibility, something else must supervene. The whole of existence at any moment faces the future, therefore, with untold possibilities. Each of them, if started on the road toward realization, has its path determined, but from the point of view of potentiality, all are equally possible. The determined path presents us with all the elements of a necessary connection, but we look in vain for such connection when we seek among the untold possibilities the one which is in effect to be. Something new must add itself, must emerge, as it were, out of non-existence into being. An arbitrary point of departure must arise, and when once it has arisen, the movement proceeds with definiteness. It is thus, whether we like it or not, that the doctrine of chance originates. To adopt again the argument of Aristotle, the elimination of chance is the elimination of the potential. For if therc had always existed the elements necessary to transform the potential, it would have always been transformed, and so motion and alteration could have no place in the scheme of things. Chance along with the potential would thus appear to be essential elements in the definition of reality.

It is very easy to misconstrue the doctrine of chance. Too readily we conclude that it destroys the possibility of exact knowledge in all spheres of inquiry. We fail to observe that all our knowledge up to the most exact rests on presuppositions which give to it all the validity it can claim. If conclusions are always drawn from premises, if every consequent must first have its antecedent, we may well conclude that this necessity in knowledge has its significance for reality as well. Indeed, if we knew all the conditions that are necessary to any result, we should know that result. But the moment we inquire after these conditions we are led to others, until the admission is forced from us that our knowledge will never free itself from ultimate contingency. Only a lack of broad reflection on the problems of existence can lead us to ascribe this result to the imperfection of our knowledge. It is far more rational to ascribe it to the nature of reality itself, and to recognize that the elements which enter into the constitution of reality force us to admit that any result can be determined only when a point of departure is first determined, and that this determination, if original, as it must be to preserve potentiality, is something new and underived in the scheme of things. And here we are back again at the recognition of individuality from which our discussion started.

The considerations here briefly outlined have aimed at stating the problem of metaphysics in terms of its most essential elements, and in independence of its concrete content. In their light, an inquiry concerning the nature of reality appears to be an inquiry whose results are to be expressed in terms such as individuality, continuity, purpose, potentiality, and chance. The complete definition of these concepts would be a very close approach to the complete definition of reality. Their recognition would enable us, I think, to approach the solution of the problem of metaphysics with an independence and directness highly to be desired. I have confined the discussion closely to the formal side of metaphysics, avoiding as far as possible its material content. The advantages of such a procedure are evident. Before the solution of the problem can be effected, it is necessary to have its statement, to formulate its equation, as it were. We must know beforehand the conditions which our solution is to fulfill, in order to determine its correctness when attained. This general consideration applies to metaphysics with as much cogency as to any other branch of inquiry. The indication of these things was the purpose of this address.

Although this purpose has, as I hope, been in a measure attained, I should like in conclusion to emphasize in a summary form the more important points of the discussion. The concepts, in terms of which the problem of metaphysics has been stated, have been regarded as ultimate and underived. In logical terms, they have no common genus in terms of which they can be defined, and they cannot be deduced from each other or from a common conception. To adapt an idea of the Scholastics, they are to be regarded rather as ultimate differentia than as species under a common genus. The definition of them can be accomplished, therefore, only by exhibiting them in their concrete form and analysing their concrete content. It is the status of their existence and the concrete modes of their operation which have to be determined. Yet even if they are ultimate and incapable of deduction, they exist together and supplement each other. They do this as a matter of fact, and not as a matter of deduction, or under conditions which themselves need analysis and explanation. In other words, the moment we attempt to grasp reality, we find ourselves compelled to grasp it in these terms, in full recognition of their absoluteness and their supplementation. We are compelled to recognize that reality is not a term which covers something which has no irreducible internal differences, but a term which covers ultimate differences in supplementation. Finally, let it not be urged as an objection that this is to elevate as the test of reality's ultimate constitution the imperfections of knowledge, the poor, weak fact that every proposition, to convey a meaning, must have a subject and a predicate which are different. For when we say that there are certain conditions which must be fulfilled in order that knowledge may be knowledge, we must recognize that it is the constitution of reality which determines these conditions. We may ascribe what *a priori* powers we like to knowledge; but these powers would never receive an atom of significance in experience, if reality did not call them out and fit into them. We must most certainly give up the ways in which alone it is possible for us to know, if those ways will not work, and most assuredly it can be nothing but reality which is to determine which of our possible ways is to succeed. If, therefore, reality baffles us until we recognize that we must seek to grasp it in some such terms as indicated in our discussion, we may recognize in these terms the elements of the problem of metaphysics and the ultimate determinations of the constitution of reality.

THE FIELD OF LOGIC*

CURRENT tendencies in logical theory make a determination of the field of logic fundamental to any statement of the general problems of the science. In view of this fact, I propose in this paper to attempt such a determination by a general discussion of the relation of logic to mathematics, psychology, and biology, especially noting in connection with biology the tendency known as pragmatism. In conclusion, I shall indicate what the resulting general problems appear to be.

I

There may appear, at first, little to distinguish mathematics in its most abstract, formal, and symbolic type from logic. Indeed, mathematics as the universal method of all knowledge has been the ideal of many philosophers, and its right to be such has been claimed of late with renewed force. The recent notable advances in the science have done much to make this claim plausible. A logician, a non-mathematical one, might be tempted to say that, in so far as mathematics is the method of thought in general, it has ceased to be mathematics; but, I suppose, one ought not to quarrel too much with a definition, but should let mathematics mean knowledge simply, if the mathematicians wish it. I shall not, therefore, enter the controversy regarding the proper limits of mathematical inquiry. I wish to note, however, a tendency in the identification of logic and mathematics which seems to me to be inconsistent with the real significance of knowledge. I refer to the exaltation of the freedom of thought in the construction of conceptions, definitions, and hypotheses.

The assertion that mathematics is a "pure" science is often taken to mean that it is in no way dependent on experience in

* In *Congress of Arts and Science,* Vol. 1, Boston, Houghton Mifflin, 1905, pp. 313-330.

the construction of its basal concepts. The space with which geometry deals may be Euclidean or not, as we please; it may be the real space of experience or not; the properties of it and the conclusions reached about it may hold in the real world or they may not; for the mind is free to construct its conception and definition of space in accordance with its own aims. Whether geometry is to be ultimately a science of this type must be left, I suppose, for the mathematicians to decide. A logician may suggest, however, that the propriety of calling all these conceptions "space" is not as clear as it ought to be. Still further, there seems to underlie all arbitrary spaces, as their foundation, a good deal of the solid material of empirical knowledge, gained by human beings through contact with an environing world, the environing character of which seems to be quite independent of the freedom of their thought. However that may be, it is evident, I think, that the generalization of the principle involved in this idea of the freedom of thought in framing its conception of space, would, if extended to logic, give us a science of knowledge which would have no necessary relation to the real things of experience, although these are the things with which all concrete knowledge is most evidently concerned. It would inform us about the conclusions which necessarily follow from accepted conceptions, but it could not inform us in any way about the real truth of these conclusions. It would, thus, always leave a gap between our knowledge and its objects which logic itself would be quite impotent to close. Truth would thus become an entirely extra-logical matter. So far as the science of knowledge is concerned, it would be an accident if knowledge fitted the world to which it refers. Such a conception of the science of knowledge is not the property of a few mathematicians exclusively, although they have, perhaps, done more than others to give it its present revived vitality. It is the classic doctrine that logic is the science of thought as thought, meaning thereby thought in independence of any specific object whatever.

In regard to this doctrine, I would not even admit that such a science of knowledge is possible. You can not, by a process of generalization or free construction, rid thought of connection with objects; and there is no such thing as a general content or as content-in-general. Generalization simply reduces the richness of content and, consequently, of implication. It deals with concrete subject-matter as much and as directly as if the content were individual and specialized. "Things equal to the same thing are equal to each other," is a truth, not about thought, but about things. The conclusions about a fourth dimension follow, not from the fact that we have thought of one, but from the conception about it which we have framed. Neither generalization nor free construction can reveal the operations of thought in transcendental independence.

It may be urged, however, that nothing of this sort was ever claimed. The bondage of thought to content must be admitted, but generalization and free construction, just because they give us the power to vary conditions as we please, give us thinking in a relative independence of content, and thus show us how thought operates irrespective of, although not independent of, its content. The binomial theorem operates irrespective of the values substituted for its symbols. But I can find no gain in this restatement of the position. It is true, in a sense, that we may determine the way thought operates irrespective of any specific content by the processes of generalization and free construction; but it is important to know in what sense. Can we claim that such irrespective operation means that we have discovered certain logical constants, which now stand out as the distinctive tools of thought? Or does it rather mean that this process of varying the content of thought as we please reveals certain real constants, certain ultimate characters of reality, which no amount of generalization or free construction can possibly alter? The second alternative seems to me to be the correct one. Whether it is or not may be left here undecided. What I wish to emphasize is the fact that the decision is one of the things of vital interest for logic, and properly belongs in that science. Clearly, we can never know the significance of ultimate constants for our thinking until we know what their real character is. To determine that character we must most certainly pass out of the realm of generalization and free construction; logic must become other than simply mathematical or symbolic.

There is another sense in which the determination of the operations of thought irrespective of its specific content is interpreted in connection with the exaltation of generalization and free construction. Knowledge, it is said, is solely a matter of implication, and logic, therefore, is the science of implication simply. If this is so, it would appear possible to develop the whole doctrine of implication by the use of symbols, and thus free the doctrine from dependence on the question as to how far these symbols are themselves related to the real things of the world. If, for instance, *a* implies *b*, then if *a* is true, *b* is true, and this quite irrespective of the real truth of *a* or *b*. It is to be urged, however, in opposition to this view, that knowledge is concerned ultimately only with the real truth of *a* and *b*, and that the implication is of no significance whatever apart from this truth. There is no virtue in the mere implication. Still further, the supposition that there can be a doctrine of implication, simply, seems to be based on a misconception. For even so-called formal implication gets its significance only on the supposed truth of the terms with which it deals. We suppose that *a does* imply *b*, and that *a is* true. In other words, we can state this law of implication only as we first have valid instances of it given in specific, concrete cases. The law is a generalization and nothing more. The formal statement gives only an apparent freedom from experience. Moreover, there is no reason for saying that *a* implies *b* unless it does so either really or by supposition. If *a* really implies *b*, then the implication is clearly not a matter of thinking it; and to suppose the implication is to feign a reality, the implications of which are equally free from the processes by which they are thought. Ultimately, therefore, logic must take account of real implications. We can not avoid this through the use of a symbolism which virtually implies them. Implication can have a logical character only because it has first a metaphysical one.

The supposition underlying the conception of logic I have been examining is, itself, open to doubt and seriously questioned. That supposition was the so-called freedom of thought. The argument has already shown that there is certainly a very definite limit to this freedom, even when logic is conceived in a very abstract and formal way. The processes of knowledge are bound up with their contents, and have their character largely determined thereby. When, moreover, we view knowledge in its genesis, when we take into consideration the contributions which psychology and biology have made to our general view of what knowledge is, we seem forced to conclude that the conceptions which we frame are very far from being our own free creations. They have, on the contrary, been laboriously worked out through the same processes of successful adaptation which have resulted in other products. Knowledge has grown up in connection with the unfolding processes of reality, and has, by no means, freely played over its surface. That is why even the most abstract of all mathematics is yet grounded in the evolution of human experience.

In the remaining parts of this paper, I shall discuss further the claims of psychology and biology. The conclusion I would draw here is that the field of logic can not be restricted to a realm where the operations of thought are supposed to move freely, independent or irrespective of their contents and the objects of a real world; and that mathematics, instead of giving us any support for the supposition that it can, carries us, by the processes of symbolization and formal implication, to recognize that logic must ultimately find its field where implications are real, independent of the processes by which they are thought, and irrespective of the conceptions we choose to frame.

II

The processes involved in the acquisition and systematization of knowledge may, undoubtedly, be regarded as mental processes and fall thus within the province of psychology. It may be claimed, therefore, that every logical process is also a psychological one. The important question is, however, is it nothing more? Do its logical and psychological characters simply coincide? Or, to put the question in still another form, as a psychological process simply, does it also serve as a logical one? The answers to these questions can be determined only by first noting what psychology can say about it as a mental process.

In the first place, psychology can analyze it, and so determine its elements and their connections. It can thus distinguish it from all other mental processes by pointing out its unique elements or their unique and characteristic connection. No one will deny that a judgment is different from an emotion, or that an act of reasoning is different from a volition; and no one will claim that these differences are entirely beyond the psychologist's power to ascertain accurately and precisely. Still further, it appears possible for him to determine with the same accuracy and precision the distinction in content and connection between processes which are true and those which are false. For, as mental processes, it is natural to suppose that they contain distinct differences of character which are ascertainable. The states of mind called belief, certainty, conviction, correctness, truth, are thus, doubtless, all distinguishable as mental states. It may be admitted, therefore, that there can be a thoroughgoing psychology of logical processes.

Yet it is quite evident to me that the characterization of a mental process as logical is not a psychological characterization. In fact, I think it may be claimed that the characterization of any mental process in a specific way, say as an emotion, is extra-psychological. Judgments and inferences are, in short, not judgments and inferences because they admit of psychological analysis and explanation, any more than space is space because the perception of it can be worked out by genetic psychology. In other words, knowledge is first *knowledge*, and only later a set of processes for psychological analysis. That is why, as it seems to me, all psychological logicians, from Locke to our own day, have signally failed in dealing with the problem of knowledge. The attempt to construct knowledge out of mental states, the relations between ideas, and the relation of ideas to things, has been, as I read the history, decidedly without profit. Confusion and divergent opinion have resulted instead of agreement and confidence. On precisely the same psychological foundation, we have such divergent views of knowledge as idealism, phenomenalism, and agnosticism, with many other strange mixtures of logic, psychology, and metaphysics. The lesson of these perplexing theories seems to be that logic, as logic, must be divorced from psychology.

It is also of importance to note, in this connection, that the determination of a process as mental and as thus falling within the domain of psychology strictly, has by no means been worked out to the general satisfaction of psychologists themselves. Recent literature abounds in elaborate discussion of the distinction between what is a mental fact and what not, with a prevailing tendency to draw the remarkable conclusion that all facts are somehow mental or experienced facts. The situation would be worse for psychology than it is, if that vigorous science had not learned from other sciences the valuable knack of isolating concrete problems and attacking them directly, without the burden of previous logical or metaphysical speculation. Thus knowledge, which is the peculiar province of logic, is increased, while we wait for the acceptable definition of a mental fact. But definitions, be it remembered, are themselves logical matters. Indeed, some psychologists have gone so far as to claim that the distinction of a fact as mental is a purely logical distinction. This is significant as indicating that the time has not yet come for the identification of logic and psychology.

In refreshingly sharp contrast to the vagueness and uncertainty which beset the definition of a mental fact are the palpable concreteness and definiteness of knowledge itself. Every science, even history and philosophy, are instances of it. What constitutes a knowledge ought to be as definite and precise a question as could be asked. That logic has made no more progress than it has in the answer to it appears to be due to the fact that it has not sufficiently grasped the significance of its own simplicity. Knowledge has been the important business of thinking man, and he ought to be able to tell what he does in order to know, as readily as he tells what he does in order to build a house. And that is why the Aristotelian logic has held its own so long. In that logic, "the master of them that know" simply rehearsed the way he had systematized his own stores of knowledge. Naturally we, so far as we have followed his methods, have had practically nothing to add. In our efforts to improve on him, we have too often left the right way and followed the impossible method inaugurated by Locke. Had we examined with greater persistence our own methods of making science, we should have profited more. The introduction of psychology, instead of helping the situation, only confuses it.

Let it be granted, however, in spite of the vagueness of what is meant by a mental fact, that logical processes are also mental processes. This fact has, as I have already suggested, an important bearing on their genesis, and sets very definite limits to the freedom of thought in creating. It is not, however, as mental processes that they have the value of knowledge. A mental process which is knowledge purports to be connected with something other than itself, something which may not be a mental process at all. This connection should be investigated, but the investigation of it belongs, not to psychology, but to logic.

I am well aware that this conclusion runs counter to some metaphysical doctrines, and especially to idealism in all its forms, with the epistemologies based thereon. It is, of course, impossible here to defend my position by an elaborate analysis of these metaphysical systems. But I will say this. I am in entire agreement with idealism in its claim that questions of knowledge and of the nature of reality can not ultimately be separated, because we can know reality only *as* we know it. But the general question as to how we know reality can still be raised. By this I do not mean the question, how is it possible for us to have knowledge at all, or how is it possible for reality to be known at all, but how, as a matter of fact, do we actually know it? That we really do know it, I would most emphatically claim. Still further, I would claim that what we know about it is determined, not by the fact that we can know in general, but by the way reality, as distinct from our knowledge, has determined. These ways appear to me to be ascertainable, and form, thus, undoubtedly, a section of metaphysics. But the metaphysics will naturally be realistic rather than idealistic.

III

Just as logical processes may be regarded as, at the same time, psychological processes, so they may be regarded, with equal right, as vital processes, coming thus under the categories of evolution. The tendency so to regard them is very marked at the present day, especially in France and in this country. In France, the movement has perhaps received the clearer definition. In America, the union of logic and biology is complicated—and at times even lost sight of—by emphasis on the idea of evolution generally. It is not my intention to trace the history of this movement, but I should like to call attention to its historic motive in order to get it in a clear light.

That the theory of evolution, even Darwinism itself, has radically transformed our historical, scientific, and philosophical methods, is quite evident. Add to this the influence of the Hegelian philosophy, with its own doctrine of development, and one finds the causes of the rather striking unanimity which is discoverable in many ways between Hegelian idealists, on the one hand, and philosophers of evolution of Spencer's type, on the other. Although two men would, perhaps, not appear more radically different at first sight than Hegel and Spencer, I am inclined to believe that we shall come to recognize more and more in them an identity of philosophical conception. The pragmatism of the day is a striking confirmation of this opinion, for it is often the expression of Hegelian ideas in Darwinian and Spencerian terminology. The claims of idealism and of evolutionary science and philosophy have thus sought reconciliation. Logic has been, naturally, the last of the sciences to yield to evolutionary and genetic treatment. It could not escape long, especially when the idea of evolution had been so successful in its handling of ethics. If morality can be brought under the categories of evolution, why not thinking also? In answer to that question we have the theory that thinking is an adaptation, judgment is instrumental. But I would not leave the impression that this is true of pragmatism alone, or that it has been developed only through pragmatic tendencies. It is naturally the result also of the extension of biological philosophy. In the biological conception of logic, we have, then, an interesting coincidence in the results of tendencies differing widely in their genesis.

It would be hazardous to deny, without any qualifications, the importance of genetic considerations. Indeed, the fact that evolution in the hands of a thinker like Huxley, for instance, should make consciousness and thinking apparently useless epiphenomena in a developing world, has seemed like a most contradictory evolutionary philosophy. It was difficult to make consciousness a real function in development so long as it was regarded as only cognitive in character. Evolutionary philosophy, coupled with physics, had built up a sort of closed system with which consciousness could not interfere, but which it could know, and know with all the assurance of a traditional logic. If, however, we were to be consistent evolutionists, we could not abide by such a remarkable result. The whole process of thinking must be brought within evolution, so that knowledge, even the knowledge of the evolutionary hypothesis itself, must appear as an instance of adaptation. In order to do this, however, consciousness must not be conceived as only cognitive. Judgment, the core of logical processes, must be regarded as an instrument and as a mode of adaptation.

The desire for completeness and consistency in an evolutionary philosophy is not the only thing which makes the denial of genetic considerations hazardous. Strictly biological considerations furnish reasons of equal weight for caution. For instance, one will hardly deny that the whole sensory apparatus is a striking instance of adaptation. Our perceptions of the world would thus appear to be determined by this adaptation, to be instances of adjustment. They might conceivably have been different, and in the case of many other creatures, the perceptions of the world are undoubtedly different. All our logical processes, referring ultimately as they do to our perceptions, would thus appear finally to depend on the adaptation exhibited in the development of our sensory apparatus. So-called laws of thought would seem to be but abstract statements or formulations of the results of this adjustment. It would be absurd to suppose that a man thinks in a sense radically different from that in which he digests, or a flower blossoms, or that two and two are four in a sense radically different from that in which a flower has a given number of petals. Thinking, like digesting and blossoming, is an effect, a product, possibly a structure.

I am not at all interested in denying the force of these considerations. They have, to my mind, the greatest importance, and due weight has, as yet, not been given to them. To one at all committed to a unitary and evolutionary view of the world, it must indeed seem strange if thinking itself should not be the result of evolution, or that, in thinking, parts of the world had not become adjusted in a new way. But while I am ready to admit this, I am by no means ready to admit some of the conclusions for logic and metaphysics which are often drawn from the admission. Just because thought, as a product of evolution, is functional and judgment instrumental, it by no means follows that logic is but a branch of biology, or that knowledge of the world is but a temporary adjustment, which, as knowledge, might have been radically different. In these conclusions, often drawn with Protagorean assurance, two considerations of crucial importance seem to be overlooked: first, that adaptation is itself metaphysical in character, and secondly, that while knowledge may be functional and judgment instrumental, the character of the functioning has the character of knowledge, which sets it off sharply from all other functions.

It seems strange to me that the admission that knowledge is a matter of adaptation, and thus a relative matter, should, in these days, be regarded as in any way destroying the claims of knowledge to metaphysical certainty. Yet, somehow, the opinion widely prevails that the doctrine of relativity necessarily involves the surrender of anything like absolute truth. "All our knowledge is relative, and, therefore, only partial, incomplete, and but practically trustworthy," is a statement repeatedly made. The fact that, if our development had been different, our knowledge would have been different, is taken to involve the conclusion that our knowledge cannot possibly disclose the real constitution of things, that it is essentially conditional, that it is only a mental device for getting results, that any other system of knowledge which would get results equally well would be equally true; in short, that there can be no such thing as metaphysical or epistemological truth. These conclusions do indeed seem strange, and especially strange on the basis of evolution. For while the evolutionary process might, conceivably, have been different, its results are, in any case, the results of the process. They are not arbitrary. We might have digested without stomachs, but the fact that we use stomachs in this important process ought not to free us from metaphysical respect for the organ. As M. Rey suggests, in the *Revue Philosophique* for June, 1904, a creature without the sense of smell would have no geometry, but that does not make geometry essentially hypothetical, a mere mental construction; for *we* have geometry because of the working out of nature's laws. Indeed, instead of issuing in a relativistic metaphysics of knowledge, the doctrine of relativity should issue in the recognition of the finality of knowledge in every case of ascertainably complete adaptation. In other words, adaptation is itself metaphysical in character. Adjustment is always adjustment between things, and yields only what it does yield. The things or elements get into the state which is their adjustment, and this adjustment purports to be their actual and unequivocal ordering in relation to one another. Different conditions might have produced a different ordering, but, again, this ordering would be equally actual and unequivocal, equally the *one* ordering to issue from them. To suppose or admit that the course of events might have been and might be different is not at all to suppose or admit that it was or is different; it is, rather, to suppose and admit that we have real knowledge of what that course really was and is. This seems to be very obvious.

Yet the evolutionist often thinks that he is not a metaphysician, even when he brings all his conceptions systematically under the conception of evolution. This must be due to some temporary lack of clearness. If evolution is not a metaphysical doctrine when extended to apply to all science, all morality, all logic, in short, all things, then it is quite meaningless for evolutionists to pronounce a metaphysical sentence on logical processes. But if evolution is a metaphysics, then its sentence is metaphysical, and in every case of adjustment or adaptation we have a revelation of the nature of reality in a definite and unequivocal form. This conclusion applies to logical processes as well as to others. The recognition that they are vital processes can, therefore, have little significance for these processes in their distinctive character as logical. They are like all other vital processes in that they are vital and subject to evolution. They are unlike all others in that thought is unlike digestion or breathing. To regard logical processes as vital processes does not in any way, therefore, invalidate them as logical processes or make it superfluous to consider their claim to give us real knowledge of a real world. Indeed, it makes such a consideration more necessary and important.

A second consideration overlooked by the Protagorean tendencies of the day is that judgment, even if it is instrumental, purports to give us knowledge, that is, it claims to reveal what is independent of the judging process. Perhaps I ought not to say that this consideration is overlooked, but rather that it is denied significance. It is even denied to be essential to judgment. It is claimed that, instead of revealing anything independent of the judging process, judgment is just the adjustment and no more. It is a reorganization of experience, an attempt at control. All this looks to me like a misstatement of the facts. Judgment *claims* to be no such thing. It does not function as such a thing. When I make any judgment, even the simplest, I may make it as the result of tension, because of a demand for reorganization, in order to secure control of experience; but the judgment *means* for me something quite different. It means decidedly and unequivocally that in reality, apart from the judging process, things exist and operate just as the judgment declares. If it is claimed that this meaning is illusory, I eagerly desire to know on what solid ground its illusoriness can be established. When the conclusion was reached that gravitation varies directly as the mass and inversely as the square of the distance, it was doubtless reached in an evolutionary and pragmatic way; but it claimed to disclose a fact which prevailed before the conclusion was reached, and in spite of the conclusion. Knowledge has been born of the travail of living, but it has been born as knowledge.

When the knowledge character of judgment is insisted on, it seems almost incredible that any one would think of denying or overlooking it. Indeed, current discussions are far from clear on the subject. Pragmatists are constantly denying that they hold the conclusions that their critics almost unanimously draw. There is, therefore, a good deal of confusion of thought yet to be dispelled. Yet there seems to be current a pronounced determination to banish the epistemological problem from logic. This is, to my mind, suspicious, even when epistemology is defined in a way which most epistemologists would not approve. It is suspicious just because we must always ask eventually that most epistemological and metaphysical question: "Is knowledge true?" To answer, It is true when it functions in a way to satisfy the needs which generated its activity, is, no doubt, correct, but it is by no means adequate. The same answer can be made to the inquiry after the efficiency of any vital process whatever, and is, therefore, not distinctive. We have still to inquire into the specific character of the needs which originate judgments and of the consequent satisfaction. Just here is where the uniqueness of the logical problem is disclosed. With conscious beings, the success of the things they do has become increasingly dependent on their ability to discover what takes place in independence of the knowing process. That is the need which generates judgment. The satisfaction is, of course, the attainment of the discovery. Now to make the judgment itself and not the consequent action the instrumental factor seems to me to misstate the facts of the case. Nothing is clearer than that there is no necessity for knowledge to issue in adjustment. And it is clear to me that increased control of experience, while resulting from knowledge, does not give to it its character. Omniscience could idly view the transformations of reality and yet remain omniscient. Knowledge works, but it is not, therefore, knowledge.

These considerations have peculiar force when applied to that branch of knowledge which is knowledge itself. Is the biological account of knowledge correct? That question we must evidently ask, especially when we are urged to accept the account. Can we, to put the question in its most general form, accept as an adequate account of the logical process a theory which is bound up with some other specific department of human knowledge? It seems to me that we can not. Here we must be epistemologists and metaphysicians, or give up the problem entirely. This by no means involves the attempt to conceive pure thought set over against pure reality—the kind of epistemology and metaphysics justly ridiculed by the pragmatist—for knowledge, as already stated, is given to us in concrete instances. How knowledge in general is possible is, therefore, as useless and meaningless a question as how reality in general is possible. The knowledge is given as a fact of life, and what we have to determine is not its non-logical antecedents or its practical consequences, but its constitution as knowledge and its validity. It may be admitted that the question of validity is settled pragmatically. No knowledge is true unless it yields results which can be verified, unless it *can* issue in increased control of experience. But I insist again that that fact is not sufficient for an account of what knowledge claims to be. It claims to issue in control because it is true in independence of the control. And it is just this assurance that is needed to distinguish knowledge from what is not knowledge. It is the necessity of exhibiting this assurance which makes it impossible to subordinate logical problems, and forces us at last to questions of epistemology and metaphysics.

As I am interested here primarily in determining the field of logic, it is somewhat outside my province to consider the details of logical theory. Yet the point just raised is of so much importance in connection with the main question that I venture the following general considerations. This is, perhaps, the more necessary because the pragmatic doctrine finds in the concession made regarding the test of validity one of its strongest defenses.

Of course a judgment is not true simply because it is a judgment. It may be false. The only way to settle its validity is to discover whether experience actually provides what the judgment promises, that is, whether the conclusions drawn from it really enable us to control experience. No mere speculation will yield the desired result, no matter with how much formal validity the conclusions may be drawn. That merely formal validity is not the essential thing, I have pointed out in discussing the relation of logic to mathematics. The test of truth is pragmatic. It is apparent, therefore, that the formal validity does not determine the actual validity. What is this but the statement that the process of judgment is not itself the determining factor in its real validity? It is, in short, only valid judgments that can really give us control of experience. The implications taken up in the judgment must, therefore, be real implications which, as such, have nothing to do with the judging process, and which, most certainly, are not brought about by it. And what is this but the claim that judgment as such is never instrumental? In other words, a judgment which effected its own content would only by the merest accident function as valid knowledge. We have valid knowledge, then, only when the implications of the judgment are found to be independent of the judging process. We have knowledge only at the risk of error. The pragmatic test of validity, instead of proving the instrumental character of judgment, would thus appear to prove just the reverse.

Valid knowledge has, therefore, for its content a system of real, not judged or hypothetical, implications. The central problem of logic which results from this fact is not how a knowledge of real implications is then possible, but what are the ascertainable types of real implications. But, it may be urged, we need some criterion to determine what a real implication is. I venture to reply that we need none, if by such is meant anything else than the facts with which we are dealing. I need no other criterion than the circle to determine whether its diameters are really equal. And, in general, I need no other criterion than the facts dealt with to determine whether they really imply what I judge them to imply. Logic appears to me to be really as simple as this. Yet there can be profound problems involved in the working out of this simple procedure. There is the problem already stated of the most general types of real implication, or, in other words, the time-honored doctrine of categories. Whether there are categories or basal types of existence seems to me to be ascertainable. When ascertained, it is also possible to discover the types of inference or implication which they afford. This is by no means the whole of logic, but it appears to me to be its central problem.

These considerations will, I hope, throw light on the statement that while knowledge works, it is not therefore knowledge. It works because its content existed before its discovery by the knowledge process, and because its content was not effected or brought about by that process. Judgment was the instrument of its discovery, not the instrument which fashioned it. While, therefore, willing to admit that logical processes are vital processes, I am not willing to admit that the problem of logic is radically changed thereby in its formulation or solution, for the vital processes in question have the unique character of knowledge, the content of which is what it claims to be, a system of real implications which existed prior to its discovery.

In the psychological and biological tendencies in logic, there is, however, I think, a distinct gain for logical theory. The insistence that logical processes are both mental and vital has done much to take them out of the transcendental aloofness from reality in which they have often been placed, especially since Kant. So long as thought and object were so separated that they could never be brought together, and so long as logical processes were conceived wholly in terms of ideas set over against objects, there was no hope of escape from the realm of pure hypothesis and conjecture. Locke's axiom that "the mind, in all its thoughts and reasonings, hath no other immediate object but its own ideas," an axiom which Kant did so much to sanctify, and which has been the basal principle of the greater part of modern logic and metaphysics, is most certainly subversive of logical theory. The transition from ideas to anything else is rendered impossible by it. Now it is just this axiom which the biological tendencies in logic have done so much to destroy. They have insisted, with the greatest right, that logical processes are not set over against their content as idea against object, as appearance against reality, but are processes of reality itself. Just as reality can and does function in a physical or a physiological way, so also it functions in a logical way. The state we call knowledge becomes, thus, as much a part of the system of things as the state we call chemical combination. The problem how thought can know anything becomes, therefore, as irrelevant as the problem how elements can combine at all. The recognition of this is a great gain, and the promise of it most fruitful for both logic and metaphysics.

But, as I have tried to point out, all this surrendering of pure thought as opposed to pure reality, does not at all necessitate our regarding judgment as a process which makes reality different from what it was before. Of course there is one difference, namely, the logical one; for reality prior to logical processes is unknown. As a result of these processes it becomes known. These processes are, therefore, responsible for a known as distinct from an unknown reality. But what is the transformation which reality undergoes in becoming known? When it becomes known that water seeks its own level, what change has taken place in the water? It would appear that we must answer, none. The water which seeks its own level has not been transformed into ideas or even into a human experience. It appears to remain, as water, precisely what it was before. The transformation which takes place, takes place in the one who knows, a transformation from ignorance to knowledge. Psychology and biology can afford us the natural history of this transformation, but they can not inform us in the least as to why it should have its specific character. That is given and not deduced. The attempts to deduce it have, without exception, been futile. That is why we are forced to take it as ultimate in the same way we take as ultimate the specific character of any definite transformation. To my mind, there is needed a fuller and more cordial recognition of this fact. The conditions under which we, as individuals, know are certainly discoverable, just as much as the conditions under which we breathe or digest. And what happens to things when we know them is also as discoverable as what happens to them when we breathe them or digest them.

But here the idealist may interpose that we can never know what happens to things when we know them, because we can never know them before they become known. I suppose I ought to wrestle with this objection. It is an obvious one, but, to my mind, it is without force. The objection, if pursued, can carry us only in a circle. The problem of knowledge is still on our hands, and every logician of whatever school, the offerer of this objection also, has, nevertheless, attempted to show what the transformation is that thought works, for all admit that it works some. Are we, therefore, engaged in a hopeless task? Or have we failed to grasp the significance of our problem? I think the latter. We fail to recognize that, in one way or other, we do solve the problem, and that our attempts to solve it show quite clearly that the objection under consideration is without force. Take, for instance, any concrete case of knowledge, the water seeking its own level, again. Follow the process of knowledge to the fullest extent, we never find a single problem which is not solvable by reference to the concrete things with which we are dealing, nor a single solution which is not forced upon us by these things rather than by the fact that we deal with them. The transformation wrought is thus discovered, in the progress of knowledge itself, to be wrought solely in the inquiring individual, and wrought by repeated contact with the things with which he deals. In other words, all knowledge discloses the fact that its content is not created by itself, but by the things with which it is concerned.

It is quite possible, therefore, that knowledge should be what we call transcendent and yet not involve us in a transcendental logic. That we should be able to know without altering the things we know is no more and no less remarkable and mysterious than that we should be able to digest by altering the things we digest. In other words, the fact that digestion alters the things is no reason that knowledge should alter them, even if we admit that logical processes are vital and subject to evolution. Indeed, if evolution teaches us anything on this point, it is that knowledge processes are real just as they exist, as real as growth and digestion, and must have their character described in accordance with what they are. The recognition that knowledge can be transcendent and yet its processes vital seems to throw light on the difficulty evolution has encountered in accounting for consciousness and knowledge. All the reactions of the individual seem to be expressible in terms of chemistry and physics without calling in consciousness as an operating factor. What is this but the recognition of its transcendence, especially when the conditions of conscious activity are quite likely expressible in chemical and physical terms? While, therefore, biological considerations result in the great gain of giving concrete reality to the processes of knowledge, the gain is lost, if knowledge itself is denied the transcendence which it so evidently discloses.

IV

The argument advanced in this discussion has had the aim of emphasizing the fact that in knowledge we have actually given, as content, reality as it is in independence of the act of knowing, that the real world is self-existent, independent of the judgments we make about it. This fact has been emphasized in order to confine the field of logic to the field of knowledge as thus understood. In the course of the argument, I have occasionally indicated what some of the resulting problems of logic are. These I wish now to state in a somewhat more systematic way.

The basal problem of logic becomes, undoubtedly, the metaphysics of knowledge, the determination of the nature of knowledge and its relation to reality. It is quite evident that this is just the problem which the current tendencies criticized have sought, not to solve, but to avoid or set aside. Their motives for so doing have been mainly the difficulties which have arisen from the Kantian philosophy in its development into transcendentalism, and the desire to extend the category of evolution to embrace the whole of reality, knowledge included. I confess to feeling the force of these motives as strongly as any advocate of the criticized opinions. But I do not see my way clear to satisfying them by denying or explaining away the evident character of knowledge itself. It appears far better to admit that a metaphysics of knowledge is as yet hopeless, rather than so to transform knowledge as to get rid of the problem; for we must ultimately ask after the truth of the transformation. But I am far from believing that a metaphysics of knowledge is hopeless. The biological tendencies themselves seem to furnish us with much material for at least the beginnings of one. Reality known is to be set over against reality unknown or independent of knowledge, not as image to original, idea to thing, phenomena to noumena, appearance to reality; but reality as known is a new stage in the development of reality itself. It is not an external mind which knows reality by means of its own ideas, but reality itself becomes known through its own expanding and readjusting processes. So far I am in entire agreement with the tendencies I have criticized. But what change is effected by this expansion and readjustment? I can find no other answer than this simple one: the change to knowledge. And by this I mean to assert unequivocally that the addition of knowledge to a reality hitherto without it is simply an addition to it and not a transformation of it. Such a view may appear to make knowledge a wholly useless addition, but I see no inherent necessity in such a conclusion. Nor do I see any inherent necessity of supposing that knowledge must be a useful addition. Yet I would not be so foolish as to deny the usefulness of knowledge. We have, of course, the most palpable evidences of its use. As we examine them, I think we find, without exception, that knowledge is useful just in proportion as we find that reality is not transformed by being known. If it really were transformed in that process, could anything but confusion result from the multitude of knowing individuals?

To me, therefore, the metaphysics of the situation resolves itself into the realistic position that a developing reality develops, under ascertainable conditions, into a known reality without undergoing any other transformation, and that this new stage marks an advance in the efficiency of reality in its adaptations. My confidence steadily grows that this whole process can be scientifically worked out. It is impossible here to justify my confidence in detail, and I must leave the matter with the following suggestion. The point from which knowledge starts and to which it ultimately returns is always some portion of reality where there is consciousness, the things, namely, which, we are wont to say, are in consciousness. These things are not ideas representing other things outside of consciousness, but real things, which, by being in consciousness, have the capacity of representing *each other*, of standing for or implying each other. Knowledge is not the creation of these implications, but their successful systematization. It will be found, I think, that this general statement is true of every concrete case of knowledge which we possess. Its detailed working out would be a metaphysics of knowledge, an epistemology.

Since knowledge is the successful systematization of the implications which are disclosed in things by virtue of consciousness, a second logical problem of fundamental importance is the determination of the most general types of implication with the categories which underlie them. The execution of this problem would naturally involve, as subsidiary, the greater part of formal and symbolic logic. Indeed, vital doctrines of the syllogism, of definition, of formal inference, of the calculus of classes and propositions, of the logic of relations, appear to be bound up ultimately with a doctrine of categories; for it is only a recognition of basal types of existence with their implications that can save these doctrines from mere formalism. These types of existence or categories are not to be regarded as free creations or as the contributions of the mind to experience. There is no deduction of them possible. They must be discovered in the actual progress of knowledge itself, and I see no reason to suppose that their number is necessarily fixed, or that we should necessarily be in possession of all of them. It is requisite, however, that in every case categories should be incapable of reduction to each other.

A doctrine of categories seems to me to be of the greatest importance in the systematization of knowledge, for no problem of relation is even statable correctly before the type of existence to which its terms belong has been first determined. I submit one illustration to reinforce this general statement, namely, the relation of mind to body. If mind and body belong to the same type of existence, we have one set of problems on our hands; but if they do not, we have an entirely different set. Yet volumes of discussion written on this subject have abounded in confusion, simply because they have regarded mind and body as belonging to radically different types of existence and yet related in terms of the type to which one of them belongs. The doctrine of parallelism is, perhaps, the epitome of this confusion.

The doctrine of categories will involve not only the greater part of formal and symbolic logic, but will undoubtedly carry the logician into the doctrine of method. Here it is to be hoped that recent tendencies will result in effectively breaking down the artificial distinctions which have prevailed between deduction and induction. Differences in method do not result from differences in points of departure, or between the universal and the particular, but from the categories, again, which give the method direction and aim, and result in different types of synthesis. In this direction, the logician may hope for an approximately correct classification of the various departments of knowledge. Such a classification is, perhaps, the ideal of logical theory.

NATURALISM AND HUMANISM*

PHILOSOPHY, declining through acquired modesty or by compulsion the position of chief of all the sciences, may still rightfully claim an historical function. For that complex of human performances which we call civilization turns out, as we examine it closely, to be a changing and shifting scene which has none the less a definable background. To discover that background, and to exhibit the varied lights and shadows as thrown up from it, is a proper task for philosophy. Indeed, each of us has such a background. Using other imagery, we may call it character or soul or personality, but what we mean by the words is some relatively fixed and fundamental body of habits and dispositions lying back of the rich phantasmagoria of our lives. There sits the helmsman, his hand on the tiller. When we are unconscious of his directing, we speak of our destiny or our fate; but when in the stress of things we suddenly grow aware of the definite pointing of our course, we boast of personal triumph. The background is thus the important factor, at once conservative and propelling. There, still to keep to our nautical figure, the log is kept, the reading of which is the true biography of any individual life.

Times as well as individuals have their backgrounds, a fact which leads us to speak of society as an organism and to ascribe a character to an age. Or we use the phrase "the spirit of the times," indicating thereby a kind of temporal destiny somehow responsible for the characteristic trend of events. At times it may be dreaded, as in 1848, when governments slept uneasily while the spirit of revolution stalked abroad. Or it may be hysterically welcomed, as in crusading days, when a continent could surrender itself to a visionary task. How such backgrounds are constituted and how they operate to afford the symptoms of a time's disease or health,

* In the *Hibbert Journal,* Vol. VI (1907), pp. 1-17.

are questions about which philosophy may properly busy itself. The general theme is well worth our study; but yielding to the current demand for the concrete and the specific, we may seek some insight into the general theme by a study of a particular case.

History did not have to preserve Cicero's cry, "O tempora! O mores!" in order to teach men to be critics of their own times and their own manners. So we today hear, on all sides, the cry, uttered now with shame and regret and now with enthusiasm, that our age is materialistic and industrial, that it has substituted utility for principle, that it has surrendered to mechanism and lost the idealism of the fathers. An age of naturalism, in short, which pictures man caught in the machinery of nature and forced to learn at his imminent peril the lesson of efficiency. The cry resounds from government halls and from the busy street, from platform and from pulpit, and has been heard along the length and breadth of our systems of education.

The cry suggests a contrast. Nay, more; the contrast has raised a conflict where individual estimates and judgments become uncertain holdings. The contrast which naturalism suggests is summed up in the word humanism. The conflict, so we have been told, is a struggle to preserve the humanities, to keep alive the classic literary heritage of the race, to preserve art and religion for ideal uses, to keep morality from sinking into mere opportunism, to make education minister to the spirit and not simply to serve the body's wants.

We are all familiar, from the words of the teacher or from the newspaper or the magazine, with the many battles of this war; but what may be said of the background of the modern spirit? How comes it that naturalism and humanism stand out from it competitors in the interest of human happiness? It was once customary to dismiss serious consideration of such questions with a joyous optimism which regarded the whole conflict as academic merely. Full of the abundance of goods, this optimism could claim that nature and man could stand in no unfriendly relation to each other. The stern critic, full of caustic disapproval, was pointed out as an embittered and unfortunate misanthrope looking with ill-concealed jealousy at the fortunate man of the times, and we were warned from his path as one leading to contempt. We were assured of the essential soundness of the modern man, and told that he took Homer or Emerson with him on his travels and carried poems in his pocketbook. Now the creed of optimism is sound, else why should life result in values to be prized? But the professions of optimism in our day have, unhappily, proved untrue. To proclaim that

> God's in His heaven,
> All's right with the world,

may have been once the utterance of a satisfied faith, but it now sounds a challenge to a distressed civilization. God may be in His heaven; but the world—who living in it, noting the events of the day, his eyes open upon man and his works, will venture the cry, "All's right"?

What we need is a clearer vision and less clamour. The call to the educated is to reflection rather than to panaceas or nostrums for our ills. We need to know how we stand and what our possessions really are. We need to see the background of our life, to find its controlling forces and so gain control ourselves. I do not mean that we should set our hopes on a multiplication of philosophers, for, with the best intentions, that could not be an unmixed good. Philosophers are seldom statesmen, as Plato discovered, and was consequently led to place the perfect city, not on earth, but in heaven. There, where the main joy is supposed to be contemplation, the state might safely be entrusted to the lovers of wisdom. On earth, however, there are affairs, and philosophers must, therefore, be content to see men of affairs inherit most of the earth. But Plato made another discovery which his perennial influence has repeatedly demonstrated, namely this, that one of the chief uses of philosophy is education. The sun must be shown to the ignorant dweller in the cave, even if the vision is at first blinding. And I am convinced that our education today needs new methods and curriculums far less than it needs a new philosophy. That is why I take it that our need is primarily to see the background of modern life.

Then, when it is seen, affairs may be more intelligibly illumined and the handling of them less perplexing.

This background is undoubtedly a highly complex thing, which fact makes some restriction necessary for the present study. I propose to deal only with some of its intellectual ingredients, and I shall begin by a study of naturalism.

I begin with it because it was the aggressor in the conflict and is now in the ascendency. It found science neglected, and, what little science there was, quite insensible to the evident fact that nature has a history. It found a morality that thought mainly of precepts and little of the concrete goods of life. It found an art, beautiful indeed beyond compare, but secured and made possible in its monumental expressions at the cost of unmerited and unrequited human suffering. It found a religion busied in saving men's souls for another world in a manner neither complimentary nor humane, while it cared little for their sad estate in this. It found an education that prized the making of verses more than it prized the discovery of the laws of nature. So it declared war.

Geography, however, is necessary for war. You can not invade with great hopes of success unless you have first spied out the land. Once learned, the geography is soon taken as a thing for granted, and its importance as a factor in the conflict forgotten. Some error in the road is necessary for its reestablishment. The map which naturalism made was nature. It was drawn with new lines and showed unexpected elevations and depressions. It revealed man's place in nature in a new and contrasted light, reducing him from pre-eminence to insignificance. That change in man's place has become one of the essential ingredients in the intellectual background of modern life. It is worth attentive regard.

Recall the words of the Eighth Psalm:—

> O Lord our Lord, how excellent is Thy name in all the earth! who hast set Thy glory above the heavens.
>
> Out of the mouth of babes and sucklings hast Thou ordained strength because of Thine enemies, that Thou mightest still the enemy and the avenger.
>
> When I consider Thy heavens, the work of Thy fingers, the moon and the stars which Thou hast ordained;

What is man that Thou art mindful of him? and the son of man that Thou visitest him?

For Thou hast made him a little lower than the angels, and hast crowned him with glory and honour.

Thou madest him to have dominion over the works of Thy hands; Thou hast put all things under his feet:

All sheep and oxen, yea, and the beasts of the field;

The fowl of the air, and the fish of the sea, and whatsoever passeth through the paths of the seas.

O Lord our Lord, how excellent is Thy name in all the world!

Surely, so thought of, man was thought of nobly. Yet the modern man considering the heavens can utter no such outburst of praise. Hear Huxley, for instance:

Our reverence for the nobility of manhood will not be lessened by the knowledge that man is, in substance and in structure, one with the brutes; for he alone possesses the marvellous endowment of intelligible and rational speech, whereby, in the secular period of his existence, he has slowly accumulated and organized the experience which is almost wholly lost with the cessation of every individual life in other animals; so that, now, he stands raised upon it as on a mountain top, far above the level of his humble fellows, and transfigured from his grosser nature by reflecting, here and there, a ray from the infinite source of truth.

We may be convinced that what Huxley says is true, but we can not wholly escape the feeling that his words are an apologetic for human dignity. He sends man to us with a recommendation.

The contrast between the words of the Psalmist and the words of Huxley reveals in part the great change in intellectual background which naturalism represents so far as man's place in nature is the thing we are attending to. Man appears no longer as the Creator's last and supreme act, with all nature made for his conquest and dominion. He has become a part of nature, her master only as he has first become her attentive and obedient servant. She nourishes him in her bosom, but sedulously conceals from him the amount and length of her concern; her greatest child, but questionably her favourite. As a part of nature he can claim only a natural origin and destiny; he can no longer spontaneously believe that he can survive her. Being a part, he must measure himself up against the whole, laying his little stature off as something practically negligible in the vastness of things. There is such an overwhelming magnitude of universe to which his existence is entirely irrelevant that he can no longer instinctively regard human civilization as the supremely important event in the history of that universe. It may be supremely important for him, but to say that it is supremely important in nature appears like uttering an untruth or an absurdity.

Now this altered estimate of our natural importance has become a widely diffused intellectual habit in the background of the thought of the modern man. It has dropped from the realm of speculation and become a controlling disposition. This is pre-eminently true of those who have had a modern education, but it is quite generally true of the mass of men who reflect at all. Is it surprising, then, that we should view things under the form of opportunity rather than under the form of eternity? Is it a thing to be wondered at that moral and religious convictions which have withstood the vicissitudes of centuries should, within our own memory, crumble in decades? Is it not a mark of superficial reflection to regard the materialism and utilitarianism of the times as a symptom of moral decadence, instead of regarding it as the natural expression of an altered background? Is it not a desperate situation when morality and religion make their appeals as if the old background were still intact, while education goes on in cordial recognition of the new? There never was a time that did not need reforming. Our own, certainly, has not enough excellences to let us rest content. But that reformer is chasing an illusion or wickedly wasting our emotions and our strength who does not reckon with the intellectual background of the modern spirit.

The historian of philosophy in trying to understand this spirit can not, however, rest content with noting simply that the view of man's place in nature has radically altered, for the modern view is not new. It was the natural and instinctive view of the Greek mind, and that mind produced the most exalted ethics and the greatest philosophy that human ingenuity has devised. The more clearly it envisaged nature the more intelligently it conceived human excellence, for nature with the Greeks still led a preferential life of which man was the most signal exhibition. But we have altered not only the view of man's place in nature, but also the view of nature herself. It is important, therefore, that we inquire what sort of nature it is of which man is conceived to be a part; for here lies the deeper source of the symptoms of modern naturalism.

Two factors, mainly, have shaped our conception of nature—the theories of modern physical science, and the part that machinery has played in our industrial and social development. These two factors, one of which is theoretical and the other practical, have led us to think of nature as a sort of vast machine controlled only by mechanical methods. The history of the science of mechanics is suggestive reading for the student of civilization, for it shows how a study of appliances has been turned into a theory of the universe. Men like Archimedes were interested in mechanics that they might make pumps and useful structures. But men like Galileo, Copernicus, Newton, and Laplace were interested that they might understand the processes of nature. Had Galileo used his knowledge as an architect might, or as an engineer, there had been no trial of him as a man hateful to God and dangerous to his fellows. Instead of being content to make machines, he essayed to make a world after a machinist's manner, and that was blasphemous. The tower of Pisa, illustrating in its wonderful structure many a mechanical law, was something to delight in and was assuredly no offence to Church or State. But Galileo, mounting its steps to drop his weights from its highest gallery, was a revolutionist. His offence, however, lay not in his ideas; they might have been pardoned, as were those of many another, had he not been measurably successful in his practice. Nature was responsible for his overthrow, for she answered readily to mechanical treatment.

From Galileo's time to our own day stretch several centuries. They mark in our intellectual history the steady and successful advance of the mechanical view of things, until today we can speak of the mechanism of thought and use no metaphor. To be sure, physical science is but a fraction of human knowledge; and the facts of life and mind do not readily yield to purely mechanical expression, yet mechanism has become the ideal of science. Indeed, our time does not lack historians who would make it the ideal of history also. In philosophy, idealism has made a valiant fight, but it has been a fight of defence. Its logic and dialect produce a sense of bewilderment, while mechanism produces profitable industry.

Furthermore, the mechanical conception of nature has ceased long ago to be a speculation of scientists. It has become a popular conviction. The encyclopedia, the lecture, the magazine have brought the view within reach of everyone who can read. Your morning paper announces the latest scientific discovery as well as the latest divorce. The average man in the street knows as much about radium as the average college graduate. Galileo, in his day, was the exception. Today he is the exception whose view of nature is not essentially that which Galileo ventured to affirm. And this view has become a settled habit of thought. Who today thinks of the San Francisco earthquake as an act of God and not as a mechanical occurrence?

In our industrial and social development mechanism has ruled fully as much as in our intellectual development, for we have become dependent on machinery and organization. In such things we have put our faith, and that not without good reason. It is machinery that has made modern civilization with all its variety and effectiveness possible. That is a common enough remark which one could reinforce with a wealth of illustration. But what is not so commonly remarked is the intellectual habit which our civilization has engendered, namely, the habit of demanding the appropriate machinery to make a cause effective before the cause itself may have an attentive hearing. We are no longer spontaneously visionary or romantic, but regard the man of visions and romances as mildly insane or as a man cultivating a pose. We may stand for ideas, as the saying is, but we are apt to do it from a sense of duty or from the desire to create an impression. We are not apt to do it instinctively as the free and natural expression of our settled habits; for our settled habits have been formed while we have conquered nature not through ideas, but by machinery. Attempts in that direction have been so abundantly justified both by theory and by practice that we no longer think readily of nature as a source of spontaneity and inspiration. We think of her rather as a vast machine.

Our background contains, thus, an altered view of man and an altered view of nature. Not only has man been dethroned from his exalted position as the lord of creation and made a part of nature, but he has been made a part of a machine. Wherever he turns, it is mechanism which confronts him and mechanical methods which commend themselves. He has by no means thought the matter out to a liberal acceptance of it and its consequences. It has been forced upon him without his free consenting, as a thing inevitable, aggressive, and dominating. Did we consult our inclinations and preferences we might choose a more personal world, peopled with divinities responsive to our moods and their expression; but such inclinations on our part are rudely inhibited by our intellectual habits. To personify the world with success, it must be done instinctively and spontaneously, with no meddling intellect to stop the free impulse; but how can one personify the world if he is convinced that it is essentially mechanical?

I have likened the background to the geography which is often neglected in a campaign because knowledge of the land is taken for granted. So I would not suggest that it is my opinion that we are living our lives, meeting our problems and our promises with the philosophical proposition currently on our lips, "Nature is a mechanism, and man is a part of that machine." I mean, rather, that what that proposition signifies has become a settled intellectual habit about which we do not think because it is a habit, but which, for the same reason, controls our actions and attitudes, colouring all that we instinctively and spontaneously do. I have tried to indicate how this habit has been formed and what its justification has been. I have suggested that what is often condemned as our materialism, utilitarianism, and loss of ideals, is not a negative matter signifying a sinful deterioration of human nature, but a positive matter, the natural expression of an altered background forced upon us by the progress of events. All this I have done professedly in the interest of philosophy and education, convinced that what we need in these days of so much agitation and reform is a clear knowledge of the controlling forces of our civilization.

In spite of its significance and its justification, naturalism has not been, however, emotionally satisfactory. Our greatest poets have been blindly optimistic, like Browning, or despairingly reflective, like Arnold. The social influence of the two men is interesting. Browning's poetry produced clubs to make of him a cult and to preserve his philosophy through sectarian discipleship. Arnold's poetry produced strong individuals tenderly yet critically appreciative of human interests, but incapable of arousing great enthusiasm. He was by far the sounder thinker of the two; but he drew his inspiration from a past he could not justify, seeing in the future the intensity of human need more than an assured promise of good. Emotions, however, are not kept young and vigorous by clubs designedly constituted for raptures, or by beautiful expressions of despair; they must well up spontaneously from the background, and be so natural that they will need no cult and so instinctive that they will need no justification. It is just here that naturalism has failed. A mechanical world is emotionally bankrupt. In such a world one star does not differ from another star in glory; the difference is to be expressed directly in terms of mass, and inversely in terms of the square of the distance. To speak of glory in such a world is to speak theatrically.

Had not naturalism been marked by such emotional poverty, it would doubtless never have found humanism arrayed as its enemy. In that event humanism might have been enlarged or its best elements incorporated in a new inspiration. It was destined, however, to suffer a shrinkage and a diminution of its powers, so that it could fight only on the defensive and yield fortress after fortress. Yet it has been strong enough, in spite of successive defeats, still to preserve the front of a compact foe. At the outset, humanism had a distinct advantage, for it possessed culture as a lawful inheritance. That human treasure was not acquired by it through violence, but came as the natural legacy of an age grown sensitive to the accomplishments of man. Remember that in the inception of humanism man had achieved little as a student of nature, while he had achieved much as a student of his own impressions and ideas. Indeed, such a study is the characteristic note and definition of humanism. Such a study had produced a wonderful literature giving expression to noble sentiments. It had embodied itself in institutions which it maintained as the treasuries of its wealth, giving to them a sanctity which history seemed to confirm. Humanism became, consequently, conservative and traditional, a tendency which naturalism forced into a habit. Remember, too, that for several centuries humanism was educationally effective. The classics presented models of statesmanship and social excellence which could serve admirably in a civilization still owning kinship with the impressions and ideas of older times. Humanism could, therefore, claim the warrant of experience when naturalism assailed its system of education. But its strongest claim has been in its emotional richness. Under the spell of literature and art, of moral aspiration and religion, the spirit of man has been quickened and ennobled. The claim is true that naturalism tends to produce efficiency merely, while humanism tends to produce character, refinement, sensitiveness, and sympathy. Even today we admire the naturalist, but we love the humanist. To the latter we still assign a kind of superior excellence as we do to gentlemen of the old school. There, indeed, is a man.

It must be set down as a misfortune that humanism has found so little to support it in the background of the modern spirit and to make it effective. But misfortunes have their causes, and we can assign as a chief cause of the steady decline of humanism its foolish educational program. I have said that it has been educationally effective, and can point to experience in proof. But its educational program has a serious defect which naturalism has not failed to make apparent. That defect resides in the fact that the materials of its education are limited and can be exhausted by a progressive age. The source of Greek intelligence and its products was not antiquity, but nature. Those ancients drew from an inexhaustible source, one not located in the past or traditionally guarded, but one surrounding them and enfolding them with wonders daily new. The moment they forgot that source, they might still teach the wisdom of the fathers to the Romans; but they ceased to be productive. They could hold up examples to imitate, but they could produce no new models. Now, humanism in its educational program has interested itself in the past of man, in what he has accomplished rather than in the immediate sources of his inspiration. It has sedulously cultivated the classic tendency. By that I mean that it has placed the foundations of human excellence in the past achievements of certain men, and not in the experience of living persons. It has shut human life up in books, making these books authoritative and forgetting that the men who wrote them wrote, not out of contemplation of the past, but out of the richness of their own experience. That is why humanism was bound to exhaust itself.

I would not be understood as not valuing history, for it is man's great teacher. Our plight would be sad indeed if we had to relearn everything. We could enjoy such a condition only if the records of the past were periodically destroyed. That might prove an interesting experiment, but it would be folly to accomplish such destruction by our volition, for we have grown too dependent for that. But history should be studied not as a record of the past, but as the story of the present, as the backward look of current experience. Then it is illuminating and instructive. America today is what lends significance to the performance of Columbus. We are guilty of a foolish anachronism when we credit him with its discovery. Similarly, our own achievements can have significance only as the future owns them as its past.

But humanism tended to seal up the past and refuse to let it have its rightful vindication. We were bidden to write commentaries on it and introductions to it, as if a man could grow strong through the perennial contemplation of his youth. Thus it was that humanism in its educational program provided mainly for reminiscence and little for the immediate sources of the imagination. It divided time into epochs, the least important of which was the present. It lived constantly in another world than its own. It thus became a producer of evil. Grant all its rich contributions to what we call the humanities, what has it done to lighten pain or poverty or disease? Why has it nearly always been impotent in the crises of history? The answer lies in its method and its educational program, for its sources were secondary, and not the primary and immediate fountains of life.

My object, however, has not been to disparage humanism any more than it has been to exalt naturalism. I have rather aimed at exhibiting their emergence from the background of the modern spirit as rival claimants for our acceptance. I have suggested that they might not have contended with each other had naturalism been able to supply that emotional uplift which is so characteristic of humanism at its best. In that case, each had doubtless ministered to the other's health. But naturalism, with its altered conception of man and nature, could see in humanism only a beautiful illusion, and, having nature to draw upon with ever-increasing justification of its draft, it has rapidly and signally altered our opinions and our practices. Without performing the interesting experiment of destroying the records of the past, we face, it seems to me, the present as men who must learn for themselves. We have returned to nature and learned the lesson of mechanism, with the result that both naturalism and humanism have become unsatisfactory philosophies of life. The times and the manners appear to be the natural expression of that result.

Philosophy, exercising that historical function of which I spoke in the beginning, might rest content with this diagnosis. But it has a critical function as well. It is never content until it has made an estimate, for in seeking knowledge it would aim at teaching wisdom. What estimates, we may therefore ask, does our study suggest? Surely it must be, after all, a high estimate we put upon the lessons of mechanism when we are mindful both of its achievements and its promise. A mechanical nature may not warm the heart or fire the imagination, but it is certainly a powerful and tractable instrument capable of being put to countless uses. It is too valuable to be neglected. Still, to deepen the consciousness that every end we may desire, every hope we may wish to see fulfilled, has, could we but discover it, the machinery appropriate to its realization, is decidedly worth while. This deepening consciousness begets a sturdy confidence. A mechanical nature is not whimsical, but a thing to be relied on, striking the proper hour at the proper time. It shelters no subtle malevolence which might elude our greatest care. It allows one no longer to have his hopes depressed and his will enfeebled by the belief that any evils are incurable. Our moral responsibility is thus put in a clear light, reinforced by a demonstration of the old saying that ignorance is the greatest of evils. For when once the appropriate mechanism for the achievement of any good is made known, no one can excuse the failure of its realization, for the condemnation is that of folly; indeed, it is a great thing for man to be able to blame his stupidity rather than Providence for the greater share of his ills. We are entering today on the full significance of this truth and its many applications. We insist, for instance, as never before, and our insistence will grow to a relentless importunity, that we be allowed to live in sanitary conditions and that our food and water shall be pure. This we do not out of humanitarian benevolence simply, but because mechanism has taught us that there is no good reason why unsanitary conditions should exist. Such insistence is a prophecy of a new social order when we shall universally demand that knowledge shall minister to the public good, conscious that none can gainsay the justice of that demand. Consider Japan. Immobile for centuries, she has suddenly acquired our science of nature and given such an exhibition of civilization that the world looks on amazed. That illustration seems to me to be typical of the future, for we have learned that the knowledge which counts is not primarily that of man's impressions and ideas, but knowledge of the mechanism of nature, which, when applied, yields its inevitable result. Yes, our estimate of mechanism must be high, convinced as we have become of its essential truth.

To deepen this conviction is the great business of education, and such education will be profoundly moral. There seems, therefore, to be no good reason to conclude that what has been called naturalism is the only philosophy of life which our altered background can afford. It appears rather to be the superficial exhibition of a profounder view of life, something bound to pass in its crudity, to be replaced by a quickened and eminently rational view of human goods and the means of their attainment. That newer philosophy might still be called naturalism, for it would own nature as its source; but it might equally well be called humanism, for it would realize that nature affords the proper mechanism to minister to the ambitions and hopes of humanity.

If the narrow and straitened humanism which we have discussed erred in its educational program, the narrow and straitened naturalism has erred in its estimate of nature. Having learned that nature works by machinery, it neglected the obvious fact that the machinery exists to support and maintain its product. The future historian will note the neglect and characterize our age as one strikingly lacking in intelligence. He will note our vast industry, and comment on the fact that while we made great machines to support and sustain the products of that industry, we could none the less regard nature as purely mechanical, with no product to exalt and sustain. We have been so afraid of the doctrine of final causes and of assigning deliberate intentions to nature, that we have forgotten that she has produced, supported, and sustained human civilization. For man is a part of nature, carried on by her forces to work the works of intelligence. In him she bursts forth into sustained consciousness of her own evolution, producing in him knowledge of her processes, estimation of her goods, and suspicions of her ultimate significance. This is a truth of nature and not a product of human fancy; and it is a truth fraught with the profoundest emotional import. Without such creatures as man, nature might well exist, but she would exist unvalued and unobserved. Her natural beauties would fire no imagination, her wonders would rouse no curiosity, the fact that her vast machinery supported and sustained a varied world would excite no comment and kindle no aspiration. Add man—ah! but you can not add him as some extraneous figure tacked on as a negligible quantity to a sum already total, for he has grown out of nature's own stuff and been wrought in her workshop. He is, then, no mere commentator on the world or spectator of it; he is one of its integrations, so to speak, a supreme instance where nature has measurably evaluated herself. His comments are nature's self-estimate.

Led by an enlightened naturalism, therefore, we cannot regard the mechanism of nature as a factory where the machines run on, but where there is supreme indifference to the product. Rather must we regard it as that which supports and maintains what we choose to call ideal products, and finds in them its significance and justification, as the germ finds its reason for existence in the life it engenders. We have been half-hearted evolutionists, seeking the causes of variation and neglecting the fact that nature is always achieving results which may justify her labours. Yes, something must be achieved. It need not be something long ago devised or originally intended, but we know it must be something with a value suited to give the struggle significance. It is impossible, therefore, for philosophy to regard the emergence of reason as but the opportunity to condemn the cosmic process as the begetter of illusions, and to convince us that the ideal aspirations of man are the one great error in the universe. Nay, rather, an enlightened naturalism will call upon reason constantly to illumine our path with ever fresh glimpses of the light of nature, so that human life may be at once natural, rational, and joyous. Such a philosophy would be also an enlightened humanism, calculated to sustain culture and give birth to impressions and ideas suffused with spontaneous emotion. And such a philosophy, I am bound to believe, is a solid foundation for enlightened educational progress.

METAPHYSICS*

THE first book to bear the title "Metaphysics" is attributed to Aristotle. If the title described or suggested the contents of the book, there might have been less confusion regarding the nature of the science. To some, however, it means the mysterious, to others, the exceptionally profound; while still others see in it an occasion for mirth. There have been, consequently, many definitions of metaphysics. The Century Dictionary gives, among others, the following: "The doctrine of first principles"; "Supernatural science; the doctrine of that which transcends all human experience"; "The science of the mind treated by means of introspection and analysis, and not by experiment and scientific observation"; "Any doctrine based upon presumption and not upon inductive reasoning and observation"; "An abstract and abstruse body of doctrine supposed to be virtually taken for granted in some science"; "Used frequently with the definite article, and generally connected with unpleasant associations, as being a study very dry and at the same time of doubtful truth." To these definitions might be added that by Professor James: "An unusually obstinate attempt to think clearly and consistently."

Such variety of definition is largely due to the fact that the title given to Aristotle's book was an unfortunate choice. It appears to indicate that when you have finished your physics, the science which was originally thought to embrace nature, you must then pass beyond physics and somehow cut loose from nature herself. After physics, metaphysics; after nature, the supernatural—that is an invitation at once to titanic effort and to Icarian folly. Metaphysics came to suggest such human possibilities. Originally, however, the term represented no more than the happy thought of an enterpris-

* A lecture delivered at Columbia University in the series on Science, Philosophy, and Art, March 18, 1908, and published by the Columbia University Press.

ing editor. For, we are told, Andronicus of Rhodes, in the first century B.C., finding among the works of Aristotle a number of loosely connected writings which the great Greek had neglected to name, placed these writings after the books on physics, and named them accordingly, τὰ μετὰ τὰ φυσικά, the books which come after the books on physics. A name which thus indicated only an editorial arrangement became the name of a department of knowledge. That is not the only time when an editor's happy thought has been the cause of mischief.

If, however, we turn from the inspiring title to the writings themselves, illusions about the supernatural character of metaphysics tend to disappear. "There is," so we are told by the Stagirite, "a science which investigates existence as existence and whatever belongs to existence as such. It is identical with none of the sciences which are defined less generally. For none of these professedly considers existence as existence, but each, restricting itself to some aspect of it, investigates the general aspect only incidentally, as do the mathematical sciences." The emphasis is thus put by Aristotle on fact and on nature, but it is put on fact and nature as we attempt to view them with at once the least and with the greatest restriction: with the least restriction, because we are invited to view nature in the light of her most comprehensive characters; with the greatest restriction, because we are invited to view her stripped of her wonderful diversity.

In thus conceiving a science whose distinguishing mark should be that it applies to all existence, Aristotle noted a fact which the history of intellectual progress has abundantly illustrated, the fact, namely, that knowledge grows in extent and richness only through specialization. Nature herself is a specialized matter. She does things by producing differences, individuals, variations. To grasp this variety, a variety of sciences is necessary. Indeed, as Aristotle estimates the achievements of his predecessors, he finds the source of their confusion, inadequacy, and limitation to lie in their habit of regarding each his own special science as a sufficient account of the cosmos. What they said may have been true under the restrictions which their limited field imposed upon their utterance; but it became false when it was transferred to other fields differently limited. Following his own illustrations we may say, for instance, that the Pythagoreans were quite right in trying to formulate the undoubted numerical relations which obtain in nature; but they were quite wrong if they conceived arithmetic to be an adequate astronomy. The soul may be a harmony of the body and thus capable of numerical expression, but to think one has exhausted its nature by defining it as a moving number is to forget the natural limitations of inquiry and to make a rhetorical phrase the substitute for scientific insight. We may properly speak of a sick soul as out of tune, but we should not thereby become either psychologists or physicians. No; knowledge is a matter of special sciences, each growing sanely as it clearly recognizes the particular and specialized aspect of nature with which it deals, but becoming confused when it forgets that it is one of many. Accordingly what we call the philosophy of Aristotle is not a single science to be described by a picturesque or a provoking name, but a system of sciences the members of which should be related to one another in the way nature rather than desire permits.

If knowledge increases thus through limitation, restriction, and specialization, if science grows through the multiplication of different sciences, must our final view of nature reveal her as a parcelled and disjointed thing? Is the desire to say something about the universe as a whole which may none the less be true of it, is that desire without warrant, something utterly to be condemned? Not, thought Aristotle, if that desire is checked and controlled by fact. We should indeed err if we thought to attain unity through any artificial combination of special truths, or by attempting so to reduce the diversity of the sciences that their individual differences should disappear. Yet we may approach unity through the same method by which the special sciences gain their individual coherence and stability, that is, by limitation and restriction of field. All things somehow exist; and because they so obviously do, we can never lose sight of the fact that existence itself is a problem irrespective of the fact whether a particular existence is that of a stone, a man, or a god. Particular existences may carry us at last to some exclusive and inalienable core of individuality, hidden somewhere and possibly discoverable, but existence itself is possessed by nothing exclusively. It is rather the common feature of everything that can be investigated, and as such is something to be looked into. Whether such looking is fruitful is a question not to be prejudiced. The fruitfulness of the inquiry depends upon the discovery whether existence as such has anything to reveal. We thus return to Aristotle's conception of a science of existence as existence, a specialized and restricted science, doing its own work and not that of the mathematician or the physicist or the biologist, or of any other investigator, a science which should take its place in that system of sciences the aim of which is to reveal to us with growing clearness the world in which we live. It was that science which Andronicus of Rhodes called "Metaphysics," baptizing it in the name of ambiguity, confusion, and idiosyncrasy.

For me it would be a congenial task to devote the remainder of this lecture to a detailed exposition of the metaphysics of Aristotle. It would be the more congenial, since the lecturer on history, by making the ancients our contemporaries, has saved enthusiasm for the Stagirite from being condemned as a mere anachronism. To call Aristotle, as Dante is supposed to have done, the master of them that know, even if they know no less than others, is still a privilege in the twentieth century. And this privilege is the one *ad hominem* argument in justification of the study of metaphysics which I would venture to suggest to an audience already made somewhat familiar with the inadequacies and limitations of human knowledge. As the congenial, however, may not be the appropriate, I proceed to sketch the general bearings of metaphysics, pointing out how, beginning with analysis and description, it tends to become speculative, and to construct systems of metaphysics which aim at complete conceptions of the universe and have a certain relevancy to science, morals, and religion. Then I will indicate how metaphysics, influenced by modern idealistic speculation, became arrogant as a theory of knowledge, and how there are present signs of its return to its ancient place as a science co-ordinated with the rest of knowledge. In concluding, I will consider how, with this return, it finds a new interest in the interpretation of the process of evolution.

Either because Aristotle developed his science of existence with so much skill or because the science is to be reckoned, as he reckoned it, among those intellectual performances which are excellent, its unfortunate name has never completely obscured its professed aims and restrictions. Too often, indeed, metaphysics has been made the refuge of ignorance, and inquirers in other fields have been too ready to bestow upon it their own unsolved problems and inconsistencies. Many have thus been led to refuse discussion of certain difficulties for the reason that they are metaphysical, a reason which may indicate that one is tired rather than that one is wise. It has even been suggested that so long as problems are unsolved they are metaphysical. Even so, the study, on account of the comprehensiveness thus given to it, might advance itself, imposing and commanding, a guarantor of intellectual modesty. Yet metaphysicians, as a rule, have not regarded their work as that of salvation. They have viewed their problems as the result of reflection rather than of emergency. And their reflection has ever seized upon the fact that nature's great and manifold diversities do, none the less, in spite of that diversity, consent to exist together in some sort of union, and that, consequently, some understanding of that unity is a thing to attempt. Metaphysics, therefore, may still adopt the definition and limitations set for it by Aristotle. We may, indeed, define it in other terms, calling it, for instance, the science of reality, but our altered words still point out that metaphysical interest is in the world as a world of connected things, a world with a general character in addition to those specific characters which give it its variety and make many sciences necessary for its comprehension.

The term "reality," however, is intellectually agile. It tends to play tricks with one's prejudices and to lead desire on a merry chase. For to denominate anything real is usually to import a distinction, and to consign, thereby, something else to the region of appearance. Could we keep the region of appearance from becoming populated, it might remain nothing more than the natural negative implication of a region of positive interest. But reality, once a king, makes many exiles who crave and seek citizenship in the land from which they have been banished. The term "reality," therefore, should inspire caution instead of confidence in metaphysics—a lesson which history has abundantly illustrated, but which man is slow to learn. Contrast those imposing products of human fancy which we call materialism and idealism, each relegating the other to the region of appearance, and what are they at bottom but an exalted prejudice for matter and an exalted prejudice for mind? And had not their conflict been spectacular, as armies with banners, what a pitiable spectacle it would have presented, since a child's first thought destroys the one, and every smallest grain of sand the other? No; everything is somehow real; and to make distinctions within that realm demands caution and hesitation.

Thus it is that the concept of reality has become an important theme in a great part of metaphysical inquiry, and that a keen appreciation of its varieties is essential to the historian of metaphysics. That science has been thought to suffer from a too close scrutiny into the idiosyncrasies of its past; but being somewhat ancient and robust, and, withal, decidedly human, it may consult the reflection that more youthful sciences have not always walked in wisdom's path, and so bear its own exposure with some consequent consolation. Yet what it has to reveal in the light of the shifting concept of reality is significant indeed. For we have come to learn that to call anything real exclusively, is to imply a preference, and that preference is largely a matter of the time in which it is born. It reflects an age, an occasion, a society, a moral, intellectual, or economic condition. It does not reflect an absolute position which knows no wavering. For me, just now, metaphysics is the most real thing imaginable, more real than chemistry or the stock exchange. In displaying some enthusiasm for it, I care not if the elements revert to ether or how the market goes. To be invited just now to consider the periodic law or the latest market quotations would irritate me. An altered situation would find me, doubtless, possessed of an altered preference, indifferent no longer to another science or to the Street. So much does occasion determine preference, and preference reality.

The historical oppositions in metaphysics present them selves, therefore, not as a mass of conflicting and contradictory opinions about the absolutely real, but as a too exclusive championship of what their exponents have believed to be most important for their times. In such metaphysicians the enthusiasm of the prophet has outrun the disinterestedness of the scientist. We may describe them as men of restricted vision, but we may not, therefore, conclude that their vision was not acute. Plato was not an idle dreamer, assigning to unreality the bed on which you sleep in order that he might convince you that the only genuinely real bed is the archetype in the mind of God, the ideal bed of which all others are shadows. Undoubtedly he converses thus about beds in his *Republic*, but he does not advise you, as a consequence, to go to sleep in heaven. He tells you, rather, that justice is a social matter which you can never adequately administer so long as your attention is fixed solely on individual concerns. You must seek to grasp justice as a principle, in the light of which the different parts of the body politic may find their most fruitful interplay and co-ordination. His metaphysics of the ideal was born of Athens' need, but his dialogues remain instructive reading for the modern man. We may confound him by pointing out the obvious fact that men, not principles, make society, and yet accept his teaching that men without principles make a bad society, exalting principles thus to the position of the eminently real.

Similarly, he who reads Fichte's *Science of Knowledge* should not forget that Fichte spoke to the German people, calling them a nation. And the response he met must have seemed, in his eyes, no small justification of his view that reality is essentially a self-imposed moral task. And Spencer, influenced by social and economic reorganization and consolidation, could force the universe into a formula and think that he had said the final word about reality. Thus any exclusive conception of reality is rendered great, not by its finality for all times, but by its historical appropriateness.

Such questions, therefore, as, What is real? Is there any

reality at all? Is not everything illusion, or at least part of everything? and such statements as, Only the good is real, Only matter is real, Only mind is real, Only energy is real, are questions and statements to be asked and made only by persons with a mission. For reality means either everything whatsoever or that a distinction has been made, a distinction which indicates not a difference in the fact of existence, but a difference in point of view, in value, in preference, in relative importance for some desire or choice. Yet it is doubtless the business of metaphysics to undertake an examination and definition of the different points of view from which those questions can be asked and those statements made. Indeed, that undertaking may well be regarded as one of the most important in metaphysics. The outcome of it is not a superficial doctrine of the relativity of the real, with the accompanying advice that each of us select his own reality and act accordingly. Nor is it the doctrine that since nothing or everything is absolutely real, there is no solid basis for conduct and no abiding hope for man. That individualism which is willful and that kind of agnosticism which is not intellectual reserve, but which is intellectual complacency, have no warrant in metaphysics. On the contrary, the doctrine of metaphysics is much more obvious and much more sane. It is that existence, taken comprehensively, is an affair of distinctions; that existence is shot through and through with variety.

But this is not all. Metaphysics discovers in the fact of variety a reason for the world's onward movement. For a world without variety would be a world eternally still, unchanged and unchanging through all the stretches of time. We might endow such a world with unlimited power, capable, if once aroused, of a marvelous reaction; but unless there existed somewhere within it a difference, no tremor of excitement would ever disturb its endless slumber. All the sciences teach this doctrine. Even logic and mathematics, the most static of them all, require variables, if their formulations are to have any significance or application. Knowledge thus reflects the basal structure of things. And in this fact that differences are fundamental in the constitution of our world, we discover the reason why all those systems of metaphysics eventually fail which attempt to reduce all existence to a single type of reality devoid of variety in its internal make-up.

The variety in our world involves a further doctrine. While all varieties as such are equally real, they are not all equally effective. They make different sorts of differences, and introduce, thereby, intensive and qualitative distinctions. The onward movement of the world is thus, not simply successive change, but a genuine development or evolution. It creates a past the contents of which must forever remain what they were, but it proposes a future where variety may still exercise its difference-making function. And that is why we human beings, acting our part in some cosmic comedy or tragedy, may not be indifferent to our performance or to the preferences we exalt. The future makes us all reformers, inviting us to meddle with the world, to use it and change it for our ends. The invitation is genuine and made in good faith, for all man's folly is not yet sufficient to prove it insincere. That is why it has been easy to believe that God once said to man: "Be fruitful and multiply, and replenish the earth, and subdue it; and have dominion over the fish of the sea, and over the fowl of the air, and over every living thing that moveth upon the earth." That is why, also, willful individualism and complacent agnosticism have no warrant in metaphysics. Since all things are equally real, but all not equally important, the world's evolution presents itself as a drift towards results, as something purposeful and intended. While we may not invoke design to explain this relative importance of things, the world's trend puts us under the natural obligation of discovering how it may be controlled, and enforces the obligation with obvious penalties. Thus willfulness receives natural punishment and the universe never accepts ignorance as an excuse.

It seems difficult, therefore, not to describe evolution as a moral process. By that I do not mean that nature is especially careful about the kinds of things she does or that she is true and just in all her dealings. But evolution is movement controlled by the relative importance of things. We consequently find such terms as "struggle," "survival," "adaptation," useful in the description of it. And although these terms may appear more appropriate to the development of living things than to that of inorganic nature, we may not overlook the fact that the physical world also begets varieties and has its character determined by their relative importance.

Thus it is that the metaphysical doctrine of final causes appears to be fundamentally sound. It is easy to render it ridiculous by supposing that things were once made on purpose to exhibit the features and manners of action which we now discover in them, or by conceiving adaptation as an efficient cause of events, as if the fact that we see were the reason why we have eyes. So conceived the doctrine of final causes is justly condemned. On the other hand, however, how superficial is the opinion that in nature there is entire indifference to results, and that there are no natural goods! Today is not simply yesterday rearranged or twenty-four hours added to a capricious time; it is yesterday reorganized, with yesterday's results carried on and intensified. So that we might say that nature, having accidentally discovered that the distinction between light and darkness is a natural good, stuck to the business of making eyes. We should thus express a natural truth, but should not thereby free ourselves from the obligation of discovering how nature had achieved so noteworthy a result. That obligation the doctrine of final causes most evidently does not discharge, because final causes have never been found adequate to reveal the method of nature's working. Again and again, some investigator, impressed by the undoubted fact of nature's continuity, by her carefulness of the type, by her preservation of forms, by that character of hers which we can properly describe only by calling it preferential or moral, impressed by these things he has attempted to turn them into efficient causes, factors operative in the mechanism of the world. And he has repeatedly failed. It is, consequently, not prejudice which leads many students of nature's processes to insist that these are ultimately what we call mechanical. It is metaphysical insight. Yet that insight may readily degenerate into the most superficial philosophy, if it leads us to forget that mechanism is the means by which the ends of nature are reached. For nature undoubtedly exists for what she accomplishes, and it is that fact which gives to mechanism its relevancy, its importance, and its high value. Thus metaphysics, true to its early formulations, finds the world to be both mechanical and teleological, both a quantitative relation of parts and a qualitative realization of goods. Some indication that this finding is correct may be discovered in our instinctive recognition that nature is appropriately described both in the formulations of science and in the expressions of poetry.

Metaphysical analysis tends thus to disclose existence as a process motived by the variety of its factors, as an evolution characterized, not by indifference, but by selection based on the relative importance of its factors for the maintenance of natural goods, as a development executed through an elaborate mechanism. It is natural that metaphysics should become speculative and attempt the construction of a system of things wherein its obvious disclosures may be envisaged with coherence and simplicity, and thus be rationally comprehended and explained. It is in such attempts that metaphysics has historically scored its greatest successes and its greatest failures. The lesson to be derived from a survey of them is, doubtless, one of grave caution, but it would be idle to affirm that we have seen the last of great systems of metaphysics. Democritus, Plato, Aristotle, Bruno, Descartes, Hobbes, Spinoza, Newton, Leibniz, Berkeley, Kant, Laplace, Hegel, Spencer—to mention only the greatest names—each has had his system of the world which still has power to affect the thought and lives of men. System is beloved of man's imagination and his mind is restless in the presence of unconnected and unsupported details. He will see things *sub specie æternitatis* even while time counts out his sands of life. It is a habit begotten of nature, to be neither justified nor condemned. It would be absurd, consequently, to regard any system of metaphysics as absolutely true, but it would be more absurd to refuse to make one on that account. For such systems constitute the supreme attempts of intelligence at integration. They propose to tell us what our world would be like if our present restricted knowledge were adequate for its complete exposition. They are not, therefore, to be abandoned because they are always inadequate, incomplete, and provisional; they are rather to be pursued, because, when constructed by the wise, they are always ennobling and minister faithfully to the freedom of the mind.

Protests against metaphysical systems are, consequently, apt to be proofs of an impatient temper rather than of sound judgment. Yet such systems often grow arrogant, and become, thereby, objects of justified suspicion. Being the crowning enterprise of intelligence, to be worn, one might say, as an indication of a certain nobility of mind, they forfeit the claim to be thus highly regarded if they are made the essential preliminaries of wisdom. Yet the too eager and the too stupid have often claimed that the only possible foundation for the truth and value of science, and the only possible warrant for morality and human aspiration, are to be found in a system of metaphysics. If such a claim meant only that with a perfect system, could we attain it, would riddles all be solved and life's darkness made supremely clear, it would express an obvious truth. But made with the intent of laying metaphysics down as the foundation of science, of morality, and of religion, it is obviously false and iniquitous. In our enthusiasm we may indeed speak of metaphysics as the queen of all the sciences, but she can wear the title only if her behavior is queenly; she forfeits it when, ceasing to reign, she stoops to rule.

Yet there is justice in the notion that metaphysics, especially in its systematic shape, should contribute to the value of science, and be a source of moral and religious enlightenment. Its greatest ally is logic. In the systematic attempt to reduce to order the business of getting and evaluating knowledge, in distinguishing fruitful from fruitless methods, and, above all, in attempting to disclose the sort of conquest knowledge makes over the world, the aims and achievements of science should become better appreciated and understood. It is still true, as Heraclitus of old remarked, that much information does not make a man wise, but wisdom is intelligent understanding.

The disclosures of metaphysics are equally significant for ethics. The great systems have usually eventuated in a theory of morals. And this is natural. Metaphysics, disclosing the fact that behavior is a primary feature of things, raises inevitably the question of how to behave effectively and well. Emphasizing the relative importance of the factors of evolution, it encourages the repeated valuation of human goods. It can make no man moral, nor give him a rule to guide him infallibly in his choices and acts; but it can impress upon him the fact that he is under a supreme obligation, that of living a life controlled, not by passion, but by reason, and of making his knowledge contribute to the well-being of society. It will still preach its ancient moral lesson, that, since with intelligence has arisen some comprehension of the world, the world is best improved, not by passions or by parties, not by governments or by sects, but by the persistent operation of intelligence itself.

After a somewhat similar manner, metaphysics in its systematic character has significance for theology. To speak of existence as a riddle is natural, because so much of its import can be only guessed. That it has import most men suspect, and that this import is due to superior beings or powers is the conviction of those who are religious. Metaphysics is seldom indifferent to such suspicions and convictions. As it has a lively sense of the unity of things, it is led to seek ultimate reasons for the world's stability. And as it deals with such conceptions as "the infinite" and "the absolute," it has a certain linguistic sympathy with faith. Consequently, while it has never made a religion, it has been used as an apology for many. This fact witnesses, no doubt, more profoundly to the adaptability of metaphysics than it does to the finality of the ideas it has been used to sustain. Yet metaphysics, tending to keep men ever close to the sources of life, fosters a whole-hearted acceptance of life's responsibilities and duties. It is thus the friend of natural piety. And in superimposing upon piety systematic reflection on what we call the divine, it follows a natural instinct, and seeks to round out man's conception of the universe as the source of his being, the place of his sojourning, the begettor of his impulses and his hopes, and the final treasury of what he has been and accomplished.

Such, then, are the general nature and scope of metaphysical inquiry. With Aristotle we may define metaphysics as the science of existence and distinguish it from other departments of knowledge by its generality and its lack of attention to those specific features of existence which make many sciences an intellectual necessity. Existence, considered generally, presents itself as an affair of connected varieties and, consequently, as an onward movement. Because the varieties have not all the same efficacy, the movement presents those selective and moral characters which we ascribe to a development or evolution. While the efficient causes of this evolution appear to be mechanical, the mechanism results in the production of natural goods, and thus justifies a doctrine of final causes. Upon such considerations metaphysics may superimpose speculative reflection, and attempt to attain a unified system of the world. It may also attempt to evaluate science in terms of logical theory, to enlarge morality through a theory of ethics, and to interpret natural piety and religion in terms of theological conceptions. Metaphysics proposes thus both an analysis and a theory of existence; it is descriptive and it is systematic. If metaphysicians often forget that theory is not analysis, that system is not description, it is not because they are metaphysicians, but because they are human. For my part, therefore, I do not see why they should not be allowed to entertain at least as many absurdities as the average reflective inquirer. Greater indulgence is neither desired nor necessary. And while metaphysicians may be hard to understand, they do not like to be misunderstood. So I emphasize again the fact that it appears to be the greatest abuse of metaphysical theories to use them to justify natural excellence or to condone natural folly. It is their business to help to clarify existence. It is not their business to constitute an apology for our prejudices or for our desires.

In regarding metaphysics as the outcome of reflection on existence in general, and, consequently, as a department of natural knowledge, I have supposed that intelligent persons could undertake such reflection and accomplish something of interest and consequence, by following the ordinary experimental methods of observation and tested generalization. I have stated that the contrast between metaphysics and other departments of knowledge arises from its emphasis on generalities and their emphasis on particulars. In doing all this I have followed ancient tradition. But much of modern philosophy has emphatically declared that such an attitude is decidedly too naïve. Keenly alive to the fact, which it credits itself with discovering, the fact, namely, that the world into which we inquire exists for us only as the mind's object, that philosophy has insisted that the mind is central in the universe, and that the nature and laws of mind are, therefore, the determining factors in the structure of the world we know.

Of this view Kant was the great systematic expounder. It was he who taught that space and time are but the forms of sense perception. It was he who declared that the basal principles of physics are but derivatives of the principles of the mind. It was he who affirmed that by virtue of our understanding we do not discover the laws of nature, but impose them. He consequently drew the conclusion that we know only the appearances of things connected according to the laws of the mind, but never the things themselves connected according to their own laws. The moral he drew pointed in the direction of intellectual modesty and an enlightened reliance on experience. But to make nature nothing but a collection of appearances in the mind, united according to the supposed necessities of thought, is really to discourage experience and bid imagination riot. For in the critical philosophy of Kant we have suggested a science which is higher than the sciences, a set of principles upon which they depend, and from which might possibly be deduced by the mere operation of thought all that is essential to their content. We have also suggested a method of inquiry which is no longer based on experimental observation and generalization, but which is controlled by principles supposed to be purely *a priori,* and thus more fundamental than experience itself. Metaphysics, by entering that supposed region of purer insight, cut itself off from all helpful competition and co-ordination with the rest of knowledge. It begot those great systems of idealistic philosophy which Professor Santayana has characterized as "visionary insolence." It produced that lamentable conflict between science and metaphysics which was so characteristic of the last century. No department of knowledge can thrive in isolation. If metaphysics, by arrogating to itself supremacy, tended to become visionary, the sciences also, despising metaphysical insight, tended to become disorganized and illiberal.

Happily in our own day there are many signs that this unfortunate antithesis between science and metaphysics is disappearing. Metaphysics itself, by a sort of inner evolution, has been working out to a more objective view of things. On the other hand, the sciences, through their own extension, have come upon unsuspected generalities and co-ordinations. Above all, the principle of evolution, which was early recognized in metaphysical theories, has served, by its general recognition in all departments of knowledge, to restore unity among the sciences. It has forced idealism to recognize that even intelligence, the mind itself, has had a natural history. Metaphysics is thus leaving its position of isolation, and returning to its ancient place as a science co-ordinated with the rest of knowledge.

But it returns not without modification and not without its own interest in evolutionary theory. It will still, as of old, seek to discover the basal types of existence and their general modes of operation. It will still ask, What can we say of existence as a whole which is true of it? But it has learned from idealism that while it may view intelligence as the instrument of knowledge, it may not hope to understand nature as a process if the place of intelligence in that process is disregarded. For to reconstruct in thought the world's vanished past and to forecast its possible future is to give to intelligence a certain baffling and perplexing importance in the scheme of things. In attacking this problem of the place of intelligence in an evolving world, metaphysics may not, however, boast that it has a method peculiarly its own. It may not hope to control the inquiry by principles supposed to be derived from pure reason and thus to have a higher warrant than the principles employed in other sciences. For metaphysics has come to believe in the evolution of intelligence because it has been so taught by the method of experimental investigation. It can not, therefore, discredit that method without discrediting its own belief.

We may, indeed, be at first bewildered by the fact that the world in which intelligence has evolved is the world which intelligence has discovered; but if we accept the discovery, we do but recognize in intelligence a natural good whose use and final cause is to make us somewhat acquainted with our dwelling-place. The world thus exists as just what we have discovered it to be, the place in which intelligence has dawned and led to a knowledge of the process in which such a great event has happened. It is natural, therefore, to claim that in reflecting on our world we may largely disregard the fact that we reflect. Realizing that in him has arisen intelligence, knowledge, understanding of the world, as the stoutest weapon in his life's warfare, man realizes that his weapon is for use rather than for scrutiny. Its excellence is to be tested by the territory won, and not by inquisitive feeling of the sharpness of the blade—especially when that blade sharpens only with its conquering use. Thus, as I say, we may largely disregard the fact that we reflect. By so doing, the world grows to clearness as the thing reflected on. Its laws and processes take shape in useful formulas. It is thus that the sciences advance to their great contributions. And why not, then, metaphysics? Why should we rather hope that by making the mind itself exclusively the object of our study, an added clearness will be given to the scheme of things?

But we can never wholly disregard the fact that we reflect, because the dawn of intelligence in the world is an event of too great interest to be accepted merely as a matter of record. If we are warranted in regarding it as a natural good whose use is to acquaint us with the world, we are, doubtless, also warranted in regarding it as the situation in which the world's evolution is most clearly and effectively revealed. If, now, we interpret this situation as differing from all others only by the fact that in it we have immediate knowledge of what it is to be an evolution, we attain a suggestive basis for generalization. From it we find little warrant to conclude that the present is simply the unfolding of a past, possibly of a very remote past, or that the future is simply the present unfolded. Evolution appears to be a process of a totally different sort. It appears to be always and eternally the unfolding of an effective present. Behind it, it leaves the past as the record of what it has done, the totality of things accomplished, but not the promise and potency of things to be. It is a dead past. As such it may be conditioning; but it is not effective, because it is accomplished. To the present alone belong the riches of potentiality and spontaneity; to it alone belongs efficiency. We are, thus, under no obligation to seek in endless regress through the past the source of the world's becoming or the secret of its variety and human interest.

If such an interpretation of evolution is warranted, that process may indeed be described as having purpose. Only we may not understand by purpose some anciently conceived plan which the world was intended to follow. We should not invoke foresight, but should recognize historical continuity. For when we have a process going on in such a manner that the present of it is continually transforming itself into the record of what it has done, writing, as it were, a cosmic history, then, surely, we have a purpose. Such a process can be comprehended only as one having meaning and significance. Its factors are bound together not only as cause and effect, but also as means and end. Shed intelligence upon any of its events, and the question, Why? will leap into being with its insistent demands. The question sends us searching through the records of the past and the promise of the future in order that the event may be estimated at its proper value. Only by such searching may we hope to discover what the world's purpose is. We may call it, in one word, achievement. And I must believe, just because achievement is wrought through an effective present, that the world, as it passes from moment to moment of its existence, carries ever with it perennial sources of outlook and novelty. And I must believe, too, that just in proportion as we free ourselves from the desperate notion that somewhere and somehow hope and outlook have been, once for all, fixed unalterably for the world's future, we shall then find in our union with nature a source of genuine enthusiasm.

Yes, we can not wholly disregard the fact that we reflect. We must note that the knowledge of the evolution of intelligence is itself a product of intelligence. Thus taking note, we may discover in the evolution of intelligence, not only the world grown to the highest point of varied and efficient action that we know, but evolution itself disclosed for what it is in its essential nature. It is the ceaseless unfolding of an effective present which carries with it the sources of what it achieves, and whose achievements have the value they disclose as discovered factors in the universal history of the world.

NATURAL TELEOLOGY*

THE operations of nature do not appear to be aimless changes. They issue in specific products the history of which can be traced and construed as the adaptation of means to ends. It is, doubtless, this aspect of nature as the producer of definite and particular results which, more than any other, profoundly stirs the imagination and provokes scientific curiosity. From of old the coming into being of things in an ordered world and their passing away has been the theme of both poet and scholar. Reflection, after it has endured disappointment and sophistication, may come to view nature with eyes less fascinated by her productivity, seeing in her nothing but an aimless and ceaseless rearrangement of elements to which chance or a human prejudice in favor of final causes imparts the illusory appearance of direction; but such is not the spontaneous vision of things. There they are, constituting the great whole we call nature, each of them with its individual history culminating through many helps and hindrances in the present product. Illustrations are so abundant that choice is baffled in selecting the most appropriate. For while living things may at first appear to be more evidently the products of directive and selective forces, inanimate nature itself—the plain with mountains about it, the river with its course motived by the character of the land through which it flows—exhibits likewise the adaptation of means to ends. And the adaptations are admirable, well-calculated, the more they are analyzed, to produce the specific results which eventuate. Thus we come to think that we have explained the origin of anything when we are able to view it as the kind of result we should expect from the operation of the factors which have produced it. But this means, of course, that these factors serve. They aid and abet the outcome in definite ways and will produce it if no obstacles

* In *Essays in Modern Theology and Related Subjects*: The Briggs Commemorative Volume. New York, Scribners, 1911, pp. 307-326.

of sufficient contrary influence thwart their natural productivity. Thus individual existence appears to be the outcome of the success of processes which help toward the realization of some specific end over those that hinder this realization. Nature is a domain, not of chaotic changes, but of definite, teleological changes pointing to particular results. In other words, in view of nature's productivity, there are helps and hindrances; things and the elements of things have specific uses.

Philosophy has not always been content to take this fact of specific usefulness as metaphysical, something to be set down as of the nature of things. Explanation has been sought of it and the question asked. Why do things have their uses, and, indeed, their specific uses? In asking this question philosophy has been stimulated by an analogy which has often proved of striking value, the analogy between nature and art. For art, like nature, produces. Its procedure is an adaptation of means to ends. Now art is controllable and its manner of operating is measurably obvious, while nature is stubborn and obscure. The building of a house is a comparatively simple process for analysis, but the factors which combine to produce a star require long searching for their discovery. To pass from art to nature thus affords knowledge the desired opportunity of passing from the better to the less known. Science has ever availed itself of this opportunity and by so doing has often attained its most signal achievements. The analogy between nature and art captivates the imagination also and has been no mean instrument in the poet's hands. And it has an obvious bearing on the problem of use. Its record in this respect has, however, been unsatisfactory. Instead of leading to accepted and intelligible opinion, it has led to bitter controversy. Instead of clarifying use, it has, more often, obscured and mystified use. Its procedure is reviewed here, not for the idle purpose of fighting old battles over again, but in the hope of securing fresh emphasis upon the obvious, but often neglected, fact that teleology is natural; that use is something on which to build, not something requiring explanation; that it is a datum in metaphysics.

I

Art, when consciously productive, evidently intends its products to be useful. A house is made for shelter, clothing for protection or adornment, pictures to delight the sense. The skill of the artist is measured by the success with which he makes his materials serve his chosen end. The finality of art appears, thus, to be an imparted and intended finality. So we find a ready explanation of the usefulness of the things man makes in the intention or design with which he makes them. Asking why the loom so successfully weaves the coloured fabric, we get the answer, it was made in order that it might do precisely the thing which we admire. Furthermore our admiration of the product passes over into even greater admiration of the skill which could contrive a machine so useful. Thus in the products of art we seem to have instances where the explanation of use is obvious. The ease of the explanation readily begets a habit of thinking about use generally, leading us to regard all uses as designed for the ends they serve. Since the hand is so useful for grasping it may be thought of as made in order to grasp. Since the adaptations of nature grow more wonderful the more they are perceived, nature may be thought of as directed by a skill commensurate with such wonder. The analogy between nature and art thus easily constituted is reinforced by human necessities. For man needs the useful in order that he may live long and well. His life is a struggle for help. Nature, too, appears to struggle and its products, like man himself, fail if help is not attained. Indeed, so profoundly may this analogy between nature and art affect the mind, that it becomes incredible that the uses of nature have any other explanation than in a power great enough and intelligent enough to contrive their manifold adaptations. Thus philosophy is led to explain natural use by design and to see in the varied adaptations of means to ends in nature proof of intelligent direction. Nature becomes thus a work of art.

If this explanation of the uses of things, this thinking of nature as somehow a work of art with its adaptations admirably contrived, does not settle down into an unquestioned faith, it suffers in its satisfactoriness from further reflection. For no work of man's art is so perverse as nature. The spider and the fly have afforded a favourite illustration of this. How admirably adapted is the spider's web for catching flies! But shall we also say, How admirably are flies adapted to be caught! Such a summer's day illustration may provoke a smile at the ease with which philosophy may embrace a hasty conclusion. The tragedies of life, however, the tragedies which arise out of these same adaptations which we have been asked to admire, provoke amazement and leave the mind bewildered. Expected harvests blighted in a night, lives of promise lost through no discoverable fault, even the kindnesses of men turned to cruelty when blame can be lodged at no one's door—these and a multitude of similar instances make nature as a work of art irrational and perverse. Indeed, if philosophy has found it easy to accept the adaptations of nature as evidence of intelligent contrivance, it has also found it easy to tear that evidence to shreds. Count only the gains, the seed breaking upward towards the life-engendering sun, and the inference to design looks easy; but count the losses also, the frost that kills before the blossom, and the inference is hard. If, when all is considered, belief in design still lingers, it is belief in a design the purposes of which are past finding out, and clearness of philosophical vision gives place to profound bewilderment. Nature, as a work of art, becomes, thus, an inscrutable mystery.

There are other considerations besides nature's perversity which disturb the opinion that use may be explained by intelligent design. The analogy between nature and art may be preserved while the inference to intelligent direction is abandoned. For the products of art often turn out to have uses which the artist neither intended nor suspected. In breaking stones, man discovered fire. In trying to make gold, he found what gold could never buy. But there is no need of striking illustrations, for accidental advantage is one of the commonest attendants of directed activity. Now this fact may be generalized as well as that of intelligent direction, and use be, consequently, explained as an accident, as something which attaches to things not by design or for any ascertainable reason, but, as we are wont to say, by chance. Incredible as such an explanation often appears when first proposed, it grows in credibility as it is steadily contemplated. For, contradictory as it may seem, the appeal to chance tends to become, when attention is focused on the thing that happens, an appeal to necessity. Long ago Democritus noted that the orderly arrangement of the sand, the pebbles, and the stones upon a beach was not due to any designed selection, but was the necessary result of the coincidence of these things and the action of the waves. So, too, while the arrangement of plants in a garden may show the gardener's taste and skill, the distribution of vegetation about the shores of a lake, although no less remarkable in its arrangement, needs no gardener for its explanation; for, again, the fact that water and soil have happened to meet there under certain natural conditions excludes any other explanation of the resulting order. And it has not been difficult to extend a similar explanation to the marvellous structures and functions of animals. Its apparent incredibility when so extended steadily diminishes with greater familiarity with the facts and with increased experimentation, until it becomes no longer easy—it may, indeed, become impossible—to think of nature as a work of art. Its uses and adaptations appear rather to be accidental, because they simply befall under the conditions which happen to exist in any given case. They appear also to be necessary, because, given these conditions, no other results than the actual appear to have been possible.

The explanation of use by design founded upon the analogy between nature and art finds thus a rival explanation in the contention that use is the outcome of chance and necessity, a rival founded upon the same analogy. The first is a generalization from intended use and the second is a generalization from unintended use. Yet the second has a certain superiority over the first. The perversity of nature, as we have seen, reduces the generalization of design to a mystery, making the purposes of nature inscrutable. But it is just this perversity which the contrasted generalization appears competent to explain. For, if there is no design in nature, but advantage and disadvantage fall out as the conditions happening at the time determine, perversity in nature is something to be expected.

Life will be quickened under the sun's grateful warmth, but be destroyed by the sudden frost. As nature works for no hoped for or expected results, its results are simply those that happen. Thus within the limits of their definitions, within the limits, that is, set by the facts from which they are generalizations, the inference to design is inferior to the inference to chance and necessity. Yet the conviction that things must be as they are is a potent means of obscuring what they are, and the appeal to chance is often only a device to end our curiosity. To conclude, therefore, that the teleology of nature has been explained, may not, after all, be an exhibition of wisdom.

There lurks in the argument which, in contrast to the argument from design, may be called the argument from chance and necessity, an obscurity regarding what it has really achieved which is seldom sufficiently emphasized. The argument is essentially negative. It insists that there is no valid reason for appealing to design in explaining the adaptations of nature; it points out that these adaptations, when clearly seen, appear to be the natural outcome of the conditions under which they arise; when applied to specific cases, it often succeeds in tracing admirably the history of the adaptations involved. These are admitted services. But it may not claim that use has been explained, that a world of useless things could by chance or by necessity become a world of useful things. Its most ardent supporters would hardly venture to make such a claim. Yet the suggestion of it serves to show the limits within which the argument moves. Chance, that is, can operate to produce adaptation only under conditions where that adaptation is already possible. A variation can turn out to be useful only in an environment where it has a possible use. It would be quite profitless, for example, for an organism to develop eyes in a world where there was nothing to see. Thus chance and necessity can operate to secure adaptation only in a world where things have their specific uses, only in a world already essentially teleological. The uses and adaptations of nature remain, having lost nothing of their teleological character from our efforts to explain them or to explain them away. Nature may not be a work of art. It may not be a work of chance. It is a domain of uses where chance and design may operate, but it is a domain of uses first.

Still the analogy between nature and art may be preserved, but it should now be less ambitiously construed. Art and nature both produce and their products are both useful and instances of the adaptation of means to ends. But in neither case is use itself something produced. Not to be sufficiently conscious of this fact is to run the risk of confusing the analogy and indulging in unwarranted speculations. Art makes useful things and may make them with or without intention, but it never makes things useful. That fact alone renders the argument from design or from chance logically illegitimate. Since the sun's warmth is grateful, it may be thought of as graciously bestowed. Life would indeed be poor if such a sentiment were forbidden; but sentiment is not reason. It is one thing to call the sun gracious because its effects are grateful, but it is quite a different thing to regard these effects as evidence that the sun acts with a motive. Poetry and science are separated by that difference. It is imperative in science that evidence should be evidence, that the facts cited should be unequivocal in their import. But in the illustration it is clear that the sun's warmth would be grateful even if it were bestowed with malice or with no motive at all. To be sure a generous gift implies a generous giver, but the thing given is not a gift because it has the quality of being generous. It is a gift for other reasons, and no connection is discoverable between these reasons and that quality which warrants an inference from the one to the other. So too with respect to use; if a thing is useful, it is useful irrespective of the causes which produced it, and no connection is discoverable between its use and its causes which warrants an inference from the one to the other. It is not because it is a work of art that a watch is useful; and it is not because the adaptations in nature may be the work of chance that they are useful. The use of anything is, thus, no evidence whatever of the character of its origin. A thing may originate by art or it may originate by chance, but whether it is useful or not is not thereby determined. Since, therefore, there is no ascertained connection between use as use, on the one hand, and chance or design, on the other, the arguments which have been considered lack the kind of evidence required by science. Use is, accordingly, to be set down, not as a product of nature or of art, but as a factor in their productivity. Art and nature are, therefore, alike in this, that in their productions use is discovered and applied.

II

The argument thus far pursued points to the conclusion that use, when it exists, is not produced, but discovered, that, in the last analysis, it is an original property of whatever possesses it. Teleology is natural, something to build upon, not something to be explained. There is, as Aristotle insisted long ago, a final factor in every instance of production, and thus a final factor among the factors of evolution. But it may be urged that thus to regard use as natural is not to provide knowledge with a valuable category. It is the business of knowledge, one may claim, to study how things do and may go together. It is causes and not uses which constitute the object of scientific research. To look for them with an eye on use is to rob science of its disinterestedness. For use is detected only as means and ends are distinguished, while causes operate independent of such distinction. If, therefore, it is affirmed that use is a factor in nature's processes, must it not also be affirmed that nature distinguishes between means and ends? And does not this latter affirmation imply that nature, after all, operates intelligently, and so open the door again to visionary speculation?

But there is no peculiar sanctity attaching to the category of causation, just as there is no peculiar sanctity attaching to any category of thought. Consequently, when it is asserted that nature must operate intelligently if means and ends are to be naturally distinguished, there is a ready retort in the assertion that nature must also operate intelligently if causes and effects are to be naturally distinguished. Yet it is not good philosophy to dismiss an objection simply by pointing out that it shares the difficulty which it raises. For simply to put one's argument and objections to it in the same boat is not to be well assured of a prosperous voyage. Reason may be better served by a consideration of her chart, for her voyage is not arbitrary, nor her port self-chosen. To drop the figure, the mind cannot create the distinctions which it discovers. Were there no causes and effects discoverable in nature, nature would never be construed by the mind in those terms. And the same is true of means and ends. That ends are reached in nature through the utilization of serviceable means is as simple and unsullied a fact of observation as any other. It is not read into the order of things; and surely disinterested inquiry should not read it out for the irrelevant reason that intelligence is necessary in order to observe it. The sole question to be raised about any category of thought is the extent of its applicability. Now to claim that the distinction between means and ends is known only when intelligence operates is not the same as to claim that the distinction exists only when intelligence operates. Indeed, as has already been pointed out, there is no discoverable connection between intelligence and use which warrants an inference from the one to the other. The category of use is not, therefore, necessarily limited in its application to the field where intelligence operates. Philosophy is amply justified in supposing that a world of useful things could exist, characterized by the adaptation of means to ends and yet unillumined throughout its whole extent by the presence of thought. Only, let it be added, such a world would not be our world.

Our world is illumined by thought. By such illumination the distinction between means and ends, together with all other discoverable distinctions, gains in significance. The gain, however, is still natural. It is another instance of natural teleology. For nature produces thinking beings as well as whirling stars. It is, consequently, no more astonishing that men should philosophize than that bodies should fall; that nature, through its products, should operate intelligently, than that it should operate unintelligently. There are, doubtless, difficulties in tracing the natural genesis of intelligent beings, but these difficulties are not reasons for concluding that their genesis is not natural. Men are not dropped into the world from without. Nature may, therefore, be said to be intelligent, but the statement should not be rendered absurd by a misuse of the concept of totality. One may speak of nature as a whole if one's intention is to be as inclusive as possible in one's utterances. For nature as a whole is simply nothing left out, but nothing more. As a whole, nature allows no other descriptive predicates. It is simply the domain where predicates are specific in their application. To affirm, therefore, that nature is intelligent, is to affirm that among the total of its specific operations intelligence is to be included. Since nature appears to be intelligent in this sense, since our world is illumined by thought, the distinction between art and nature turns out to be a distinction within nature itself, a distincion between nature as intelligent and nature as unintelligent. It points to a specific instance of the adaptation of means to ends. It is a special case of use. Thus, far from creating the distinction between means and ends, intelligence is one of its most significant illustrations.

In metaphysics, moreover, the category of use would appear to be indispensable. Here, at least, where the aim is to define the factors which enter into existence generally, our view of things is warped by a too exclusive emphasis upon causation. Metaphysics may be limited in the appeal it makes, and our chief business in life may remain the discovery of the quantitative value of the factors which combine to effect any change; but only a mind long habituated to the disregard of all but the quantitative can be content to construe the world generally only in quantitative terms. The quantitative is only so much, and always so much of the concrete and the qualitative, of sugar and salt, of gold and silver, of space and time, of motion and electricity. Furthermore, all our skill is unable to discover any connection between the quantitative value of a cause and the peculiar character of its efficiency. The quantity of food required to sustain life does not resemble the quality of the life sustained. And while we may consider such a generalization as the conservation of energy to be among the triumphs of scientific induction, its value consists, not in rendering the characteristic efficiency of any cause intelligible, but rather in showing that all causes appear to be connected and subject to control. Consequently philosophy can never be satisfied with the attempt to regard the qualitative features of the world as negligible in any effort to construe existence generally. For this purpose the category of causation is inadequate, because it is colourless. Moreover, it is useful only because, in its application, it presupposes the characteristic and qualitative efficiency of the factors with which it deals. To define a world, therefore, solely in terms of the dimensions of energy, is to define another world than ours. The vision of things is only distorted when their qualitative features, their æsthetic character even, are regarded merely as the incidental byplay of factors which have no other law than the equation.

III

The justification of the category of use has, thus far, been mainly negative. The attempt has been made to show, first, that there is no relevant connection between the fact of teleology and the operations of chance or design; and, secondly, that intelligence may not be regarded as the source of the distinction between means and ends, because it cannot be credited with creating the distinctions it discovers, and because it is itself an instance of teleology. These considerations do not, however, amount to a positive definition. They produce at best a negative conviction and so serve to warn us that teleology is to be reckoned with. But if teleology is natural, how is it to be naturally construed and worked out? This study would be incomplete if no attempt were made to answer the question. For the baffling thing about the distinction between means and ends is that it is a distinction which points towards the future; and to regard an end not yet attained as an efficient factor in producing present changes has never been productive of generally convincing reasoning. Historically the progress of knowledge has often been arrested by some fresh and fascinating appeal to final causes, but knowledge has usually proceeded again unmodified by the appeal except in so far as it has directed attention to new methods of obviating the difficulties it raises. The science of biology is a pertinent illustration of this. Its history is marked by repeated appearances of vitalism in some form, but its great gains have not been made by the use of that hypothesis. There is, thus, in the fact noted, cause for inquiry and caution. The appeal to final causes always commands interest, but it is always regarded with suspicion. The interest appears to be due to the fact that the appeal forcibly calls attention to the habitual presupposition of finality in tracing the course of any natural process. The suspicion appears to be due to the fact that the appeal insists that what the presupposition involves should be regarded as an efficient factor during the process. The issue thus raised is more of a logical tangle than a question of fact. Its analysis may serve to indicate that a definition of natural teleology must recognize an ultimate diversity in the character of the factors with which we have to deal. Use is always specific use.

The bare statement that the attempt to trace the life history of a given organism is the attempt to follow the movement from its germ to its matured form, is sufficient to indicate that the finality of the movement is presupposed. For the germ is not the germ of an organism in general, but the germ of a particular organism. A kernel of corn is not a grain of wheat. And, to transfer the illustration to the inorganic world, carbon is not oxygen. Consequently, whether we are dealing with elements or with complexes, with dead things or with living things, these factors, if they are to enter into the production of any future result, are never conceived irrespective of the particular part they are to play in that production. Their finality, their serviceableness in the production of definite ends is presupposed. Without the presupposition inquiry could not go forward, but, when once made, the presupposition may be disregarded without any damage resulting to the explanation. To conclude, however, that teleology does not exist or that it has been explained is unwarranted. It both exists and is unexplained. An appeal to final causes directs attention to this fact. But it goes further. It insists that an additional cause should be incorporated among the already ascertained factors in any process. It invokes some "end," "form," "idea," "entelechy," "psychoid," "soul," to account for the fact that specific ends are reached. The situation thus produced is ambiguous and confusing. If one asks what is the specific function of the final cause, the answer is, obviously, to give the product its specific character. Since, however, the product must first exist before its specific character is realized, and since this character has already been presupposed, the answer appears to mean nothing at all or an absurdity. An acorn is not an oak, but to put an oak into the acorn in order to explain why acorns grow into oaks instead of into fishes, is like putting an explosion into gunpowder in order to explain why it explodes when ignited. In other words to put the end of a process into the beginning of it in order to explain why that end is reached, is either meaningless or absurd. For, assuredly, if the end existed at the beginning we should need more than all our wit to distinguish the one from the other. A world so constituted would be a world where nothing could happen, a perfectly static world. If it is urged that this is only a caricature of the doctrine of final causes, the reply may wisely be made that that doctrine is only a caricature of the facts. For little more is gained besides a kind of mystification of the mind by expressing the doctrine in terms less gross than those here employed.

Yet something is, perhaps, gained, although a more refined expression is not necessary to secure it, and although the gain is not a gain for the doctrine itself. The appeal to final causes calls as we have seen, attention to the fact that teleology exists, but is unexplained. Its own explanation is devoid of force because it turns the necessary presupposition of teleology in any movement toward a result into a cause why the particular result is reached. That is why it fails to be logically convincing. But its failure does not constitute a reason for rejecting teleology. It points rather to the fact that what is needed is not explanation, but definition. It does more. It points also to the fact that any definition of teleology must recognize an essential diversity of character in the processes involved in any change. Things and the elements of things are specifically different in their character and their operations. In terms of use, uses are always specific and in specific directions.

When we indulge in speculations about the origin of things in general we are forced to conceive that origin as capable of yielding the kind of world we discover ours to be. Such speculations may at first impose themselves upon the mind as explanations of why things are as they are, but candid scrutiny can find in them only more or less successful generalizations of the obvious. Thus our attempt to explain why the processes of the world move on in specific and distinguished directions with specific and distinguished results, amounts, in the last analysis, to a generalization of the fact of specific difference in a dynamic world. In biology, for instance, the problem of the origin of species is always the problem of the origin of particular species, and its solution is not an explanation of the existence of species generally. The solution is rather the fact of specific differences generalized and refined in view of the conditions under which they exist. By this is not meant, of course, that biological species must always have existed, but that ultimately specific differences in the factors dealt with must exist if specific differences in the results of their operation are to be made clear. Expressing the matter once more in general terms, recognition is here asked of the fact that uses are specific and operate in specific directions. In other words, to claim that things are generally useful is not to exhibit the fact of teleology in the processes of nature. The particular—and, indeed, many—ways in which they are useful must first be discriminated if there is to be any pertinent consideration of the adaptation of means to ends. The teleology of nature is not, therefore, a general drift toward some general result, it is always in individualized directions. It is a teleology of special cases. Our world is thus a collection of concretes, so that we are always inquiring about some definite thing, a star, an atom, an element, an organism, or some specific relation of these things to one another. There is no other kind of profitable inquiry, because there is no other kind of subject-matter for investigation. Ultimately concrete and specific differences in the character and operations of whatever factors go to make up the world, appear, thus, to be the first element in a definition of natural teleology. Given such differences, any change, no matter how it originated, would be subject to them, and the resulting movement be consequently a controlled movement.

Natural teleology involves more than controlled movement. We get but an inadequate picture of things if we view them only as the arrangement of given factors under fixed conditions. For the movements of nature are marked by unmistakable gains and losses; they are helped and hindered. In view of these helps and hindrances, it is possible for us to select any one of the concrete things of the world and regard it as a centre, while the others form its varying attendants or environment. The world's processes may thus be regarded as the interaction between a thing and its surroundings. Since the selection of any centre is at our pleasure, this procedure has a certain universality about it, so that the complete natural history of anything would be a history of nature itself. Yet many such histories would have to be written, for the world as a whole has no possible single history, because it has no possible environment with which to be related. But one may say that it has many histories, because, as a whole, it is but the sum of all possible distinctions between a thing and its environment. Thus we come once more upon the fact of ultimately specific differences, but we come upon it under new aspects. For to construe the world as the environment of any chosen thing as its centre, reveals the world as contributing, not only in different ways, but with unequal success to the processes of that thing. The elements in the environment are not all useful, and those that are useful are not all equally so. Any thing's existence presents itself thus as a kind of survival, as a centre where the useful in a given direction has been in excess. While attempts to explain survival are not usually successful because they have a fatal tendency to reduce themselves to the simple statement that things do survive, it is evident that only in a teleological world is the concept of survival appropriate. Indeed, when the concept is critically examined, it appears to mean primarily that all things are not equally useful in supporting individual existence. Natural teleology involves, therefore, the recognition that use is comparative. Things and the elements of things differ in their teleological importance. Deductively expressed, one might say: Given a world made up of specifically different elements in dynamic relations and of different values with respect to any processes which might occur, these processes would result in specific products the existence of which could be construed as survivals, as the adaptations of means to ends, as the success of processes which help more over those that help less. The deductive expression ought not, however, to blind our eyes to the fact that it is not an hypothesis invented to explain the world. It is only a generalization of familiar facts.

The third element in a definition of natural teleology is a corollary of the preceding. Uses are not only specifically different and of comparative value, they also persist and accumulate. The eye, when it appeared, afforded, not a temporary glimpse of the world, but a continuing vision of it. This persistence and accumulation, however, should be construed under the general limitations already set for the definition. That is, we do not appear warranted in speaking of progress in general; we may speak only of specific and individualized progress. Consequently, when we affirm that natural teleology is progressive, we affirm that factors of greater teleological importance have continued to operate. The fact of such continuance is the fact of progress. It is possible, therefore, to imagine that a given thing, if it met with no hindrance in the progressive appropriation of the useful, would present an instance of the steady approach towards complete adaptation to its environment and towards a conquest of the uses of the world. The Malthusian rabbit might thus become sovereign of the universe. It is, therefore, not unnatural to believe that, if there is any dominating direction in the appropriation of the useful, that direction must be due to the operation of some individual being. But sober thinking is reminded that the directions in which use is appropriated are many and diverse, and that hindrances consequently oppose complete adaptation. There is war in the world and sovereignty there is hazardous. The most dominating of beings may succumb to the most insignificant, as man may be destroyed by the animalcule. Yet sober thinking must also recognize that the symbol of war is appropriate, and that uncertainty in the tenure of supremacy does not obscure the fact that there are genuine victories.

The definition of natural teleology involves, therefore, besides the recognition that uses are specific, in specific and controlled directions, and of comparative value in view of these directions, the further recognition that uses are progressive. Let it be insisted once more, however, that the definition is not proposed as an explanation of teleology in the world's processes, but as a generalization from facts which we can, in wisdom, neither overlook nor explain away. While no attempt has been made to question the right of any science to employ the categories it finds best adapted to its specific aims, the attempt has been made to justify metaphysics in the employment of the category of use.

IV

There are, doubtless, various applications of the general definition of natural teleology which has been here proposed. These lie outside the scope of this discussion. There is, however, a special instance of teleology which may serve to throw the definition into sharper relief, and which affords inquiries of special interest—the teleology of consciousness. That it is useful to be conscious is palpably evident in spite of the difficulties one may encounter in defining just how thought can change the world. These difficulties can not obscure the significance to be attached to these moments in the world's history when its teleology becomes a conscious teleology and is reflectively considered. The significance may at first be emotional. Consciousness may be a "lyric cry"—to adapt Professor Santayana's phrase—involving joy over discovered uses or sorrow over frustrated aims. But the deeper significance lies evidently in the direction of foresight and knowledge. To anticipate advantage or disadvantage, and to know the means by which the one may be gained and the other avoided, presents the most signal instance of natural teleology that can be cited.

The conception of a world like ours in all respects save the presence of thought has already been suggested as philosophically warranted. Such a world would have a past and a future, and its history would display the facts of comparative use and progressive adaptation which have been embodied in the general definition of natural teleology. Yet it would appear to be impossible to assign to these facts or to the past and the future any characteristic efficiency. This statement does not mean that such a world would lack continuity in its development, that any given factor in it would be what it is irrespective of its past, or that its future would be out of relation to other future factors. But it does mean that the teleology in such a world would be only a characteristic of it, indicating the appropriation of use, but that this characteristic would not be detached from the specific instances of its operation and thus become itself a factor in that world's processes. This, after all, is but a way of saying that a world so conceived lacks consciousness, that its processes go on uncomplicated by any recognition of their uses, actual, prospective, or retrospective. Yet it may serve to indicate the kind of complication which the presence of consciousness introduces. The spider may spin its web unconsciously and produce thereby a product useful to it; but if it spins consciously, the past and future have entered into its activity in a new and significant manner. It may even be led to contemplate the miserable fate of its prey. Without consciousness, yesterday is only today's past, tomorrow only today's possible future. With consciousness today's changes occur in view of yesterday and of the possible tomorrow. With consciousness the processes of the world become at once retrospective and prospective in their operation.

There is, therefore, design in the world. Only, as we have seen, that design may not be invoked to explain the world's teleology, because it is one instance of that teleology. But the fact that it is such makes it unnecessary to seek further for the ground of moral distinctions or for a rational confidence that nature is sufficient for the demands design may make upon it. Responsibility is not imposed from without. It arises from no authoritative command. It is, rather, the inevitable consequence of design. For to plan and put the plan in operation is to become the cause of the issuing result, the point where responsibility is definitely lodged. So we do not hold rocks responsible because they fall, but we do hold men responsible because they think. Because they think today is changed in view of yesterday and tomorrow, and consciousness being the possibility of such a change takes upon itself the thoughtful construction of the issue in the light of the world's natural teleology. That is the essence of morality. Man was not made moral by the prohibition of an apple. The fruit was good to eat, and the conscious discovery of its use turned man into a designing being. Thereafter he must learn the natural uses of things and turn them to his advantage, but at the risk of reciprocal demands. Thus, with consciousness, the world's teleology is a moral teleology. Given the world, which is not that world unillumined by thought which philosophy in its freedom may imagine, but a world among whose factors conscious beings must be numbered as instances of its productivity, these beings may not be surprised that their world is moral. Its moral character impresses them as again something necessary, something for the absence of which they can discover no reason. What the sun is to the movements of the planets, that justice is to the movements of design.

Perfect justice, like perfect equilibrium, may be unattainable, but justice is not a visionary ideal, unsupported by the teleology from which it arises. For, as we have seen, uses are specific, cumulative, and of comparative value in their operations. Justice has, therefore, for its exercise, not only the distinction of the useful and the useless, the good and the bad, but also the distinction of the better and the worse. Accordingly, while design may despair of success in eliminating evil, it ought not to despair of success in attempting to achieve the better. For these attempts are supported by the world's natural teleology, by the comparative value of the uses of things. Knowledge thus ministers to morality in a twofold manner, by the localizing of responsibility and by the conscious discovering of the more useful. The end of such discovery is most evidently beyond our vision. Every new scrutiny of the world's uses reveals new and unsuspected possibilities, and warrants the conviction that the better is attainable and attainable with a diminution of injustice. The world may not have had its origin in reason, moral progress in it may waver, great gains may there be lost, and civilization go backward, but the world affords of itself the vision of its own rational conquest. To fix responsibility and to promote science appear thus to be the primary essentials of moral progress. To entertain, therefore, the vision of the world's rational conquest is not to be an optimist by temperament, but an optimist by conviction. We may not proclaim out of an abundance of well-being that this is the best possible world and that all things work together for good. For the moral lesson of natural teleology is that the world can be improved. Ours is the best possible world only because it has the capacity to engender and support the effort to make it better.

Yet enthusiasm is not to be denied to philosophy. To envisage the world in the light of reason is to beget emotions for which the impersonal categories of knowledge afford inadequate expression. These emotions, too, are natural, responses to provoking stimuli as much as the vibrating chord to the finger's touch. Man may, therefore, sing the praises of nature and be devout or fearful in her presence, for to personify her is but to accord her the filial recognition that persons are her offspring, born of her body, and nourished at her breasts. To refuse emotional responses to her revelations because they do not involve an explanation of her origin or of her destiny, is not a sign of wisdom, but of insensibility. For the contemplation of the stars has other natural uses besides the advancement of astronomy.

Indeed, man can hardly be indifferent to the fact that nature evokes from him emotional responses as well as intellectual curiosity. But it is impossible for him so to divorce emotion and reason that his thinking and his feeling may remain unrelated and independent activities. For consciousness is comprehensive in its scope, including in its survey the fact that we live fully as much as the fact that we fall. It is also reflective, embracing, as we are wont to say, its own operations as something of which it also takes cognizance. This is, however, only the affirmation that consciousness is consciousness, that the existence of facts is not the considering of them. But it serves again to render conspicuous the particular use to be assigned to consciousness, the use of rendering the past and the future connectable and continuous now. It is creative of nothing but comprehension, and is subservient to the materials it finds. Its task is thus the rational organization of this material in its entirety. While, therefore, its exercise may discover emotions, we may not say that it is because we are conscious that we rejoice or fear, just as we may not say that it is because we are conscious that we have a certain specific gravity. The emotional life presents itself, thus, as one object for intelligent control and organization. But it does present itself as such an object. To claim, therefore, that teleology is natural and that consciousness is its most signal illustration, is not thoughtlessly to discard the obligation to seek for the emotional life its appropriate support and the befitting sphere of its operation. It is, rather, to urge that the search be conducted with an intensified appreciation of the immediate sources by which that life is quickened and refined.

EVOLUTION*

THE subject to which I ask your attention requires a preliminary statement if it is not to appear at the outset too vast and vague. My purpose is to express the opinion that evolution is history; that antecedents and causes should consequently be historically construed; that evolution is pluralistic, implying many histories, but not a single history of the world; that man writes the history only of his own world; that, however, since he discovers his world to be a history, he may have a science of history or evolution which is universal, and that this science indicates that evolution is progressive. Because I am expressing an opinion and not trying to prove a thesis I have indulged in many assertions.

I take it that the term "evolution" in so far as it indicates any natural fact, indicates initially no more than the fact that things have a past, that they have a history. It would indeed be but another name for history if we were willing to extend our conception of history to denote all discovered and discoverable changes. As indicating a rational enterprise the term appears to express the attempt to recover the history of things by generalizing for the past the conditions, types, factors, and rates of change which are discoverable. If this is so, it would seem clear that the only point where the doctrine of evolution in general is questionable, is in its method of procedure. If we are not justified in extending to the past the discoverable principles of change, the attempt to do so might be interesting, but it would deserve no special commendation. It is, however, unprofitable to question this method of evolution, because it is the only method which can be checked and controlled. No alternative method is open to us except the arbitrary method of making what suppositions we choose about the past, and in

* In the *Philosophical Review,* Vol. XXI (1912), pp. 137-151. Delivered as the presidential address before the Eleventh Annual Meeting of the American Philosophical Association at Harvard University, December 28, 1911.

that case all suppositions can be made equally good because none of them can be tested. The evolutionary attitude needs, therefore, neither apology nor justification. It may need advocacy because it is easier and often more congenial to make mythologies than to write history.

The acceptance of the evolutionary point of view is, however, no guarantee that mythology has been abandoned. Speculations about energy and force, about the origins of variation, about heredity, about nature and nurture, as well as such controversies as often mark the engagements between vitalists and the supporters of mechanism, or between the adherents of epigenesis and of preformation, seem frequently to indicate that mythology still finds a place among the general doctrines of evolution. I do not mean to imply that these speculations and controversies point to no problems in need of solution. I mean only that they too frequently display a tendency to turn the characteristic operations of things into causes why things so operate; to assign a superior efficiency to the past than to the present; to make evolution a substitute for a creator; and, in general, to suppose that the causes rather than the history of the world have been discovered.

When, for instance, we ask, Why does a hen sit on eggs? we are often forbidden to give the natural and obvious answers, Because she wants to, or, In order that chicks may be hatched; and are urged rather to give the mythological answers, Because she has an instinct to sit, or, Because her ancestors sat. Now the first of these latter answers is the attempt to turn the characteristic behaviour of the hen into a cause why she so behaves, and the second is the attempt to regard her past as more efficient than her present. One might as rationally say that a clock goes because it has an instinct to go or because its antecedents went. It seems, however, that when we ask such a question as has been proposed about the hen, we desire an answer which will make clear to us the result to be attained by her behaviour, whether that result be a bodily satisfaction or future offspring, or we desire one which will disclose what it is that induces the hen so to behave. We do not desire, or rationally ought not to desire, an answer which will disclose why the hen sits irrespective of the end to be attained by her behaviour or of the stimulus which excites her. In other words, unless we are mythologists, we do not expect to be told why in a world like ours it is characteristic of hens to sit. To be sure, we do want to discover what that characteristic behaviour is, what stimulates it, what the hen's structure is, how that structure has come about, and what results from her activity, and there our rational interest stops. To suppose that the answers to any one or to all of these questions will give us an explanation of the fact or possibility of sitting hens in a world like ours is totally to misconceive their import. There are hens, they do sit, they thus perpetuate their kind, and they have had a history which is measurably ascertainable; but hens must be given first, if there is to be any investigation of them or any discovery of their evolution. If there were no hens, or never had been any, all our science and all our philosophy would be irrelevant to their consideration. Evolution, that is, discloses and is the history of what exists or what has existed, but it is always with the existent that it begins. To suppose, therefore, that any state of the universe, however remote or distant, has a metaphysical superiority to any other, or a greater right to ontological eulogy, or is possessed of a more potent efficiency, is, to my mind, radically irrational.

The opposite opinion is not unfamiliar. Although it may not be as widely held as formerly, it is still current, clouding our intelligence, depressing our energies, and weakening our responsibilities. We have been frequently told that if we knew completely the state of the cosmos before hens existed, we should then be able to set the date for the first hen that would eventually appear, we should be able to tell, that is, whether there would ever be such things as hens in this world of ours because we should have become cognizant of all the causes of its evolution. Perhaps such a statement can not be refuted. Every attempted refutation may be met with the rejoinder that our knowledge is as yet too incomplete to make the prediction successful. It may be asked, Do you really mean to affirm that if we knew the cosmos through and through we should not then know its possibilities and its eventualities? Does the fact that we must wait for events to happen before *we* can discover their causes give us the slightest warrant for supposing that those causes, even before we discovered their effects, were not competent to produce them, would not, in fact, produce them? And if so, is it not simply nonsense to affirm that we could not have predicted what those causes would produce if we had really known what those causes were? Is not such an affirmation one more instance of the stupid failure to distinguish between the *ratio cognoscendi* of things and their *ratio essendi* or *fiendi*?

Questions like these may impose upon the mind, but they do not clarify it. To be sure, if we knew the full competency of things and how and when that competency would be exercised, there would be nothing left to discover. This we do not know and we may confidently say that we never shall know it. That we shall not does not indicate a defect in our faculties, some limitation which we vainly try to leap over. It indicates rather that our knowing is itself an event, one of nature's happenings, an item of history. The *ratio fiendi* and the *ratio cognoscendi* look strange, do they not, when applied to the fact of knowledge itself; if they force us to affirm that if we knew—let us say, the primeval condition of all things—we should then be in a position to state what our knowledge of it would eventually be and whether that knowledge would be correct or not. We owe idealism a profound debt for that piece of dialectic, even if we charge idealism with the failure to profit by it. It, too, imposes upon the mind even if it does not clarify it. What intelligible meaning can be attached to the statement that if I knew the antecedents of my present knowledge, I should then be able to tell from those antecedents what my present knowledge is? The antecedents of my present knowledge are not my knowledge, and the antecedents of the hen are not the hen. And I have not been able to discover any wisdom or profit in putting my present knowledge into its antecedents in order to explain how that knowledge originated, nor in putting the hen into her antecedents in order to explain her.

Our researches acquaint us with the natural history of the things into which we inquire and they acquaint us with nothing else. Knowing their natural history we may be led to entertain certain expectations about their future, but it is important to remember the conditions of such expectations. Now I take it that while the fact that we expect anything has its antecedents, these antecedents are not themselves expectations or anything like expectations. Because the sun has risen so invariably, I may expect it to continue invariably to rise; but its performance does not account for the fact that I expect it to do anything at all. That performance may lead me to expect a rising and not a setting sun, but it does not lead me *to expect* that the sun will do anything. In other words what our expectations about things concretely are may be due entirely to the things, but it is not due to them that we meet them in the attitude of expectation. Expectant beings must first exist before anything is expected of things. To be sure, expectant beings have a history, but what can it possibly mean to affirm that any knowledge of that history short of their existence would lead us who are expectant beings to expect that such beings would one day exist? I am not trying to say that the origin of consciousness is one of the riddles of the universe. I doubt that it is. To suppose that its origin may one day be discovered appears to me to be neither visionary nor absurd. I am trying to say, however, that the origin of consciousness, its evolution, is a matter of history only. We expect things to do what they are in the habit of doing. Because plants grow from seeds, we expect them so to grow. If they dropped from the clouds like rain, we should expect that of them. If they behaved in a way to baffle all expectation, we should expect them so to behave. If, therefore, we discovered that matter produced thought, we should expect it to produce thought. This does not mean, however, that if we knew the constitution of matter, we should expect matter to produce thought. It means rather that we can not construe matter without taking thought as an item in its history. To say, therefore, that if we completely knew the past condition of all things we should then see that the present is its fulfillment, can mean only that we are construing the present historically. It can not mean that we have discovered a condition of affairs which, irrespective of the present, would, by a kind of unfolding, produce the present, because irrespective of the present that condition is not only not discoverable, but it does not even exist. Antecedents are only antecedents and evolution is history.

But antecedents are antecedents. That means, naturally, that they can not be isolated or defined out of relation to the historical movement in which they occur. The past is undoubtedly dead. It is unalterable because it is dead and exists no longer. But this does not allow us to construe the past independent of the continuing processes of things. When we say that the past can not be changed, all we can profitably mean is that prior to a given date the events that have occurred are not altered by the events that occur subsequently. We can not mean that our appreciation of what the past was is fixed or that the significance and efficacy of the past as an item in the world's history is completed. In other words, it is only what the past was that is unalterable. What it is, undergoes constant change. What it was, is impotent. What it is, has efficacy. Or, to speak epigrammatically, there always was a past, but never is one. This means, I take it, that antecedents are definable only in view of the history to which they belong and as items in that history; they are, neither from the point of view of our knowledge of them nor from the point of view of their own efficacy, fixed and finished things. Even the principle of inertia must be expressed in terms of a *continuance* in a state if it is to be comprehensible and a principle of things. It should, therefore, be apparent that what the antecedents of anything are, not what they were, is never fully ascertainable nor fully existent except as we arbitrarily fix a date and refuse to pass beyond it. A world which has had a past is a world which will have a future. Undoubtedly its past was what it was and its future will be what it will be, but in so far as it is an evolution which has continuously a past and a future, its past is alterable and its future therefore indeterminate. Evolution as history is thus not simply the record of accomplished events with all their principles and laws; it is rather, let us say, history as an object, a continuing process whose past is recoverable and whose future is conjecturable, but which, as a process, can not be construed as the result or eventuation of anything.

In a certain sense, then, there is no evolution. If we conceive of the simple unfolding of potentialities once resident and determined in some primitive condition, there is no evolution. As a substitute for a creator, there is no evolution. As a set of laws or principles which, somehow controlling the stuff of things, causes that stuff to produce a world, there is no evolution. As the growth of a cosmic seed, there is no evolution. Nature defies and gives the lie to all these conceptions. She proclaims again and again that everything that happens has had a history, but that nothing happens because it has had a history. Clocks do not go because they have had a history. Hens do not sit because they have had a history. Matter does not perform its manifold functions because it has had a history. To say that the world is what it is because it has had a history is to say something meaningless. It is meaningless for two reasons: first, because the history of a thing is never the cause of it, and secondly, because the world has no history at all.

These statements may be more irritating than convincing. I am sensible that they appear to obscure an issue. It may be readily admitted that the history of anything is never its cause, since so to affirm is to confuse facts with their record. But the thing has causes and its history reveals what those causes are. The history of a house may not be the cause of a house, but its history does reveal the men who built it. Assuredly; but this is to construe causation as well as evolution historically. It is evident that builders do not build houses in a world where houses are not built. Causes do not operate where they do not produce effects. In other words, no effect points to its causes as isolated antecedents of that effect. If there is no effect without a cause, there is also no cause without an effect. Only existent things have causes. To impute causation, therefore, to anything irrespective of its effect, is to impute an entirely meaningless conception. We may say, that is, that whatever conception of causation we entertain, it should be historically construed to be made intelligible. To make evolution the cause of anything is, therefore, meaningless, for evolution as a cause can not be historically construed. It has no effects over against which it can be indicated as a cause. To say that it causes the history of things is unintelligible, for that is to say that it causes itself. So, I repeat, causes are never causes absolutely and in isolation. They are causes only in an historical series. Their nature and efficacy are never given except in their eventualities, and when these occur, the causes as causes have ceased to be. A spark may cause an explosion, and there may be no explosion without a spark; but where there are no explosions, sparks, even if they exist, are not their causes.

And the world has no history. I appeal to the philosopher of Königsberg. The world is a collective idea which we can frame because we can group things and because things are grouped in nature. To extend the act of grouping, however, until we have the idea of a group from which no fact remains uncollected, and then to suppose that there corresponds to this idea an object of which we may ask, Has it a beginning in time, an extent in space, a history or an evolution? is to enter the realm of illusion. No; the world as a useful concept must be used distributively. It must mean, Take any item you like, but not, Take all items together. It must be regulative and not constitutive. Evolution as history is always the history of items. Yet no limit can be set to the extent of any such history. A flower in a crannied wall may carry other than a poet far, leading to the construction of every discoverable event as significant in the light of its career. But no one of such histories, however comprehensive, may claim cosmic preeminence over any other. The world is no more matter's world than it is the spirit's, and no less; no more man's world than the microbe's, and no less. Individuals may compete for their lives, but cosmic histories are free from rivalry. No one of them exists as a history to the prejudice of any other. The history of the stars is not the history of man. So to conceive it is to make the history of man contributory and incidental to astronomy, and this man as the writer of histories can not succeed in doing. He can write other histories only as he is willing to become an observer of the world but not a factor in it. He can regard himself as something incidental to another's history only through a kind of forgetfulness of his personality, or by substituting for it a kind of dummy which behaves as he would, but without his reasons.

Xenophanes, we know, sought to disparage man by saying

that if lions had hands and could paint they would paint their gods as lions; and this truthful remark has many times since been taken in that same sense of disparagement. Maeterlinck, on the other hand, has represented a dog as calling a boy his god. He thereby made the dog as stupid an animal as the men who call dogs their gods. We may say, consequently, that Xenophanes had the finer poetic feeling, but he appears to have missed altogether the profundity of his remark. Man can construe the world eventually only as his own history. His doing so is saved from egotism, however, so long as he knows what he is doing and why he does it. That knowledge is inconvenient at times. It often disturbs man's mind with thoughts of the rights of other histories. Consequently, he may often attempt to quell this disturbance by trying to write a history of the world which will be totally impersonal and inhuman. Then he becomes a materialist. Or he may convert the fact that he can write only a human history into an epistemology. Then he becomes an idealist. Or he may call upon evolution to explain it all. Then he becomes superstitious. Yet through all his blundering he has sounded the depths of his philosophy. He has discovered the world because he has discovered his history. That means that he has discovered the world to be a history and that any discovery of the world would be the discovery of a history.

Evolution is, therefore, pluralistic, and man tries to write many histories even if eventually he succeeds in writing only his own; but no history of evolution can be written. Every attempt to write one always gives us something other than a history and something other than an evolution. It converts the world into a product or into an effect of causes, and must at last confess its inability to find the producer of that product or the causes of that effect. Its failure does not indicate a lack of intellectual power, but a misdirection of intellectual effort. It proves that evolution is pluralistic, not that monism is necessary. Yet the attempt to write many histories with a clear consciousness that histories are the theme, may disclose the fact that all histories have common categories. That is the discovery of metaphysics. In other words, the attempt to tell what history is, or what evolution is, may not be inept or futile. That is, since we discover the world to be an evolution, it ought not to be impossible for us to analyze that discovery and state what it is to be an evolution. Whatever success we may attain in such an enterprise, it is not necessarily vitiated by any human limitation. It is universal. Only, I repeat, it is not universal history. It is not the portrayal of an evolution. It is the science of evolution. So while there can be no history of evolution, a science of it may be attempted and projected. In no other sense may we venture to claim that evolution is monistic. As a history it is many; as a science it is one.

It should be apparent that the science of evolution, just because it is not a history, will not deal in origins. It will disclose no genesis of the world and discover no causes of its existence. It will disclose, however, or we should expect it to disclose, principles, laws, types, groupings, connections, characteristic efficiences. Briefly, we should expect it to disclose the factors and method of evolution, but nothing more. We should expect, too, that such a science would not only be universal, but might also be restricted to as narrow a field as we might choose. That is, we may have not only a science of evolution, but also a science of any particular evolution. If it is legitimate to inquire into the nature of history, it is also legitimate to inquire into the nature of matter, or of life, or of consciousness, or of anything that can be denoted as subject-matter for analysis and study. Only we should remember that its science discloses its nature and not its history; and that its evolution discloses its history, the record of its existence, and not its nature.

The contrast thus stated is stated, perhaps, with too great simplicity. The science of any history is a science of *a history*, that is, it is a science of natures which may themselves have a history. This fact can not be disregarded. It is evident, therefore, that when we say that the evolution of anything discloses its history, but not its nature, we should not prejudge the possibility that there may be things the nature of which is only historically definable, the nature of which is, we may say, just their concrete history. A grain of wheat in its chemical and physical composition is a thing quite different from what we call a seed, the grain of wheat which implies what only its history can make apparent at the time of harvest. It is conceivably possible that we might know the chemical and physical composition of all seeds without any nook or corner left unexplored; that we might then be able to detect differences in their composition which would allow us to classify them with accuracy, so that one kind of seed could be distinguished without error from any other kind; and yet that we might find nothing which would indicate what the nature of those seeds is as displayed in their growth. It is considerations like this that give to vitalistic theories their recurring interest. Yet we should emphasize two things: first, that under the supposition we have made, vitalism is scientifically unnecessary; and, secondly, that vitalism would be scientifically necessary only if after fully ascertaining the composition of all seeds we were unable to distinguish between them or to classify them as of different kinds. It may well be that every living thing in its germ has a mechanical constitution as specifically and individually distinct as the specific form and individuality which its maturity reveals. The evidence points that way, and as long as it so points, vitalistic theories are naturally viewed with suspicion. No; the supposition I have ventured to make, has not been made in order that we may entertain once more a theory which retreats defeated again and again after every fresh appearance, but to emphasize the fact that the nature of a thing may be progressive. Time may enter into its substance. Our problem then becomes to discover and trace that progress, not to look for causes of it. Why should we look for them? The argument against so doing is old. If progress has causes we must invoke time to delay their operation, to keep the world from being finished at a single stroke. But then what causes can we invoke for time's delay? It avails us not. We shall end by affirming that causes are progressive, and then, perhaps, delude ourselves into supposing that we have discovered the cause of progress itself. That some natures are progressive seems certain; that all are seems doubtful. And that, I suspect, is why we find the distinction between the organic and the inorganic so natural and so helpful. I venture to suggest that the triumph of mechanism would involve, not the reduction of the organic to the inorganic, but the removal of the distinction or the restatement of it in terms of a time function.

Evolution is thus discovered to be progressive. All our attempts to explain why this is so, all our appeals to energy, force, will, design, vitality, appear to be but the obscure recognition of that discovery. Or they are introduced to help out an initial misconception, the conception, namely, that the nature and efficacy of all causes are fixed and determined irrespective of the time it takes for those causes to operate. Such a conception implies to my mind a world where nothing could occur without the intervention of some new power to make it occur. But we have the best of evidence that it is not some such mysterious power which operates, but rather simply the continuing in operation of the concrete factors with which we deal.

If evolution as a natural fact is thus progressive, it is apparent that evolution as a rational enterprise, as the attempt to recover the history of things by generalizing for the past the conditions, types, factors, and rates of change which are discoverable, is itself an instance of progress. That the past is thus recoverable can be no less a natural fact and no less significant for evolution than the existence of the past itself. If it is unprofitable to construe evolution otherwise than as history, it is also unprofitable to construe it irrespective of intelligence, to suppose that the mind has had no history or that it is irrelevant to the world it contemplates. We should not say that it creates that world or serves as the ground of its character or existence. Yet we should say that it makes that world discoverable and prospective so that in intelligent beings we find a discovered and a prospective evolution. We find the contrast between what might be and what was and is. We find the progress of history alterable in the interest of what is desired, hoped for, and imagined. We find nature submitting to be idealized and evoking the spiritual enterprises which enlarge the happiness of men.

In the light of evolution, intelligence is seen thus to have the kind of operation which does more than excuse the vagaries of intelligent beings. Their attempts to construe the world as itself a rational process and to read the mind into its substance and into its every operation; their making of mythologies even; their superstitions, their blunders, their faiths, their hopes, their ambitions; their irrationalities also; their sciences, their philosophies, their poetry, and their art; their morality and their religion; their likes and dislikes; their loves and their hates; their cults and their ceremonies; their societies and their utopias; their nationalities and their politics; their laws and their institutions; their comedies and their tragedies; their impotence and their strength—all these things are no less ontological than nebulæ and ions. They are as much factors in evolution as anything that can be named. They have to be reckoned with as much as climate and soil. They are as dignified as electricity or gravitation. That the world should have become the home of the imagination is no less cosmically important than that it should have become the home of stellar systems. If man was destined to be an instance of physics and chemistry, he was also destined to be an instance of the "life of reason."

That intelligent beings should recover their history is no reason why they should repudiate it, even if they find many things of which to be ashamed; for they are examples of the recovery of the past with the prospect of a future. In reading their own history, they may find that they may smile at that which once they reverenced and laugh at that which once they feared. They may have to unlearn many established lessons and renounce many cherished hopes. They may have to emancipate themselves continually from their past; but note that it is from their past that they would be emancipated and that it is freedom that they seek. It is not a new form of slavery. Into what greater slavery could they fall than into that implied by the squandering of their inheritance or by blaming their ancestors for preceding them? They will be ancestors themselves one day and others will ask what they have bequeathed. These others may not ask for Greece again or for Rome or for Christianity, but they will ask for the like of these, things which can live perennially in the imagination, even if as institutions they are past and dead. He is not freed from the past who has lost it or who regards himself simply as its product. In the one case he would have no experience to guide him and no memories to cherish. In the other he would have no enthusiasm. To be emancipated is to have recovered the past untrammeled in an enlightened pursuit of that enterprise of the mind which first begot it. It is not to renounce imagination, but to exercise it illumined and refreshed.

It would appear, therefore, an error to consider intelligence solely as the instrument of truth or the rule by which propositions are proved and disproved. It is such an instrument and such a rule, but it is more. It is an instrument for the recovery of the past in such wise that the past is doubly effective, effective in view of its own continued nature and effective in view of what intelligence conceives and imagines. To that double effectiveness knowledge is subsidiary. It is a means to an end, not an end in itself. How the whole of philosophy witnesses to that conclusion! We call ourselves by differing party names. We rush to different colours to contend under them for the truth of propositions. It is a battle for the strong, and it is good to engage in it. Let the hosts be drilled and the conflict test our strategy, for truth is worth fighting for. Yet it is worth fighting for because there is one truth which none of us can successfully assail, the truth that intelligence provides "a technique for generating a chosen future out of a given present."[1]

I made my summary at the beginning. I there stated that it was my purpose to express the opinion that evolution is history; that antecedents and causes should consequently be historically construed; that evolution is pluralistic, implying many histories but no single history of the world; that man writes the history only of his own world; that, however, since he discovers his world to be a history, he may have a science of history or evolution which is universal; and that this science indicates that evolution is progressive. Such an opinion is, I believe, liberalizing. It frees intelligence for its own progressive operation untrammeled by any suspicion of its rights. It suggests that the discovery of the world is not principally or essentially the discovery of what it has been, and not at

[1] W. T. Bush, "The Emancipation of Intelligence," *Journal of Philosophy, Psychology, and Scientific Methods,* Vol. VIII (1911), p. 178.

all the discovery of causes which, irrespective of its history, have produced it, but the discovery of its implied possibilities, a discovery which is the surest foundation for the ideals of men and which allows them to look upon their present and their future as something far richer than an illustration of their past.

STRUCTURE*

We speak of the structure of buildings, poems, plants, animals, machines, states, and even atoms. The fact denoted by the term is of such importance for our knowledge and use of things that nearly all inquiry is devoted to the discovery of structure in specific cases. Moreover, this discovery has an obvious finality about it. Its explanatory value is high and satisfying. For whatever the end may be which any operation serves and whatever the cause may be which initiated the operation, our curiosity is largely satisfied and our efficiency is enhanced when we have discovered the structure to which the operation conforms. A watch may be made to keep time; if we ask why it keeps time, we are not satisfied by saying because it was made for that purpose by a watchmaker, but we are satisfied by knowing its structure. Having this knowledge we are able to increase the precision of watches. The eye may have been made in order that we might see, but, if so, we do not thereby understand vision. We understand it rather when we have discovered optical structure. Then, too, we are in a position to improve defective vision. The fact of structure is obvious. Illustrations of it, however, even if they are trite, may serve to emphasize the fact in some of its apparent varieties.

The user of materials may do many things with them provided that his use of them conforms to their structure. This is well illustrated in any problem of maxima and minima, as, for instance, the problem of determining what areas may be enclosed by a line of given length. Here the particular areas are limitless in number, but they are all limited by a single

* In the *Journal of Philosophy, Psychology and Scientific Methods,* Vol. XIV (1917), pp. 680-688. Delivered at the meeting of the American Philosophical Association, December, 1916.

principle. This principle defines precisely the structure to which the operation conforms and within which, so to speak, it is confined, so that we know that the minimum area is the line and the maximum area the circle. This illustration may be paralleled indefinitely. Proper selection from among the illustrations would lead to recognized sciences which set forth the discovery of the structures within which are confined the operations with which these sciences deal. Mechanics would be one of these sciences. And it is clear that no matter how much mechanics may vary in its concrete discoveries or in the terms and instruments it finds best suited to its use, it will not vary in its attempt to discover the structure to which the equilibrium and displacement of bodies are confined. So far as this structure is concerned our conception of what bodies "really" are seems quite irrelevant. They may be the concrete things we perceive them to be, they may be "masses of matter" or "congeries of sensations," they may be molecules, atoms, or what not, their equilibrium and displacement conform to a precise and definite structure. Mechanics thus testifies to the fact of a structure of a particular kind within which and subject to which numberless operations of a particular kind can occur.

Chemistry affords another example. Not only do elements combine in definite ways, but the same elements subjected to different structural arrangements seem to produce an almost limitless variety of compounds. Ultimately, all chemical structures may be discovered to be mechanical. In that event we should recognize a welcome scientific simplification and an extension of the domain of mechanics. Such a possibility ought not to be prejudged even if in many chemical operations time appears to be a different factor from what it is in mechanics generally. To the latter science time seems to be relevant only as it is measured in terms of simultaneous displacements, while in chemistry successive or genuinely temporal displacements often seem to be involved. Although a remark of this kind ought not, in the present state of our knowledge, to be accepted as final, it serves, nevertheless, to indicate the possibility that structures may be matters of time as well as of space.[1]

Biology seems to confirm this possibility. It has advanced in recent years to remarkable determinations in detail of the structure of living beings and of their operations. Recent experimental work on heredity, instinct, growth, and descent has revealed to us what we may call living structures with a fullness hardly suspected fifty years ago.[2] And it is these structures rather than any assumed vitalistic principles which, as we are wont to say, "accounts for" the variety of forms and operations. But since living is not something spread out in space, but something enduring in time, living structures seem to be characterized temporally in a way different from mechanical and chemical structures. A cell is not simply what it appears to be under the microscope. It seems to have also what we might call a suspension in time which can be ascertained only by allowing to it its proper duration. It is not only so much chemical substance encased, so to speak, in a particular mechanical structure, but it is also so many minutes or days of a specific kind of growth. Accordingly, its growing seems to be subject to a structure suspended in time fully as much as the displacement of its parts is subject to a structure extended in space. Conformably with the latter it may divide and conformably with the former its successive divisions result in a typical living form. In biology, therefore, we apparently meet with structures which, while they exhibit definite mechanical and chemical characteristics, exhibit also characteristics which can not be defined in these terms. These structures are of *kinds*; and when we exhibit definitely the kind in any instance, we point not only to a particular mechanical and chemical fact, or series of such facts, but also to a life history.[3]

Psychology, at present, is following the lead of biology,

[1] "The present physical and chemical structure of organism must be explained not only in terms of atoms and molecules, but also in terms of the history of living matter upon the earth." Comstock and Troland, *The Nature of Matter and Electricity*. New York, Van Nostrand, 1917, p. 194.

[2] See, for example, T. H. Morgan's *Mechanism of Mendelian Heredity*. New York, Holt, 1915, with its extensive references.

[3] I suspect that it is a confused recognition of the fact of life histories, as different from one another as different chemical compounds, that leads so re-

especially when the latter science deals with highly organized living beings. Many of the operations which we call mental are so evidently vital that a distinction between the mental and the vital is more often confusing than helpful. If we are to make a sound distinction at all, our considerations hitherto might lead us to make it in what we may call structural terms. In other words, if there are operations or activities of living beings which indicate a structure different from the mechanical, the chemical, or the biological, then we may have a means of distinguishing mental from vital processes which may be advantageous. Such a difference appears to be the fact, for we recognize a kind of structure which we call logical. Whichever of the current attitudes toward logic we may take, we seem to be confronted with the fact that the operations of thought are subject to a structure which is not like that involved in the displacement of bodies, or in chemical combinations, or in life histories. The syllogism may be an inadequate expression of this structure, but it is an historically instructive one and shows how different the structure of thought is from the other types of structure we have considered. Every examination of the operation of implying or inferring seems to show the same difference. Ideas and propositions, whether spoken or unspoken, are subject in their movement to structural principles as definite and precise as the principle involved in the simple illustration of the line and the area with which we started. And these principles have that kind of aloofness from time and space which we indicate by the ordinary word "mental" and the extraordinary word "transcendental."

The foregoing illustrations naturally suggest the generalization that a structure of some sort is characteristic of all operations universally. In other words, whatever else the world or the universe or "reality" may be, it is at least a structure or a system of structures. Or we may say that it has structure as something genuinely, universally, and metaphysically characteristic of it. Whether it has one structure or many will be left here unconsidered. We shall be content to follow

peatedly to vitalistic theories in biology, just as it is the failure to recognize the structural character of life histories which makes many "mechanical" interpretations of life so unsatisfactory and so unconvincing.

the lead of our illustrations and say that it has at least spatial, temporal, and logical structures which may be reducible to one type, but which will be left here without any attempt so to reduce them. Nevertheless, we shall speak in what follows of the fact of structure generally without distinguishing its apparent kinds.

Structure is a discovery and not an hypothesis. Naturally the discovery in particular cases may be generalized for cases not yet examined, so that belief in the universality of structure becomes a controlling belief. It may lead us to refuse the supposition that there is any operation which is structureless. But we do not begin inquiry by first supposing that there must be structure and then find that our supposition is borne out by the facts. Structure is met with in quite a different way. It is met in action and practice, by setting one stone upon another, for instance, and finding that stones must be set in certain ways if they are to stand up as a wall. The fact found out in such ways as this imposes itself on us, so to speak, confronts us, obstructs us after the manner of a brute fact, so that we must regard it as belonging to the subject-matter into which we inquire and as independent of the fact that we discover it by inquiry. If we apply to it the distinctness current in philosophical usage, we must say that it is objective and not subjective, that it is *a posteriori* and not *a priori*, that it is empirical and not transcendental. In short, it is not an hypothesis invented by the mind for purposes either of explanation or control. It is a fact discovered, and discovered like other facts, as, for instance, that Saturn has rings.

Consequently there are many philosophical considerations irrelevant to it and on which it in no way depends. Its status as a genuinely discovered fact is independent of realistic and idealistic theories. It confronts materialism and spiritualism equally and unequivocally. Every brand of epistemology must bow to it, no matter how each brand may attempt to account for it, since each brand discovers it first and attempts to account for it afterwards. These statements need no other evidence than the recognition that the philosophical considerations implied by them, if they deal with structure at all, deal with it as a discovered fact which they attempt to elucidate or explain. In that sense only are they at all relevant to it. But they are in no sense relevant to its obviousness, its obstructiveness, or its bruteness. Any of these philosophies may be entertained without any alteration in the fact of structure either as a discovery of a general nature, or as a discovery specific in characteristic details. It stands out thus as one of the absolute metaphysical facts to which all speculation is subordinate.

Although philosophers may busy themselves with attempts to explain structure, there is no explanation of it, if by explanation we mean the finding of a reason why it should be. Of course there is explanation in the sense of making plain what structure is in specific cases and even what structure is in general. There is explanation also in the sense of showing what consequences flow from the fact of structure itself. But there is no explanation in the sense of showing why there is structure or why there is structure of any particular kind. A watch has a particular structure by virtue of which it keeps time; but if we ask why it has that structure, it is difficult to make clear precisely what we mean by the question. We can hardly say that the watch has its structure in order to keep time or because it keeps time, for manifestly its structure and its time-keeping go together simultaneously and not successively—the one is in no sense because of the other or for the sake of the other. To be sure, watches have been made in order that time may be kept, and that fact may show us why watches have come to be, but it does not show us why a watch in order to keep time or in just keeping time, has a structure of a particular sort. The discovery of what the structure of a timepiece is or has got to be, if time is to be or is kept, is a very ultimate kind of discovery. It does not lead beyond itself. And what is true of the watch is true generally. God may have made all things after the manner in which a watchmaker makes a watch, for the purpose of having certain things done, but his purposes could not explain to us why things have the structure they are discovered to have. His purposes explain only what uses of structure he has chosen. And so the discovery that all things have structure is a very ultimate kind of discovery. It is absolute because the consideration of origin is quite irrelevant to it. No matter how things have been produced nor when, no matter whether they were ever produced or not, structure is an absolute fact about them, the kind of fact that does not lead beyond itself. There is no explanation of it because it is the kind of fact that does not require explanation.

All this is saying again that structure is really a discovery and a discovery of an absolute kind. That is, the inquiries which lead to the discovery of structure terminate absolutely in that discovery. Has structure been discovered or not? If it has been discovered, that ends the matter. From which it is clear that structure is not imposed upon things, but is something constitutional to them, so to speak. A watch does not have its structure imposed upon it by its maker. Neither does anything else. This is really saying again that structure needs no explanation, that the question why anything has structure is an idle question, but it is saying it in another way. Since structure is a discovery it may, like other discoveries, often be a surprise. Historically it seems to have been a surprise when made on a large scale. That things are fluid, so to speak, structureless, a kind of flux without law or order, subject to whim and caprice, is not an unnatural supposition, so that the discovery of structure may come as a surprise and may lead to the question how was structure imposed upon the flux? But the discovery of structure in any specific case always disposes of this question by showing its futility. No one who understands the structure of a watch is surprised by it. We may be surprised at what is accomplished by means of the structure before it has been discovered, but when it is discovered we are not surprised that these things are accomplished by its means. Put in its most general form, the idea is this: order and uniformity cease to be objects of surprise when once structure has been discovered. There is then no longer any motive for accounting for them. They are not imposed upon the flux, but the flux exposes them in its movement. Structure is thus evidently a metaphysical discovery absolute and final.

Knowledge of structure is an eminently satisfying kind of knowledge. It reduces impressions, opinions, convictions, and beliefs to what we call science. Never do we understand anything more completely and finally than when we understand its structure. Such knowledge is in the highest sense explanatory, because it leaves nothing to be explained. By that I do not mean that it puts an end to all intellectual interest or that the discovery of structure is not progressive. I mean rather that did we know the structure of things thoroughly, all our intellectual interests would become practical and inventive. Science would become dogmatic while art would flourish. Since such complete knowledge would enable us to predict the consequences of any structural combination, all our ingenuity would be employed in inventing new combinations adapted to secure desired ends. All arts foreshadow such an ideal and especially the mechanical arts. For even if the principles of the classical mechanics are now under suspicion, it is clear that their acceptance as so much settled dogma has been marvelously fruitful in inventions for man's use and comfort. And so it is that knowledge of structure gives us the great desiderata of all knowledge, namely, science and prediction, on the one hand, and control in the interest of desired ends, on the other.

Such complete knowledge, even if attained, would probably not put an end to attempts to conceive existence generally in terms which will satisfy human aspiration. But these attempts would not increase knowledge or add a new department to science. They would not, therefore, be either needless or profitless. They would be instances of an art which transforms existence by refining, beautifying, and ennobling it as does a picture or a song. In a world where pictures are painted and songs sung, it would be quite ridiculous to say that the imagination ought not to leap to a vision of providence or of a moral order. For a knowledge of structure would show that poetry and religion, as clearly as anything else, are not miraculous, and that they are not unnatural. But it would show also that they are not scientific, and that they do not increase our knowledge. Yet they do beautify existence and enhance the control of it. They put into the world heavenly pictures, so that he who contemplates them may be the more at home in this physical world.

There is apparently little difference, if any, between structure and what is called substance by metaphysicians. The latter term is more ambiguous in its usage and has associated with it many conflicting ideas. Yet when we speak of substance as that which exists in its own right, or as that which persists through all changes, or that which is defined in its own terms, or that which stands under, or as that which has attributes, or as that the knowledge of which is conclusive and final, we are using expressions which seem equally applicable to structure. Indeed, when the term substance is used to identify anything beyond the particular subject of discourse at any time, it seems to carry us to much the same conclusions as a consideration of structure carries us. But the term structure has the advantage of freeing us from many perplexing associations. To speak paradoxically it is less substantial. It means something absolute without meaning God. It means that without which nothing can be or be conceived without meaning something which should be eulogized or made an object of emotional attachment. It is more expressive than the term substance is of an ultimate fact actually discovered. But our habit of thinking of structure as something possessed by the world or by things suggests the advisability of linking it more closely with the older term. For although we may say that a watch has a certain structure we do not thereby mean that the watch is more ultimate than the strucure it is said to have. And so with the world—it does not possess its structure, but is rather its structure when we wish to express a final and absolute fact about it.

This linking of the terms structure and substance enables us to speak of structure more naturally as a subject to which predicates may appropriately be attached. We may then say not that the world has structure, but that structure is the world. In other words, the attempt to form a conception of all things together or to speak of the universe or nature generally is an attempt which does not successfully carry us to the recognition of a single complete and self-enclosed whole of things, but rather to the fact that however endless the succession of events may be, or however manifold the number of identifiable things may be, ultimately there is unity of structure. And it is this discovered fact of unity of structure rather than some supposed wholeness with nothing left out which may properly be called the world or the universe. We might then say that beyond structure there is nothing, without meaning that within structure everything past, present, and to come is already somehow included. We should mean rather that all there is to structure is completely knowable because structure is itself complete, but that it is the only thing of which this can be said.

Linked with this completeness of structure is its principal attribute—as I should like to call it, still using substantial terms. That attribute is inertia. I have already indicated that structure is discovered as a brute fact. It is met with not by way of hypothesis or conjecture, but by way of opposition or resistance. Everything that happens conforms to it, but it of itself does nothing. Our original illustration is here again suggestive. The structural principle of the many areas is a principle to which each of them must conform. Figuratively speaking, it sets a limit beyond which they can not go. But it produces no single area, although an infinity of areas is producible. As over against them structure is absolutely inert. And this seems true generally. Structure is the inert principle of all existence. On this fact itself I do not now dwell, although the derivatives of it are interesting and illuminating. I wish rather to venture one further generalization, namely, the identification of structure with matter when matter is metaphysically conceived. When so conceived—and here again we seem forced into paradoxical statements—when so conceived, matter loses its material qualities. These qualities, like solidity, fluidity, etc., as well as all the so-called secondary qualities, have long appeared to men as convertible into one another and to afford no absolute basis for exact determination. Even the conception of chemical elements is seriously attacked on both theoretical and experimental grounds. But the conception of structure remains intact and to this conception still cling the so-called primary qualities of matter like inertia and those which are only quantitatively and relationally expressible, like weight. If the materials of things are convertible, it seems evident that in no sense can any of them be more final and primary than any other; but if all are convertible in terms of changeless structural principles, these latter would appear to give us just that absolute conception of an inert factor in existence which has long borne the name of matter. This proposed identification of structure with substance and with matter is here only suggested. I hope at another time to elaborate it.

Indeed the points put forward in this paper are all in need of elaboration. But it has occurred to me that they might prove suggestive as indicating a field of metaphysical inquiry apparently free from the controversial questions of much recent philosophy. The considerations here suggested seem to me to afford scope for inquiry and discussion independent of mooted questions about the truth of perception or the possibility of knowledge.

MIND DISCERNED*

"WE HAVE said that those objects which can not be incorporated into the one space which the understanding envisages are relegated to another sphere called imagination. We reach here a most important corollary. As material objects, making a single system which fills space and evolves in time, are conceived by abstraction from the flux of sensuous experience, so, *pari passu,* the rest of experience, with all its other outgrowths and concretions, falls out with the physical world and forms the sphere of mind, the sphere of memory, fancy, and the passions. We have in this discrimination the *genesis of mind*, not of course in the transcendental sense in which the word mind is extended to mean the sum total and mere fact of existence—for mind, so taken, can have no origin and indeed no specific meaning—but the genesis of mind as a determinate form of being, a distinguishable part of the universe known to experience and discourse, the mind that unravels itself in meditation, inhabits animal bodies, and is studied in psychology."[1]

This passage from Santayana's "Reason in Common Sense" is quoted for homiletical rather than critical purposes. I confess, however, that I have found no little difficulty in attempting to construe it intelligibly and systematically. There is apt to remain with me a residuum which is ambiguous and obscure. For, if the genesis of mind is the consequence of a discrimination which, in its turn, is made by processes of conceiving and abstracting, there seems obviously to be presupposed as already generated or existing a mind which discriminates in that manner. And if such a mind is to be presupposed, it is not easy to make out whether it is mind in the transcendental sense without origin or specific meaning, or whether

* In the *Journal of Philosophy,* Vol. XVIII (1921), pp. 337-347.

[1] *The Life of Reason,* by George Santayana, Vol. I, pp. 124-125.

it is the mind known to experience and studied in psychology. Both seem to be logically excluded. For a mind which discriminates by conceiving and abstracting can hardly mean the sum total and mere fact of existence, and a mind which, as a consequence of such discrimination, becomes a determinate form of being, can hardly be the mind which, by discriminating, leads to that consequence. Yet mind as mere fact of existence and mind as a determinate form of being seem to exhaust the whole domain of mind as defined in the passage and its context.

These considerations I naturally believe are as obvious to Santayana as they are to me, and that belief makes me suspect that the passage was not written to provoke an excursion into dialectic. I suspect that his presentation of a flux of experience coming somehow to be discriminated into material objects—making a single system which fills space and evolves in time—and a sphere of memory, fancy and the passions, is an attempt, not to raise metaphysical problems, but to tell in a fairly accurate way after all, how, in an individual's life, his personality and the world he lives in come to be sharply set over against each other. Such, at any rate, was my understanding on first reading the passage. Later readings brought out and emphasized the difficulties to which I have given expression. They have led me to do something more, to consider afresh the question of mind in the transcendental sense and the mind which is studied in psychology. And it is because they have done this, that I now approach the question with this introduction.

It is to be emphasized that what now follows is neither criticism nor exposition of the quoted passage, although its words may frequently recur. I can not easily escape their haunting suggestiveness and have no desire to. The mind which inhabits animal bodies and mind in that sense in which the word is extended to mean the sum total and mere fact of existence, set forth a contrast which is not easily escapable when one remembers the writings of philosophers. Moreover, reflection quickly leads to the recognition that no matter how absolute the varied determinations of being may be taken to be, determinate forms of being are discovered in the course of one's personal history. The universe which we investigate is, in a very genuine sense, a universe of discourse—certainly, a universe discoursed about—a sort of total object of thought, the totality of which seems to be in no wise impaired by any of the distinctions discovered or set up within it. The mind which is studied in psychology as a determinate form of being exists in this universe of inquiry alongside other determinate forms of being from which it is distinguished. Both it and they are in some sense objects of thought and their being so does not in any way seem to exclude either them or the distinction between them from the total universe of inquiry. In other words, the world of material objects and the mind which inhabits animal bodies lie, as it were, discriminated in a single universe of discourse and may be subjects of thoughtful inquiry even if such inquiry may seem never to occur except with the presence of some animal body with a mind inhabiting it. Shall we say then that the total universe of discourse to which all distinctions and discriminations are relevant is mind in the transcendental sense, the sum total and mere fact of existence? An affirmative answer could identify itself with several recognized systems of philosophy. But it is not any such identification which is here sought, but rather what understanding, if any, is to be given to such an affirmation.

Let us consider the total universe of discourse, that realm in which all determinate forms of being lie, so to speak, side by side in their manifold relations. We may give to this universe other names, such as the world of phenomena or the sum total of experience. Naming it is, however, apt to disclose some prejudice about it or some theoretical construction of it, of which it itself may be innocent. If it is named a world of phenomena, the term "phenomena" may imply no more than that it appears as just what it appears to be; but the term may also imply that its items are phenomena or appearances of something else and thus involve a relation not possibly given within the universe we are considering. For clearly the total realm of being does not contain within itself a relation to something not contained within it, and a relation to something wholly exterior to it would not be a relation open to investigation. Propositions involving such a relation would be mean ingless. Again, if the universe we are considering is named the sum total of experience, the term "experience" may mean only that we are considering it, talking about it, regarding it in any way we can regard it, or making trial of its many factors; but the term may also mean that the universe of discourse is the result of some anterior process by which it is generated and comes to be the kind of universe it is. In this latter sense "experience" is not an item within its boundaries, and can not be explored. The expression "the total universe of discourse" may involve similar difficulties. It has, however, the advantage of suggesting primarily logical considerations. It brings at once to the front the fact that what we are concerned with are those realms of being which are objects of study and inquiry, the universe of the chemist and the physicist as well as the universe of the moralist and the psychologist. It emphasizes subject-matter as over against speculation and hypotheses. It calls before us the natural attitude of the man who finds a purse and looks to see what is in it. So men find rocks and trees, seas and stars, memories and fancies, and look to see what these things are and what can be said about them. All inquiry starts in this way and not with "phenomena" or "experience" or "sense-data." These may be arrived at later as interpretations or explanations of what it was with which inquiry started, but they are not original with its inception. It is, therefore, in the hope of keeping close to the initial act of inquiry into definite, concrete subject-matter that I speak of the total universe of discourse, using the term "total" to mean no more than the attempt to leave out no instance whatever of such inquiry.

This universe in its totality—meaning by totality what I have just defined—might conceivably be the object of a single individual's consideration. We have a sense of that whenever we enter a library which contains measurably all that men have ever said or discovered about this universe. With time and patience enough one might read every book and learn what purses had been found and what treasures within them. But it is not the magnitude of the information possibly to be derived in this way that is in point here, but rather the fact that such a reader, were he asked to note it, would observe an underlying continuity in his readings. He would observe for instance that the physicist and the psychologist were both studying sounds even if the former said they were waves of air and the latter sensations; that the moralist and the economist were both investigating goods even if the former called them objects of desire and the latter commodities of exchange. In sum, he would observe that in all his reading he was confronted with a world to be interpreted and with interpretations of that world. The latter might vary from Genesis to Einstein, but the former would seem to be invariable. Such a reader might leave the library with what I conceive to be a very simple, but also a very fundamental piece of metaphysical wisdom, namely, that in spite of the varieties of interpretation, there is, logically speaking, but one subject-matter to be interpreted. The physicist and the psychologist have the same subject-matter although they interpret it differently, likewise the moralist and the economist, likewise everybody. That is, all inquiry is ultimately relevant to the same subject-matter, the same universe of discourse. It is the continuity of this subject-matter, underlying all interpretations of it, which makes it possible for the reader to detect what he is reading about.

To strip this universe of every shred of interpretation is not easy. For, in the first place, some interpretation has apparently laid hold of it before one is led to the attempt so to strip it. And, in the second place, any stripping is inevitably fraught with the danger of being itself an interpretation of some sort. On this double difficulty one might dwell at length, for the search for what is called "the immediate" has been long, labourious, and unconvincing. Yet, as I take it, the search is ill-advised. We are not called upon in our investigations to divorce subject-matter and interpretation in any way which would force upon us two wholly disconnected universes. That puzzling obligation does not as a matter of fact confront us. We might with greater truth assert that any attempted divorce would be meaningless, since interpretation itself involves the identification of the subject-matter to be interpreted. This assertion seems to be valid when followed out in detail. For what are sounds? The physicist and the psychologist both answer the question and it is quite clear that they are both telling us what sounds are. There is no difference of subject-matter between them. There is something to which their replies, however different, are relevant and that something is identified by them and their hearers. If some lover of the pure immediate should interpose with the claim that to call that something "sound" is already to interpret it, we should have no difficulty in recognizing that he was talking about the same item in the universe of discourse about which the others were also talking. In short, subject-matter needs no divorce, either absolute or relative, from interpretation in order to be identified. If it did, it is quite clear that the visitor to the library could not understand a single book he read, or discover any differences of interpretation or opinion among the authors.

Consequently it would appear that we can tell what subject-matter is either by identifying it or interpreting it. Asked what sounds are, we either produce them or refer to physics and psychology. This fact recalls many familiar contrasts of philosophy, such as knowledge of acquaintance and knowledge about, fact and meaning, existence and explanation, object and idea. That such contrasts should so naturally and constantly recur is good evidence that they are metaphysically sound. They indicate that the universe of discourse, that is, again, the universe within which all inquiry occurs and proceeds, is characterized fundamentally by the contrast of subject-matter and interpretation, or, we may say, of object and idea.[2] Although we may be enticed by various considerations to attempt to divorce the terms of this contrast so that they may constitute initially two distinct realms of being which are subsequently united by some secret agency, we never really succeed. Man has contrived their union only through hypotheses which are ultimately either unintelligible or *petitones principii.* We might better side with those who say, "What God hath joined together, let no man put asunder." For no inquiry into the universe of discourse has ever succeeded in separating it into a universe of objects apart from ideas and a universe of these ideas absolutely apart from objects. In the words of Spinoza:

[2] This I take to be Spinoza's doctrine of the attributes of extension and thought, and the basis of his axiom, "A true idea agrees with its object."

Ordo et connectio idearum idem est ac ordo et connectio rerum.

Since the universe of discourse is a universe of this kind, we might give to it with some appropriateness the name of mind. Such a name would be used in the transcendental sense, for it would be used to indicate possibilities, the possibility of knowledge, of inquiry, of discursive thinking. It could not mean that *a* mind was taking thought of *a* world. In this latter sense the name could have no specific meaning. Neither could such a mind be said to have an origin. One might reluctantly admit that the universe of discourse itself might have an origin, that it was not self-sustained and self-sufficient, but mind in the transcendental sense could have no origin within it, since mind in that sense is but a name given to the universe's salient character. And that name would indicate the sum total and mere fact of existence as constituting the universe wherein inquiry is active and productive.

Clearly this mind is also not a determinate form of being, a distinguishable part of the universe known to experience and discourse. It does not inhabit animal bodies and it is not studied in psychology. Nor does it explain the universe it constitutes, for it is not a substance which supports that universe, nor a cause of which that universe is an effect. It is a name for the fact that object and idea are already married whenever their union is open to consideration. It is a protest against the divorce courts of epistemology. It may be more, indicating a type of structure which the metaphysician must recognize in any dealing with being in its ultimate character.[3]

What then is the mind studied in psychology? Clearly it is not mind in the sense we have been considering. No argument is needed, I imagine, to support this statement, for the mind studied in psychology is a mind which remembers, imagines, perceives, reasons, is disturbed by passions, moved by desires, and, above all else, inhabits animal bodies. It is a biographical and not a transcendental fact. It is a determinate form of being. It has a genesis and an origin. It is studied in psychology and to that study it must largely be left here. Since, however,

[3] I have suggested this in an article on "Structure." See *Journal of Philosophy*, Vol. XIV (1917), pp. 680-688.

the passage from Santayana which led us to it is a summary of its genesis, we may consider that topic in the light of our previous discussion. I am fairly content to let Santayana's account of its genesis stand, for, as already indicated, that account calls us to note how the sphere of memory, fancy and the passions falls out with the physical world, and forms a sphere by itself although still in touch with what it has left. Every individual can, I imagine, discover some such genesis in his own life if he studiously looks for it. And assuredly the things which for an individual do not make up the physical world are the things which are studied in psychology. Santayana's account may, therefore, stand. What is said in the following is neither exposition nor criticism, but only considerations which are in line with the previous discussion and which are prompted by the statement that there is a genesis of mind in the psychological sense. But strictly it is not with its genesis specifically that I shall be concerned, but with something relevant to its genesis, namely the possibility of it, as a determinate form of being, interpreting the universe in which it finds itself.

The mind studied in psychology inhabits animal bodies. Whether it inhabits all such bodies is uncertain, but the question whether it does is one of the best proofs of its habitat and a clear indication that its definition is ultimately biological. It is distinguished in the body not in the way the head, brain, or any anatomical part of the body is distinguished, but in the way the life of the body is distinguished. It is not a part of the body in the sense that the fingernails are a part of it. If we call it a part at all, we tend to follow Aristotle and say that body and mind are parts of the living individual, and are more like an axe and cutting than they are like an axe-head and an axe-handle. Disembodied spirits seem unable to function without a medium, and souls, if they survive one body, seem forced to seek another. So that even if we say that the mind is not a part of the body in the anatomical sense, and even if we fancy that the mind can be without a body, it must have a habitat to be effective, to be communicated with, and to be studied.

Now the animal bodies which mind as a determinate form

of being inhabits are items in the universe of discourse. They themselves belong to the total domain of things which can be investigated and are objects of inquiry like all other objects in the same domain. Asking what they are, we say, among other things that might be said, that they are the habitations of mind, and that being such they think and reason. They interpret the world in which they live. They say, among other things, that sounds are waves of air and also that they are sensations; that goods are objects of desire and commodities of exchange. I am not concerned here with their justification in saying these things, but with the fact that they do say them and with the possibility of saying them that lies back of that fact. Of our interpretations of subject-matter we say that some are sound, others unsound, some correct, others incorrect, some true, others false. But it is quite clear that back of such affirmations and fundamental to them is the possibility of making any affirmations at all. On what does that possibility depend? In other words, how are we to construe the fact that animal bodies, in so far as they respond to the world about them by interpreting it, are said to be inhabited by a mind?

This question of possibility ought not to be so handled that in place of possibility we have impossibility. Yet this, I suspect, is what is too frequently done when the question is considered. For instance, the possibility of interpreting sounds as waves of air can not lie in the initial existence of waves of air as subject-matter to be interpreted. Yet our books are full of attempts to exhibit the possibility of interpretation generally in terms of some specific interpretation which itself rests on that possibility. Nor can we successfully flee from the universe of discourse altogether and say that the possibility is outside of it or arises from the union of factors in themselves alien to it. Yet this too has been repeatedly tried, with only ultimate confusion as a consequence. Indeed just now I can think of only two answers which promise anything like conclusiveness. The first is that the possibility resides in the fact that mind as a determinate form of being inhabits animal bodies; and the second is that it resides in the fact of the universe of discourse itself defined as mind in the transcendental sense as we have defined it above.

Yet I must regard the first answer with suspicion. Its sole title to accuracy, so far as I can discover, resides in the fact that the universe of discourse is considered and inquired into only, so far as we know, by animal bodies inhabited by a mind. Because it is bodies of this sort that do the interpreting and write the books in the library, and because without them interpretations are apparently not made, nor books written, it is natural to conclude that the possibility resides in them. But this turns out to be a rather queer conclusion when once it is attentively examined. For my own animal body is one of the many objects of my study, and while I may discover that it is different from other objects in many ways, I do not discover that *as an object of study* it differs at all from them. It lies side by side with them in the total universe of discourse. It is, to be sure, what Bergson calls a privileged object since its movements and activities enlarge the range of my inquiries, but this fact is one of the discovered differences between it and other objects and does not put it in a different universe from them. I know that its health and integrity are prime factors in successful study. As in imagination I rob it successively of what are called its faculties, I find that the universe of discourse is for me progressively impoverished, but I do not find that it ever wholly disappears. I know that to the blind this universe is not luminous as it is to me and that to the deaf it is not sonorous, but I know that I myself neither see nor hear without adequate stimuli thereto. In other words such differences as are thus indicated appear to be differences due to the constitution of the universe as a whole and imply no more than the interdependence of its parts. They are not differences which can be intelligibly construed as ultimately disrupting its continuity. The difference between an animal body which can see and one which can not, is like the difference between one which can fly and one which can not. Such facts as these, together with the other that I can not even in fancy abolish the universe and leave anything to consider, make the conclusion look queer to me that the possibility of interpretation resides in the fact that a mind inhabits animal bodies.

In other words, I can make nothing intelligible out of the attempt to start with animal bodies fully equipped in their animality and then by adding a mind to them construe their thoughtful consideration of their world in terms of this addition only. The attempt has been made many times, but it has always been wrecked ultimately by our inability to exhibit what animal bodies are without any implication at all of mind. The attempt moves wholly within the total universe of discourse. It is never free from the distinction between thing and idea. Its enticement, as has already been said, lies wholly in the fact that without animal bodies the attempt itself is not made, but this fact must be offset by the recognition that there are other things, such as digesting food, which are not done without animal bodies, and that we are not wont to construe the possibility of doing them by adding to the body a factor in which the possibility resides. Significant, therefore, as the fact may be that without animal bodies inhabited by a mind inquiry into the universe of discourse does not occur and no interpretation of it is made, the attempt to construe the possibility of such interpretation in terms of the inhabiting mind —the mind studied in psychology—is here rejected. We turn to the other locus of possibility, namely the fact of mind in the transcendental sense.[4]

Those who deal with the natural history of mind in the psychological sense point out how that history keeps pace with the natural history of animal bodies, but they have never been able to discover a point at which mind may be said definitely to enter, at which it precisely takes up its habitation. The reason is, perhaps, not that they have not been acute enough to discover it, but rather that there is no such point to discover. A mind inhabiting a body may involve a procedure wholly unlike that of a tenant inhabiting a house. The latter leases his dwelling from an owner who has a prior right to possession. It is difficult, however, to think that a mind leases a body from nature and then moves in on some appointed day. It seems to dwell in its habitation, if we are to keep up the figure, more as the house's outlook dwells in it, something

[4] It may be unnecessary to point out again how radically different the transcendental mind is from the psychological. The former can not be defined in terms of conscious processes or behavior. It is neither substance nor cause. I conceive it to be, as indicated in the article "Structure," one of the structural facts of existence generally.

congenital and not alien. It would seem as if animal bodies become seeing, thinking, remembering, imaginative, and passionate bodies in much the same way as they become digesting, breathing, walking, and reproductive bodies. Just how they become this latter sort of bodies we do not very well know, but we do know that in actually being bodies of this sort they do no more than react to a world which is itself congenial to their reactions. They react, that is, to a world which makes the specific character of their reactions possible, but this possibility they do not create. Chemistry may be said to inhabit them and unravel itself in digestion, but the possibility of such a determinate, individualized, and organized form of chemistry clearly resides in the fact that the world in which they are is in a very genuine sense a chemical world. Should all animal bodies cease to be, digestion might also cease, but since the process of digesting did not create the chemistry which made it possible, we could not affirm that what we might call the chemical structure of the world also ceased to be. We might rather venture to say that the possibility of chemistry as a determinate form of being, inhabiting animal bodies, and unraveling itself in digestion resided in the fact that there is chemistry in the transcendental sense.

Our attitude toward the question of the possibility of interpretation, of thinking, of knowledge might advantageously be similar. For thinking, like digestion, is a reaction to a world congenial to it. Just as we do not affirm that by digestion the possibility of chemistry is created, so we ought not to affirm that by thinking the possibility of mind is created. We ought rather to affirm that the possibility of mind as a determinate form of being inhabiting animal bodies resides in the fact that there is mind in the transcendental sense. Such a view makes of the genesis of the mind studied in psychology something wholly natural—I know of no better word—as natural as digestion or breathing. With the death of all animal bodies thinking itself might cease, but that which made thinking possible would not cease. This latter would remain something characteristic of the world in which animal bodies had come to be. That is, mind in the transcendental sense can have no genesis. The term when so used does not indicate an individual existence whose days may be numbered. Like mechanism, chemistry, and what in general we call the laws of nature, it indicates a type of structure or a system of connections, a logical structure it might be called, or a system of logical connections. To this structure living beings conform in much the same way as they conform to other structural facts. As by conforming to the mechanical structure of things they maintain their equilibrium, so by conforming to the logical structure of things they think in propositions, they make distinctions and so finally come to discover themselves as distinct from their world, recognize themselves as the habitations of mind, and undertake the study of psychology.

MENTAL DEVELOPMENT*

THE habit of conceiving the life of the mind as a development has become fixed through the influence of evolutionary ideas. We speak of stages in intellectual growth with a conviction and naturalness seldom questioned. For we become wiser, it is to be hoped, through experience. We leave behind us outworn ideas and views of life, and can regard our past as a succession of periods through which we have passed, which form a continuity, each period moving into its successor by a discoverable transition. To exhibit this transition and show how it has been motived would thus be to write the history of the mind. This done, we might see the events of life as something more than a wonderful spectacle. We might see them rather as an ordered series which we had come to understand because we had discovered its laws. Intellectual development would then be explained in the sense that its stages and their connections would appear to us to be natural because they would appear to be regular and many times repeated. They would appear, that is, to be just the kind of stages and connections which our larger knowledge would lead us reasonably to expect. Our wonder at life might not be abated, but it would be transformed. We could adapt to it Aristotle's remark that the ignorant are astonished because the diagonal and side of a square are incommensurable while the geometrician would be astonished if they were not. So for us the order and development of life might still appear wonderful, but we should say that it would be more wonderful if life were not orderly.

There is much to support this view of mental development. The journey from youth to age has long since been divided into epochs. The parts and scenes of life's drama have passed from poetic imagery to psychological exposition. The child's inheritance has been sketched in lines increasingly more dis-

* In the *Journal of Philosophy,* Vol. XXI (1924), pp. 449-456.

tinct. Its varying responses to the play of stimuli upon it have been correlated with changes in its bodily structure. They have been closely followed from infancy, through adolescence and maturity, to the old age in which they end. The innocency and sweetness of childhood still charm us, but they can also appear to us as the natural expressions of that age. The youthful lover may still command the affection of all the world, but he can also be the inevitable incident of the years of adolescence. And so through all the chances and changes of life their typical representatives offer themselves, not only as things to be admired, but also as the natural outcome of the factors and conditions which from day to day motive and control the evolution of life itself. The individual grows. The growth is a development which sufficient knowledge might exhibit as an orderly evolution.

From the individual we pass to the race. The picture becomes epical and magnificent. Yet the researches of anthropology would reduce it to an orderly series of events, marked by successive periods which unfold, as it were, into one another by natural and discoverable transitions. By observing savages still living and by studying the remains of men long dead, we frame a conception of man in his primitive state. We follow him through the vicissitudes of the centuries. We write his history as a continued story, with the chapters sometimes ending in breathless suspense, but held together by a plot which discloses their natural connections. No doubt we often piece out the tale, as a novelist might, with an eye to æsthetic fitness rather than to scientific accuracy, but our intention is to be truthful. The lapses into romance indicate our impatience with our lack of information, our haste to get on, but not any deliberate intention to deceive or any desire to be edifying at the risk of being inexact. The story will have to be rewritten many times, but we have little doubt that we have discovered the kind of story it is.

He has discovered how to make fire and has found his natural weapons, the club and the stone. Hitherto he had been only an animal among other animals, meeting nature as they do, face to face, and body to body, the cunningest wrestler, no doubt, but risking his life in every clinch. Now he has put his art between himself and everything else. It is no longer his muscles, but the fire which holds the preying beasts from his throat. It is no longer his body, but his club that receives and turns the impact of their spring. He now walks the earth without an equal upon it. The possibilities of civilization have become his, for civilization is just that intervention of art of which the fire, the club, and the stone are now symbols. The height of his civilization will be marked by the extent and complexity of his art. For he grows in power, not like Antæus, who drew his strength directly from the earth with every fresh contact of his body with it, but by keeping his body aloof and by indirection unlocking the forces of nature. His possibilities are embodied in the conception of a God who could create the world by speaking.

From the fire, the club, and the stone, to the creative word —thus we may indicate in something more than a figure the reach of man's development. His civilization increases just in proportion as he has made nature the slave of his bidding. That means that the original face to face and body to body contact with nature, which mark him only as one animal among many, has steadily decreased. The importance of his body has been progressively minimized. The importance of his mind has been progressively magnified. He is continually converting nature into a piece of machinery which he can command. His development is thus an intellectual development and his history an intellectual history. To speak of his history as natural is to run the risk of forgetting his civilization. Here we play with terms well calculated to trick us. Nature may be as much or as little as we please. So, to deny man a natural history may be an absurdity. Yet it may also be the means of keeping clear the distinction which we may not wisely avoid, the distinction that indicates that he has developed, as no other creature has, through the intervention of art between himself and his world. In so far, then, as "art" and "nature" spell a contrast, the history of man is a history of art and not a history of nature.

Man's art is varied. We use the term when we speak of agriculture and when we speak of music. We may use it also when we speak of ideas. This extension is not metaphorical.

It goes rather to the heart of the whole matter. For art, as we have already seen, is both a kind of instrument and a symbol. It is something which intervenes between man and what he controls. We may say crudely that it is a sort of substitute for his body, yet touching both his body and nature. The club again may serve us as an illustration. He wields it with his arm and it bruises his foe. It does what his body without it would have to do. It is thus a real instrument. And it is also a symbol. It represents combat even when it is not used. A panoply of arms on the walls of a museum is as much a picture as a painted canvas. The latter we may call a finer instrumentation, but at bottom it is of the same kind. It is a substitute for immediate vision, making it unnecessary for the eye to behold directly what the picture symbolizes. Otherwise looking at nature would be the equivalent of looking at pictures. Ideas condense symbolism as no other material of art can. You can pack into one volume the words that express all that has been expressed. Every form of art is supplemented with language and ideas to prevent it from becoming utterly inarticulate. Without this supplementation it reverts to nature simply, becomes emotion and activity directly, and loses all its symbolism. Music which does not symbolize a dance, but which makes one dance, is not art except metaphorically. It is art in the power of him who uses it to produce the effect it is calculated to produce. It is not art for the dancer any more than the club is art for the bruised animal. Ideas are thus the things that keep art from being only an instrument. But they are themselves instruments as well as symbols. They are substitutes for the things they signify, so that a sentence uttered may take the impact of a blow. And so between man and nature intervene the whole symbolism and instrumentality of his ideas. They mean and they fend. They suggest and they control. They represent and they operate. They are the supreme intervention of art, at once the highest form of instrumentation and the highest form of symbolism.

Once more we glimpse the truth that the development of man is an intellectual development. His history is the history of his ideas. It is the exhibition of the way he has put between himself and nature the symbols which are also his instruments. It is the record of how he has met nature not directly with his body, but indirectly with his mind. In setting forth this history, we divide it into periods. We ascribe to mind a kind of immortality from age to age, so that we can think of it as a continuous development displaying each stage as the outgrowth of its predecessor. In each we seek the factors which change it into its successor and the laws which these changes follow. The items in individual growth are transferred to racial growth, and thus we come to speak of the childhood of the race, its youth, its maturity, and its age. The transfer is supported by many analogies; the savage is like an overgrown child, the intelligent man like a child grown mature. Step by step we trace the progress of the race in all its vicissitudes until we reach the culminating present and then look back upon the long march as a continued and connected series of events in the life of the mind. Psychology would appear to offer us the key to the connections and transitions, and so we seek to solve the problem which confronts us by trying to discover the origin of ideas and the principles of their association. We piece out our lack of information by conceiving that the individual in some measure recapitulates in his own history the history of the race and by comparing the behaviour of animals under experimental control with the behaviour of man himself. Stages in intellectual development appear to be established for the race as well as for the individual.

Yet our conviction in this regard deserves scrutiny. It is immediately apparent that in construing the history of man as a continuous development—and it should be remembered that this continuity may admit of cataclysms—we run the risk of an over-simplification. The continuity we display is a selected continuity and it is continuous only because it is selected. It is necessary to forget many things as we pass from age to age if we would picture successfully the growth of intelligence as one process running through time. To interpret Roman ideas in terms of Greek ideas—as a sort of continuation and modification of them—has its fascination, but in so doing we must forget that the Roman mind did not begin in Greece. In viewing modern civilization as the outcome of ancient civilization with its roots in the East, we must forget that modern civilization began in the forests of Germany and not in Palestine. In other words, the intellectual heritage that an academic tradition has preserved and certain Augustinian ideas about the history of mankind have reinforced does not represent, except to the forgetful, any actual sequence of events. The intellectual traditions with which we have grown familiar are not histories of anything besides these traditions. The boy set at his history books may still begin with the Babylonians, advance to the Greeks and on through the Romans, the Middle Ages, and Western Europe to America, but he is not studying the history of man. He is studying little more than a selected series of events which an historical tradition has correlated with the calendar. It is this correlation more than any discovered principle of connection that imposes upon him the idea of a continuous history. We are doubtless in no better case when, helped by the anthropologist, we sketch the primitive condition of man and picture his progress through stage after stage of his evolution up to the highest pitch of his civilization. We are writing no actual history, but establishing a new historical tradition, no better than the Augustinian, or we are selecting a continuity which we do not find.

In still another way the selected character of our supposed continuity is apparent. We discover history backwards, so to speak, but we write it forwards. We start with some event or circumstance and seek its past. Our guiding thread is fixed to the thing from which we start. Clinging to it we make our way among the mazes of the past and on our return do an astonishing thing. We write the history of our wanderings not only as if they began in the distant past we reach, but as if the event or circumstance we would understand had there its origin and had moved steadily forward to its consummation! We forget that that event or circumstance has had a thousand different pasts and proceed to debate as to which of its histories is correct. Of course, such a statement as this may easily become extravagant, but the essential point is that the writing of history is an over-simplification and a process of selection. What, for instance, is the history of New York? Is it a continuous story since the settlement of the Dutch, a true sequence of events single lined to the present? Or does it rather continue the history of many different places and peoples and find for itself manifold beginning in the ends of the earth? Its continuity is a product and not an evolution. It is a selection and not a process of development. So, too, with our history of man; when we write it we write of the many things he has done or of the many scenes in which he might conceivably have been an actor, but to construe all this as his development is simply to select him as the centre of many converging influences. The continuity of his achievements is not the law of his evolution.

Comments similar to these about racial development may be made about individual development. They may seem less apt, at first, because for the individual the body serves so admirably and so concretely as the conserver of the individual's experiences. The physical continuity of the race, although no less real, perhaps, than that of the individual body, is not so immediately imposing. It is broken up and individualized, as we say, and its parts, having become severed and detached, pursue severed and detached careers. It would be meaningless, or little more than a figure of speech, to say that this physical continuity of the race conserved the experiences of the race as the physical continuity of the body conserves the experiences of the individual. For to express ourselves after that manner involves the conception of the race itself as a kind of individual and the loss of that distinction we would make when we contrast the race and the individual. It means something to say that the Jefferson who signed the Declaration of Independence was the Jefferson who became president of the United States; but it means little to say that the human race which achieved the constitution of Cleisthenes became the human race which won the Magna Charta. This latter expression is too evidently a striving to conceive as an individual a thing which can exist only as many individuals, to impose upon us as any important truth. Indeed, it is primarily the physical continuity of the body and the fact that an individual is the offspring of other individuals that lead us to conceive of the race itself as having any continuity at all. The development of the race is thus metaphorical. The conception of it involves a transfer of meaning and in that transfer loses the features that give it distinction. Individual men may grow, but man, being a metaphor, grows only metaphorically. Even the biologist who supposes that the germ cells of a species of living things form a virtual physical continuity, finds it difficult to assign to the germ plasm itself any development in the strict sense. It can not acquire characters. It can not be influenced by its environment. To assign to it an inherent principle of directive change independent of any stimulus seems preposterous. For all purposes of evolution its changes are accidental. Its variations become factors in succeeding evolutions, but are not the results of the evolutions which precede them. The continuity of the germ plasm may be a fact, but if so, it is a fact which has not yet been successfully conceived in terms of evolution. Thus, again, it would appear that while the development of the individual may be real the development of the race is metaphorical.

But in what sense, after all, is the development of the individual a real development? In speaking of it as real is there no over-simplification and no selection similar to that which we find in speaking of the development of the race? Individual and racial development have this at least in common, both are the successive interventions of art. This common feature is, in case of the individual, emphatically reinforced by education. He does not inherit the traditions and experiences of his ancestors. He is taught them. Consequently, he has little development apart from society. It is common enough to observe the effects of a new sky even upon the mature. The traditions, habits, and modes of thought of immigrants to this country change with a rapidity astonishing enough when one thinks of the centuries of tradition behind them. The native children of foreign parents are foreigners in every sense to their cousins abroad. We may call this a development, but it should be more properly called a response to new stimuli. If it is called a development, where did that development begin? Surely we cannot say in the ancestors. It has no continuity with the individuals' past. They rather have become factors which continue a past to which hitherto they have been strangers. To speak of these continuities as *their* development is, consequently, highly figurative. It is again the fact of their bodily continuity and the possibility of correlating their experiences with their successive birthdays that evoke the inference that we are dealing with processes and events that unfold. The child that develops into the man is a child over-simplified and selected. It is a child which is but the centre of many converging lines which have many different beginnings. In speaking of this development as a continuous evolution, we are simply pointing him out as successively just such a centre.

It would thus appear that the conception of mental development and of stages in that development is largely metaphorical whether we have in mind the development of the individual or the race. When we speak of the growth of the mind we are, it would appear, speaking really of something else, namely, of the growth of art. We are setting forth incidents in the life of these beings in whose reactions art is a factor and trying to follow those incidents in their manifold connections. And their connections are manifold. The incidents form no continuous series unless a selection is made and that selection localized in a centre which is physically continuous—a place on the map or an individual body which may be had when required. But viewed in time these incidents become centres from which radiate into past and future countless series of connections. They have, these centres, no one past and no one future. They are points in which many pasts converge and from which many futures diverge. By the aid of the place or the body to which they are attached and by the aid of the calendar with which changes in that place or in that body may be correlated, we can arrange them in continuous series which we call the histories of a certain people, place, institution, or individual. The result is never an adequate account, but always an over-simplified and a selected account.

We should not, however, conclude that these accounts are, therefore, useless, or that they are, therefore, false. It is too evident that they are neither. They have precisely the advantage that simplification and selection have. They introduce precision and clarity where otherwise precision and clarity would be lacking. They promote comprehension and appreciation. The simplified and selected continuities which they present should not, however, be construed into an absolute evolution which reveals its own causes and factors. They do not constitute a philosophy of history or an evolutionary metaphysics of the mind. They reveal rather that reaction, simplification, and selection are themselves prime factors in motivating all change and all succession.

BEHAVIOUR*

THE dependence of the way things behave on the way they are put together seems to be sufficiently proved. Every act, from the movement of a body in space to the movement of thought in an inference, seems to be done by an agent in which can be found a structure, constitution, or organization without which the act is not done. Specific activity and specific structure go together. This, as I have said, seems to be sufficiently proved. Obviously, however, it has not been discovered in all the particular instances to which the general principle might apply. We are very far from that. It is, therefore, not unnatural perhaps to be tempted at times to see in instances of peculiar difficulty exceptions to the general rule. That certain chemical compounds live while others do not, that germs so evidently alike in their composition produce creatures so radically different in kind and in modes of behaviour, may tempt us to appeal to other than structural determinations for an understanding of how things behave as they do. And this temptation is reinforced by the fact that the completest analysis of structure affords no indication whatever of consequent behaviour. We may be convinced that without brains we could not think, but to expect a brain to think seems to be about as unreasonable an expectation as one can entertain. Indeed, Hume's analysis of cause and effect and necessary connection, in spite of its metaphysical, psychological and historical limitations, ought to convince anyone that, while specific behaviour may habitually be inferred from specific structure, there is nothing discoverable in that structure to warrant that inference. Perhaps, were it not for this fact, we should be less tempted to conclude that what we have not yet discovered is proof that we shall never discover it. For it is easy to argue that since there is no necessary connection between structure

* In the *Journal of Philosophy,* Vol. XXII (1925), pp. 402-411.

and behaviour, even those cases where the dependence of behaviour on structure is proved require additional principles to explain how the structures involved behave as they do.

It is not my purpose, however, to try to deal with the problems which this situation is often supposed to generate. That seems to me to be futile. I admit that there is often a rare delight in trying to do what can not be done, but there is little or no profit for metaphysics in so trying. For my own part, I have not found that the conversion of Hume's analysis into a problem of epistemology or the attempt to add non-structural principles on to structure in order to explain specific behaviour, have enlightened us in any respect with regard to the subject-matter with which they have dealt. They have historical and biographical interest. But I can not discover that they have any metaphysical interest. This inability of mine should be recognized in what I have here to say. The lack of what Hume called necessary connection between what a thing is and what it does is here admitted and taken for granted without suspecting that this lack obliges us to try to make it good in some way or other.

In saying this, however, I would avoid, if possible, any suspicion of giving aid and comfort to those misguided souls who seem to identify behaviour with structure. I fear that I do not understand them, and may impute to them opinions they do not hold. So incredible does such an identification appear to me that I find it difficult to convince myself that those who appear to make it really do make it. That specific modes of behaviour may exhibit what may be called specific patterns, I think I can understand. But to read these specific patterns into antecedent structural conformations which respond to stimuli is for me wholly unintelligible. It looks to me so much like reading into a man's legs a map of the walk he takes on the highway that I am left bewildered. Perhaps I have wholly misunderstood the matter. I am willing to admit that. Yet I suspect that the current science of behaviour is not as conscious as it might be of apparent contradictions which so often mar its presentation. However that may be, I wish it might be clear that, in refusing to add metaphysical supplements to structure in order to explain behaviour, I am not trying to enlarge specific structures by imputing specific behaviour patterns to them. Indeed, I see no real difference between saying that specific structures are animated by a specific directing principle and saying that they possess a specific pattern of response. It seems clear to me that while a man will not walk unless he has legs, his excursions in this world are very little determined by his anatomy. So also, while he will not speak unless he has an apparatus, the pattern of his discourse is very little determined by his vocal chords and his nervous system.

All this has been said not simply for the negative purpose of dismissing certain considerations, but for the more positive purpose of defining a point of view. It has been said for the purpose of suggesting that since there is no necessary connection between what things are and what they do, an examination of behaviour should be conscious of that fact. It defines a point from which inquiry should go forward rather than backward. It gives us a metaphysical datum the consequences of which are perhaps more interesting and instructive than any attempt to get back of it. To some of the consequences which seem to follow from it, attention is here asked.

Although specific behaviour is dependent on specific structure—meaning by dependence here that without the structure the behaviour does not occur—differences in behaviour are not defined in terms of differences in structure. This is only another way of saying what Hume said, that although behaviour may be habitually inferred from structure, there is nothing discoverable in the latter to warrant the inference of the former. But resaying it in the altered manner leads to asking how differences in behaviour are defined. Such differences are recognized and defined, and it is quite clear, if we consider the historical order of our knowing, that they are usually recognized and defined before their relevant structures are discovered. The discovery of structure has been slow and labourious. The incentive to it is unusual even if the accomplishment of it is always remarkable. For our interest in the behaviour of things is naturally more immediate and practical than our interest in their structure. Important as the fact is that only with a knowledge of their structure can the behaviour of things be adequately controlled, the fact has to be learned with much disappointment and experience. Our practical interest is in what things do and in discovering what they can do before we discover the mechanism by which they do it. So I repeat that differences in behaviour are not defined in terms of differences of structure. They are defined in terms of what results from the behaviour. This is so evident that I think it needs neither proof nor illustration. But it may need emphasis. It may need emphasis especially in view of the dogma, so readily accepted by many, that teleological considerations should have no place in the mind of a sober and thoughtful man. For behaviour is a teleological matter and without considerations of ends reached no differences in behaviour are recognizable or definable.

I would not deny that teleological considerations are tricky and dangerous, nor that they have often stupidly held back recognition of important discoveries and often stood in the way of progress. But I am forced to maintain that the behaviour of opium is still defined in terms of what it does and if we wholly disregard that fact we can not distinguish its behaviour from that of any other drug on the market. The elimination of teleological distinctions reduces all behaviour to the bare abstraction of activity. It forces us into the position that there is such a thing as behaviour pure and simple, a position which may indeed be serviceable if it leads us to seek the differentiations of behaviour, but which, if it does not so lead, is quite devoid of illumination and significance. Structure and behaviour may indicate ultimates in metaphysical analysis just as force and matter may. As such they may tell us where it is wise to stop and where it is fruitful to begin. But they hold no magic. Operation with them involves the specific and the determinate. They themselves are distinguished for a purpose, and a purpose which is justified by every analysis and every experiment we make. Since this is so, the moral is to regard and not disregard teleological considerations. If ends attained are essential to the discrimination of types of activity or behaviour, the indication is clear that teleology is something with which we can not wisely avoid reckoning. There are ends in nature as well as means, eventualities as well as actualities, purposes as well as causes, and the outstanding evidence of it all is the fact of behaviour itself. Our business is not to deny the fact in fear lest we get mixed in our thinking, but rather to accept the fact whether we get mixed or not. It is hard for me to see how we human beings could so ardently strive for ends in a world in which ends themselves are entirely irrelevant.

Behaviour being so pre-eminently a teleological matter, the science of behaviour might well be called a teleological science. But I am acutely aware of the storm of protest that making such a definition might raise. If I made it, I should have to confess that malice largely prompted it. For I am quite willing to confess that the only genuine science of behaviour seems to be that which embodies the discovery of the structures that so behave. I would avoid provoking a discussion of terms only. Yet it seems clear to me that in so far as a consideration of behaviour involves a consideration of ends, we ought frankly to admit that we have entered the realm of teleology and that there the analysis of structure is not helpful. That much I would claim and claim it in the interest of our attempts to construe nature intelligibly and to live both rationally and hopefully. For these are teleological enterprises, sufficiently justified by the facts that the forces which made us made us what we are and that our behaviour, like the behaviour of anything else, is not irrelevant to the world in which we behave.

Behaviouristic distinctions are teleological distinctions. That is one thing worth emphasizing. It merits a discussion commensurate with its importance. Failing that, we may at least recognize the fact and free our minds from needless confusion regarding it. For example, if behaviour is a teleological matter, if it is wholly unintelligible without a consideration of ends, it does not necessarily follow that we must conclude that ends operate. The polemic against final causes, although it often misconceives what final causes are, is justified in denying what it does deny. It seems to me foolish to deny that there are ends in nature, but it also seems foolish to affirm that these ends operate to determine the structure and constitution of things. Although it is obvious to me that a spider spins its web in order to catch flies—and even that combustion occurs in order to produce heat—I can discover in the obvious fact no reason whatever why spiders should exist or be what they are. Knowing what they do I may discover that their structure is appropriate to their behaviour, but it seems quite clear that this appropriateness does not operate to produce them. Employing final causes to explain the operations of nature has always been futile and for a simple reason—what things do, tells us nothing at all about how they do it. Undoubtedly a thing has the power to do what it does, but this power of doing is not a force resident in it independent of the things to which it reacts. Its power is exercised only in co-operation with other things, and when we examine the means and occasion of this co-operation we discover only structural determinations. To admit teleology does not, therefore, necessarily involve the admission that ends operate.

And it is not wise to be troubled by dialecticians who advise us to consider which is nature's end, the chicken or the egg, the acorn or the oak. For it is clear that we are never confronted with such an alternative when we plot out what the behaviour of a given thing accomplishes. Still less should we be troubled by the fact that an egg may end in a chicken or a breakfast. For the behaviour of a thing, involving as it does co-partnership with other things, is plotted accordingly. We may admit that the dialectic is interesting. We may admit also that it may be useful. But its use is by way of criticism. It may warn us of legitimate limitations which should be kept in mind when we speak of ends, pointing out that any consideration of ends in general is formal rather than material and undertaken in the interest of making distinctions, not of destroying them. Indeed, the principle of relativity generally, whether it is applied to ends or other matters, is the clear indication that nature owns distinctions. That the motion of a body is relative to that with respect to which it moves is the absolute fact of motion, not its undoing. So the relativity of ends is the confirmation, not the denial, of their existence.

Let us turn to more constructive considerations. The teleological character of behaviour constitutes the intelligibility of nature. I am conscious here of considerable verbal difficulty. Most of our terms which denote knowing and comprehending are ambiguous in their use, yet we must use them to distinguish their ambiguities. But I hope I shall not be misunderstood when I say that we understand what things are only in terms of what they do. We may understand how a sewing machine is put together, how it works, so to speak, but clearly we have no intelligent understanding of what it is until we know that it sews. Rob it of its use and purpose and it becomes unintelligible. I can not escape generalizing so homely an illustration. Analyze things to their atoms and attempt with the analysis to rob them progressively of their behaviour, and we approach not clearness but obscurity, not order but chaos, not intelligibility, but absurdity. This conclusion, I can not escape. I think it could be demonstrated, although I am not prepared to give that demonstration. I may, however, say this. In our analyses of things we tend constantly to approach the quantitative and the mathematical. Now, we may say, that just in proportion as we approach the quantitative and the mathematical we understand nature and are able to control it. I am willing to admit that. I am willing to admit even that did we know thoroughly what the structure of things is, our knowledge would have reached its limit. And I think we might gain in clearness by saying so. But granted that completion of knowledge, it would still be what the vast mechanism did, what it accomplished, what ends it served, that gave it life and meaning and intelligibility. From the structure alone the finality could never be inferred, but given the finality, the discovery of structure is illuminated and comprehended by it. Otherwise how could we possibly admire the adaptations of nature, find the hand appropriate for grasping, and the eye for seeing, and why should every explorer of nature, no matter what his philosophical creed, be haunted by some form of the maxim, "nature does nothing in vain"? It is the absence of this vanity which is the presence of intelligibility.

To speak of the purposes of nature is not necessarily to imply that nature is animated by a directing agency which, foreseeing ends, deliberately works for them. Such an implication is beset by difficulties which only increase the farther it is pursued. It involves that conversion of final causes into operating agencies to which I have already referred. It is quite a different implication that is worth considering. If it is because of nature's purposes that nature is intelligible, we may well be tempted to find in that fact some clue to the mystery of our own minds. Sometimes I think we have made our minds needlessly mysterious. Robbing nature of finality, stripping her to the bare bones of mechanism, and reducing our bodies either to a physical machine or a chemical formula, we have been driven to account for mind and to perform miracles in the accounting. A world without finality would be a world in which a mind would have nothing to understand. That is a stupid remark, but I risk it for the possible contrast it implies. It is not altogether stupid, however, to remark that in a world where ends may be attained a mind would have much to comprehend. Perhaps, if we are to account for mind at all, we may say that in a world of final causes mind is a natural consequence of behaviour, a specific concretion of it, so to speak, exercised by a specific structure which, like all other structures, holds no magical resident power, but which, like them, finds the exercise of its power in co-operation with other things. What I have just said may sound like a jumble of words, but this much seems clear to me—in a teleological world mind would be natural and at home, while in a non-teleological world it would be irrelevant and absurd. Consequently, if we feel ourselves under compulsion to explain mind, it would seem that the explanation could be approached better by some methods of reducing teleology in general to teleology in particular, than by the method of adding on to what is not teleological a factor which produces only an illusion of ends.

To sum up what has thus far been said: starting with the fact that what things are is not an indication of what they do, I would observe (1) that behaviouristic distinctions are made not in terms of structure, but in terms of the ends accomplished by behaviour; (2) that behaviour is consequently a teleological matter implying a natural teleology; (3) that the admission of natural teleology does not necessarily involve either the doctrine that ends operate or the doctrine that structures contain resident powers by virtue of which they do what they do; (4) that the relativity of ends is confirmation of teleology and not its undoing; (5) that natural teleology constitutes the intelligibility of nature; and (6) that mind may be construed as an instance of teleology rather than the cause of it.

Analysis of structure reveals no reason for behaviour and the intelligibility of structure resides in the fact that ends are reached by behaving. Perhaps, however, we do not do well when we say that analysis of structure reveals no reason for behaviour. Whether we do well or not depends on the emphasis. If the fact is emphasized to warn us that structure and reasons ought not to be associated, I think we do well. If, however, it is emphasized to arouse the suspicion that while structure reveals no reason for behaviour, it ought to, and that if we knew enough it would, then I think we do not do well. The reason, therefore, for saying that structure does not yield reasons is the illegitimate expectation that it ought to or might. What structure yields is control. There is no need to prove that. And if we would keep this positive profit, there is apt to follow only confusion of thought if we go on and affirm that with increased control we are not better off as regards reasons. For an affirmation of that kind is ungentlemanly at least. It suggests a snobbish attitude toward those who spend their lives discovering structure and an estimate of them which is not flattering. It is also intellectually slovenly. It is the easiest thing in the world to make much of what we don't do and to harp on the shortcomings of mankind. There is no royal road to learning for those who leave structure out of account. Moreover, the affirmation in question is not true. With increased control we are better off as regards reasons. This, too, is in no need of proof, for it is plainly evident that increased control reveals the ends, purposes, and uses of nature as nothing else does. To be sure, it does not make clear to us, as some moralists seem to think it should, what we ought to do, but it does make strikingly clear to us what we might and also what it is utterly useless to try to do. It opens the highway to freedom. But I am here more interested in metaphysics than in morals. And that interest leads me to say that the fact that control is progressively attained through the progressive discovery of structure, is perhaps the crowning instance of natural teleology. Accordingly, if we ask, as we are sometimes tempted to do, what is the ultimate reason for the existence of things, the only intelligible answer we can give is something like this: things exist to be controlled for ends through the discovery of their structure. If we are tempted still further to ask why they should so exist, the question is meaningless. For any answer to it involves these two absurdities: first, the denial that nature is teleological, and, secondly, the attempt to make nature teleological in spite of the denial. Theologians who have solved the problem of God's last end in creation have solved it by confessing that his last end is himself. Translated into metaphysics the solution might well read, the reason why things exist as they do is their existence.

This obvious solution of so weighty a problem is valuable only in terms of what is made of it. By itself it is worth no more than any other question turned into its own answer. Applied to relevant subject-matter, however, it may serve to keep us aware of the fact that it is the structural concatenation of things which determines the limits of possible behaviour from the movement of an ion to the thinking of a man, while only actual behaviour, from the movement to the thinking, discovers what those limitations are. This does not indicate that structure is more fundamental than behaviour. It indicates rather that any attempt to reduce behaviour to structure is futile. Structure and behaviour seem to be ultimate. But if we should, as we sometimes do in the hope of greater clearness, suppose things to be differently constituted than they are, we might suppose that structure in all its manifold intricacy came first. Then we might conclude that any behaviour in so vast a scheme would search out the possible from the impossible and produce a much diversified world. And that is just what seems to happen. We act and so discover the world to be an intricately complicated structure with a wealth of possibility beyond our dreams. Yet we soon realize that we must dream according to that structure if our dreams are ever to come true. That is why structure tends to become exalted and admired, why necessity puts into a man what in ordinary speech we call the love of beauty and the fear of God. It is with a sound instinct that we try to see things *sub specie æternitatis,* for so seen, the possibilities of structure would be completely revealed and behaviour would have been freed to reach its goal.

CREATION*

I

It is not the aim of this article to add to a popular controversy. It is rather to consider a doctrine which, whether it is sound or not, is worth respectful attention. The doctrine is not new. It has commanded respectful attention repeatedly in the past because its foundation is an obvious fact of experience which, when followed far, has the power to provoke the consciousness of things spiritual. Creating itself the sense that something has been said which is both significant and profound, it may affect the mind as a revelation, calling for hearty acceptance and averse to doubting criticism. It has had that effect. There is about it a simple yet subtle beauty, which the imaginative are quick to appreciate and which even the dull may feel with a vague sense of a mystery too high for them. It is thus an accessible doctrine. It requires little learning to feel its force and may admit much learning with no diminution of its power. Its æsthetic quality is so high that a connoisseur in doctrines might wish to keep it a precious possession even when he did not embrace it as his faith.

As I have said, the foundation of the doctrine is an obvious face of experience. Its expressions, consequently, have not necessarily been confined to any particular time, place, or people. One might be led to it independently, through reflection, without the bias of dogma or tradition. Scholars have traced its ramifications far. Yet for most of us, on account of our history and education, the most popular expression of the doctrine is found in the Bible and particularly in the first chapter of Genesis. "In the beginning God created the heaven and the earth. And the earth was without form, and void; and darkness was upon the face of the deep. And the Spirit of

* In the *Atlantic Monthly,* Vol. 137 (1926), No. 3, pp. 335-342.

God moved upon the face of the waters. And God said, Let there be light: and there was light."

Few of those to whom these words have been familiar since childhood will recall any doubt or difficulty connected with their first hearing. I can not trust my own memory of them. When I attempt to recover their first impression, I am acutely conscious that I am reading them in the light of subsequent study and reflection. Yet I venture to believe that I believed them, not because there was lacking in my knowledge and experience the ground for a competing belief, but because my experience supported them. It is, however, probably improper to speak of believing them at all, for speaking of them in that way seems to imply that they were subjected to scrutiny, made a matter of reflection, and then accepted because they seemed warranted. This, it is reasonably certain, did not happen. When I speak, as I just now did, of believing them—not because there was no experience against them, but because experience was on their side—I am speaking as a man trying to recover an impression of childhood and find a natural motivation for it. Very likely if I had been told with the competent authority of my parents something else about the beginning of things, I should have accepted it with a similar absence of questionings. Their business was, among other things, to instruct me. They were a living encyclopaedia for children, lacking in patience at times and at times amused over questions asked in no sense of humour, but they were never inadequate in knowledge. They knew enough to name the animals when asked, so that a child could hardly be surprised at Adam's similar skill. Their speech was creative. At their command things appeared and disappeared, doors were opened and shut, lights were lit and put out. They said, Let there be dinner: and there was dinner. Let us go for a walk: and we went for a walk. Let us make a house of these cards: and of these cards a house was made. They could do whatever they were willing to say they would do, and answer any question they were willing to answer. So while I might readily have accepted any answer they might have given to a question about the beginning of things, it could have been no surprise to learn that

God spake and things were made. The creative power of speech has warrant in the experience of a child.

Whether this is a correct rendering of an experience of my own childhood—its reasonable psychology, so to speak—I do not know. But this I know, that repeated readings of the first chapter of Genesis in later years have progressively exalted its doctrine about God's voice, so that when I now try to recover the impression which the first attentive hearing of it may have made upon me I find myself wondering at its doctrine, undisturbed by problems of natural history. Indeed, in this respect I must confess to what may be considered a prejudice, for I can neither hear nor read a controversy between Genesis and science without feeling that it is a perversion of something essentially sublime. In saying this, I would not be misunderstood. I can not take the chapter as an equivalent or substitute for science. I can understand how the unintelligent might, finding a story instead of a doctrine. And I can understand how the unimaginative might, tying the doctrine to the literal details of the story. But I must confess again, and this time doubtless with a show of intellectual egotism, that for me a controversy between Genesis and science is one in which only the unintelligent or the unimaginative will engage. I could rejoice in all the trouble and perturbations of mind they will enjoy, were it not for the conviction that they are engaging in something trivial and absurd, and needlessly defacing something beautiful. The doctrine that speech is creative, that existence is evoked with words, that chaos commanded is order, is a doctrine so engaging that the first chapter of Genesis impresses me, not with puerilities in natural history, but with sublimity in spiritual insight.

II

Under the power of this impression, I can readily believe that, if we are to entertain a doctrine of creation at all seriously, it will be to the doctrine of Genesis that we are ultimately led. For we seek the adequate expression of existence. Like children bringing animals to parents to see what they would call them, we bring the items of existence to the wise to see how these items are most appropriately voiced. We would be told what they are. And the wise are supposed to be competent for the telling. Their voice brings light. This is an experience so familiar and useful that we may ask questions, go to school, read books, write them, and spend a lifetime in inquiry with little wonder at the simple fact that all this enterprise of learning is an attempt to get existence into words—a faith that things are what they are ultimately said to be. They have names—such an astonishing variety of them when we consider the diversity of human speech, and such a preposterous jumble of them when their makers become extravagant, that we can easily assent to the opinion that names are conventional marks, "wise men's counters," but "the money of fools," and yet, when we ask the astronomer what that bright star in the zenith is and he says it is Vega, the most intelligent among us enjoys the illusion that he has learned something. He has felt the evoking power of the voice. Even when words are so arranged that they mean nothing or are contradictory, it is hard to escape the impression that something has been said. Philosophers have invented subsistence for the round square, believing that, since the thing can be named, it must somehow be. The power of words is great.

We may deny them omnipotence. They are easily stilled, like Hamlet's voice, by a scratch from poisoned steel. But Hamlet's last words are the thrilling commentary on the fact —"the rest is silence." Rob existence of the voice, let there be no expression, no utterance anywhere, let nothing ever be said in the beginning; then the rest—is it even silence? The voice has to be evoked to name its absence. In a dumb world there may be power, brute and inarticulate. We have the habit of saying so even when it passes all our wit to tell what that power is, to name it otherwise than in terms of its expressions or in terms like "the unknowable," which imply no more than the obvious fact that without expression it is unexpressed. The "unknowable," the "infinite," the "absolute," "God," are all imposing words like "the rest is silence." They create in us the vast sense, ushering us into the presence of immensity. Unless, however, they carry with them the implication of possible expression and possible utterance, they are empty sounds, or leave us, like the Ancient Mariner, desperately aloof.

> O Wedding-Guest! this soul hath been
> Alone on a wide, wide sea:
> So lonely 't was, that God Himself
> Scarce seemèd there to be.

We may deny words omnipotence, yet without them omnipotence means nothing at all. Nor does anything else. The fact is obvious, as obvious as the questioning child who takes a dog to his father to see what he will call it. The power of words is evocation, and this power boasts omnipotence when it claims to tell in a book what heaven and earth are.

Perhaps the writer of the first chapter of Genesis did not have all this in mind, but the reader of it may. I like to think that he did. I like to think of him pondering over what happened in the beginning and being driven to say: "A Voice." That would make him a poet at least. He would then write a beautiful story of creation, telling how, in the beginning, God spoke and there was light, enough for evening and morning, enough for the first day; enough too, we may say, for God to see by to do what remained to be done as evening and morning came round again—a week's work, naturally, with the last day to rest in and think it over. Thus the heavens and the earth were finished, and all the host of them. The last deed was man, made in God's image, after His likeness, a second voice which would tell again and again to children how heaven and earth are made, and which will never be content with the telling until this vast scheme of things is adequately voiced in human speech. And God saw, by the light He had first created, everything that He had made, and it was very good. It is a story which children and poets can understand.

And I can imagine the poet's consternation when somebody asked him, in earnest or in scorn, if he seriously thought that God had a voice-box with vocal cords in it. Did God speak to chaos in English? Evidently the poet had not thought of that difficulty. Forced to think of it, I can imagine that he became a little afraid for his story, foreseeing times when some men in fear and even in reverence would nickname the story itself

God's Word, while others would set it down as an interesting contribution to the mythology of the race. But, being a very great poet, he was willing to let it go its way. He knew it would be read, at least by children and poets, and that was a fairly large audience. He knew too that, as a doctrine of creation, it was sound.

Of course these are my imaginings, literary devices to win the attention of a reader. But, dear reader, I have no desire to deceive you or trick you with pretty phrases. I would share my enthusiasm for a doctrine of creation which is the profoundest that I know, but I will satisfy no man's curiosity as to whether I believe it or not. That is not an important matter. And I am not sure that any doctrine of creation is an important matter. What things become in the end is much more interesting and probably much more important than what they were in the beginning, as it is better to die well than to be well born. Perhaps heaven and earth were never created, but if they were—if there was once brought into being this solid and substantial scheme of things which all our science is now trying to render intelligible in human speech, fondly believing that, by saying what existence is, darkness gives place to light and chaos to order—by what name shall we call that omnipotence which wrought so great a work? Saint Thomas says: "This is what men call God." But how did God create? "He spake, and it was done; he commanded, and it stood fast." Otherwise how could it ever happen that, by man's speech, what God had created would be called into the light of knowledge? Creation is response to a call. This is the doctrine of saints and poets and philosophers.

III

If one will not have a doctrine of creation, one need not therefore hastily dismiss the doctrine of the voice. For, whatever else the first chapter of Genesis may be believed to be, it is man's speaking glorified. That is a matter worth attention. The greatest of all miracles is human speech, and he who is convinced of this one will rarely be tempted to ask for another. But we are so familiar with it that contempt is bred, leading us to say that silence is golden, while for speech we use the metaphor of the baser metal. The vain babblings of men, their silly talk, their absurd opinions absurdly expressed, their sentimental blessings and profane cursings, and the shrieking discord of unmusical voices ragtimed with the gear of eating, may drive us to take refuge in a silence which is really golden. But it is their silence, not ours. We escape to talk with more congenial souls or, best of all, possibly, with ourselves. And who can fully confess this latter intimate conversation? I would not suggest that it is unprintable. At times it may be, but enough has already been printed by confessors to make further publication of that kind superfluous. I speak of a golden silence. The noises of the world are stilled. We are alone with ourselves. We speak. We listen. Beauty, truth, goodness, joy, terror, evil, anguish, despair, hope—desperately trying to say what it is to be, and this in a world where atoms combine by law—it is the miracle of the voice. I do not mean by this that we must set it down as an infraction of what we call the laws of nature. It is sheer wonder that from the world in which we are born and shall die, and in which we are such little bodies, we may escape into that private communion with ourselves in which we sense the limitless reaches of what might be said. It is our voice that speaks. It speaks with an egotism ridiculous, pathetic, and sublime—*my* wife, *my* children, *my* home, *my* neighbour, *my* doctor, *my* banker, *my* minister, *my* publisher, *my* country, *my* world, *my* life, *my* fate, *my* God! The privacy of our own voice is the possession of what it utters.

I talk with my neighbour. There is public conversation in which good taste would suppress egotism by translating the personal pronoun into the more objective article even when we distractedly say that *the* world is too much with *us*. But we would speak to our neighbour objectively. We would tell him the truth, or at least have him believe that the truth had been told; not *my* truth, but *the* truth unshadowed by any personal slant. That is what I am doing here. Dear reader, you are not at all at liberty to suppose that the words I have here set down are but the record of my own babblings. They are my words only because I am the agent of their utterance. The meaning they convey is not mine, but something quite independent of me. I discovered it and I am expecting you to discover it similarly. You are expected to understand what I am saying from the fact that I am saying it. If you do not, the fault may be mine because I am not clear, or yours because you are stupid. But neither you nor I believe that the truth of what I am saying is ultimately determined by your authority or mine, or, if you will forgive me, that your understanding has anything to do with the matter. Neither has mine. Both you and I may not understand what Professor Einstein has to say. Sometimes I am tempted to think he himself does not understand. But you and he and I are at least under the illusion that he has said something which we might understand and which may be true. Impersonal conversation, objective speech, makes its own startling claim. The writer of Genesis did not say, "It seems to me."

We may test the effect of objective speech by the simplest experiments. "My heart leaps up when I behold a rainbow in the sky." Wordsworth's heart, yes—but how about yours and mine? Change "my" to "the" and "I" to "anybody" with the appropriate verb to follow—the line then loses in poetic form, but it gains a power it did not have before, the logical power of objective speech. It is unimportant who said it. It is important only if true. If true, its truth may be enhanced by the personal form, winning thereby a lyric outburst, but if it is not true the personal form expresses only an idiosyncrasy. Here, then, is the miracle of the voice a second time. Changing Aaron's rod into a serpent pales before changing "my" into "the." The former smacks of magic, for the Egyptians could work a similar miracle; and, although Aaron's serpent swallowed theirs, the change from "my" to "the" swallows his and forces us to look for truth. It does not matter what our tests of truth may be. Let us be as pragmatic as we will, the fact still stands that the objective world is called to our attention by the voice. By simply dropping personal forms of speech we find ourselves transported into a world which we dare no longer call our own. It is The World. It possesses us. From it we came and to it we shall return. It holds our family, our doctor, our country, our fate, our God, in the hollow of it-hand. I speak truthfully with my neighbour, and he becomes no longer mine and what we say is no longer ours.

I speak to the world; in questions, to be sure, but in the confident belief that, if these questions are properly framed rightly to guide my eye and hand and thought, the world will answer in its own way and with singleness of meaning. It is the common belief of men. They seem never to have been taught it and never to have acquired it. It is simply the voice operating. They evidently acquired, during their natural history, the human sounds and particular words they use, as we acquired the speech of our ancestors or learn a foreign tongue; but the power to make a noise is not the expectation of an answer to a question. It is not the interrogative mood. Inquisition is as natural to the voice as oxidation is to the air. Our first words and even our first inarticulate cries are explorations calling for something quite different from their own echoes. Answers will come to them either as yes or no. And the answers that have come to man's questions—his science, his literature, his art, his institutions, his religion—have eventually determined his excellence and his power. Through them he comes into and justifies his dominion. This is a platitude of his pride, but it suggests again the miracle of the voice.

But that he should believe it! Although that belief is natural, untaught, and unacquired, although it is simply the voice's operation and effect which we habitually accept without scrutiny or surprise, it is the belief that the whole of existence might be rendered in words, that there is possible an adequate utterance of what all things are. The change of "my" into "the" is perhaps far less wonderful than the change of things into words and of words back again into things. Or if we will have it that words themselves are things, since they are either sounds in the air or the equivalents of these in our bodies, we still face the fact that, among all the sorts of things there are, there is one sort which presumes to dictate to all the rest, to tell them what they are. Adam's success in naming the animals was a trivial achievement compared with that which he would come to believe was in his power. He would name everything else—the flowers of the field, the stars in the sky, the minerals in the earth, elements, ions, protons, complexes. His chief interest, however, would continue to be in the animals. Brooding over the chaos of living forms, he would speak, expecting light and order. He would put into words a story of how these forms came to be and call it "The Origin of Species" or "The Descent of Man."

IV

It would seem, therefore, that words deserve metaphysical as well as literary and rhetorical cultivation. At least they deserve moral respect. I gladly give them that because, as the president of the Canadian Pacific once reminded me, I have made my living by them. They have economic value. The vendor of them, he who sells this food of the soul, usually enjoys a much higher social recognition than he who sells the food of the body. Writers have always been more preciously esteemed than farmers, butchers, or grocers, in spite of the fact that without these latter the former could not live. And yet an immortal butcher is a contradiction in terms. This might very well be cited as another illustration of the miracle of the voice. The wonder of it grows. But I am now trying, as a scientist ought, to strip the voice of its wonder, explain the miracle, and reduce it to the simple fact that it is. We are done with poetry and are coming to sense. So we stress the economic value of words as a first step in the direction of sanity.

We must rate it high, but high not as a matter of economics and not as a matter of morals or social estimation. The exact computation of it has, so far as I know, never been made, but it is clear that it would run into billions and exceed that of any other commodity. Writers have the false impression that publishers get most of it because publishers are able to pay writers and still have a good deal left for their own consumption. But it is bankers and financiers generally who profit most. That is why there is so much popular criticism of them. They eventually get the money. And it is natural that they should. For all this dealing with words, this buying and selling of them, this asking and paying for a loaf of bread at the baker's, is in the last analysis a dealing in promises. It is a mistake to suppose that the banker makes money by dealing in money. He often has very little of that commodity. He deals in promises, and promises sometimes come very high and can be negotiated with only a promise to secure them. We are wont to say that a man's word is as good as his bond, forgetting that proverbs so often reverse the order of experience. A bond is only as good as a word somewhere. If a man has command of that word, only then does he have a bond. This is a natural fact by which bankers profit. They profit by it so enormously—winning, apparently, command of both industry and civilization—that it is not surprising that the rest of us should so often look at them in envy or in fear.

A promise is a promise either to pay or to do. Unless the something promised is either paid or done, or unless there is belief that it will be paid or done, the promise is worthless. This fact, however, should not make us blind. It should not lead us so to exalt the things promised that we forget that their viability, their passing from hand to hand, their going here and going there, their proximate and ultimate exchange, are all effected through an elaborate machinery which would crumble to pieces if promises were not kept. It does crumble in part at times, so that men may suffer panic and disaster although nothing whatever may have happened to the material riches of the earth. Men may starve in the presence of plenty simply because a promise has not been kept. The reason is that words are the prime medium of exchange. Economists have a habit of saying that money is that, although they know well enough that a dollar may be printed as well as coined. They ought not to be surprised at the childlike faith of the buncoed rustic who, believing that he has bought from his swindler a genuine plate from the Bureau of Engraving, believes also that bills printed from it are not counterfeit, but genuine currency, so that his own moral fault is negligible compared with the benefits he can confer without really harming anybody. Governments in their despair often fall back on this faith as their last financial resource. And it is quite clear that if promises were always kept we should need no other money than recorded words, so evidently are they the medium of exchange.

Their economic value is but one instance of their logical power. When they are literally bought and sold, like commercial notes, or even this article, they are more than ink and paper. They effect first of all an exchange of ideas. There is no need of deep philosophical insight to see that this power of them is behind and fundamental to their economic value. It carries us out of the market place into metaphysics. All things are exchanged for words and words for all things, as goods for gold and gold for goods. Old Heraclitus said it long ago. He spoke of fire, using that element as the glowing symbol of the word, so convinced was he that existence is consumed in speech. We seem unable to get away from the miracle after all. But we should try. Our spiritual business, the enterprise which we put on top of our buying and selling in the market, on top of our producing things to be bought and sold there, and on top even of our loving beauty and fearing God, is to render the world intelligible. But how can the world be rendered intelligible if it is not intelligible in the beginning? Who simply by speaking can create the logic which so holds his words together that his neighbour can understand them and translate them back into their powerful intent? Who creates the intelligibility of the world by talking to it? Surely neither you, dear reader, nor I. Neither you nor I made understanding, even if both you and I are egotistical enough to believe that we can promote it.

There seems to be but one conclusion. This exchange of things for words and words for things is a very real exchange. The world is evidently composed in a manner congenial to it. It is put together on the principle of exchange: oxygen and hydrogen for water and water for oxygen and hydrogen, goods for money and money for goods, food for growth and growth for food, life for death and death for life, things for words and words for things. In this exchange we speaking things are caught. We are examples of it—fleeting examples, to be sure, but in that fleeting moment darkness gives place to light and chaos to order through the power of articulate speech. Only then can it be said with any sense that heaven and earth *are*. In the language of metaphysics, being is a predication. To be is to be something, to be something is to be expressed, and to be expressed is to be exchanged, one thing for another, with the one intelligible and illuminating medium of exchange, the voice. Heaven and earth may never have been created. That may be left as it was. But this remains. Whether or not they were once evoked by speech in the beginning, in the end and always they are evoked by nothing else.

SUBSTANCE*

In his *Dialogues in Limbo*, Mr. George Santayana has made Democritus the spokesman for substance in a manner to arrest the attention of philosophers. The case is there stated with simplicity, directness, and clearness rarely, if ever, equalled. The statement, as the Dialogues themselves indicate, may not carry conviction to every mind, but, as they also disclose, it can hardly fail to leave upon the mind of an attentive listener an impression of inevitability. Substance is the ground and antithesis of every dream or illusion just as health is the ground and antithesis of every form of disease. And dreams are no more dispelled by further dreaming than disease is dispelled by falling ill again. One must wake up from the dream just as one must get well, if illusion and disease are to depart. The waking and the cure are both wrought by substance which itself wrought also the dream and the disease. For dreaming and sickness can not be affirmed to be unnatural since both duly occur in the order of nature, but since they do occur in that way, that order or constitution of nature by means of which they arise can itself be neither visionary nor sick, but is antithetical to them, as substance is to appearance. To construe the order of nature in terms of appearance is, therefore, madness. The way of substance alone is the way of sanity.

This is an old doctrine. It is doubtless as old as Democritus, as Mr. Santayana would have us believe, even if in individual cases it may not "sit crowned with all the snows and wisdom of extreme old age." Modern philosophers have generously accorded it antiquity. They have, however, often looked upon it as evidence of an immature rather than a ripened wisdom. For they, like Locke, whom they have followed closely or from afar, have seen in substance "something I know not

* In the *Journal of Philosophy*, Vol. XXV (1928), pp. 685-691.

what" instead of something to which the knowing mind clings in the practical interest of a sane and ordered life, or in the theoretical interest of maintaining continuity in an evidently divided and shifting world. The difference between the two attitudes is considerable. It is easy to reduce knowledge of substance to profound ignorance of it, if one will adopt a method appropriate to that result. The thing has been done many times with always the same bewildering outcome that ignorance is somehow established with no clear indication of just what it is of which we are ignorant. Bradley, for example, looking for substance in a lump of sugar, could not find it. He found rather that even in so homely a commodity which the taste acknowledges as sweet, the eye as white, and the fingers as hard, the distinction between a thing and its qualities carries us nowhere with satisfaction. But of what are we then left in ignorance? Bradley's analysis may leave us bewildered. It leaves sugar, however, precisely what it was and something to be analyzed by a chemist in quite a different fashion. And the fashion of the chemist does not leave us bewildered and confused. It leaves us rather enlightened both in practice and in theory. The analysis of the philosopher and that of the chemist are thus quite different in their effects—a difference which one might urge is the rather radical difference between ignorance and knowledge. For even the philosopher, when *in extremis*, seems forced to admit that anyone desirous of really knowing what the substance of sugar *is*, must ask a chemist to tell him. Knowledge as over against ignorance, being awake as over against dreaming, reality as over against appearance, carry us to atoms and the void, to substance as it is actually explored in utter disregard not only of passionate and moral distinctions, but also of those reputed logical distinctions which would force even upon substance itself a division between it and its attributes. In other words, we may dream as much as we like and construe nature in moral or passionate terms which are agreeable to our imagination, hopes, and fears, but we are awake and sane only when we construe her in terms of atoms and the void.

This is what Democritus seems to say in the dialogues. Atoms and the void are terms obviously dear to him and ought not to trouble the modern reader who may suspect that they are antiquated. The modern disciples of Democritus have other terms equally dear to them. But with him and them alike, they are terms for substance, for that which is determined and determinable with an indifference absolute and complete to any wish or hope or fear, to any liking or disliking, to any good or bad or right or wrong, even to any truth or error, if this last distinction implies anything beyond the acceptance of the fact of substance itself. So Democritus seems to say. And all of us, no matter by what adjectives we qualify our philosophy and no matter to what faith we give our allegiance, all of us seem driven at one time or another to say the same thing, even if we say it in different words. We confront and are confronted with substance, not as a vague hypothesis, nor as an epistemological assumption, nor as a limitation of knowledge, but as something recognized and to be explored—the positive fact which is negatively expressed by saying that out of nothing nothing comes. But since something comes, something which is a confused collection of good and evil, beauty and ugliness, peace and war, truth and error, that from which all this comes must refuse for itself these passionate distinctions which it generates. These distinctions, no doubt, are—for do we not experience them?—but they are as qualities of events that happen, not, however, as qualities of that from which events spring, but qualities of substance which by possessing them makes some vessels for dishonour, others for honour. From atoms and the void came earthquake and fire upon the city, not in order to punish its wicked inhabitants while the good also perished, nor yet, by making some suffer, to provide for others an opportunity for showing mercy; they came because they came. So we are driven to acknowledge substance, not that thereby we may solve philosophical problems, but that, thereby, we may keep ourselves awake and from going wholly mad. Otherwise we should awake from dreaming by dreaming again and get well of one disease only by falling into another. Substance seems inescapable.

But consequences of a profoundly interesting sort follow upon the recognition and acceptance of the inevitability of substance. That recognition may lead one to love, as it led

Spinoza, to laugh, as it led Democritus. It has diverse effects. In the dialogues the argument of Democritus is left unimpaired, but its effect on the Stranger is the telling of a beautiful and pathetic story, and on the others, except Democritus, the making of a new religion for which, when he understands it, he supplies the ritual. The effect on himself is too powerfully expressed to be summarized in a phrase.

Alcibiades. Aristippus and Dionysius are enemies of science, and you, Democritus, are a believer in it. Being no judge in the matter, I will not pronounce between you, but I can conceive that a man who has spent his whole long life distilling herbs and grinding stones into powder should believe that he knows something of their substance. Nevertheless, intense study, too, is hypnotic, and might not the lucid theory of nature which you think partly awakens you out of the dream of life, be but a dream within a dream and the deepest of your illusions? My whole career seems a myth to me now in memory; yet when I interpret it in terms of your philosophy and imagine instead nothing but clouds of atoms drifting through a black sky, I seem to be descending into an even deeper cavern of reverie. Suppose I was dreaming of a chariot-race, hearing the shouting crowds, blushing to be myself the victor, and reining in my quivering steeds to receive the crown and suppose that suddenly my dream was transformed, and Olympia and the sunshine and myself and my horses and my joy and the praises of the Athenians turned to atoms fatally combined—I am afraid that, like the child in the Stranger's tale, I should burst into tears at that change of dreams.

Democritus. Do you think I should blame you? Is the sublimity of truth impatient of error? I know well the shock that comes to innocence on discovering that the beautiful is unsubstantial. The soul, too, has her virginity and must bleed a little before bearing fruit. You misconceive my philosophy if you suppose that I deny the beautiful or would madly forbid it to appear. Has not my whole discourse been an apology for illusion and a proof of its necessity? When I discover that the substance of the beautiful is a certain rhythm and harmony in motion, as the atoms dance in circles through the void (and what else should the substance of the beautiful be if it has a substance at all?) far from destroying the beautiful in the realm of appearance my discovery raises its presence there to a double dignity; for its witchery, being a magic birth, is witchery indeed; and in it its parent nature, whose joy it is, proves her fertility. I deny nothing. Your Olympian victory and your trembling steeds, spattered with foam, and your strong lithe hand detaining them before the altar of Apollo, while you receive the crown

—how should science delete these verses from the book of experience or prove that they were never sung? But where is their music now? What was it when passing? A waking dream. Yes, and grief also is a dream, which if it leaves a trace leaves not one of its own quality, but a transmuted and serene image of sorrow in this realm of memory and truth. As the grief of Priam in Homer and the grief of Achilles, springing from the dreadful madness of love and pride in their two bosoms, united in the divine ecstasy of the poet, so all the joys and griefs of illusion unite and become a strange ecstasy in a sane mind. What would you ask of philosophy? To feed you on sweets and lull you in your errors in the hope that death may overtake you before you understand anything? Ah, wisdom is sharper than death and only the brave can love her. When in the thick of passion the veil suddenly falls, it leaves us bereft of all we thought ours, smitten and consecrated to an unearthly revelation, walking dead among the living, not knowing what we seem to know, not loving what we seem to love, but already translated into an invisible paradise where none of these things are, but one only companion, smiling and silent, who by day and night stands beside us and shakes his head gently, bidding us say Nay, nay, to all our madness. Did you think, because I would not spare you, that I never felt the cold steel? Has not my own heart been pierced? Shed your tears, my son, shed your tears. The young man who has not wept is a savage, and the old man who will not laugh is a fool.

If, then, we are to take the dialogues in which Democritus figures, as a veracious document—and I think we must—and if we are, with an open mind, to consult human experience, there seems to be an unescapable conclusion; substance is not the end of something, but the beginning. I am tempted to say that it is not the last word in philosophy, but the first. By that, I do not mean that the later words will unsay the first or so respell it that it will sound with a different tone. It is neither to be unsaid or respelled. And I can believe that unless this is generously and whole-heartedly recognized, there is no wisdom to be sought by philosophers. Substance is a first word; yet nothing is clearer than that there has followed upon its admitted spelling such things as religion and laughter and love. Granted that from the indifferent determinations of substance we have come to be what we are, and, being what we are, we are confronted with substance as the first word which spells all the difference between dreaming and waking, between ignorance and knowledge, there seems to be no intelligible appeal back again to substance for what may then eventuate. On this I must insist in the face of everything that may be alleged against it. It is easy to say that substance is still at work, that what eventuates upon its summons from sleep is still to be credited to its operations, but Alcibiades has the ready answer that this is only to sink into a deeper dream. This will not do. The situation is one which dialectic confuses and does not relieve. Facts are more potent. And the fact is, by whatever standard we apply, that being awake to substance is a liberation. If we ask for evidence, it freed Democritus to laugh and Spinoza to love. To be confronted with substance is to be confronted with an opportunity. What happens after this experience is not construable in terms of what happened before. The recognition of necessity, which is only the recognition of secure knowledge as over against insecure ignorance, opens the door to freedom, to use, and to exploitation. There are few better attested facts. Secured knowledge does not determine what a man does, but reveals him as determining what follows upon it, from the building of a bridge to the building of a church.

This may be a last word, as Democritus and Spinoza would evidently have us believe while still insisting that medicine and society are worth the attention of a liberated soul, not for its own sake indeed, but for the sake of the sick, whether they suffer from ills of the body or those other ills which bondage to the passions generates in gregarious mortals. It may be that we should stop here, admitting that liberation happens and that a consequence of it, besides laughing and loving, is service. Yet one may neither laugh nor love, and, doing either, one may not serve, although the instances I have given are actual and daily verified. The liberated soul may embrace instant death, which Democritus recognizes as a radical cure for every form of madness, but does not prescribe. He withholds it for the subtle reason that it substitutes for all blatant errors "one great mute and perpetual error: the total ignorance which besets the atoms regarding the patterns and the dreams which in fact they generate." But the choice is possible no matter what logical substitution of error it may imply. Its absurdity is, perhaps, the least impressive thing about it. Its impotence is more impressive. That the first exercise of liberation should be absolute surrender looks like something unmatched in futility. It is as if a physician should discover the cure for a dread disease only to destroy it thereupon forever. But it is not wholly like this, for the physician might have enjoyed a curious glory in keeping the discovery to himself, or might have concluded it were better for men to suffer or that they were not worth release from their pains. Such considerations are denied the free choice of instant death. If the embrace of it involved the simultaneous destruction of substance —which is indestructible—it is difficult to conceive a choice which would have a higher recommendation. But substance, like the old woman in the Stranger's tale, is not disturbed by any death.

Perhaps we should not stop with the unparalleled futility of the absolute surrender. For to be free to die is for the liberated soul the recognition that substance makes no claim upon it that it should live. That's what its liberation means. It is free for laughter, for love, for service, but it is also free for death; and the atoms and the void yield not the slightest indication of a preference. Phrase the fact as we will—and philosophers have invented many ways of phrasing it and turned it into perplexing problems which they have vainly tried to solve—the indifference of substance to us is a genuine indifference only when confronted with the chance to choose. What possible sense is there in denying purpose to nature, or hope or fear or care or anxiety or striving or recompense or vengeance, unless in view of the possible exercise somehow of what has been denied? These operations are denied to substance although there is some specific arrangement of atoms and the void whenever they occur. To admit this is to be awake and alive to truth. It is to avoid illusion and madness. But it is to end nothing. Substance may be the first word in sanity, but it is not the last word either in wisdom or in life.

We might venture a proof of this beyond the fact itself, although we should have to admit that such a proof was a speculative diversion which borrowed all its force from the fact it would establish. We might say, for example, that the indifference of substance if really native to it, having its original seat in atoms and the void, would operate so that we should suffer without anguish and enjoy without enjoyment. The energies of substance would simply be exhausted or transformed in what was done, just as we imagine them to be in the movements of the stars or when an acid eats a metal. There could be birth and death, growth and decay, and such seethings as when water boils or chemicals combine to explode. Nature might then be infinitely diversified, but it would be indifferent through and through. No place could be found for illusion or for the waking from a dream. The indifference of substance would not be the indication of a difference, but only a universal character attached to every event. Or we might suppose that substance was not indifferent and affirm that it really cared about what it generated. We should then need more wit than we have to understand why its care was not effective, and to keep us from imputing to it either wickedness or insanity. Indeed, as we well know, to impute care to substance is to turn substance itself into an illusion. Such proofs as these suggested ones, are, as I have said, speculative diversions. Since, however, we may make suppositions contrary to fact, they may help to show that the indifference of substance is something which finds no place in atoms and the void.

Substance, then, as substance simply—atoms and the void, ions and electrons, matter, nature, necessity—substance is not indifferent to what we do. It has that moral character in its own right no more than any other. It is indifferent, that is, not in its own terms, but in terms of something else. It is indifferent only when in its terms we seek grounds for approval and justification of what we do. Then it fails us. And because it fails us, or better, when we become well assured that it fails us, we turn it into the uses of laughter, love, service, and death. For such uses we find it well adapted. Even Democritus can join in the ritual.

Substance is, then, not the end. It is not a last word, even if without it, nothing can be nor be conceived. Indeed, to take it as such is to sink into the deepest dream and entertain the greatest illusion. For in any philosophy of human life, laughter and love and service—without which death is defeat

—are more ultimate words. Spoken by souls liberated through being awake to substance, they have produced—in a sense perhaps more profound than Democritus guessed—that witchery which, being a magic birth, is witchery indeed. This no free man would willingly exchange for atoms and the void unless, perchance, having found in substance the faithful servant of his freedom, he had suffused it with his laughter or his love.

THE PROMISE OF PRAGMATISM*

THE conviction grows upon me that pragmatism might have had and still may have a more fruitful influence on philosophical thinking than it has yet enjoyed. As itself a philosophy, it is now more a memory than a force. It is referred to more frequently than it is celebrated. Many of us have become pragmatists in one sense or another, but few of us claim to be pragmatists in the sense that we have found in pragmatism a philosophy of human living, a theory of knowledge, or the key which unlocks the mind. It looks, indeed, as if pragmatism had taken a comfortable and respected place among those intellectual enthusiasms which have historical as distinct from permanent or progressive interest. The reason is not hard to discover. Pragmatism originally appeared as an attractive name for a method of clarifying our ideas, "a new name for some old ways of thinking," as James himself phrased it. Ideas, we were advised, can be clarified by finding their meaning in the procedure in which they are employed. We were cautioned against meanings independent of procedure or supposedly antecedent to it. Arbitrary definitions were to confess the fact that they were arbitrary and were not to be allowed to encourage dialectic when it was out of place. Freedom and flexibility in thinking, the habit of seeing how ideas are generated and modified by following the lead of subject-matter, an analysis of how our thinking operates as it passes from station to station in its progress—such as these were the aims which pragmatism professed to further. There was promise in it. This promise was speedily put into a position of minor importance. Pragmatism became a controversy about the nature of truth. Instead of encouraging analyses of the meaning of terms and ideas in the contexts wherein they occur, it encouraged a debate about the foundations of belief and

* In the *Journal of Philosophy,* Vol. XXVI (1929), pp. 541-552.

the criteria of truth and falsity. How can we determine when our ideas are true, became a more important question than How can we determine what they mean. The promise of pragmatism had, except in rare instances, little illustration of its fulfillment. It remained, for the most part, expressed in very general terms, a hope, an aspiration, a piece of advice, but found little expression in terms of specific analyses of procedures applied to varying subject-matter.

The reasons why pragmatism became a controversy may be left here unconsidered. The fact is probably more important than the reasons, for the controversy diverted attention from what was fruitful to what was fruitless. It led to antipathies between minds which were, ordinarily, not antipathetic. The combatants convicted each other of nonsense although they otherwise respected each other. They said in their haste what they probably would not have said at their leisure. It has to be admitted, I think, that "truth" is essentially a controversial matter. What is truth? Those who stay for an answer are pretty sure to stay for a quarrel. Pragmatism tried to alter the question, to ask instead for samples of truths or for a consideration of the adjective rather than the noun. But unhappy and unfortunate phrases got in the way. The slogans of pragmatism were perilous. When it was claimed that an idea is true because it works, the rejoinder was ready and well-nigh inevitable that an idea works because it is true. "Working" was something that had to be defined, but the best of definitions never seemed competent to settle the question whether truth was the consequence of working or working the consequence of truth. Undoubtedly there is something suspicious about any identification of the truth of ideas with their effectiveness either in discourse or experiment. It would seem that the effectiveness must be of a particular kind. And that particular kind, when it takes on an adjective to qualify it, always seems to clamour for the adjective in dispute. Beliefs are obviously effective when they are not true, and no "long run" of their effectiveness seems adequate to remove them from suspicion. So long as the qualification of effectiveness must be the true qualification, it is difficult to find another adjective which will do as well, even if the dear adjective is elusive. It ought not to be said that the opponents of pragmatism were successful in removing that elusiveness. To equate truth with consistency or with the agreement of ideas with objects, was as perilous as to equate it with effectiveness, especially when a pragmatist was one's opponent. There were nasty questions to answer. How are ideas found to be consistent? How are they found to agree with objects? The answer seemed to be: Is pragmatism true because it works or does it work because it is true? The answer was, in other words, to renew the controversy. There was not settlement of it. It wore itself out. The unfortunate consequence was that it left pragmatism to be remembered mainly as a controversy, a debate, brilliant at times and at times bringing with it matter of importance, but a debate without an issue. Tired of trying to tell what truth is, the combatants turned to a more promising occupation, that of trying to tell what other things are.

I would not say that pragmatism was nothing but a controversy. Rarely is anything nothing but. I am saying rather that its effect was controversial and predominantly so. It provoked dissent, and that provocation obscured its major contention. Instead of leading to an embrace of its promise, it led to a contention about irrelevancies. I think this can now be said. Pragmatism, as a way of thinking, had no more and no less to do with truth than any other way. These ways are known by their fruits—a remark which sounds like a pragmatic slogan—and their fruits may be truth incidentally, but they are, first of all, clarifications of the procedure of thought. They may clarify that procedure to a point where the question of truth becomes pertinent, to the point where questions find or do not find answers which answer them. The clarification is primary. And clearly it was primary in the claims of pragmatism. Moreover the claim was not of the kind that can be settled by debate or by considerations in general. The question, whether the claim that the method of pragmatism can clarify ideas is a true claim, could be answered only by finding out whether the method did or did not. There was no other possible answer and the answer was bound to be in specific cases, final. In no other sense had truth anything to do with the matter. The important thing was the way of thinking recommended. Its importance was discovered by trial and should be evaluated by trial. In this respect, pragmatism was anything but a controversy. It was a recommendation to experiment. Rarely did it happen, even in those controversial days, that that recommendation, when studiously followed, was fruitless. It is worth recalling what the recommendation was.

It was not of something new, but of something readily and often habitually forgotten, and of something, too, of which the need of a reminder seems to be periodic. It was the recommendation to remember that whatever meaning an idea may have independent of a given context, it has a discoverable and often an altered meaning in that context. Consequently it is clarified by discovering the way it operates in the context given. Pushed further, it was the recommendation to remember that although an idea may always have the same meaning in every context to which it is relevant, it has no meaning at all apart from any context. Pushed still further, the recommendation may turn into a dogma. Pragmatism, as I understand it, claimed or certainly seemed to claim, that apart from operation in discourse and experiment, ideas not only have no meaning, but are non-existent; and that, consequently, the function of ideas is not to represent, stand for, or duplicate objects in some way, but to mediate the processes of discourse and experiment. If I am not mistaken, it was this dogma which was the prime motivator of the controversy which ensued. As I do not wish to revive the controversy, I leave the dogma without other comment than this: It is a dogma which might very appropriately submit itself to pragmatic analysis. Much obviously depends on the meaning of "idea."

Pragmatism, then, recommends that we think in terms of what we do: that we think of measures in terms of measuring, of values in terms of evaluating, of ideas in terms of the way they operate. The recommendation was timely when it occurred. It afforded a needed stimulus to a reconsideration of philosophical ideas and problems which persisted more because of the historical momentum they had acquired than because of their clear relevancy to contemporaneous inquiry. At the lowest estimate, it afforded a rigorous and interesting diversion, in response to which much that was old was considered anew.

Its appropriate estimate deserves to be made in other terms, in terms, namely, of its repeated application. Its claim to be able to clarify ideas is, as I have said, a claim to be tested, not by discussion, but by trial. What, for example, did Euclid mean by a point; or, if one will, what was his idea of a point? He defined a point as "that which has no parts." Is this a direction to try to think of something that has no parts? Is everything that has no parts a point? Is a point something physical or conceptual? Is it something concrete or abstract? Is it real or ideal? Is it something found or something assumed? Students of geometry are familiar with such questions as these and with controversies arising from them. In contrast with these questions and controversies, we may ask the pragmatic question: What is a point in Euclid's procedure? In that procedure, what is it that has no parts as over against other things in that procedure which have parts? Then an answer seems to come of itself. Euclid meant by a point, first of all, the ends and intersections of lines. Other meanings, as of "a point above a line" or of "a point without a circle" seem to be derivatives of the original meaning. Now the ends and intersections of lines do not have parts in the sense that lines and what is made up of them or inclosed by them have. A line can be divided, but the end of a line can't. Euclid's definition does not clarify his procedure, but his procedure clarifies his definition. With the definition so clarified, one is not likely longer to debate whether a point is abstract or concrete, ideal or real. Indeed, there are many controverted questions which one will then no longer debate. A similar clarification of other definitions and the application of pragmatic analysis to Euclid's procedure generally, have a similar effect. Clearness of a definite and genuine sort is attained.

In an example like this there may remain the question—and a similar question may remain in similar examples—whether a point as clarified in terms of Euclid's procedure is a point as Euclid conceived it in his own mind or as it ought to be conceived in any mind. An answer to this question seems to me to be irrelevant to the value of pragmatic analysis. Nor can that analysis answer it. But it is in just these considerations that the merit of the analysis is discovered. To turn it into a means of revealing hidden thoughts or into a metaphysical determination of absolute meanings is to distort it. The important thing is that ideas, concepts, categories, definitions and the like, no matter what meanings may be given to them independent of their use in the exploration of some subject-matter, have a discoverable meaning in every such exploration. They have a meaning when they are at work which can be discovered from the way they work. Example after example can be given. Chance, for instance, is a troublesome category. To define it first and then seek for instances which the definition covers, involves a very ambiguous performance. It is easy to say there can be no such thing as chance. It is easy to affirm that its recognition is a consequence of ignorance. Yet when chance is used as an operating category in the various fields where it is employed, it has a discoverable meaning which rarely permits us to say there is no such thing or that the recognition of it is due to our ignorance. Multiplying illustrations of the pragmatic meaning of ideas is some revelation of their character. Let us believe, if we want to, that in themselves they are as absolute as any ardent Platonist could wish, with fixed and unalterable meanings which we labor to discover, pragmatic analysis can still convince us that when they appear in discourse and experiment, they have a working meaning. They expose themselves in connection with very concrete performances and lead our thought on to very definite implications. Seen in the light of the procedure in which they are involved, they gain in precision, definiteness, and effectiveness. Our understanding of the subject-matter about which they are employed is heightened. The merit of pragmatic analysis lies in its freedom from those entanglements which arise when ideas are otherwise analyzed and defined.

The illustrations given, sketchy as they are, seem to me to be a clear indication of this merit. The controversies to which pragmatism gave and may give rise in no way affect the advantage gained by analyzing the meaning of ideas in terms of the procedure in which they are involved. Meanings derived from context are as genuinely meanings as those derived in any other way. They operate and there are discoverable consequences of their operation. They often become controlling in the progress of an inquiry. They often lead thought to conclusions which can not be understood unless in terms of their operating meaning. We are, as a consequence, repeatedly confronted with statements, conclusions, and beliefs which mean one thing in their own context and quite a different thing, or nothing at all, when transferred to another context. The pragmatic analysis is pretty sure to bring relief in this situation. It is an old way of thinking in the sense that logic anciently advised thinkers not to mix up their universes of discourse. It is new, with a new name, whenever the need of its exercise becomes significantly recognized. Its need seems to me to be eminently evident. The outstanding illustration is the rapidity with which ideas have been shifting in our theoretical interests and particularly in the field of physics. That there is abundant confusion needs no proof and that this confusion is largely due to contexts in rivalry is evident.

When, for example, Professor Whitehead writes: "The most successful example of community life exists where pure instinct reigns supreme. These examples occur only in the inorganic world; among societies of active molecules forming rocks, planets, solar systems, star clusters,"[1] a reader, like myself, may be pardoned if at first he wonders whether Professor Whitehead is writing nonsense or poetry. The wonder might be dispelled by application of pragmatic analysis. I might be brought to see that Professor Whitehead is writing neither. When the possibility is suggested to me by Professor Eddington[2] of sending out messages tomorrow and receiving the answers today, I am at a loss to know whether to laugh or to cry. The laugh, I guess, was expected, but could not one cry if the best physics can do is to give us the prospect of a world so bizarre? If there is sense in it, I can see no other way of finding it than by pragmatic analysis. What, in the procedure to which Professor Eddington is committed, is the meaning of "messages," "today," and "tomorrow"? So long as I can not make that out, the book is no more illuminating to me about the physical world than is the *Shaving of Shagpat* about a barber-shop. Again: in terms of my habitual ideas, it is quite

[1] *Symbolism,* p. 62.
[2] *The Nature of the Physical World,* p. 57.

conceivable to me that, when measured, I shall be found to be shorter standing up than when lying down; but I can not conceive this if, at the same time, I am expected to admit that the rod which measures me is of different lengths in different positions. If I am six feet lying down and five feet ten standing, then the rod which measures me must, when measuring me standing, extend two inches clear above my head. I can readily suspect that when either the rod or my body is turned from a horizontal to a vertical position, something happens to it which should seek expression somehow in terms of measurements of length, but if I am to be clear about that somehow, it is useless for me to follow the lead of my habitual ideas; I must find out by pragmatic analysis what "differences in length" mean in a procedure which claims that a rod is shortened when it moves in the direction of its own length. What is "its own length"? What is it to "move in the direction of its own length"? What is it for "its own length to be not so long when moving in the direction of its own length"? How can a rod have a length of its own? If it can not have such a length, how can moving it in that direction shorten it? If its length is its length in a context, what is it that is shortened in another context? My habitual ideas are of little or no help in trying to answer such questions. In terms of them, these remarkable new ideas about the rod are simply silly. I cannot, however, believe that they are silly simply because I do not understand them, any more than I can believe that this article is silly if some dear reader fails to understand it. My trouble—and the dear reader's—is an invitation to try pragmatic analysis.[3]

My trouble, however, leads me to say with conviction, even if the expression of this conviction sounds extravagant, that many of the recent attempts to make clear to what is called "the intelligent reader," new ideas about space, time, motion, mass, matter, etc., are misguided and essentially unintelligible. They seriously raise the question whether the authors are clear in their own minds. They are misguided because what

[3] I can readily believe that the FitzGerald contraction is real, but like Professor Eddington, I want to know in what context it is real and what it means to be a real contraction in that context.

their authors have to say about space and time can not be said in terms of the space and time with which the intelligent reader is familiar. His space and time definitely belie what is said about them. To be sure, it may be replied; for what is said is said not about *his* space and time, but about *the* space and time of the physical world; he ought to be intelligent enough to see this. I reply—he is. He is also—I venture this—intelligent enough to see that many of the illustrations, and often the crucial illustrations, that are given to him to help him understand, are illustrations in terms of *his* space and time and not in terms of *the* space and time of the physical world. That is why he suspects that those who offer the illustrations are themselves a little confused. He knows that t may be $+ t$ or $-t$ or t^2 or t^{-1} or even πt, but he knows also that yesterday, today, and tomorrow are not matters of this kind. He knows that things look different from different points of view, but he knows also that he can not see how an observer who sees an elevator with its mechanism carry him to the top of a building can construe that ascent as the building going down. The building may be going down and he not know it, while the observer does, but that is not the difficulty. The difficulty is the elevator. The intelligent reader strongly suspects that the observer is seeing him carried up in an elevator in a building which is going down. It may justly be said that such illustrations as are here given ought not to be used. The fact is that just such illustrations are used. They promote confusion instead of clearness. They create the suspicion that there is confusion in the minds of those who use them.

The passage in thought from the world of yesterday, today, and tomorrow and from the world in which we go up and down, in which we go here and there, and in which we do one thing at the same time another does another thing, the passage in thought from this world to the physical world is a difficult passage. I doubt whether all the strange behaviour of clocks and rods to which attention has been directed has made that passage clearer than it was before that strange behaviour was promulgated. The very fact that we speak of the *physical* world ought to warn us that the ideas which go to make it up ought to be made clear, not by illustrations drawn from another world, but in terms of the procedure which is employed in discovering the physical world. In this way alone, as I see it, can we hope to reach a position from which the passage in thought to the physical world can itself be made clearer. I have no doubt at all that there is the physical world, or that explorers of it are saying, even when they say things very strange to me, relevant things about it. I believe it is a world without which nobody could be born or die. But it is difficult for me to believe that anybody either is born in it or will die in it. Without it, the sun could not go round the earth, nor the earth go round the sun. In it, neither does either. But I should have to use pragmatic analysis to make these unintelligibilities clear.

Of all the recent books I have read which have been written for the intelligent reader about the physical world, I like Professor Bridgman's the best.[4] It impresses me as having rendered a great service in helping to make ideas clear. It uses pragmatic analysis. I hope I do not misrepresent it when I say that I learned from it that when we speak of the distance from the earth to the sun and take into account how that distance is arrived at, distance does not mean quite the same thing it means when we speak of the distance between the top and bottom of this page and take into account how this distance is arrived at. With this lesson learned, I thought I saw quite clearly that the distance between bodies at rest, the distance between bodies in motion, the distance between opposite sides of a street, the distance between the earth and the sun, the distance between the Battle of Marathon and the Battle of Bull Run, the distance between a note and its octave, the distance between white and black, and the distance between good and evil, might all be distances but that *distance* was probably distance between nothing at all. As an historian, I sensed at once the age-old distinction between the universal and the particular, but under Professor Bridgman's influence, I sensed it in a fresh way. I was not at all ready to deny that there is such a thing as *distance* which is not a particular distance. Logic had taught me that *distance* can not be a particular distance, that *distance* can not be *the* distance between the

[4] *The Logic of Modern Physics.*

earth and the sun. And I have never been able to agree with those who would, therefore, deny being to distance or those who try to explain it away by some psychological juggling. I suspected Professor Bridgman of saying that there may be a formula for distance which is neither the distance between opposite sides of a street nor between the earth and the sun, but from which both these distances, when the proper transformations are made, can be derived. I had long suspected that there might be such a formula, because I had been taught that from $D = \sqrt{x^2 + y^2}$ one could derive either the side of a square or the circumference of a circle and that the formula was also a formula for distance. If I could derive from it or from something like it the distance between the earth and the sun, perhaps I could also derive from it the distance between two events like the Battle of Marathon and the Battle of Bull Run. Why not then go on to good and evil? Everything pointed that way even if I could not follow. Since, however, x and y could be anything and could be held together in such a way as to yield such different things as distances, squares, circles, sines, and roots, why should it not yield much besides? And it seemed quite clear that the more it yielded the less it would be anything it yielded. In fact it would never be anything it yielded. In yielding the distance between opposite sides of a street, it was never that distance. If it yielded good and evil it would never be good or evil. So the distinction between distances and what can yield distances by some operation or other seemed clear to me. There was concrete illustration of it, and, I thought, quite unequivocal illustration. It was an easy jump to the physical world—at least it seemed easy. The physical world is that which can be so formulated as to yield with the relevant operation a man's birth or death, but, obviously, in that world he neither is born nor dies, any more than the distance between the earth and the sun is in the world of $\sqrt{x^2 + y^2}$.

But I had not intended to air my ideas—or the ideas to which my reading has led me—about the physical world.[5]

[5] The "physical world" is an ambiguous expression, as one can readily detect by putting "physics" and "physiology" side by side or by reflecting on a current demand that "physiology" should be more "physical." The adjective "physical"

What I have said may be taken as some further illustration of pragmatic analysis. By the use of that analysis in a variety of cases it has become increasingly obvious to me that the physical world is a discovery and a discovery which can not be identified with that out of which it is discovered. Professor Eddington's two tables confront me. There is a table which can be so explored that the explorer is led into the physical world

---

has not kept a tight and uniform meaning throughout its history. The "physical world" once meant, among other things, the world to which "physics" is relevant. "Physics" has come to mean, among other things, the systematic measurement of that world. In systematizing the measurements, it would seem that another world has been discovered which is coming to be called, more and more restrictedly, "the physical world" or "the world of physics." The "world of physics" may be that without which nothing can be measured in a coherent and systematic way; but is it anything that can itself be measured? Can *the* measure be measured? Is not an identification of *the* measure with what is measured a source of much current confusion? Is not an identification of the "world of physics" with the "physical world" made again and again without sufficient analysis of the meaning of the terms which mediate the identification?

Take this for example: "The speed of 299,796 kilometers per second which occupies a unique position in every measure-system is commonly referred to as the speed of light. But it is much more than that; it is the speed at which the mass of matter becomes infinite, lengths contract to zero, clocks stand still. Therefore it crops up in all kinds of problems whether light is concerned or not." Am I quite foolish—thinking of some kinds of problems—if I wonder if my clock is now going with the speed of light because it has stopped? Of course I know it is out of order and so has stopped. I shift my wondering: if my clock were not at all out of order and should stop, would it be going with the speed of light? Could it go with the speed of light and stand still, with the mass of matter become infinite and lengths contracted to zero, and still be a clock and my clock at that? I can't believe it. Yet I can still believe that "the speed of light" occupies a unique position in every measure-system. Indeed, I could even venture into the realm of pure rationalism and say: since light is essential to every measure system, the speed of light *must* have a unique place. I find it however, very difficult to believe that the speed is 299,796 kilometers per second if at that speed lengths—kilometers?—contract to zero. In short, it is easy to believe in the world of physics, but difficult to believe that it is the physical world. How comparable—and in what way comparable—are masses, lengths and times in the world of physics with clocks, kilometers, and seconds in the physical world? How do we pass from the latter to the former? Surely not by making the behavior of the latter unintelligible. Nor, as I see it, do we need a theory of knowledge to help us out. The passage is made. It is made by doing certain very definite, repeatable, and learnable things. It involves a procedure. We need pragmatic analysis of it, and in detail. This we need far more than expositions which try to tell us what the world would look like if we travelled with the speed of light, if we observed it under conditions under which it could not possibly be observed. If there is a world impossible of observation, it ought not to be exploited in terms of observation, even if it is by observation that we are led to it.

to discover there something which may also be called a table when we keep in mind the manner of its discovery, but which, independent of that manner, would never be called a table at all. The physical table is not the table with which we start, but the table at which we arrive. It is not the beginning of an exploration, but the end of one. The evidence for this seems to me to be too strong to be refuted. The table with which we begin has been familiar for centuries; the table with which we end has taken centuries to discover and may not be the table we discover next week. Yet the fact that we continually discover a second table is good proof that a second table there is. We might stop here. We might even generalize the matter. We might say that by exploration of a world constantly familiar we are led into another world which is not constantly familiar, which changes in familiarity with our explorations, in which, however, we confidently believe. We might, I say, stop here. Pragmatism would advise us to stop long enough, at least, to become quite clear about the situation, to be quite clear that it is a solid outcome of procedure even if it may not be the final outcome. The table we write on, when explored, leads to the discovery of a table to which writing on is quite irrelevant as an expression of what it is. That's a good place to stop and get accustomed to before going on, because it is so solid and so uncontrovertible. The fact that when we go on we so frequently fall into controversy and say things astonishingly strange and often so difficult to believe ought to fill us with supreme caution. One of the commonest things we are apt to do when we go on is to say and try to believe that the unfamiliar table is prior to the familiar table. In spite of the fact that the unfamiliar table has no discoverable precedence, we often make it precedent and look upon the familiar table as its disguise. Were it not for the garb which the unfamiliar table wears when we see the familiar, we should see the unfamiliar table! This may be true, for it is a mighty curious world in which we live. I can not believe it, however, and for several reasons. Some of them may be personal, others, I think, are not. A personal reason is that if I believed this, I could believe almost anything; few beliefs would impress me as quite unwarranted. Among other reasons is this: every attempt I have made and have found made by others to deal with these tables in terms of priority, results in a controversy. Bias for the unfamiliar table turns the familiar into something called appearance, and bias for the familiar turns the unfamiliar into a convenience for the imagination or practice. Each of these positions becomes a matter of debate, and yet each is discredited by any test which is relevant to a trial of them. If the appeal is to experience, then experience robs neither table of its genuineness. More emphatic still is the reason that the unfamiliar table is discovered by dealing with the familiar one. So I must take both tables as equally genuine. But I can not take the discovered table as identical with the table from which it is derived. Making them identical seems always to lead to saying about the familiar table what is said about the unfamiliar, and this results in something paradoxical and bizarre. If I identified them and were sensitive about it, I should be sensitive about moving my familiar table about even if I am advised that it is not big enough or small enough to be seriously affected by the changes going on in the unfamiliar table. No: I must, at least pragmatically, keep my two tables from merging into one, if I am not to lose either them or sanity. This may not be the end of the matter, but it seems to be the beginning of anything subsequent that matters.

There should be, I suppose, a conclusion to this article. But its conclusion would be its point, namely, that pragmatism held out the promise of helping to clarify our ideas and that promise has been too much obscured by the controversy which made of pragmatism a debate about truth. The debate may never be ended, but the promises can be fulfilled; at least, whether it can be or not, is a matter of trial. The trial seems to be poignantly recommended when rocks become social, when clocks and rods behave remarkably, and when religion is encouraged by exploration of the nature of the atom. What do all the new ideas mean? It seems useless trying to define them in terms of old ideas. They need definition in terms of their operation in discourse and experiment. One can not begin with space, time, and matter, or with ions, electrical charges, and space-time. One has to begin with something else, with defi nite concrete operations, often with laboratory experiments, and, following them out, find out what the new ideas mean as revealed in and by the procedure. Until this is done, there is no use in asking whether the new ideas are true. Pragmatism may never arrive at truth, but it can minimize confusion. If my illustrations have not illustrated this clearly, the fault is mine, not the method. The more the method is tried in specific and limited cases, the more likely is it that we shall be clear in our dealings with cases at large.

EXPERIENCE AND DIALECTIC*

EVEN a misguided comment on Professor Dewey's philosophy may be instructive. Opinions have a social as well as an individual character, with the obvious consequence that one man's understanding of another is at least one instance of how that other is understood. Otherwise, why should we comment on great philosophers, and tell the world what they thought, when they have already told the world themselves? In the present case, malice could suggest that a philosophy should be defined and judged in terms of the effects it produces, but malice would be confused if confronted with a multiplicity of effects, and might find the criterion that a philosophy is what it is experienced to be, forcing it, in the interest of justice, to distinguish between appearance and reality. A commentator is embarrassed in making the distinction, for what he finds the philosophy to be is what he concludes it to be. His commentary is, then, at least as instructive as personal revelations usually are. He exhibits himself. He is an appearance. If the reality, as it may very well do, mocks him, that is the penalty of being an appearance, and, perhaps, some justification for being it, some evidence that the reality is antecedent to the appearance and should control it. Haunted by this perplexing circumstance, I proceed with this paper. I shall state what I have to say in summary at the beginning, and then illustrate it in two particulars.

Professor Dewey has had an eminently practical effect. He has profoundly influenced the way many people think and act and teach. When his writings are stripped of dialectic and controversy, and freed from contact with certain of the traditional problems of philosophy, there remains a positive and substantial pronouncement on human life in its immediate

* In the *Journal of Philosophy,* Vol. XXVII (1930), pp. 264-272. Read at the meeting of the American Philosophical Association in New York, December 30, 1929.

practical character. This pronouncement has had on many minds the effect of a genuine liberation from obstacles which warped their thinking and clogged their action. It proposes to substitute courage for uncertainty and hopefulness for fear. That is a very practical substitution. Certainty, or the claim of it, might have been offered as the substitute for uncertainty, and courage might have been offered as the substitute for fear. This, however, is not what the pronouncement offers. The soul is not to be cured of uncertainty and fear by becoming certain and courageous. It is to be made immune to its vices by means of a revised alignment of opposites, an alignment revised in view of the exigencies of living. The shift involved is naturally described as a shift from the theoretical to the practical. And I suspect that the major difficulties found in construing the philosophy of Professor Dewey arise from attempts to justify that shift on theoretical grounds. It is difficult for me to think that Professor Dewey himself does not attempt to provide such a justification. I find this less in what he affirms than in what he denies. His affirmations impress me as keeping close to a progressive development of a central theme. His denials, however, often impress me as requiring the acceptance of the opposite of what is denied as the ultimate theoretical ground which supports the practical affirmations. I seem at times to be asked to substitute courage for certainty on the ground that there is no certainty, and hopefulness for fear on the ground that there is nothing of which to be afraid. In such moments I find myself involved in a dialectic of theories of knowledge and existence. I become myself a controversialist, and find myself leaving the solid ground of experience.

There are two sentences in *Experience and Nature*[1] which express concisely and without controversial implications that pronouncement on human life to which I have referred. They are these:

> Because intelligence is critical method applied to goods of belief, appreciation, and conduct, so as to construct freer and more secure goods, turning assent and assertion into free communication and sharable meanings, turning feeling into ordered and liberal sense, turning

[1] Pages 436-437.

reaction into response, it is the reasonable object of our deepest faith and loyalty, the stay and support of all reasonable hopes. . . . What the method of intelligence, thoughtful valuation, will accomplish, if once it be tried, is for the result of trial to determine.

I have said that these sentences are without controversial implications. They receive, moreover, in Professor Dewey's manifold expansion of them, an emphasis which puts them in a position of philosophical dignity. They are not left without an expert analysis which aims to make them of primary importance, and to exhibit their entire independence of any attitude which can be defined as antecedent or more fundamental. This analysis, when freed from dialectical and controversial entanglements, impresses me as wholly convincing. The attempt to bring intelligence to bear on life in the manner described, is an attempt which is, and can be, made, without first having solved any antecedent problem whatever. Least of all does it wait on the solution of such problems as the existence of God, immortality, freedom *versus* necessity, mechanism *versus* teleology, and the like. Problems do not exist to be solved before we can live: they arise in the process of living, and in that process are solved and resolved. Professor Dewey has driven that fact home with untiring persistence; and he has made that fact the starting point of all fruitful thinking. As a consequence, he has made many of us intolerant of any other attitude. He has made it quite impossible for many of us to believe that life can generate any problem the solution of which would be life's undoing. And he has made this impossible because he has shown us in a wholly convincing manner that if we are to philosophize profitably we must begin with the concrete operations of intelligence as these promote more satisfactory living, and not with some antecedent scheme of things which is supposed to explain or justify these operations. Life with its exigencies is fundamental, and this fundamental can not be explained by any solution of life's problems, nor deduced from any system of things which our ingenuity may devise. Whatever one thinks of all this, it is a very definite and a clearly intelligible philosophy. And it is natural for it to recommend courage in the face of uncertainty and hopefulness in the face of fear.

It is natural, too, perhaps, that among its analyses it should give a prominent and even a distinctive place to the analysis of reflective thinking and the operation of ideas. Its premise, it may be said, forces it to look upon thinking as inquiry, and upon ideas as the intellectual instruments of inquiry which find their validity in what they effect or accomplish. Here is a thesis which can stand on its own bottom. It seems to be a major thesis of Professor Dewey, which he uses to frame a logic of practice, to give moral tone to actions, and to humanize education. In his development of it, however, he seems to me to support it far less by an appeal to its natural source, than by using it dialectically to confound every analysis of knowledge which implies an antecedent reality to which intelligence must conform in its operations if it is to be successful. Now, the question I would raise here is not whether there is such an antecedent reality, nor whether there are grounds for believing that there is. Such questions, like Professor Dewey's major thesis, seem to me to stand on their own bottom. Surely we can ask with as complete intelligibility as we can ask any question, whether or not reflective thinking implies an antecedent reality to which knowledge must conform to be successful. It is a question to be settled by inquiry fully as much as any other. To make it a wholly illegitimate question, and to read the whole history of philosophy down to very recent times as if it were vitiated by attempted answers to this question, give to Professor Dewey's thesis a character extraordinarily difficult to construe. I repeat, the question is not whether there are objects antecedent to knowledge to which knowledge must conform to be successful. The question is, rather, whether Professor Dewey's thesis would be vitiated in proportion as one believed in such objects and operated accordingly, and whether, if there were such objects, that thesis would be wholly destroyed? I ask the question because I have failed to discover that the existence or non-existence of such objects has anything to do with the essential character of the thesis. I can not find that the problem of their existence has to be settled first, before validity can be claimed for the thesis. Yet I am forced to believe that Professor Dewey thinks that such a settlement is essential. As I follow his settlement, I find myself in a dialectic which sets antecedent objects over against eventual objects to the confounding of both.

To be more specific, in *The Quest for Certainty*[2] Professor Dewey says in italics, *"only the conclusion of reflective inquiry is known."* This forces me to reply, "The conclusion of reflective inquiry is currently said to be knowledge; am I then to identify knowledge with the known?" If I do this, I am thrown into the arms of the idealists, whose embrace I dislike. So I distinguish between knowledge and its object; I conceive the object to exist prior to its being known. Then I am confronted with the charge that this robs knowing of practical efficacy. To avoid this I must recognize that objects of knowledge exist only after the act of knowing; they are eventual objects. That there are eventual objects after the act of knowing, and that, unless there are such objects, the acting of knowing is futile, are propositions which are for me both clear and acceptable. But if any objects whatever are known, it seems to me to be irrelevant whether they exist prior or subsequent to the act of knowing. What knowing eventuates in is a known object. I suppose no one disputes that, at least no one disputes it so far as the intent of knowledge is concerned. If that eventuation is made to depend on the prior settlement of the problem of antecedent as against eventual object, I can see nothing left but a dialectic which settles nothing. I do see, however, that an analysis of knowing as a concrete operation with subject-matter, makes such a dialectic quite unnecessary. Why, then, play eventual objects over against primary subject-matter, making of the former reconstructions of the latter, and making these reconstructions the objects of knowledge? I am quite ready to agree that it is the important business of knowing so to deal with subject-matter that more satisfactory objects are substituted for less satisfactory, and that, thereby, greater security, control, and happiness are secured; but I fail to see how this warrants the statement that "only the conclusion of reflective inquiry is known." That statement seems to me to come from another source. To find that source I am driven back on Professor Dewey's dialectical and controversial arguments. These drive me, in spite of all he says, to try to frame

[2] Page 182.

some conception of existence which is wholly independent of the act of knowing, and yet the justification of that act and the source of its efficacy. Yet this seems to be precisely what I am forbidden to do by the dialectic.

The matter may be made still more specific. In the chapter on "The Seat of Intellectual Authority" in *The Quest for Certainty*, Professor Dewey uses the example of a physician called in to diagnose the disease of a patient. He has the physician do what a physician would do, examine the patient and bring to bear his medical knowledge on the case. But the whole discussion drives me to ask: Must we conclude that it is only after the physician has found out what is the matter with the patient that the patient has anything the matter with him? So to conclude would be to caricature. Is, I venture to ask, the caricature only the result of the reader's stupidity, or is it the result of being forced to decide whether antecedents or consequents are the objects known? One must ask: Do what things are and the ways they operate depend on the eventuation of inquiry? Must we conclude that they do so depend because intelligence does, as a matter of fact, participate in the order of events, and so operate that more satisfactory objects are substituted for less satisfactory? Is this caricature? What saves us from the confusion here involved except a metaphysics of the kind which the dialectic of prior and eventual objects tends to destroy?

The questions are not asked to try to convict Professor Dewey of contradiction. They are asked because one reader at least finds no clue to an answer to them except in the dialectic, and that clue leaves him in the dialectic. The best he can do is to conclude that existence is essentially dialectical, and that the dialectic is incidentally resolved by the practical operations of intelligence. This may be a sound conclusion. If, now, we try to settle the question whether it is or not, we discover in ourselves a close intellectual kinship with Plato, Aristotle, Spinoza, Locke, Kant, Hegel, and all that array of names which the history of philosophy holds up for admiration.

Again I take sentences from *Experience and Nature*.[3]

[3] Pages 68-70.

A naturalistic metaphysics is bound to consider reflection itself a natural event, occurring *within* nature because of traits of the latter. . . . The world must actually be such as to generate ignorance and inquiry, doubt and hypothesis, trial and temporal conclusions. . . . The ultimate evidence of genuine hazard, contingency, irregularity, and indeterminateness in nature is thus found in the occurrence of thinking. The traits of natural existence which generate the fears and adorations of superstitious barbarians, generate the scientific procedures of disciplined civilization.

Sentences like these abound in Professor Dewey's writings. They impress me as being fully as characteristic of his philosophy as the instrumental doctrine of intelligence. At times, they impress me as more characteristic, because they define an attitude from which instrumentalism may be derived, but which itself is not derived from instrumentalism. It is a challenging attitude which nowhere else in my reading have I found so vigorously set forth.

It is not unusual among philosophies to be what is called anthropomorphic. It is very unusual, however, to be that in Professor Dewey's sense. There is a vast difference between constructing nature out of human traits and finding in human traits clues for inferences regarding what nature is. According to Professor Dewey's attitude, we are just as much forbidden to put man over against nature as an ultimate contrast as we are forbidden to put the sun, the moon, or the stars, over against it as such a contrast. If the latter are good grounds for inference, so also is man, and every part of man's make-up and activity.

I dislike to leave this feature of Professor Dewey's philosophy with so bare a statement of it. The importance of it is so great that it deserves far more attention than it has received. It involves an attitude difficult to describe by those pet isms with which we philosophers love to deal, and in which we think we feel at home. And "nature" is a very troublesome word. One thing, however, seems clear. Limited by our location and by our length of days, we do try to form some conception of that context within which we ourselves are so evidently incidents. "Nature" may not be that context; it may be only a part of it; but who is going to decide for us all?

Shall we let a word cramp the challenging significance of an utterance which affirms that man, when he tries to pass beyond the limits of the evident situation in which he finds himself, must not neglect anything within that situation? Let us, then, for the present at least, accept "nature" as the name for that which includes us as events within itself. What, then, is nature like? The answer is, it is, in some measure at least, like what we are. If we are unstable, there is instability in it; if we are contradictory, there is contradiction in it; if we are hopeful, there is possibility—one might dare to say, hope—in it; if we err, there is something like error in it; if we are incomplete, there is incompleteness in it. And all this does not mean that we are the exclusive instances of all such traits of nature. We are samples of them. In short, man is a sample of nature, and just as good a sample as the solar system or an atom. Consequently, we should never suppose that the latter afford better grounds for inferring what nature is like than the former affords. Here is a road which philosophers rarely travel with unencumbering luggage.

The acceptance or rejection of this conception of nature is not here in question. Nor is the method by which it is approached. These matters are left to the disputatious. The thing that troubles me is the limitation which Professor Dewey seems to put upon what we are entitled to infer from the samples of nature which we may study and analyze. Clearly man is not the only sample. There is the solar system also, and, if not the atom, at least that which admits an atomic theory. Why, then, should inference to anything permanent and unchanging be forbidden? Such inferences may be unsound, but they suggest themselves repeatedly as we explore the varied samples of nature. I do not find, however, that Professor Dewey rejects them because there is not evidence for them. He seems, rather, to argue them into illegitimacy. The ground of the argument seems to be, I repeat, not lack of evidence; it seems, rather, to be the conviction that any recognition of the permanently fixed or unchanging is bad. It implies a disastrous preference. *The Quest for Certainty* seems to me to read the history of philosophy in terms of that disaster, and to turn that history into an argument against the recognition of anything but relative permanency. And in *Experience and Nature*[4] we read: "One doctrine finds structure in a framework of ideal forms, the other finds it in matter. They agree in supposing that structure has some superlative reality. This supposition is another form taken by preference for the stable over the precarious and incompleted." Are we to conclude, therefore, that to avoid disaster, we must take a preference for the precarious and incompleted? Why is one preference better than the other, and why should the question be one of taking preference at all? I get no answer in terms of evidence of the same kind that warrants the emphasis on change. I get a dialectical answer, as if dialectic, and not the method by which nature is inferred, is to decide what inferences are to be admitted. And when I examine the dialectic, I find it motivated by the insistent claim that the recognition of the permanent gives it a metaphysical superiority to the changing. This makes it possible to play the one off against the other in the interest of proving that the permanent is but the relatively stable in a nature which is change through and through.

Now nature may be just that. I am not questioning that conception of what nature is. I am only pointing out that I find that conception supported finally, not by empirical evidence, but by a dialectical argument. That, again, may be the way to support it. If it is, then I am forced to conclude that dialectic is a better sample of nature's processes than any other. This also may be true. Then, to consider its truth, I find myself owning kinship with Heraclitus and Parmenides and their illustrious followers. I must carry the debate into that atmosphere; and when I do, I find no help whatever in terms of that practical procedure which marks the development of securer knowledge.

Such are the two illustrations I venture to give of the general statement I made in the beginning of this paper. They represent a conclusion I am led to by reading the writing of Professor Dewey. It is what his philosophy ultimately looks like in my own mind: a philosophy with a doctrine of experience and nature which admits of a positive and progressive development in its own terms, which stands, as I have said, on

[4] Page 72.

its own bottom; but which, in spite of this, is made to depend on a dialectic which runs back in the history of philosophy very far indeed. We should expect, as I see it, a metaphysics which is wholly inferential. We have, instead, a metaphysics which is a matter of preference. And this preference—we may even say that the empirical fact of preference—implies that nature is essentially dialectical, and that one way, at least, by which the dialectic is incidentally obviated, is through the practical procedure of intelligence. Experience appears to be, therefore, not something which is justified by its fruits, but which is justified by a dialectic which determines what experience is like.

IMPLICATIONS OF THE GENETIC METHOD*

THE genetic method is applied to processes which, whether they are planned or not, exhibit a plan which is progressively exposed as the processes continue. Its aim is to discover the factors which operate in this progressive exhibition. These factors are found within the context of the process selected for examination. This fact gives a certain priority to the plan of the process. In terms of the observed plan the processes to be examined are identified and distinguished. In terms of it continuities from origin to product are discriminated. In terms of it the contributions of the factors are analyzed. In all these respects the plan can claim priority, for without it, to begin with, the relevancy of these identifications, distinctions, discriminations, and contributions could not be determined. Genetic inquiries are thus confronted at the outset with an observed teleology in the subject-matter with which they deal. The processes involved go on from origin to product as if they were arranged to produce the results which characterize them. From Aristotle's day to the present such processes have repeatedly suggested a comparison between nature and art, and raised the question whether factors recognized in art are to be recognized in nature also. The question has provoked much controversy.

The teleology in art seems to be a relatively simple matter, for the plan involved, both in its conception and execution, can be assigned to an artist. There may be difficulty in understanding how a plan conceived can be turned into a plan executed, but, miracle or not, the artist is there to work it. In construing natural processes as processes of art also, the finding of an artist presents a difficulty. It has, however, been

* In *Proceedings of the Seventh International Congress of Philosophy*, Oxford Univ. Press, 1930, pp. 65-69.

greatly exaggerated. It seems as easy for the plan of a frog to be in a frog's egg as it is for the plan of a house to be in an architect's brain. The choice of artists, therefore, does not seem to be restricted. Vitalistic theories, consequently, ought not to be condemned out of hand on the ground that they make an absurd transfer from man to nature. Before that transfer can rightly be called absurd, either of two propositions must first be proved. One is that the plans of men are not controlling factors in what they do; the other is that only in men are plans controlling factors. Neither of these propositions has ever been proved or disproved. It is far from clear what would constitute a valid proof or disproof of them. They are matters of argument or controversy. Experimental evidence is not decisive because its probative force depends on some antecedent theory of the relation between the factors in dispute. If the term "soul" is used as Aristotle used the term Ψυχή, to distinguish *a* life from *any* life, the distinction between body and soul confronts the observer at every turn; and what he makes of the distinction will determine for him the value of experimental evidence.

Attempts to settle the controversy between mechanists and vitalists in favour of either seem, therefore, to be hopeless. It is to be noted, however, that the discoveries of the mechanists can not be set aside except by finding errors in their experimental procedure. Genetic experiments, however interpreted, are like other experiments in this respect. And the claim of mechanists that vital factors are irrelevant to their procedure seems sound and just. Their procedure aims at what can be experimentally identified and measured, and has been so successful that it is not fair to blame mechanists for not doing what they do not intend to do. The terms "mechanism" and "mechanical" may be offensive, but their meaning in experimental procedure is free from disrespect. It is not an insult to digestion to explore its chemistry, nor to vision to explore its physics. The mechanists rest on the solid fact that, no matter how processes are labelled, chemistry and physics are discoverable in them.

What, then, is it that either party to the controversy does, to which the other objects? The mechanists evidently claim that vital factors can not, and ought not to be, introduced into experimental procedure because their introduction robs the procedure of experimental control. This claim seems to be just, in spite of the experiments of vitalists in support of their own view. Such experiments seem to do no more than define a context within which experiments may be performed; and within this context experimentation seems to reveal precisely the kind of factors on which the mechanists insist. The claim of the mechanists seems, therefore, to be justified.

The vitalists evidently claim that the mechanists do not, and can not, solve the teleological problem. This claim seems to be just also. I am not sure that mechanists generally think they are solving that problem, or are interested in trying to solve it. They may claim that a solution is irrelevant to what they are doing. My reading, however, convinces me that an appearance on their part of trying to solve it, or the belief or fear on the part of others that such an effort is made, is the primary source of the controversy. I can not find that the facts brought to light by the mechanists are any more disputable than the facts brought to light by the experimental method generally. The dispute seems to bear wholly upon the use of these facts to explain that observed teleology without which the genetic method would have no subject-matter to explore.

If this is true the controversy is simplified and set in a more general context. If an explanation of teleology is sought, it is pertinent to ask what sort of an explanation would suffice. The answer seems to me to be the usual one. In all my reading and reflections I find no other. The only sort of explanation of teleology which would suffice is one that involves the imposition of a teleological principle upon factors which are not teleological in their own right. Again the appeal is to the artist, only now the artist is not a co-worker with the adaptable possibilities of his materials, but a separate agency, without which those materials would be quite devoid of import or possibility of adaptation. If teleology is not accepted as a metaphysical datum, but requires first an explanation, then it seems that the only sort of an explanation which would suffice is a theory which provides somehow for the imposition of teleology on an existence otherwise totally devoid of it.

I do not find that the genetic method implies any explanation of this sort. It takes the plans of processes as it finds them. Its analyses may lead to a better understanding of the operations involved, and to some control of them, but these consequences are the normally expected consequences of inquiry generally. "Explanation" may be defined in terms of them without at all implying that teleology is thereby accounted for. Finding the co-operating factors in the production of a result which has a specific character is quite different from finding a principle which produces that character. Now, as I see it, failure to observe the distinction here involved, or the suspicion that it is overlooked, gives the impulse to vitalistic theories. It is so clear that mechanism does not account for teleology that any suggestion that it does leads repeatedly to a protest. The protest is valid enough, but it is not itself a counter-explanation. The failure of mechanism to explain teleology does not imply that vitalism or anything else will explain it, or even that it is in need of some explanation. Yet, judging from history, the denial of mechanism is readily turned into an affirmation of vitalism.

Something can be said in its favour, for vitalism involves an appeal to specific powers or energies. Such powers are hard to deny. What things do, they obviously can do. This, their ability, is their power. Nature is a domain of just such powers. But there is considerable difference between acknowledging powers and converting them into teleological agencies. The eye has the power of vision, but to convert that power into an agency which produces eyes in order that the power of vision may be exercised, is a procedure difficult to match in futility. Clearly such an agency would have to create an instrument with which to see, and act, thus, after the manner of a man who makes a microscope and observes how the instrument works. It leaps the bounds of credibility that an agency must first see in order to make an eye in order to see. Why make an eye at all, if vision operates without one? Into such strangeness of conception on a total scale vitalism seems to fall when offered as an explanation of teleology. Powers are unmistakably evinced in the operation of their instruments, but this is the fact of teleology, the fact observed, and not its explanation. Since the exhibition of powers is what is observed in the operation of instruments, the way the instruments work becomes a matter of the instruments solely.

The genetic method, then, leaves the fact of teleology precisely where it finds it, as an observed trait of the subject-matter with which it deals, without explaining teleology, or explaining it away. Perhaps it would be profitable to stop trying to explain it, and turn to an exploration of its consequences and implications. A universe—if I may speak after the manner of philosophers—a universe in which plans are actually worked out is probably more interested in working them out than in provoking the question why it is that kind of a universe. To seek the purpose of a purposeful world looks like seeking the good of what is good, the evil of what is evil, the beauty of what is beautiful, the meaning of what is meaningful, the truth of what is true, or the divinity of what is divine. A teleological universe merits these adjectives in its own right, without imposing the necessity of finding some principle or principles by virtue of which these adjectives are warranted. These adjectives express in our human speech what the universe discloses as of importance in its concerns; and man, who can only equivocally be called its chief concern, exhibits this importance convincingly.

A less massive statement of possibilities is desirable. Teleology may throw some light on the nature of inquiry itself. There has been controversy among philosophers over the relation of inquiry to subject-matter, of knowledge to objects. To settle the controversy it would seem necessary to exhibit knowledge and objects in a context in which they could be independently identified. Such a context is not accessible. We can deal only with the operation of inquiry as it formally proceeds. Then it is exhibited as itself a genetic process. It is an instance of teleology. A theory of knowledge, therefore, can hardly be expected to reveal a context which is antecedently irrelevant to the teleological character of inquiry itself. Knowledge is not the attempt to apply a logical framework to existence in order to see whether it fits. It is rather a genetic process, which, moving within what frameworks there are, discloses them with increasing clarity. A theory of knowledge would seem, therefore, to involve something else than an attempted explanation of the relation of subject to object, or an attempted justification of the validity of knowledge. It would do for inquiry generally something analogous to what the genetic method does for living creatures. It would be as much debarred from beginning with an original antithesis between subject and object, a world to be known and a mind to know it, as the theory of genetics is debarred from beginning with an original antithesis between inorganic matter and an organic principle to quicken it.

THE NATURE OF MAN*

HISTORIANS of philosophy would have us remember Hegel, with honour and thankfulness, during this hundredth anniversary of the year of his death. In the situation in which I find myself, I must remember Fichte. I am compelled to. I know well that Hegel has influenced the development of philosophy much more and more deeply than Fichte. Today, however, I am not thinking of this development. I am thinking rather of our obligations, our necessities, and above all of our imperative need as men to learn what we can about our nature and our destiny. Surely a philosopher—and I must add, an American—who in Germany would venture to speak about the nature of man, must remember Fichte. He can not do otherwise. Fichte's time, like ours, was a time when the problem of human destiny lay heavily on men's minds. It is true that Fichte spoke to the German nation, but his voice carried beyond national boundaries and was heard by alien ears. His book *Die Bestimmung des Menschen* has become a book for mankind. It can be read today.

It may, however, be read in two ways, either to get an understanding of the philosophical ideas of Fichte's time, or to become intimate with a beautiful spirit. He who reads it in the first way can easily miss the experience which he who reads it in the second way is sure to have. The man Fichte impresses me as far greater than the peculiarities of his philosophy. I doubt if there are many thinkers today who can take seriously Fichte's own development of doubt, knowledge and belief. It sounds a little too immature and outmoded. Its social, scientific, and literary background is different from ours. Yet

* In the *Columbia University Quarterly*, Vol. XXIII (1931), pp. 402-419. Inaugural address as Visiting Roosevelt Professor of American History and Institutions in the University of Berlin, 11 November, 1931. English translation, by the author, of his address as originally written in German.

doubt, knowledge, and belief remain. Human life is not yet rid of these three. They endure. Fichte wrestled with them to get a blessing. To illuminate them, he brought the best he knew and the best he could find. And he did illuminate them. He made them live. He challenged men to busy themselves seriously and deeply with doubt, knowledge, and belief. He challenges them today, when he is read in the light of his purpose. Man's nature demands a commitment. A man may doubt as he pleases and know what he can; but to be a man involves something more. What do we look like, when we observe ourselves and when, with an emancipated mind, we reflect on our journey in the noisy world and on our companions in that journey?

These are questions for philosophy. They are also questions which every man asks who is not content to view his life as a senseless event in the world. He expects philosophy to give him light and leadership. What may be said then of the philosophy of the present day? I fear that it has until recently shown timidity, when these questions are asked, and a threefold timidity.

First, it has shown timidity when confronted with the belief in something supernatural in the nature of man. It is not necessary today to exhibit in detail the powerful influence which this belief has had on all branches of philosophy. It is sufficient to note that it has fixed the controlling terms which philosophy uses when it considers what is peculiar in the nature of man. We discuss whether we are heavenly or earthly creatures. To find what is heavenly, we turn to religious doctrines or to the assertion that thinking itself puts man somehow in a position above nature. To find the earthly, we turn to the natural sciences. These alone should determine what we are to understand by nature. But the language of these sciences is not the language of the soul. Their words are not the words we use when we reflect on life and death. Yes; we discuss what we are. We rarely directly and positively inquire. Philosophy, when busied about humanity, is usually controversial. It should cease to be that. It should cease to waver between an idea of man and an idea of nature which are opposed to each other from the start. Is it really possible to believe that man is something which must be put into one or the other of two antecedently prepared worlds?

Philosophy has also shown itself timid in the face of the positive sciences. We are accustomed to boast that these sciences are the greatest intellectual achievement of modern times. This they are beyond a doubt. But this they are because they are positive. They have taught us that we can hope to find the laws of nature only as we are willing to be impartial toward events; and that the finding of the laws of nature puts us in a position to plan and enjoy with a purpose. The success of the positive sciences could easily raise the suspicion that philosophy itself should be equally positive. To be sure, there is a wide-spread positivism. It impresses me, however, as not strong enough, as not thoroughly positive, and as not relentlessly carried out. It regards human life, and particularly the life of the soul, in much the same ways as any idealistic philosophy regards them. It sees in the soul a source of error and foolishness, the moment we regard the soul as a source of genuine information regarding the laws of nature. Idealistic philosophy, on the other hand, seems to be content with posing as an unanswerable criticism of positivism. This is easy, because it is obvious that we win knowledge and control of nature only through the exercise of the soul's activities. So for decades we have had systems of philosophy at war, and the war has always had a cautious eye directed toward the positive sciences. Both sides have been afraid of them. Positivism will do nothing to hurt them, and idealism will let them go their own way in isolation and undisturbed. Only about the beginning of the century has philosophy, with self-consciousness and energy, tried to become fully as independent and positive as the natural sciences. It has begun to be less fearful of what they have to say and to take them at their face value. It will no longer allow that they alone determine either what man or what nature is.

There is a third example of timidity. When I was a student in Berlin in the last century, it was common to hear that psychology had become at last a positive and experimental science. Since that time psychology has made extraordinary progress. Its pace has been so rapid and its changes so dramatic, that one often wonders what will eventually become of it. Until recently, the other sciences were content to leave the study of the soul wholly to psychology. The soul lay beyond their territory. Psychology itself has changed this attitude. In its positive development it finds the need of physiology and physics. It turns to the study of animals, the apes and insects. It would become biological. It seeks help from the new biophysics and biochemistry. Its scope becomes constantly broader and its relations to other sciences increasingly closer. One result of this remarkable development is that psychology seems to have lost the human soul. Perhaps it would be better and more proper to say, that the soul has been progressively transformed, until it has at last become no more than the physiological, physical, and chemical behaviour of human beings. We no longer have a soul or the soul is no longer a thing we can have. It is rather what we do, our activity as a whole. Philosophy has often regarded this progress of psychology as the progress of a lost son, although few psychologists seem anxious to return to the parental mansion. But we may well ask, has the effort of psychology to become an independent natural science been a gain or a loss for philosophy? Faced with this question philosophy seems to be timid. Only recently has it tried with a clear consciousness to see what it can make out of a man without a soul.

It is natural to man to form opinions about the world and to try to orient his life within its boundaries. So philosophers have affirmed many times. The affirmation amounts to much more and has a deeper meaning than a justification of philosophy. It means that philosophy is in no need of justification at all. It needs a justification as little as do the singing of birds, the blossoming of plants, or the velocity of light. Whatever is natural to anything in nature, is natural to it. In this respect all things and all procedures are equal. There is no privileged procedure. This we should have learned. As we learn it and value it, we gain a clear consciousness that philosophy is not an answer to the question, Why is there a world with men in it, but an analysis of such a world, with basal emphasis on the fact that the world contains men for the same sort of reasons as it contains birds and plants and light. It holds them all together. There are not two worlds, to be played off against each other, one with men and one with all sorts of other things. I find it impossible to think that the world is divided into two the moment a man perceives it or thinks about it. If that were true, then I should have to believe that the world is so divided the moment the sun shines or an electron swings. I can not look upon the activity of man as an exception. Our philosophy should be wholly positive.

I am not thinking of a revival of the positivism of the nineteenth century. I have already said that kind of positivism was essentially a handmaid of the positive sciences. It was also the handmaid of cherished educational, social, and political theories. It was not independent and free. It boasted that it looked upon man as a natural being, but when it was through with man's life, it saw in all that is most characteristically human little more than visionary dreams, the natural sciences alone excepted. Man lost thereby his natural rights. Yet animals, plants, and atoms were left to go their natural way in the world. The demand that philosophy be positive calls for something quite different. It is a demand for independence, freedom, and a release from timidity.

That book of Fichte's closed with belief. We often ask, what should we believe? This is not, I think, as a first question, the question suited to the intellectual temper of the present. We have accustomed ourselves to disbelieve. We doubt, and even about knowledge itself. But why? That is the first question. The answer is not hard to find, although it lies deep down in the history of the western world.

We hear of the decay of the western world. But what is it that has really decayed? It is impossible to find in the whole history of the human race a century which can compare with ours in the mastery of those material forces and means which are the foundations on which a noble and brilliant civilization can be erected. Here there can be no thought of a decay. Here we stand on a height of which others have dreamed, but which none has ever reached before. The suspicion of decay touches only our spirituality. Education, politics, morals, society, the give and take among men, and art itself—all exhibit nervousness, vacillation, and folly. They seem to have fallen into an extreme of confusion. They are not quickened and inspired by ideals like those—so many believe—that quickened our ancestors, even when they departed from them. It is hard, however, to believe that we are really worse men than our ancestors. The evidence may well point the other way. Yet it is not to be denied that daily there are fewer and fewer people who believe as our fathers believed. To have such a faith has become well-nigh impossible. The reason lies, not in a decay of human nature, but in the character of the history of the western world.

Our ancestors believed what they were taught to believe. They had to go to school, and to a school wherein they were not taught to consider their own experience and thereby gain ideas and ideals that were appropriate to it, but to a school in which they were taught the ideas and ideals of other peoples, ideas and ideals which had their source in a different civilization and were appropriate to a different experience. These alien ideas and ideals floated before their consciousness as the norms which should determine what their experience ought to be. They ought to think like Greeks, plunder like Romans, and pray like Christians. But they were themselves something different. Every now and then they became conscious of this, and then there was a revolution. The history of the western world, intellectually considered, is the history of the education of new peoples, but an education which would compel them to think and to feel like the peoples of a foreign world, and which through this compulsion sowed the seeds of revolution. The current opposition between old and new is not the ordinary opposition between parents and children, but something much deeper. It is the opposition between a tradition of foreign origin and the desire to be oneself. The western world takes no delight in speaking Latin, it prefers to speak its own languages. It would lead its own life. It does not seem strange, therefore, that today we would rather free ourselves from history than learn from it. It is not strange that we have become so unsettled and vacillating. We will have our own experience. But who knows what that experience is or should be? What should we believe? The answer can still wait a little.

What should we not believe, if we would really learn something from our history?

When I consider the results of the historical criticism of human opinions, philosophical, religious, or otherwise, and also the results of positive inquiry into natural events, I am compelled to conclude that we should not believe that man is an exception in the natural history of the world. He comes from nature and to nature he returns. He comes and goes like any other event in the world; and the world exists for his sake as little as it exists for the sake of anything else. We should not believe differently. There are many who will believe differently. But they will to believe; and the "will to believe," although it may often be a comfort, is not an attitude which is intellectually grounded. I would not fight about words. A philosopher like William James, for example, may hold that all knowledge is at bottom a belief, but the distinction between what is believable and what is not believable remains. What I would affirm is this: in the face of all our discoveries, it has become intellectually impossible to believe that man is not a natural being in the same sense as animals, plants, and atoms. We may put this unbelievable thing away in the interest of hopes and fears, but we can not think it away, when we thoughtfully and purposefully plan for our daily life.

This negative attitude should be transformed into a positive attitude. It is not enough to believe that we are not otherwise than we are. We should believe that we really are what we are. The development of a thoroughly naturalistic philosophy seems to me to be essential, if philosophy is to point out to modern men what the love of wisdom really means. Naturalism is becoming daily more popular. This fact, however, witnesses neither to its truth nor its solidity. It witnesses rather to the profound impression, which the results of modern criticism and research have made upon modern living and popular thinking. What we call "Modern" is no longer a matter of literary or artistic eccentricity. It is a spirit which has permeated the whole of our social, moral, economic, and religious life. The new is sought, the old is discarded. We repeatedly hear that the age-long institutions of mankind are no longer suited to the needs of the day. They have confined and repressed the natural desires and enjoyments of men, although it is only with the fulfilment of desire that life finds satisfaction. Naturalism is becoming increasingly popular.

It is, however, rarely confident and relentlessly carried out. With us it is a young philosophy and often youthful. It exhibits excitement, rather than depth. The bonds of tradition and authority fall away, and there comes a sense of freedom, which would let every man lead his life as he pleases. It demands social, moral, and economic arrangements which will insure favourable opportunities for living. Yes, insurance of living is what is demanded, and even government is expected to provide it. There is little serious thought about the question. What does it really mean to be a child of nature? What is the nature of man?

Few philosophers and still fewer psychologists have attained a clear knowledge of the fact that this incorporation of man into nature is of the greatest metaphysical significance. They seem to be content with the conclusion, that something thereby has happened to man. He has been changed. His relatives have been changed. He is no longer a child of God and an inheritor of the Kingdom of Heaven. His once high position in the cosmos has been abased. His relatives have become the animals, the plants, and the atoms, and this is taken to mean that the nature of man is to be found at last in the nature of the atom. There are a few who can find in Heisenberg's principle of indeterminism the hope that there is yet a Promethean spark of freedom in the world, but beyond this the incorporation of man into nature is a profound transformation of what he is, a change of his destiny and his relationships.

The popular attitude agrees with this conclusion. It is thought that naturalism gives to men chiefly their animal rights. Man has become an animal. His intelligence is only an instrument of his animal life, to be used to find channels through which his natural impulses may healthfully and freely flow. This is what both the followers and the opponents of naturalism usually affirm. In this affirmation the former find joy and hope, and the latter shame and destruction.

Shall we, however, make haste to become either followers or opponents? It is still possible, even in these revolutionary times, to find an hour for a little deeper reflection on the whole matter. The current conclusion from naturalism is not the only conclusion, and perhaps not the most correct, that may be drawn. The incorporation of man into nature may well do something to man, but it must also do something to nature. It is impossible that the word "nature" can mean the same after this incorporation that it meant before. The incorporation is really revolutionary. It does not permit us to think of nature as if it were wholly predetermined, irrespective of man's incorporation into it. What has naturalism really done to man? It has most certainly changed him. But how? It has changed him from an illustration of what nature is not, to a profound illustration of what nature is. He reveals what nature is fully as much as any other natural event. The nature of man and the nature of nature go together.

This truth is the lesson taught by the whole history of philosophy. Thinking about man and thinking about nature have always gone together. In the history of thought, nature and man have always formed either an opposition or a unity. When they are opposed, then it is obvious that the nature of man can not be found in the nature of nature. When they are not opposed, then it is equally obvious that what nature is, is closely and basically bound up with what man is. The failure to recognize this, or the fear of the consequences of recognizing it, has been responsible in large measure for the vacillations and follies of naturalism. Otherwise how could it be possible for any one to believe that animals, plants, and atoms are better and more important examples of what nature really is than man himself? How could naturalism be looked upon as a debasement of man and not an elevation of nature? How could so many naturalists believe that physics and chemistry, rather than metaphysics, reveal nature's character? I must affirm that the incorporation of man into nature restores metaphysics to freedom, independence, and confidence. It regains its position as the primary discipline which lies at the basis of any reflective consideration of existence.

The nature of man and the nature of nature go together.

A thoroughgoing naturalism will not separate them. It will not allow us to think of nature as something first created or first discovered, and then man added to introduce confusion. It forbids the myth of creation and also that substitute for it which is so often constructed on the foundations of what we call the natural sciences. Since there are men and atoms, nature can be no more adequately defined without men than it can be without atoms. Man himself discloses the kind of nature in which atoms can exist fully as much as atoms disclose the kind of nature in which man can exist. A naturalistic philosophy should not think of nature as something first created or first defined, which only tolerates the existence of man in some mysterious manner. Does nature tolerate the atoms; or the vegetables; or the birds? Such questions are absurd. For nature is equally tolerant of everything that happens and everything that happens is equally tolerant of her. And that means that she can not be something first created or first found, to be followed by whatever happens. She is something quite different. She is what events together disclose in their mutual relations to one another—activity illustrating law. Man explains nature only in the sense that he discovers her, and he discovers her only as a consequence of the fact that his whole life from birth to death, from waking to thinking, is a genuine co-working with what she is. The question why and how man lives, how and why he walks and thinks, is, in principle, the same sort of question as why and how the atoms move. This does not mean that the movement of atoms is the thinking of a man, or that thinking is some curious addition to motion, but that both motion and thinking are a co-working with nature under controlling laws. A thorough naturalism may not think of something already prepared for the happening of events. It demands not only an emancipation from a traditional conception of man, it demands also an emancipation from a traditional conception of nature.

I hope I have now made clear my own attitude toward naturalism. When I speak of my own attitude, I do not think of a personal discovery. I mean the attitude to which I have been led by the study of the history of philosophy and the movements of thought in our time. Naturalism is a discovery with me only in the sense that it impresses me as the philosophy which thinking men would gladly accept, if only they could believe it. We do not like to look upon nature as our enemy. Our daily life seems so obviously to be an opportunity to accomplish something lasting and worth while; and life is the only thing we know that seems to offer such an opportunity. This is fact. It is not speculation or a dream. It is not even a belief. It is fact. Belief arises only when we reflect on the fact and wonder if it forces us to break the world in two. Two, we would rather not have. It is our errors, our difficulties, our embarrassments, which incline us to divide the world. Yet without these we could not be co-workers with nature. Without them possibilities would be impossible. I would not admit a division, I would believe in a unity. I must believe that nature reveals herself in man more adequately than in anything else, that in him her laws come to expression and meaning, that human life is not set over against nature, but is nature illuminated and inspirited. And then I turn again to history.

Naturalism is not an historically new philosophy. The modern kind is new only in the sense that it is not founded on the naturalisms of the past, but is a product of modern science, modern psychology, modern criticism and the technological demands of modern life. It is a challenge to us to revolutionize our traditional thinking. The first consequence is not surprising. Man feels himself changed, he asks what he has lost and what he has gained. He does not first ask what nature has lost and what she has gained. But it is just this question which he must ask at last. Then he may well turn to history. Then he may find a genuine interest in the naturalisms of the past.

I select from the nature philosophies of the past, and particularly from that of Aristotle, a principle to emphasize. I would call it the principle of propriety. In his exposition of nature as something dynamic and progressive, Aristotle used two principles which have profoundly influenced subsequent thinking, the principle of natural powers and the principle of natural proprieties. We usually think that the principle of the conservation of energy has freed us from the first. I doubt if we are right, but that may be left here unconsidered. To the principle of proprieties we still hold. On it depends the discovery of the lawfulness of nature. Or I would rather say, that it is the discovery of proprieties which leads us to the formulation of the laws of nature. We seek everywhere for what is peculiar or proper to the operation of things. When we find it we formulate a law. I doubt if examples are necessary. Perhaps it is enough to say that we try to find, not any velocity, but the proper velocity of light, which can be held to be constant when we formulate the laws of what we observe. On the discovery of this proper velocity, much depends. Determinations or characteristics like this together make up the propriety of nature.

We might therefore define nature as a realm or sphere or even an assemblage of proprieties. I prefer the word "realm," not because it is poetic and suggests a government, although these are good reasons enough, but because it carries with it all that law implies. When, however, I define nature as such a realm, I do not imply that nature was once upon a time teleologically arranged. I am fond of teleology, but not of a teleology of that sort. Teleology is what the events of nature reveal and without it these events would not be intelligible to us. We understand a thing when we have discovered what it can do in relation to other things. In different relations it acts differently, but in every case with a definiteness in accord with its propriety. Its operation in specific cases is a specific operation which none the less illustrates its proper action. If this is not teleology, I wonder what teleology can be. In this kind of teleology, we find the usefulness and usability of things; and the source of these characters is not in us, but in the proprieties of nature.

Now what have these observations, which are for the most part obvious and naïve, to do with man and the nature of man? Much, I believe. Guided by the philosophy of naturalism we have incorporated man wholly within nature. This now means that, with respect to human life, there is propriety in nature fully as much as in any other instance. Man, from his lowest physiological functions to the highest aspirations of his thought, illustrates the propriety of nature. The world in which he lives is controlled not only by physical and chemical laws, it is controlled also by logical, moral and spiritual laws. Otherwise how could man doubt or know or believe? When a man walks, we readily admit that nature is appropriate to his walking. When he sees or thinks, should we say something different? Should we say something different even when he prays? He is doing what is natural. A thoroughgoing naturalism can not avoid the conclusion that nature is as adapted to the life of man as it is to animals, plants and atoms. To be so adapted, nature must be so arranged and ordered that the spiritual life of man is not alien to her. The nature of man and the nature of nature coincide.

It seems possible, therefore, that philosophy can develop a valid positivism, a valid realism, a valid naturalism, which will teach that the world does not exist for other purposes than its own. It exists as something to be experienced in order to discover the possibilities its existence offers. Metaphysically considered, the world is very much like what children, poets, and the man in the street take it to be—something out of which something can be made; and to make something out of it is what everything in it seems bent on doing, from atoms to man. Nature is not a creation, but the challenge and the opportunity to create. She is the enemy of nothing. She is like a God who loves all his children equally, in order to show his love unequal only as the impulse to create extends wider and wider. We may well remember the words of Aristotle: "Even the stone would become a doorstep; and all things strive after the divine."

Such a philosophy may be lightly dismissed as childish and poetic. But there are children and poets in the world as well as hydrogen. It may be condemned as anthropomorphic. Old Xenophanes is credited with the remark: "If oxen and lions had hands and could paint, oxen would paint gods as oxen, and lions as lions." He forgot the important matter, namely, that neither oxen nor lions have hands. They do not paint. He who has hands and can paint is a man. And who dares affirm that oxen and lions exist in order to cheapen men? This childish and poetic philosophy is of that kind which has always quickened and inspirited the strivings of men. And I often wonder why some of us seem to be uncomfortable when confronted with the childlike and poetic. It is not, however, because this philosophy is childlike and poetic that I turn to it. It is because it impresses me as grounded in the nature of things. What I have here expressed in poetic language, could also be expressed in language which would sound scientific. But the language which sounds scientific does not reach to the full extent of man's nature. The birds can be scientifically analyzed. Still they sing. They are machines, if we will; but they are singing machines, and he who forgets the singing has not discovered what birds naturally and really are.

I believe that naturalism is a good philosophy for mankind. To have a philosophy of some sort belongs to the nature of man. When, however, we consider the leading nations and peoples of the present world, what do we find? Do they see eye to eye? Are they at one in the desire to honour man and to care for him? Have they the same respect for him as they have for chemistry? Has the modern world a vision, like that of Christendom, which can inspire men even when they depart from it and sin against it? Perhaps some will say yes. There is democracy, there is socialism, there is communism, there is capitalism, there is fascism. But what do these names name? Surely not ideals of human life, but different methods of administration. There is no doubt that our happiness and well-being are bound up with methods of administration, but there is also no doubt that the successful carrying through of any method depends, not on its character, but on the character of its administrators. Communism as well as capitalism can ruin mankind. One can not overlook the fact that the modern world cries to heaven for a strong, orderly, and wise administration. With that which is current we have not gone very far. We are suffering from eccentricities, fears, and egotisms. We are suffering from the common human failing of blaming others for our own negligence. Mankind always suffers when it has neither a religion nor a philosophy to quicken and inspire.

> Das Wahre war schon längst gefunden,
> Hat edle Geisterschaft verbunden,
> Das alte Wahre, fass es en.

Yes, we suffer from administration and from conditions which are socially, politically, and economically extraordinarily complicated. But who can be so foolish as to believe that any administration can be invented which will automatically free men once for all from suffering? We must hold fast to the old truth. Human salvation lies in inspiration, in a conception of the nature of man, which rises above his daily life to become its ideal and its judge. Man must see something in the sky, which illuminates his earthly pilgrimage and criticizes it.

What can a man see in the sky? A naturalistic philosophy should teach that he can see all that the astronomer sees through his telescope and elaborates with the help of mathematics. But that is not all. He can also see how the sky affects his sensibility—the impression of infinity upon infinity, the consequent lifting and humbling of his spirit, the impulse to reflect and reflect until he feels himself incorporated in the whole, the consequent awakening in him of the suspicion that his life is committed, committed to possibilities which reach far beyond his daily joys and sorrows, hopes and fears—he can see that it is this kind of seeing that makes him a man, and reveals to him what it really means to live with other men and to live with nature. Looking through a telescope is not the only valid experience which nature allows. Spiritual experience is also an experience of nature, and it is this experience alone which quickens and inspires living. So should naturalism teach when it tries to be a philosophical guide to mankind.

Perhaps I should say something about the practical applications of a philosophy like this. But I have thought, that on this occasion an expression of my philosophical point of view would be expected. I can bring this together in a sentence: It has become impossible for me to believe, that a world in which perceiving and thinking and longing actually exist as facts can be a world which must be philosophically divided because these facts exist in it. So far as practice is concerned, I will emphasize only the obvious. We should learn from what our experience of nature is. That is our duty. It is a real duty, because our inclination is to have experiences, instead of learning from them. Really to learn involves the setting aside of what is visionary or deceptive or only egotistical. It involves the sustained criticism of life in the presence of life's emergencies. I venture to use the war as the best example that could today be chosen.

With good reasons we speak of it as the World War. That means something far deeper than the fact that nearly all the peoples of the world became involved in it. It means that through the war we have all had a profound common experience which should teach us something about the needs of the modern man. Historians may search for the causes of the war. That is undoubtedly interesting and important. But what the war has to teach does not depend upon its causes. Causes concern its beginning, but not its end. In 1914, the observer asked, who started the war and why, who would be victor and what would the victor gain? In 1918, where were observers to be found? Then the question was: To what purpose? The nations feared not only each other, they were afraid of themselves. How could this terrible disease be brought to an end? How could the exhausted nations recover? Such were the great questions. They remain the great questions still. When they are forgotten, the terrible disease again threatens. To be sure the war revealed the rivalry and self-seeking of the nations, but there was no need of a war to reveal that. That we knew well enough without seeking a proof of it. The important thing which the war revealed was that rivalry and self-seeking of nations are things unsuited to modern times and to modern life. The war showed that they are antiquated. Against them are arrayed the forces of our time, which are daily growing and which will control in the end. That dreadful and common experience has demonstrated that the claims of men have passed far beyond the claims of nations, and that the nations must change their mode of thinking if they are to save and to serve the modern world.

This is easy to say and it is often said. Men dreamed long ago of a parliament of the world, but it has been of a parliament that they have dreamed. Is it really any longer possible to believe that a parliament like those of the past is really suited to our needs? If we would learn from the experience of the war and from its consequences, we should begin with men. We should go from the home to the nation and not from the nation to the home. I do not doubt that questions of national boundaries, national armies, national navies and national security are weighty questions, but I doubt much more whether these are the questions with which the modern world should begin or which concern its permanent good. We are afraid of another war. But is it not worth while to ask if it is not really dangerous to let the opposition between war and peace be the determining principle of our thinking and planning? Shall we discuss the carrying of guns when we sit around a table? We should think of other things, of labour, of business, of education, of the nature of man. What advantage does the modern world get from victory or defeat? The victors may easily go to ruin and the defeated become a sore. The war has clearly shown that labour, business, and education are the things on which the welfare of the modern world depends. These are the things which are determining more and more the internal and external policy of the nations. The history of mankind has brought us to this position, and the war has made this movement of history clear. It was a terrible experience, but it ought not to be profitless to have had it. We should not think in terms of having it again, but in terms of its lessons. This is what philosophy should teach. But it should be taught inspired by an ideal of human life which like a vision, will reveal that labour, business, and education are good, because through them man comes nearer to what he calls divine. And to be divine is not to conquer other men or even nature. It is to honour both.

A new world—that we would gladly have. The forces of our time are bent on having it. These forces have their source not in political theories, but in the occupations and needs of human life. Mankind will have a new world. Its will is set upon this with increasing clearness and increasing power. But what kind of a new world? Shall philosophy sit still and leave mankind to be enticed by all sorts of administrative theories, theories which encourage the hope that, through their adoption, we shall automatically come to happiness and salvation? Shall philosophy not rather teach that no administration can be successful if it is not inspired by a consciousness of the natural destiny of man which reveals that human life is a commitment, that nature has so determined it, because she has disclosed in man what can be made out of her adaptability? In man she has revealed what her forces can accomplish; in him she has become visible; in him she has become knowable; in him she has awakened the desire to bring his life to a consummation which justifies itself and over which a God might rejoice. In him she has fostered the belief that life itself is a demand and a need of nature. These are the foundations on which philosophy should build.

What should we believe? The voice of Fichte still speaks. It summons us to consider our character and our destiny, and to believe that these can never be divorced from the character and destiny of nature at large. They go together; and in the hearty acceptance of their going together is to be found the quickening of the human spirit.

THE UNIVERSE OF LIGHT*

Sir William Bragg has given to a book on optics a brilliant title, *The Universe of Light*.[1] The opening sentences of the first chapter are these: "Light brings us the news of the Universe. Coming to us from the sun and the stars it tells us of their existence, their positions, their movements, their constitutions and many other matters of interest. Coming to us from objects that surround us more nearly it enables us to see our way about the world: we enjoy the forms and colours that it reveals to us, we use it in the exchange of information and thought." The reader's attention is then called to the rightful and reasonable extension of the meaning of the word "light" to cover the wide range of invisible radiations, the great conveyor of energy from place to place, radio transmission, Röntgen rays, rays from radio-active substances, and, possibly, cosmic rays.

> These greatly differing phenomena are all manifestations of one principle, the magnificent inclusiveness of which has grown clearer continuously as we have studied the nature of light. . . . Even the atoms themselves seem to fall, in certain aspects, within the same great category. Light, therefore, using the full meaning of the word, transmits energy which is the mainstay of life, and gives to living beings the power of observation: and it is akin to the matter of which all things animate and inanimate are made. The universe is its sphere of action. We do it no more than justice when we speak of the Universe of Light.

Clearly we do it no less, if light is a principle of such magnificent inclusiveness. After reading the book, however, I am prompted to ask whether it should be read in the light of the title or the title read in the light of the book? What is it tha

* In the *Journal of Philosophy*, Vol. XXXI (1934), pp. 15-21. Read at the meeting of the Eastern Branch of the American Philosophical Association, Amherst College, December, 1933.

[1] New York, Macmillan Company, 1933. xi + 283 pp.

has been illuminated and made clearer and more understandable, the universe or the messenger that brings us the news of it? Is the book about the messenger or does it contain his message, in part, at least? If the latter, what then is the universe like? The book leads me to ask these questions, and not this book alone, but books on light generally. Sir William's book, by its suggestiveness and his competence, has made them more interesting than ever. I do it and him, I hope, no injustice by using it as a text for comment.

This particular book is chiefly about the messenger's way of travelling. It is essentially an introduction to optics for the general reader and is a revision and enlargement of the Christmas Lectures of 1931, given at the Royal Institution by the author, under the same title.

> I have taken as the thread of my story [Sir William writes in the Preface] that old rivalry between two theories of light which has been one of the most powerful contributions to the development of science. The corpuscle and the wave, associated always with the names, respectively, of Newton and Huygens, have each in turn seemed to be finally victorious. The struggle is ending in a manner as unexpected as it is illuminating. There is to be a reconcilement of hypotheses which we had thought to be mutually exclusive; and the fact warns us of the danger of allowing our mental imaginings to become fixed beliefs. We still find it difficult to understand how these two theories can both be true; yet we are forced to do so by the mass of good evidence which can be brought forward in support of each of them. We conclude that what at one time may be beyond our understanding may later become clear, not only through the acquisition of fresh knowledge, but also by the training of our minds to new ways of thought.

A theory of the way a messenger travels may have little to do with the news he brings. The radio brings us news from the ends of the earth, but a theory of radio transmission would hardly be that news. There is considerable difference between the way a messenger goes from one place to another and the message he brings. This seems to be conspicuously true in the case of light. Whether it travels by way of wave or corpuscle or by way of both together, its message, at least for those who see, is that the visible world is the chief object and source of all their knowledge. In this world light and darkness alternate, and it is easy to think of light travelling in it and dispelling the darkness, although, since Aristotle, we have been repeatedly cautioned about thinking so. Professor Bridgman has said that "light as a thing travelling must be recognized as a pure invention."[2] Yet it is natural to think of light as travelling, for lamps, when lit, seem so evidently to send out their light, mirrors reflect it, prisms refract it, and lenses focus it. The lantern to our feet carries its horizon of illumination along as we walk. Shadows fall. There are opaque bodies through which light does not seem to pass. Something that travels, although we never see the traveller, is a conception of light difficult to avoid when we consider the behaviour of a lighted world. It is, however, the conception of something not identified. The distinction between what we ordinarily call light and darkness is like the distinction between day and night, one which does not reveal an agent which makes the difference, unless the agent be something like the sun or other glowing or radiant bodies. They are not the light of theory. We are consequently forced, in dealing with light as something that travels, to deal with it indirectly, not with it itself, but with its manner of travelling. Does it travel like a projectile or like a wave? Hence the rival theories and the current attempt to reconcile them. This is the story th book tells.

One can not read the story, even in the condensed form i which Sir William relates it, without being profoundly im pressed by the brilliancy and skill shown by those who hav contributed to it. Here is one of the masterpieces of moder physics. Can I be pardoned the apparently impudent questio What is it all about? I intend no impudence. I was once co tent with the answer that it is all about light, but am no longe content, and the more I read, the less content I am. My ac miration for the intellectual skill which has marked the deve opment of the theory and the remarkable experimental ver fication of deductions from it is greater than it was when took my first lessons in it years ago. I do not put such ma ters in question. What I have seen done before my eyes an read in books written by responsible men is too evident to b

[2] *The Logic of Modern Physics.* New York, Macmillan Co., 1927, p. 153.

gainsaid. It is the success of the theory which baffles me—the success attained by dealing with modes of travel without an identifiable traveller. A projectile that flies through the air like a bullet from a gun, the movement of waves in a pan of water, the impact upon balls in series, and all the many means, aided by mathematical calculations, which are used in building up the theory, make clearer and clearer modes of travel, but obscurer and obscurer the traveller itself. My knowledge of corpuscular and wave propagation increases, but as knowledge of light it is like knowledge of a light that never was on sea or land. The Light, the light that warrants our speaking of the Universe of Light, although it remains unidentified as corpuscle or wave or both somehow together, is that which reveals that there is a visible world accessible to observation and experiment. Its actuality is declared by the alternation of day and night and by opening and closing the eyes. It is that which brings us news of the universe.

If the news, or part of it, is optics, what then is the universe? The answer seems to me to be this: it is something whose framework, when we attempt to model or conceive it, is modelled and conceived in an optical way. In other words, if optics is news, then models, maps, plans, patterns, designs, systems, or conceptions of what the universe is like, as containing all that is, are bound to be of a sort which an observer might possibly see. Otherwise considerations of shape, size, distance, position, motion, orbit, and the like seem to lose meaning. Space seems to disappear. If it is characteristic of the universe that the angle of incidence equals the angle of reflection, the model must be congruent with that principle. If we consider whether the universe is contracting or expanding, whether it is limited or unlimited, it is an optical model which gives point to the consideration. In short, if optics is valid news, then models and conceptions of the universe are formed in terms of an optical system. The universe, whatever else it may be, is optical.

The acceptance of this conclusion raises many interesting questions. I would mention a few of them. One of them is the sort of question Professor Royce dealt with in his *World and the Individual.* I ask it with reference to the conclusion just reached. What is to be said of a system or universe which is delineated and conceived in an optical way? Any answer to this question seems to me to be, in principle, like Professor Royce's answer, irrespective of the particular use he made of it. Modelling and conceiving such a system in optical terms are themselves determinations or delineations of what such a system is. This strikes me as both obvious and profound. It is obvious that optical systems are thought of in optical terms, angles in terms of angles, distances in terms of distance, positions in terms of position, and so on. The repetitions and correspondences which are therein involved, make it impossible, however, to limit and frame the system itself in terms of angles, distances, positions, and so on. Such terms are limited in their application in such a way that they are not applicable to the system itself. This is, perhaps, profound. We are dealing with a system which, if delineated at all, must be delineated in terms of optical models which its character imposes, but which are not replicas of that character. These models cannot be placed side by side with the system and then compared. They serve in exploring the system, but they do not embrace it. This does not mean that the system is so vast that no model can embrace it, nor that it is greater than any conceivable model. It means rather that optical frameworks are in the system, but the system is not in any framework at all. Space is in it, but it is not in space.

From this conclusion, another seems to follow, namely, that there can be in the universe no uniquely privileged observer, no observer, that is, who can compare what he observes with the universe itself. Although light brings us the news, it does not send it. The difference is considerable. The acknowledged and evident effect of its coming is its message and that message is not about a transmitting station which we might occupy and then observe whether the message received was the one intended to be sent. Optics forbids such a privileged station. Why, then, I would rhetorically ask, attempt to construe the universe as if there were a uniquely privileged observer somewhere? If there is no such observer, why suppose that optical perspectives are anything else than necessities of an optical system? Why imagine that the intellectual extension of the terms of delineation like straight line, angle, rotation, etc., reveals what such an observer would see if there were one? Why suppose that the universe can be spatial without at the same time being optically instrumented? I leave the questions in their rhetorical form. If optics is news that the universe is optical, it seems to me to be quite superfluous to try to get back of the news and find an observer who can tell us whether the news is correct. It seems futile to ask what the news would be for an observer independent of the types of the optical behaviour of an optical world.

Taking optics, then, to be news of the universe, I would venture to amend one of the sentences quoted from Sir William Bragg's book. Speaking of light he says: "The universe is its sphere of action." I would say: Its sphere of action is the universe. Light acts; then the universe is a sphere whose centre is anywhere and whose circumference is nowhere. Hence space as optically determined, hence the inevitability of optical models and frameworks without an embracing framework, and hence the absence of a uniquely privileged observer.

Light brings us other news besides that of a universe optically instrumented or schematized. "Coming to us from the sun and the stars, it tells us of their existence, their movements, their constitutions and many other matters of interest." It lights up the universe, makes it visible at least in part, revealing that there are sun and stars in the sky, and minerals, plants, and animals on the earth. Perhaps this kind of news is not the more important, but it is certainly the kind which most absorbs our attention. It is a dramatic kind of news, as if light were exhibiting what it can do to waves and corpuscles by illuminating modes of travel. Then there is splendour and scenery to behold and the drama of life and death. One ought not to expect to find this vision in a book on optics, but books on optics rarely fail to mention it. Vision is too evidently the major consequence of letting light be. Without this consequence we should never speak of a universe of light or of getting news of the sun's existence; books on optics would never be written. The books do vision no more than justice by making at least a bow.

What this particular book says about vision, I have found

perplexing and exciting. It says the usual thing, but not in the usual way. The usual thing is that there is a device in the eye "which gathers together the waves coming from each and every external point, and converges them upon a corresponding point on the retina. Thus all the details of the view are impressed upon the retina in their proper places relative to one another, and each with its proper character. The whole is then referred to the brain by way of a complicated system of nerves, and is there interpreted" (p. 38). If this were all, it would be the usual thing, leaving the question open whether the "interpretation" is vision. But light as a news-bringer is constantly stressed and stressed in such a way that I can not regard the expression as a pretty metaphor. "When light enters the eye it brings news of the source from which it has come, and of its experiences on the way. In particular it tells of the last encounter with a material object before entry into the eye, and so enables the owner of the eye to 'see' that object" (p. 38). Such expressions make it hard for me to identify vision with an interpretation in the brain. I can think of light as informing the brain that there is a sun in the sky, but I find it difficult to think of the brain as seeing a sun in the sky. And I should find it just as difficult if I substituted for "brain," "mind" or "consciousness" or "soul."

I find this difficult because I must believe that eyes and not brains are the organs of seeing, just as ears and not brains are the organs of hearing. Consequently, to identify interpretation in the brain, or in the mind, with vision seems to me to be curiously unintelligible. I say curiously unintelligible because such identification would involve either vision without eyes or the reversal of the process which generated the interpretation, going back to the retina, through the lens and ending with that last encounter of light with a material object before entry into the eye. In the latter case, it would seem as if the brain looked back over the course by which light had come to it, and looked back not with the eye, but through it. Newton[3] thought that God had vision without eyes and Molyneux[4] exclaimed: "He that made the eye shall see!" It

[3] *Optics,* Queries 28, 31.
[4] *Dioptrica Nova,* Part I, Prop. 28.

is, perhaps, possible that a being having vision without eyes could make them, but he could hardly make them in order to see. That would be a little ridiculous. If, however, he lived in a world where eyes were necessary for vision, it would not be surprising if he invented a microscope. I can readily accept brains without a visible world, but I can not similarly accept eyes. And it is neither brains nor eyes that make the world visible, but the light itself. So far as I can make out, all that the brain does with the help of the eye is to co-ordinate our activities in an optical world made visible by the light. It is that world that is interpreted and not a nervous disturbance in the brain.

Accordingly, with little reservation and with possible misconstruction, I can repeat the words: "When light enters the eye it brings news of the source from which it has come, and of its experiences on the way. In particular it tells of the last encounter with a material object before entry into the eye, and so enables the owner of the eye to 'see' that object." Yes: the man who has eyes and brain sees the visible world, but that world quite evidently is not in his eye, or in his brain, or in his "mind." It is in the light.

AN APPROACH TO THE THEORY OF NATURE*

WESTERN philosophers have inherited from ancient Greece the idea of theories of nature. They were prevented by the course of history from discovering it themselves and from using a language of their own for its approximate expression. They have employed Greek words which expressed thoughts often novel to them and have spent no small part of their time in trying to find out what the words they use really mean, for the domestication of an alien speech is difficult. The Greeks seem to have been more fortunate. Their language had attained remarkable transparency in the social use of it before it was turned to professedly intellectual purposes. They knew what they meant before they understood it and considered understanding to be the development of their ordinary knowledge into a comprehensive view of it. This came to be called θεωρία and Aristotle could think of the theoretical life as not unlike the life of a god who beholds existence without interfering with it. *Theory* is thus a Greek word and its exaltation to such a height is a fine example of the passage of a word from social to philosophical usage, from the theatre to the study and the laboratory. So it passed in Greek. A spectator at a play and the spectator of existence were kinsmen in attitude. Detached from what they beheld, they had a clearer and more comprehensive view of it than would be possible otherwise. Could a man see the spectacle of existence as he sees a play in a theatre, he might understand what existence is, get the gist of it and in the moment of that beholding be like a god who sees the world wag, but keeps himself aloof. To know what theory is, a Greek had only to go to a theatre. To make the

* Howison Memorial Lecture, given at the University of California, Berkeley, California, February 8, 1935.

world a stage and behold atoms playing in the void, or earth, water, air, and fire, those well-known levels of existence, playing with one another true to their characters, was to attain the theoretical vision. A boy or girl in school today, studying Euclid's geometry and seeing how figures drawn with rule and compass illustrate the control of principles, may see what a theory is without being told and get a glimmering of that theoretical life which can make a man forget that he is human.

The Greeks, in spite of an abundant egotism, did not normally forget their humanity. Aristotle had something to say about the effect of going to the theatre upon the spectators. The moment of divine aloofness with its cleansing of laughter and tears or of pity and fear is followed by a return to existence shared with others. Only God can keep his isolation intact and serene. Men must work, get on with one another, and manage cities. Perhaps they can do all this better after they have had the theoretical vision. At least they ought to understand better what they are about and be wise about it instead of foolish. They can get on without the vision just as they can get on without the theatre, but it is unlikely that they will get on as well. Men may know how to run a city as they want to, but they may run it better if they understand what a city is. Men can not help knowing nature because, like plants and animals, they live with it the whole course of their lives, but they may live better if they understand what nature is.

Nature is not a Greek word, so it is idle to ask what the Greeks meant by the use of it. We may use it, however, to indicate what they would comprise in a complete theoretical vision. This was no less than what was contained within the familiar horizon of their daily lives, earth and sky with all that goes on within the sphere they ostensibly form. To the going-on they gave the name of *φύσις* to express their knowledge that the going-on is energetic and productive, a growth of things from what they once were to what they eventually become, a tireless coming and going within an horizon which could be identified by looking at it. To look at it with theoretical detachment was to have a theory of nature.

This idea of a theory of nature with which the influence of Greek thought has had so much to do, might conceivably be entertained independent of that influence. That is conceivable, but it has not happened in the western world. Subsequent philosophers accepted it, acknowledging its source and its possible independent character. They too would have a theory of nature, believing it to be admirable in itself and calculated to make a man wise. They too would turn the intimate knowledge they have of earth and sky gained by living on the one and under the other into an understanding of it all by means of a vision as complete as attainable. They would turn the vision of the eye into a vision of the mind, for a better understanding of what goes on under the sun.

Since the day of John Locke, however, philosophers have been increasingly critical of the idea of a theory of nature. They have called in question both its character and its validity. That peculiar detachment which the theory suggests is very equivocal. Attentively regarded, it looks too theatrical, for, whereas a man may, by looking at a play without acting in it, gain an understanding of its plot, he can not look at nature in like fashion. Here he is both actor and spectator and his detachment is, therefore, illusory. This he may forget and then he presents the ridiculous spectacle of trying to fashion a world suited to his own eventual appearance in it. He becomes a theologian without knowing it, sporting with the doctrine of creation. Many theories of nature look like that, attempts to create a world ready for the appearance of man. Obviously divine detachment is impossible and no man can frame a theory of nature free from attention to his own existence. He only deludes himself when he tries. Philosophers have also questioned the validity of that familiar knowledge of earth and sky with what they contain which we normally accept without any question at all. They have found in it something confusing, deceptive, and superficial. It concerns only the surface of existence and does not penetrate to its depths. This surface is at best a useful symbol of what lies beneath it and at the worst the soul's dream of its own career. Our existence is a veiled existence and unless that veil is penetrated or torn away, all our knowledge rests upon uncertain foundations.

In view of such difficulties, the matter of the approach to a theory of nature has become increasingly important. In spite of the difficulties, it is not likely that men will drop the enterprise. One can not imagine them continuing to live without trying to understand the world in which they live. Defeat does not stop them. Doubt does not stop them from writing books with titles like *The Universe around Us*, *Mind and the World Order, Process and Reality, The Universe of Light,* nor does it stop readers from reading such books in the hope of finding their persistent questions answered. The Greeks may have started the fashion, but it is not because they started it that we keep it up. And we keep it up because we are alive and not dead. There is no other reason at all for keeping it up. Because we go from here to there, because we breathe, digest, and reproduce, because we look up at the stars and dig down into the earth, because we remember and plan, because we build schools and churches, because we set up governments and try to make living secure—because we *do* all this, we are impelled to try to understand it. If we did not want to see the other side of the mountain and know that by climbing we could do it, there never would be a theory of nature at all. No amount of argument, no accumulation of doubt, and no repetition of failure can alter that obvious and inescapable fact. Why not then, I ask myself, approach a theory of nature from emphasis on this evident fact of life and not from an emphasis on doubt, perplexity, and possible illusion? Can we leave life out of nature and then expect to understand what nature is? Can we turn the generator of all our problems itself into a problem and hope to say anything sensible? Have philosophers ever said anything sensible about it when they have made that turning? Not making it is not immunity from follies, but it can be a prophylactic.

I would suggest, then, that the fruitful approach to a theory of nature is from an initial emphasis on life. By "life" I mean that evident and explorable organization of our activities which makes us out as individuals who are born and die, who eat and reproduce, rejoice and suffer, hope and fear, see and hear, accept and reject, affirm and deny, and try to gain an understanding of the world in which all this is done. I mean, consequently, nothing obscure or hypothetical, no "vital principle" invoked to explain why bodies live and behave as they do. Nor do I mean a "consciousness" which is put into them to make them aware of what they do, for what they do and their awareness of it are interwoven; they are not like two things that can be taken apart or put together or laid the one on top of the other. Their consciousness is an exhibition of their life fully as much as their digestion is. When we insist on difficulties about consciousness and ask for reasons for doing what we do, we should remember that it is no less difficult and just as unreasonable to digest a sandwich as it is to see the moon. With emphasis on life in the concrete and evident sense, the distinction between ourselves and nature is equally concrete and evident. By living we are factually distinguished within a common context from the houses in which we live, the gardens we cultivate, and the stars at which we look. They and their companions are our environment and are nature as distinct from us, but they and we together, in the intimate interplay between ourselves and our environment, are nature as comprehending both them and us. We are of a piece with nature, not beings put into it from outside, nor beings with something put inside of us to help us get outside of our skins. Outside of our skins are those houses and gardens and stars and we never get at them by getting outside of our skins, but by going about among them in our skins. It is this evident and acknowledged fact of being living individuals, distinguished from their environment and yet united with it in intimate interplay, communion, and communication, that I would suggest as the basal fact from which a theory of nature should start. Here and nowhere else is the situation which generates theories of nature. Its initial acknowledgement, free from underpinning or overloading, is crucial and entitled to the highest respect.

Emphasis on this situation is not simply an arbitrary or capricious return to the Greek attitude. It need not be neglectful of philosophical criticism. The long subjection of theories of nature to an initial criticism of knowledge has, doubtless, been good for them, for by effectively exhibiting the limitations of that criticism, it has made philosophers more sensitive to the obligations they owe to those who explore nature untroubled by epistemology, and by pointing out how easy is the road to scepticism, it has had some influence in making those happy others less confident in their dogmatism. To be critical of the manner in which we build up systems of the world is to exhibit an intellectual virtue. It is only when the attempt is made to set knowledge at a distance from life and make it its own object that theories of knowledge become theories of nothing at all. A theory of nature and a theory of knowledge may well go hand in hand, for the employment of life for enlarged and more penetrating views of that with which life is employed is an exercise of life's possibilities under conditions which control that exercise. Thereby seeing is made better and farther seeing without ceasing to be seeing, and the discovery of nature is enlarged without discovery ceasing to be discovery or nature ceasing to be nature, for nature understood is no less nature than nature not understood any more than nature dry is less nature than nature wet. Growing into an understanding of what nature is, surely seems to be the attainment of a natural status fully as much as growing into a plant or an animal.

Throwing initial emphasis on life seems, therefore, to have the promise of keeping the theory of knowledge and the theory of nature together. The difference between them would not be a difference in subject-matter, but a difference in attention. The exhibition of the principles which govern the understanding in attempting to gain a comprehensive view of nature would be a theory of knowledge. It would also be a theory of nature because those principles would exhibit characters of nature by which the understanding is governed and without which the attempt to understand would not itself be understood. Understanding, being as natural a performance as any other, would derive its comprehensiveness from those features of nature which are comprehensive, like space, time, and communication. In this respect a theory of nature and a theory of knowledge would be well-nigh indistinguishable. A theory of this kind would be an initial discipline which might help to keep our wayward speculations in wholesome check, and enable us to distinguish between vision and the visionary.

But is all this more than a seeming? I think something by way of answer may be had from a consideration of some of the motives and consequences of throwing initial emphasis on knowledge, as if knowing were not a living exercise, but a supplement to life in need of critical examination before it can be exercised with confidence. I recall Descartes doubting that he had a living body, yet certain that he thought, and Locke, certain that he had experience, yet throwing doubt on his own account of it. Both men are typical in contrasted ways of elevating what is usually called epistemology to a position of both initial and final importance. They have had many followers. I recall many declarations like the following: We don't know what matter is, we know it only as it appears to us; we don't know the external world in its terms, we know it only in terms of our experience. I recall the pitting of nature and human nature over against each other—man and nature with knowledge a possible link between them; I the knower here, and yonder the to-be-known, and the wonder how I can go to it or it can come to me; soul and body, mind and the world order, subject and object and the former trying to know the latter; knowledge set at a distance and nature set at a distance, with a knowledge called upon to shorten the distance.

The motives for these recurring dichotomies are many and varied. They are also illusive. I find it difficult to be sure of them in many individual cases. One thing is, however, clear. Modern philosophy has given to epistemology a prominent professional status, and modern science and modern psychology have supported it in doing so. Without epistemology, many a philosopher would have little to do. If the professional motive is dismissed, we seem to be thrown back upon two basic considerations, first, the intensity of personal existence, and, secondly, the imposing character of modern physics. Often these two motives supplement each other. Reflection on our individual isolation makes us sensitive to it and the picture which modern physics has drawn of its world has imposed itself upon many as the correct picture of what nature really is, at least in its essential features. The picture gives us a world so different from that which is known by living, that what is physical and what is cognitive seem to have equivocal commerce with each other. The two tables, for example, with which Professor Eddington begins his much read book, stare each other in the face, so to speak, but without mutual recognition. The stars of the astronomer do not go to school, but we do. The heavens do not declare the glory of God unless we worship him. The nature which is a matter of energy and the nature which is a matter of life and death present a contrast like that between the natural and the supernatural; the one is and ought to be, the other also is, but ought not to be. Knowledge, such as we can have, is about nature, not of it, and could be taken away and nature left intact. Nature known is not an event in nature's history even if the knower as a physical body is. There is distilled in his brain the spirits of knowledge which must be temperately used if the intoxications of poetry are to be avoided. Algebra is the only sane language when nature is considered. The heavens declare equations.

Without the support of such a picture, the first or personal motive may raise problems of one's convictions or of the character of one's existence, but the isolated soul, although living in a baffling world, has discovered it to be baffling. The pure solipsist doubts neither his own existence nor that of others, if existence is defined to his liking. He admits existence on condition that there is an owner of it and that such ownership is impenetrable. Being an owner is not a matter of knowledge, but of being, and an owner's knowledge is knowledge of what he owns. It can not be defined in terms of anything else. So far as knowledge is concerned, the pure solipsist gets on as well as anybody else. Indeed, he may get on better, for he sees his stars in his sky and his astronomy is immediately relevant to his celestial possessions and can be talked about with his fellows, only stars and sky and astronomy and fellows and talking are all his possessions and not the conspirators of his existence. He is in the happy ownership of his world even if he is lonesome in enjoying it.

It is not worth wasting even solipsistic time in trying to refute such an ontology. The pure solipsist has done no more than discover a principle which every theory of nature is forced to contain, namely, that individual existence is the definition of an exclusive environment. This is so all the way from atoms to men; each has its own sphere of existence, which it neither gives nor takes. In that sense each is impenetrable. Surely our understanding of nature is in part the recognition of this and, untroubled by epistemology, we know it even if we know no more. It is, however, to know a good deal, for the illuminating power of the principle is illustrated in many ways. Without it the integers could not be marshalled in a theory of numbers, nor could anything be measured. Obviously one could not travel from New York to San Francisco, if the two cities had identical environments. Monadologies may be marred by the invention of many a fairy tale, but it is clear that the structure of nature admits a monadological principle.

Some appreciation of the extent and significance of the principle may be gained from even a moment's consideration of space. Here exclusive environment rigorously prevails. It was long ago expressed in apparently axiomatic fashion by saying that two bodies can not occupy the same space at the same time. If, however, we let that "at the same time" imply that they could occupy the same place at different times, we have been beguiled by the old example of filling and emptying a pitcher with its suggestion that where the water once was, there is now air. Placements and displacements are obvious enough. We know that we can fill and empty pitchers. But transform that knowledge into theory in an attempt to understand space, then it becomes clear that space can not be the environment of anything at all. It is not, like a pitcher, something that can be filled or emptied or something that can be placed or displaced. Nature exhibits the principle of exclusive environment so rigorously that to nature an environment of its own is irrelevant. Different times only emphasize the fact, for no life is long enough to find out what it means to say that either space or nature are today where they were yesterday. Pitchers may be here and there, now and then, and sometimes filled and sometimes empty, because of the relevancy of an environment. Without such relevancy there is neither here and there, nor now and then, nor plenums and vacuums. We are more familiar with this today than we were a few years ago, familiar with the identification of space with that natural integration of frames of reference whereby it is possible to pass from one to the other both in fact and in calculation. That integration has no resemblance whatever to a pitcher and is not at all a place in which we move about. So the theorist of nature may thank the solipsist for the latter's dogged adherence to an illuminating principle, the only principle which gives to the affirmation that space is infinite an intelligible meaning. The infinity of space is what having an environment amounts to. It is not a place without boundaries, which lets nature expand or contract, to dissipate itself into a gas or congeal into a frozen lump of matter. The possibilities of space theoretically beheld in terms of what observed displacements involve are of a wholly different sort. They are the possibilities of measurement and calculation and of the discovery and invention of optical instruments which enlarge the vision of the eye into a better understanding of what it is to be living and seeing beings. In the light of that better understanding we may acknowledge our eyes to be organs and instruments of vision without supposing that they work in order that we may see. To suppose that is like supposing that microscopes work in order that things may look larger than they are, or that a camera works in order that we may take photographs.

The fact that that evident and daily acknowledged world in which I personally live, is, in a very genuine sense, mine and not another's impresses me, not as a riddle requiring some ingenious solution, but as a circumstance typical of all existence. I can not think of nature free from it. I look out of my window and up the street exposed to the vision of my eyes, with automobiles stationed on either side and people moving to and fro. It is my vision of a part of nature and

I know well enough that a vision of nature is had in no other way. I know well enough that I can change that vision of mine by going out and walking up that street, by moving about as I see others moving about. Just now, as I write, and fortunately for my illustration, a fog has obscured that street, those cars, and those people, but I know that it has not destroyed them, for I have learned by a thousand repeatable experiments that there is co-operation between my vision and what goes on in its field. It is the development of this co-operation which constitutes my understanding of nature. All this seems to me to be so unmistakably so that I can not think of nature otherwise than as a system diversified after the manner in which I find it to be diversified. I can not think of it as a system initially irrelevant to what my appearance in it is like. It is diversification and co-operation that brings the fog and clears it away, and it is diversification and co-operation which brings me to knowledge and understanding.

Did our solipsisms and monadologies assert no more than this, they would not wear the extravagant appearance which they so often exhibit. They would not shut us up as knowing and understanding beings in windowless compartments looking at pictures magically painted on opaque walls, and deluded into thinking that what is there beheld is an external world. Then the principle of exclusive environment becomes something quite different from a characteristic of nature's operations.

The personal, individual, and centralized character of our experience can not, therefore, be intelligibly regarded as something so exceptional and unique that it defines either a problem of being or a problem of knowledge. It defines rather a fact of being generally and in our own case a fact out of which the knowledge and understanding of our environment grows. Personally, I can not escape that conclusion. It is for me verified by everything that we do and especially by our attempts to systematize and order our explorations of that environment. I can not see, for example, how a problem of being or knowledge is generated when we survey a tract of land and make a map of it, so long as we fix our attention on the procedure involved in doing so simple a thing. Further, I must regard that procedure as typical of all our attempts to increase our knowledge and understanding of the world in which we live. And further, if we go beyond this perfectly familiar procedure, which is so characteristic of our living, and create problems of being and knowledge supposed to be antecedent or subsequent to that procedure, I do not find that knowledge and understanding of our natural environment are thereby increased. If the other side of the mountain which I climb is not the other side of it which I discover, because theories of being and knowledge make this either impossible or problematic, I must still make my map of the country as a surveyor makes it. It is surveyors and explorers and not ontologists and epistemologists who increase our knowledge and understanding of what mountains are.

Turning the natural procedure of knowing and understanding into a unique problem requires some other motive than simply the personal or, if you will, the solipsistic character of our experience. So far as modern philosophy is concerned, the principal and generally controlling motive is, as I have already indicated, the increasing prominence given to physical science in philosophical thinking. That Descartes and Locke were the distinctive personalities promoting this tendency is clear from its history. Descartes' clear and distinct recognition of the radical difference between extension and thinking, and Locke's isolation of the world of human understanding from the world of existing bodies in space, both raised the problem of the relation of thought to a world external to thought and different from it. There was little difficulty in stating the problem formally and in citing proofs of its necessity. If the physical world defined in terms of extension or of more or less solid bodies moving and colliding in space is a world exclusive of thinking, and if thinking and all that goes with it is in its own terms exclusive of the physical world, then there is clearly a problem of how the physical world can be known. Physical science, however, was evidence that the external physical world is in some sense known. Experiment supported the discoveries of physicists in a manner too imposing to be overlooked. The evidence, however, only widened the breach between nature and mind, because it progressively robbed nature of those traits which are vitally conspicuous in human experience. The language in which nature is described and made coherent became less and less the language in which human living is described and made coherent. And yet it was in nature that human living came into existence. Here, indeed, was a problem of magnificent proportions into the profundities of which the novice could readily be admitted by pointing out the difference between what he sees and what physical science declares about light and optics. What he sees, the blue vault of heaven above him on a sunshiny day, is not what is, but something given to him by means of which, possibly, he may come to know and understand what is.

All this with its interesting variations and the speculative systems to which it has led is a familiar story to students of modern philosophy. The whole matter has, I think, been sufficiently debated, although keeping up the debate may be pedagogically and professionally useful. The consequences are the really important consideration. When I speak of the consequences, I am not proposing a pragmatic test of the truth or validity of a theory, I am proposing rather a consideration of what the theory accomplishes. Here I would emphasize first of all the thing which is, perhaps, the most significant, namely, the complete isolation of the problem as a matter of intellectual interest. It is very much a problem by itself, having, at best, a very remote or a very artificial connection with anything else. It may be initial to all inquiry as Descartes made it, or subsequent to all inquiry as Locke made it, but in between it is irrelevant. Those amateur astronomers the country over of whom our papers now and then inform us, make their home-made telescopes and their observations untroubled by it and are typical of the rest of mankind. I look at Vega, that bright star above my head, and observing it with a telescope see two stars instead of one. Here is a problem, undoubtedly, but it is not one of the relation of what I see to what I do not see, but of one vision of the sky to another. It is solved without the help of epistemology.

Illustrations of the isolation of the theory of knowledge as that theory has been notably conceived in modern philosophy need not, I think, be multiplied. The statement of it and the way that statement is supported may make it absorbingly interesting, but were it not stated at all and were it, when stated, solved or left unsolved, it is difficult to make out how our knowledge and understanding of nature as we factually explore it to the advancement of such enterprises as astronomy, chemistry, and history, would be affected as a consequence. I will not say that there are no satisfactions in regarding the problem as fundamentally important, for history shows plainly that there are. Some attitude toward the general meaning and significance of human life in the world is sure to follow and is conspicuously revealed in the names employed to designate those attitudes. A materialist and an idealist, for example, can hardly avoid having the same chemistry, but living with one may be quite different from living with the other.

A second consequence is that the problem, in spite of its statement and the support of it, is not solved. It reduces itself to a problem between two incommensurables which can be solved only by abolishing the incommensurability. This obviously can not be done directly and we are consequently driven to try to do it indirectly. All these indirect attempts seem to me to be ultimately of the same kind. They reduce the evident and familiar world to what is now usually called the given or data and then regard the given as symbolic of what is not given, as symbolic of that reality which is responsible for our existence and which sustains us during the whole course of our lives, which was before there was knowledge and will be when knowledge is no more. The evident world of human experience, although incommensurable with nature, is yet the faith by which we live in nature, but a faith to be purged of those superstitions and errors to which we are somehow disposed by the limitations of our human powers and idiosyncrasies.

These indirect solutions do not, however, solve the problem. They only set it aside. There are excellent reasons for regarding the expansion of our knowledge and understanding as due to the symbolic office which familiar things perform. Evident nature is full of signs—the smoke which is the sign of fire, the clouds which are the sign of storm, and the cry which is the sign of pain. The co-ordination of these signs is a crucial part of what our theoretical understanding of nature is. We reduce it to language, print it in books and teach it to the young. Evident nature is, as it were, perpetually saying, "Watch your step!" But it is watching the step within evident nature, and not a step from within to without. Natural symbolism is not effective in that way. To convert evident nature as a whole into a symbol is not an extension of natural symbolism at all. We go in evident nature not only from smoke to fire, but also from fire to smoke, but although we may go in imagination from that same nature as a symbol to something else which is not a symbol at all, there is no way of getting back again. Appearance may be a symbol of reality, but reality is not a symbol of anything. That is why these indirect solutions of the problem are not solutions at all, but only the employment of an analogy in one half of its application.

A third major consequence of these epistemological theories is that when rigorously pursued, they tend increasingly to beget an ultimate scepticism about their own foundations and about all our knowledge generally. The reason is this: they create by the use of the term knowledge a demand for an intellectual possession of something which the ascertained conditions and circumstances of our natural knowing forbid our possessing, and yet base this demand on those ascertained conditions and circumstances. David Hume, if I do not misunderstand him, drew this conclusion in his own time and, if I mistake not, Santayana is drawing it again today. This philosophical scepticism is not the same thing as practical uncertainty, doubt, hesitation, or unbelief. It is rather the doctrine that our systematization of the given, of those data or that evident subject-matter of observation and experimentation, are not knowledge. To be that they would have to be of a character which the circumstances of that evident existence forbid. These circumstances are evidence that all trust in experience is something generated, temporary, incidental, and superficial. It is a gift but not the giver of the gift. Our vision of the spacious firmament on high, for example, is clearly an event; it comes and goes and implies antecedents and consequents which are not given in its own occurrence. And in general given experience is shot through and through with implications of something not given and which can not possibly be given in any given experience. We live sustained by confidence in these implications of before and after, of past and future, but without the immediacy of that which they imply. We may not doubt the existence of ancient Athens, but ancient Athens is not accessible to us who do not doubt its existence. So long as what we experience is of this kind, we must fall short of knowledge.

This is a hard doctrine. That a rigorous analysis of our own experience should be its own cognitive undoing is a doctrine I find very difficult to understand. I hope I understand what it is to be ignorant and to confess that there is much I do not know, but I find my powers of understanding are taxed to the uttermost when I try to make out what that knowledge would be of which philosophical scepticism declares we are deprived. To be ignorant of reality because the character and circumstances of my experience exclude me from knowledge of it, makes me wonder what the character and circumstances of my experience would have to be to give me that excluded knowledge. Obviously they could not be what they are. That much I can understand; and that much forces me to conclude that if I had the knowledge which could relieve me of my ultimate ignorance, I would have it wholly independent of anything that could possibly be named a human experience. I might know what such an experience is, but would not have that knowledge by means of that experience.

For my part, I must follow the philosophical sceptics in their analysis of dichotomizing theories of knowledge, and follow them to the ultimate conclusions I have just drawn. Only, I must now find in that conclusion a commentary on the motivations and procedure which lead to it. One of the things which, I think, can now be said and said with emphasis is that the expression "the external world" has ceased to identify the familiar world which we explore and has become a demand for a way of being complete and self-contained. Only such a way of being would be free from the limitations of our experience. Since it is approached by way of a criticism of knowledge, such a way of being is a demand for freedom from all error and contingency. There should be little if any surprise that this demand should be supported and approximately supplied by physical science. That science, conspicuously in the modern development of it, has more and more neglected traits of the natural world which were once regarded as eminently physical, and has concerned itself with the measurable in terms of units which can be algebraically expressed and interrelated. It is well, in speaking even today of the physical world, to remember that physics and physiology once went hand in hand, and that the terms of life no less than determinations of mass, length, and time were characteristically physical, and that the title of Newton's great book was *Principia Mathematica Philosophiae Naturalis*. Modern physicists may err and be at the mercy of many a contingency, but their science defines freedom from those obstacles. The men may err, the algebra does not. It returns true to its own forms whatever is put into it. Evident nature beheld under the form of algebra is, I imagine, much like what it would be beheld *sub specie æternitatis*.

The "external world" and also the "physical world" have become very uncertain expressions, especially when they are used to identify or indicate a sphere of being in which stars shine, plants grow and animals beget offspring, and the children of men go to school to be trained up in the way they should go. Those expressions are maximally uncertain when used to identify or indicate the source from which, by means of sense organs and a nervous system, data are given to a perceiving and thinking man, which data, although not belonging to the external physical world, are none the less the data from which that man develops his conception of what is physical and external.

This maximum uncertainty ought, I think, to turn every

philosopher into a very cautious man. It should make him very cautious about regarding that which so clearly lies before his eyes when there is light enough to see by and which for him is a vision of that region in which lie the things he feels, tastes, smells, and hears—that maximum uncertainty should make him very cautious about regarding all that world before his eyes as data for knowing a different world, a world that is physical and external. He can be cautious without being absurd. His caution need not blind him to that intellectual vision to which the way of physical science leads. He can still see, if he will try, the world before his eyes in the grip of algebra and can be thankful that it is, because to find it in that grip is to find it dependable. But I think he must insist that unless it is that world before his eyes and no other which is in that grip, that algebraic world has lost every shred of meaning. Its meaning lies in being a heightened understanding of the world before him and not a substitute for it. To speak in ancient fashion, that meaning is a part of the truth of the world before his eyes, and not a substitute for that world or the source of its energy and existence.

The exercise of this excellent caution—I must regard it as excellent—is greatly furthered by approaching a theory of nature with the primary emphasis on life and not on those difficulties about knowledge which epistemologies raise. The irrelevancy of those difficulties to the work of actual explorations, their resistance to resolution, and their issue in philosophical scepticism, are weighty reasons for adopting a different point of departure from that which they define. Nature and human nature define an intelligible contrast and even an intelligible opposition when the contrast and opposition are accepted as that daily familiar scene in which there is no mistaking the difference between our living selves and the evident horizon which surrounds them. We are not in the habit of setting a moving body over against nature as if the two were so dichotomized that the body's motion defined a region discontinuous with nature's space instead of being a sample of what that space is. Why then should we set a perceiving and thinking man over against nature as if the two were so dichotomized that his perceiving and thinking defined a region discontinuous with nature instead of being a sample of what nature is? When we do the latter, philosophical scepticism becomes inevitable because we are then forced to admit that no samples whatever of what nature is, are accessible to us. Nature then becomes a name for something that never was on sea or land, a name for something wholly irrelevant and inaccessible to knowledge.

The recognition of this impresses me as a great intellectual liberation. It has become for me convincing evidence of two conclusions. One is that the distinction between nature and human nature, if taken to be an absolute and unique dichotomy, can yield no theory of nature at all. The other is that if the distinction is not so taken, then all theories of nature find in the visible world their most conspicuous and fundamental guidance. Then nature is seen, and with that vision we proceed by all the helps at our command to explore it and systematize our explorations. We go from sense as natural to intellect as natural, from the vision of the eye to that possession which we call the vision of the mind, to that which is expressible in articulated speech and can be told to one another. We see the stars and write astronomies, we see man and write anthropologies, but both in the same evident context and both by observation and experiment, and without what we see, both our astronomies and our anthropologies would be unintelligible. Theories of nature are not the discovery of its creation. They are nature systematically understood.

I am fully aware that a declaration of this kind, stated in a manner that makes the denial of it difficult, may be regarded as childishly naïve and utterly neglectful of problems which the study of perception and logic force upon us. I admit the naïvete but deny the neglect. It is largely the study of those problems that has produced that naïvete and led me to try and see those problems in a different light. I have no doubt that theories of nature should have what may be called a philosophical introduction. They need a metaphysics; only it should come before and not after, as a discipline to keep us sane in what we do after—an examination one might say of the grounds and method of intelligibility, or a general theory of nature prior to theories of special traits. When I try to work this out with the emphasis primarily on life, those problems to which I have referred seem largely if not wholly to disappear. They seem to have not natural but artificial support. For example, I must admit like everybody else that sense organs and a nervous system are necessary to the seeing of nature and the intellectual comprehension of what is seen. But I do not see how this should make seeing nature difficult, for sense organs and nervous systems are by no means all that is necessary. Light and nature's co-operation are also necessary and so necessary that it becomes quite impossible for me to take sense organs and nervous systems out of the visible world without leaving in that world what I would see if I put them back. Our seeing is elaborately instrumented, but so also is everything that happens in nature. I can not believe that that universal instrumentation is something interposed between nature and a perceiving mind in order that perception may occur. My instrumentation and nature's are neither disparate nor supplementary. Mine is not brought to bear upon its for the purpose of making me acquainted with circumstances and conditions which underlie my life and are in any sense external to it. I must doubt the validity of using the fact of instrumentation to support a doctrine of that kind, because all the evidence goes to show that nature is instrumented through and through, that no event is free from it and that the character of the event and its instrumentation are not separable. All the evidence goes to show that, and that, as I see it, is something which a theory of nature must make fundamental. Put in terms of a concrete instance, I find only a distortion of fact in the doctrine that our vision is the end result in us of a process of optical instrumentation. It is an event in nature with which an environment diversified by light has fully as much to do as an occipital lobe of a brain, especially since the latter is not the place of that environment. I find it very difficult to think that the optical instrumentation stays in one sphere of being and, operating there, puts the vision in another.

I hope the illustration will clarify what I mean when I say that vision is living and dynamic intimacy with nature and not something like a picture remotely hung; that it is not cognitive, but that within its field are displayed objects of cognition so diversified and arranged that that arrangement and diversification become for us the source of models of an optical universe. We speak of the sphere of existence, of length, of breadth, of depth, of scope, of extension, of near and far, of large and small, and, perhaps distracted by so much geometrizing which seems to exclude so much of the evident variety, we speak of realms of being, but a light of some sort seems still to shine in every realm. Without any light anywhere—but how can any but the seeing understand such words—without any light anywhere, there might be sounds and odors and the rest, but what creature could live with them as we do or think of nature as we do, we who see the bell that rings and the flowers that yield their perfume? There is little left to nature when we rob it of what it is in the event of vision. In that event, however, it is of such a character that a theory of space becomes a prerequisite in the theory of nature.

Of the logical difficulties often emphasized, I would refer to two. With propositions of a formal character the logician has only algebraic troubles. So conspicuous is this fact that since the work of Aristotle the attempt has been repeatedly made to construct a universal algebra which will exhibit the basic structure of discourse in general irrespective of its special applications. It would be idle to question either the validity or the value of such an enterprise and especially at the present time when it can claim so many significant achievements. Surely it is not violent to suppose that an analysis of whatever is said should reveal the coherency of its being said or that this coherency should find exemplification in all discourse. Violence is detected the moment that logic is made an instrument for discovery. Here, if I mistake not, the major controversies arise. They arise acutely when time and existence are taken into consideration. Here the emphasis on life impresses me as affording at least relief, for life is time and existence intimately blended. Nature as evidenced in our living is a matter of today, yesterday, and tomorrow. It is history with eventuality through and through. It will not let itself be coerced into any formal system and without it any formal system loses all intelligible meaning beyond its own algebraic coherence. What an equation is and what it is of, are not the same, and without that "what it is of," it may still be an equation but one devoid of all meaning and existence beyond the operations which can be performed with or upon it. Life and existence can not be deduced from systematized discourse because that discourse is a systematization of what is first said about acknowledged life and existence. That, although it may be taken to be obvious, is yet momentous, for one of the things that has to be said first about natural events is that they are jointly retrospective and prospective. A moving body is moving from and to, a plant is growing from and to, a living being is living from and to—every event is jointly a from and to, and that from and to can not be separated from the event itself, as if they constituted a system antecedently prepared for the occurrence of the event. Where we suppose such a thing, then motion, growth, and life with memory and imagination look unintelligibly miraculous, but when we do not, then it seems no miracle at all that we should remember and imagine.

No miracle at all, because starting with nature as eventual, with every event jointly retrospective and prospective, our being in a nature of that sort is itself jointly retrospective and perspective being. It would be a miracle if we did not remember and imagine. Why, I repeatedly ask myself, is it worth while making miracles of our knowledge of the past and our hopes of the future when the only way to do so is by supposing that our temporal being is not a sample of what all temporal being is? Whether we suppose so or not, it seems perfectly clear that a theory of time is a preliminary essential to theories of nature. With the emphasis on life one will, I think, turn to a consideration of history generally for enlightenment and not let oneself be confused by clocks and calendars. And one whose thinking has been largely controlled by physicists may find it advantageous to let it be controlled for a season by biologists and examine the evidence that their work affords that the structure and functions of our bodies are understandable only in terms of their history, of what they retrospectively and prospectively imply. That piece of instrumentation is teleologically baffling only when we make it so by some misconstruction or distortion of its time character. Whatever is jointly retrospective and prospective ought surely to illustrate that character in what it does, ought to achieve some sort of result commensurate with the possibilities of achieving it.

Emphasis on life relieves logic also in its existential troubles. There is, I suppose, some sense to saying that what things are and what they are said to be in discourse are not the same, but I must be impressed by the fact that we are all of us quite sure that language is competent to express what things are until we call that competence in question and even then go on talking in an effort to express our doubts in the matter. And I must also be impressed by the fact that in the books of a well furnished library a man has access to distant times and places more comprehensive than he could attain by travelling his life long at the highest speed we have yet attained. Imaginary travelling, according to our present views, at the speed of light would not give it to him, for the faster he travelled the nearer he would come to beholding perpetually the same scene if he beheld anything at all. If we are to play with miracles, language is undoubtedly the greatest of them all. I must believe that the sublimest story of the beginning of things ever written is that which conceives of God as creating nature by speaking. For in the light of that story all our attempts at understanding things look like attempts to translate them back again into their original expression. Creation looks like research reversed. Instead of going from formulas to things, we go from things to formulas, from what they are in this evident character to what can be said about them, and find that the latter can not maintain itself with stability and success without their co-operation. Language as a living and natural communication with nature is something quite different from a superficial articulation of words, conventionally playing over things, and requiring a leap over a gulf if it is to find contact with existence. Propositions considered by themselves may be considered as implying or not implying existence but existential propositions, propositions which declare what things are and what they are not, are not vouched for by logic but by the eventual character of nature. Surely a theory of language as distinct from a universalized algebra is another preliminary essential in theories of nature.

As I read the history of philosophy I find that a spatial world with what is exposed in vision, a temporal world with what is exposed in history, and a communicable world with what is exposed in language, have been in control of all theories of nature from the superficial to the most profound, and from the orderly to the most fantastic. In modern philosophy these evident controls have been made problematic through an emphasis on knowledge which makes them appear to be, not nature itself, but means of arriving at what nature is as distinct from them, with philosophical scepticism as the apparently inevitable result. Knowledge and understanding become thereby supplements to nature and supplements in such a way that the world daily exposed and evident in human living is set over against another world external to that life. The consequent difficulties and controversies have not, I fear, clarified or enlarged our understanding of nature. They have rather confused and narrowed it. Perhaps if we at least suspended the initial emphasis on knowledge and let it fall on life as it naturally does from day to day, letting our vision be a vision of nature's space, our eventful life a participation in its eventfulness, and our language a sharing in its communication, we might fare a little better. But we can fare better only by using the freedom gained for a reconsideration of what nature is as a consequence. That suggests a preliminary or general theory with space, time, and communication not divorced from human living, but as finding in that living, appropriate examples of what they are.

CONSCIOUSNESS AND COGNITION

WHAT IS PERSONALITY?*

ONE naturally turns to psychology for an answer to the question, What is personality? But the inquirer, unless he happens to have only a psychological interest in the matter, is likely to return with a problem to solve, rather than with an answer which satisfies. For the experiences of life, the reality of which it seems impossible to doubt, appear to be impeached, and even to have their value destroyed, by the analysis to which they are subjected. A study of this situation ought to throw some light on the nature and significance of personality.

It is common to entertain the conviction that one has a soul, the possession of which distinguishes him from others by giving him his peculiar individuality, and from things, by giving him the power to think and feel and will. This conviction forms the content of the ordinary conception of personality. To subject it to analysis is to enter the domain of psychology, and to ask, What are thinking, feeling, and willing, and what is the soul, which is the principle of individuality and the source of these three activities? The history of this inquiry abounds in interest, but that must be sacrificed to our more urgent present need of knowing the result.

Psychologists today appear to be pretty well agreed as to this result in its general aspects. Consciousness, the realm of personality, appears to be a very complex combination of elements, which in the last analysis are like the simplest colors and sounds, and are called sensations. These are of a great variety and number, and determine by their character and arrangement various kinds of conscious states or processes. Thus one grouping gives us thought, another feeling, and another will. Or to put it in a different way, if we

* In *Papers, Addresses, and Discussions at the Twenty-first Church Congress in the United States,* New York, Thomas Whittaker, 1902, pp. 125-130.

take those states of mind in which we are said to think or feel or will and subject them to analysis, we shall find them to consist of nothing but peculiar arrangements of elementary sensations; and the only difference in the character and arrangement of the sensations involved. Elements in combination, that is all. Just as water is its elements in combination and yet presents itself as something quite different from those elements in isolation, so thought, feeling, and will are only their elements in combination, and yet present themselves as something quite different from those elements as the psychologist analyzes them out and separates them. And just as water disappears with the separation of its elements, so do these mental activities disappear under the like circumstances. It is not meant that these activities are unreal. All that is denied is that the analysis discovers them to be real in any other sense than here described, that they are discovered to be realities back of and independent of their elements. They are these elements united in a very real and important way, but they are nothing more.

The conclusion regarding the soul and personality is the same. These words indicate for the psychologist nothing but the kind of correlation in which all mental activities are found. Sensations are always *somebody's*. The same is true of combinations of sensations. It is *I* that think and feel and will. Yet this *I* does not involve any new elements; it is not something new in kind. It is rather only the way in which all mental elements are found, as a matter of fact, to coexist. Remove these elements, destroy the correlation or change it, and the soul and personality are removed, destroyed, or changed. Thus the soul is not a power, a creative force, an independent existence, separate and distinct from its sensation elements. It is simply these elements in more or less stable combination. We are not to argue that the peculiar character of this combination, namely that it always presents itself as soul or personality, not *being*, but *having* sensations, warrants the conclusion that there must be therefore an independent existence back of sensations, which has them. We might as well argue, because all objects are spatial, and yet space is that *in which* objects are, an absolutely empty space must therefore exist independent of objects. No; just as space is the form in which we know physical objects to exist, a form which the removal of these objects would also remove, so is personality the form in which we know consciousness to exist. Remove the conscious elements, and the personality is also removed.

Such briefly is the psychological analysis of personality. Against opposition, against bigotry and ridicule, against personal abuse and persecution, the psychologist has fought his way to this result, until today it is the dominant conception of the psychology of personality. Those that hold it may differ widely in their attitudes toward life. They may be materialists or spiritualists, agnostics or idealists, sceptics or men of faith, yet they find harmony and satisfaction in reducing the highest manifestations of conscious life, not to entities and independent existences, but to combinations of elements. The reason is this: These men believe that, in so doing, they are but repeating in their own science the history of all science. They have learned the lesson of that history, which is this—scientific truth is advanced just in proportion as the assumption of entities behind the facts considered is discarded.

But is such an analysis adequate to the needs of life? Drop for a moment the scientific attitude of mind; go out into the world to meet its duties and joys, its evil and pain; join your fellow man in labour and progress; open your heart to the refining influences of friendship and love; and then reflect that you, you to whom these things have a value beyond all else just because they are yours, reflect that you are nothing but the form in which sensations are found in correlation! If that is so, how can I possibly take up the duties of life and quit myself like a man? How can I lift this little span of existence, which dwindles into nothing when measured by the infinity of time; how can I lift it out of its pettiness, its sordidness, its weakness up to those heights where the presence of eternal spiritual realities may brighten and purify it? How can I raise my voice in praise and prayer to a God whose personality, if He has one, must also be a psychological process of some sort? How can I, who know that the dissolution of my sensations means my dissolution, entertain the hope of eternal life? Could there be greater impossibilities than these? To substitute thus in life the psychological personality for the responsible man seems to strip life of its meaning and value, to ruin it utterly. And so we are apt to cry, psychology is wrong, totally, viciously wrong.

This emotional cry has found its champions in speculative thought. Often in the interest of some metaphysical system, often in the interest of moral and religious faith, war has been declared against science. But history records the victories on the side of science. If we are ever driven to the point where we must accept or reject the validity of scientific aims and the conditions under which it is possible for these aims to be realized, we can not hesitate long over the choice. If we understand the alternative in its full meaning, we will range ourselves on the side of science. When one has come to this conclusion, he has, to my mind, taken the first step toward freedom of life and thought.

That is the first step, but it is not the last. We can not stop the progress of any science by emotional cries, and yet the instinctive protests of life against the results of scientific analysis force upon us a problem of the greatest interest—the problem of the relation of science to life. Are these two things in inevitable opposition, or is it only our failure rightly to conceive them, that makes them appear so? Undoubtedly it is the latter. The power that knowledge gives is so great that we are apt to think that knowledge and its possession are ends in themselves, and that our most natural function is intellectual. But it is not. Our experience does not present itself as something primarily to be explained, but as something to be worked out. We study to understand our world, to explain it, to order its elements in the form of laws, not ultimately for the sake of knowledge, but for the sake of action. If we are going to achieve anything at all, we must understand as fully as possible the machinery, whether physical or mental, by means of which that thing may be achieved. And so it is that every discovery of science presents itself to the individual not only as a discovery, but also as a problem for his activity. What will he do with it? What will he make of it? He may have discovered certain conditions under which the weal and woe of society may be increased. Which will he increase, the weal or the woe? Knowledge held in isolation from practical life is the most harmless and the most useless thing imaginable. But we can not so hold it. Imagine ourselves possessed of all knowledge possibly conceivable, and, I take it, there would still be left something for us to do. And just as long as one faces life with the possibility of doing something, he is something other than a psychological personality, he is a moral being. It is true that his morality is not constituted by this result, but by the fact that he still can act. If giving free rein to science is the first step toward freedom, to recognize in one's self a moral possibility is the second step. Nay more, it is to become free.

In somewhat technical language, what philosophy and science both need to recognize is that not only are actualities real, but possibilities are real also. And it belongs to the idea of a possibility that, however real it may be, it may never become actual in the sphere of concrete experience. Consequently, if the realm of the possible is ever to be made available for our use in life, it must be laid hold of by other conceptions and other categories than those by means of which we formulate the actual in terms of positive, scientific knowledge. And it should be recognized that the attempt so to make the realm of the possible available is just as important, just as valid, just as necessary as the attempt to lay hold of scientific truth. If, then, the reality of our personality as a given psychological fact is to be made available by analyzing it into mental elements in correlation, how is the reality of our personality as a moral possibility to be made available?

How has it been made available? The answer is, in the moral ideal and religious aspirations and beliefs of the race. We read in their history how man's possibilities have been revealed to him, how he has been inspired and helped toward their attainment. In such a ministry morality and religion have found their proper function. When they have been true to it, they have won men as their friends. Only when they have been false to it have they turned men into their enemies. And they are false to it when they set themselves up as explanations of the origin of things, or to formulate the laws of natural events. Lightning and tempest, plague, pestilence, and famine have indeed a moral significance for us and for our attitude toward life, but when we attempt to explain their occurrence through moral and religious causes, we not only fail, but also subject morality and religion to ridicule and attack. Perhaps the day has at last dawned when we shall no longer look to theology, to some supposed insight into the plan of a divine being, for an explanation of why things happen as they do, but we shall look simply to the things themselves, and seek their natural causes. Many have dreaded that day, but it should be welcomed gladly; for with it morality and religion are restored to their natural and proper places in life; they become the inspiration and hope they claim to be by revealing what it is to be a moral and religious personality. And so I say that when we ask, How have the possibilities of man been made available for his use in life? we get the answer, Through the moral ideals and religious aspirations and beliefs of the race.

I do not mean to assert that man has found no help in science, or that he has drawn from its discoveries no revelation. That assertion would be absurd and untrue. Inspiration and faith are nothing without knowledge. I may have the purest and loftiest purpose, but unless I am in some degree master of the machinery by which that purpose can be realized, I might as well not be inspired. On the other hand, if I have all knowledge, and have not charity, I am nothing. What I would claim is, that the discoveries which we make from our study of the world, the events of history, and the nature of our consciousness, do but reveal to us the machinery we can use for moral ends. They do not constitute our morality. We bring that to their use. They do not give us the motives for that use. That too we must bring, clarified by our ideals and hopes. To be thus creatures who turn the discoveries they make in their world to service in the realization of their ideals, is to be moral personalities. The reality of personality is revealed, therefore, not only in the analysis of those elements which constitute the human mind, but also in the character, value, and validity which our ideals have for life.

Anything approaching a complete conception of our moral personality could be attained only by a study of these ideals in detail. But such a study is excluded by the limits of our discussion, and indeed is unnecessary before an audience like this. I should like however, to note the condition under which such a study should naturally proceed. I have said that the reality of our moral personality is revealed by the character, value, and validity which our ideals have for life. Now where should we go to study them in these aspects but to life itself? Their character, value, and validity are not determined by deduction from the propositions of metaphysics or by the analysis of human motives. They are determined by their manifestation in the great persons of history. These persons are great, simply because they have actually shown to us, by participating in a common experience, what our moral possibilities are. For no other reason are they great. In no other way have they held men to their allegiance to the uttermost. To my mind, it has not been the doctrine of the nature of Jesus of Nazareth, or of his origin, that has succeeded in winning men to His side, but the fact that men have seen revealed in Him, in a genuine human experience, what their moral and spiritual possibilities are. It is that that has won us. And until that revelation is surpassed, men will still, with freedom, with joy, with enthusiasm, call Him Master. Yes; it is to life we must go for life's interpretation, and the value and justification of any ideal or belief we may entertain are to be determined by their power so to transform life, that we are drawn to the resulting personality, irresistibly as the needle to the pole.

What, then, is personality? If by the question we mean to ask, What is the nature of personality as a given conscious fact to be analyzed? we get the answer of psychology. As such a fact personality is found to be, not a cause of consciousness, not something back of it and distinct from it, but is itself a content, an arrangement of element. But if we mean by the question, what an individual with such a content is in life, what is he as a factor in society, what is he as revealed in the fullness of human experience, we get the answer of history—to be a person is to use the materials and machinery of life in the service of ideals. Let us think of ourselves as masses of sensations, if we must; but let us never be so absurd as to forget that such masses of sensations have made human history what it is, and can, if they will, make the history of the future immeasurably more glorious. Let us not quarrel with psychology or the results of science, but let the wonder of it all possess us; that there should appear in the natural history of the world creatures whose lot in life should be constantly to reach beyond themselves in order to live at all, whose whole existence should be a world-transformation and a self-transformation in the interest of what they would have prevail, who, while they must draw the materials of their work from what they could discover of nature's constitution and their own, must none the less draw life's inspiration and motives, must get the mainspring of their activity and progress, not from what they are, but from what they might be; creatures who, under this necessity and this compulsion, should find no permanent peace until they should commit themselves freely and wholly, in complete self-surrender, to what their ideals reveal them to be—let us wonder at it. And we should be wondering, not at some theory of things, but at one of the plainest facts we know. No psychology can destroy that fact, and no metaphysics enhance the wonder of it. It is the truth of experience, and in that truth our personality is disclosed.

THE NATURE OF CONSCIOUSNESS*

THE motives which influence one interested in definitions to attempt a definition of consciousness are at present so obvious that I shall not stop to discuss them. I should like, however, by way of introduction, to indicate the point of departure from which the definition should, in my opinion, be attempted.

Locke and Kant conceived consciousness to be a kind of receptacle or receptivity set over against the things which were to give it a content. Huxley in his essay on "Sensation and the Sensiferous Organs" appears to have a similar conception. Indeed, it is mainly after this manner that consciousness has been conceived and discussed in modern theories. Yet it seems to be quite impossible to find out anything verifiable about consciousness from the point of view of this conception, because we are not able to produce an instance of the distinction between consciousness and other things which it involves. Consciousness is never discovered as one thing set over against other things which are not already its content. Consequently it seems futile to suppose that it is, and then proceed to build up a theory about it. As it is found to exist only when it has a content, I shall take my point of departure from that fact, and speak of the type of existence involved as "objects in consciousness."

No doubt this type of existence has had a history. It may have been much simpler than it is at present. But what it was like in its simpler form is so clearly an inference from what it is in its developed form that I can not regard the inference as the proper point of departure for a definition of the type of existence on which the inference depends. I therefore dismiss consideration of the conditions out of which our conscious

* In the *Journal of Philosophy, Psychology and Scientific Methods*, Vol. II (1905), pp. 119-125. Read before the American Philosophical Association, December 29, 1904.

experience may have developed. I take objects in consciousness or consciousness of objects as just that kind of existence which each one can identify and analyze for himself as readily as he would analyze a plant or a rock.

The objects of consciousness may be as varied and as variable as you please. They may be men and trees, reds and what we call mere ideas, present facts and remembered happenings, reasonings and discussions, pains, pleasures, emotions, and volitions; they may even constitute what we call the self: but all, without exception, stand out as the objects *of which* there is consciousness, but never as the consciousness itself. Just as objects in the light are not the light, so objects in consciousness are not the consciousness. There is thus a distinction between consciousness and its objects. The distinction has often been denied on the ground that we can not distinguish in a given perception between object and perceiving. Perhaps we can not, but we do distinguish between different perceptions. It is this fact, that different perceptions or objects exist together and are yet distinguished as different, which constitutes a recognizable and definable distinction between consciousness and its objects. It is the distinction involved in the existence of different things together.

Such a type of existence is very common. The three most noticeable instances of it, other than consciousness, are things in space, events in time, and individuals in species. Space is distinguished from the things in it, not by taking these things in isolation, but by taking them together as different things in space. The same is true of time and species. We have, in these instances, a distinction like that between consciousness and its objects. Consciousness should, therefore, be defined as the same general type of existence as space, time, or species. Its nature is akin to theirs.

Some suggestive conclusions may be drawn from this fact which throw a clarifying light on several controverted questions. The relation of the world of which there is consciousness to consciousness involves the same kind of problems as the relation of objects in space to space, or the events in time to time. We do not ask if space and time affect their objects casually. We should not raise the question of the causal efficiency of consciousness. We do not ask how things get into space, so we should not ask how objects get into consciousness, if we thereby imply, in any way, the previous separate existence of the two. Just as it is possible to find out about things much that is interesting which does not depend on the fact that they are in space, so also it is possible to find out much that is interesting about objects which does not depend on the fact that they are in consciousness. And just as we may have a body of knowledge built up from the fact that things are in space, so we may have a body of knowledge built up from the fact that objects are in consciousness. Finally one who has recognized that in consciousness we have simply an instance of the existence of different things together, will not engage in the controversies which are suggested by such terms as "automatism," "interactionism," "parallelism," "agnosticism," and their kindred. Indeed, he will have to renounce many so-called metaphysical pleasures.

The type of existence to which consciousness belongs makes it evident at once that there is little propriety in speaking of objects as "states of consciousness." So to characterize them involves a deal of speculation which has ultimately to reckon with the difference between consciousness and its objects, and account for it. I am, by no means, immediately aware of objects as states of consciousness any more than I am aware of things as states of space. Thus the axiom of Locke that "the mind in all its thoughts and reasonings hath no other immediate object but its own ideas," an axiom which has been the central principle of most modern philosophy through Hegel and since, has at best only a highly speculative warrant.

When things exist together, that which constitutes their being together is some sort of continuum. Consciousness may be defined, therefore, as a kind of continuum of objects. From this definition an important aspect of consciousness can be deduced, namely, the isolation of any individual consciousness. Two continuums of the same kind can not be parts of each other. They stand over against each other as closed systems, so to speak. The spaces and times of our dreams are not interchangeable with those of our waking moments. Two species are not interchangeable. Two consciousnesses also are not interchangeable. They refuse to be systematized or even grouped together under a common continuum of the same sort. We can not relate them to each other, therefore, in the ways we relate different objects to each other. We can relate them only indirectly, never directly. Another's consciousness is never given as a part of mine or related to mine in anything like the way his body is related to my body. I get into relations with his consciousness indirectly by means of his body. While his body may be in my consciousness, his consciousness never is, but is inferred by me to be in his body. The necessity of thus indirectly relating different consciousnesses to each other, or, what is the same thing, of relating the objects of one consciousness to a second consciousness is the foundation on which most theories of perception are based. The expectation of ever getting rid of this indirection by means of such a theory seems to me, therefore, to be without justification. If this is true, all speculation about the nature of consciousness which is based on theories of perception is in great danger of arriving at no verifiable results.

Besides the type of isolation just noted, consciousness has other characters, such as infinity, which are common to all continuums. I pass these by, for the present, in order to note the distinctive character of that form of continuity or connection which we have when objects are in consciousness. In this form, they become grouped and systematized in a manner quite different from their grouping in any other form. They become representative of each other. Note that it is *of each other* that they become representative, but not of anything else. They are not ideas which represent things, or phenomena which represent noumena, or things in the body which represent things outside, or states of consciousness which represent an external world. It is each other that they represent, as bread represents nourishment. Because of such representation, all our knowledge is built up; and I am not acquainted with any body of verifiable and generally accepted knowledge which is built up in any other way. All science deals solely with the systematization of this representative value of the things with which it is concerned.

The peculiar way in which consciousness connects the objects in it is, thus, the way of knowledge actual or possible. Objects are connected in consciousness in such a way that they become known. It is important to note that, while this is so, the knowledge is wholly determined in its content by the relations of the objects in consciousness to one another, not by the relation of consciousness to the objects. This latter may be the relation which makes the knowledge possible, but it is not the relation which determines what the knowledge is. In other words, we know what our objects are and what we may expect from them, not at all by considering their relation to consciousness, but to one another. The relation to consciousness is the same with each one of them, expressed by the preposition *in*, and is, therefore, not a distinguishing relation. Whatever we find out about the relation of objects is found out from them and from no other source. Their *esse* is not *percipi*. We may, if we will, identify their perceived existence with their *percipi*, but this identification would have no distinguishing significance. What they are as perceived existences, what relations still subsist between them, the laws of their occurrence, all such things are to be found out by considering them themselves, and in no other way. The fact, therefore, that knowledge of what objects are depends on the fact that they are in consciousness, in no way determines the nature of objects. We may say, consequently, that the peculiar form of connection or continuity which consciousness constitutes between objects does not affect their nature, but simply makes them known or knowable, and known with all their variety of distinctions from a thing to a thought.

That form of connection or continuum which we call consciousness is thus distinguished by the fact that it makes knowledge possible, and this knowledge, so far as its content is concerned, and that is so far as it is knowledge of anything, is determined not by consciousness, but by something else. The limits of knowledge would thus appear beyond our power to determine. Of course we can say, in a general way, that where we have no objects there we can have no knowledge, but that does not mean very much. We constantly find out new and surprising things about our objects, and to this sort of discovery it is impossible to set a limit. Just as consciousness in no way determines what we discover, it determines in no way the limits of what we can discover. There is thus no such thing in the realm of knowledge as an impossibility which consciousness determines. Impossibilities, inconsistencies, contradictions, absurdities, just as much as concrete information, are determined not by the fact that we are conscious of objects, but by the fact that objects are what we know. It is meaningless, therefore, to state that matter can not think, because that is unthinkable, unless we mean that we have actually discovered in the nature of matter something which we know must exclude thought. It is quite meaningless to urge that life could arise only from life, if our urging of this is supported by an appeal to mere thinkableness. Whether life can arise from anything else than life can never be determined by any "must" or "must not," but only when we actually find out whether it can. In general, just because consciousness is the determining factor in the existence of knowledge, there is no reason to conclude that it is in any way a determining factor in the content or limitations of knowledge. The necessity we are under to know something never determines in any way the character of what we know. Knowledge may be a synthesis or a construction, but what it synthesizes or constructs, together with the principles and laws of the synthesis or construction is discovered to depend not on the fact of consciousness as such. Clearly this seems very much like saying that in knowledge we have revealed in a very real way that which is itself independent of consciousness and knowledge. Just because we find the content and limits of our knowledge never taking their colouring from the fact that we can or must know, we seem warranted in concluding that consciousness and knowledge do actually disclose to us that which is in no way dependent on consciousness or knowledge for its existence or character. Knowledge is, thus, palpably realistic.

The most crucial instance of this realism is doubtless the discovery which we make from a study of objects in consciousness, namely, that consciousness itself is a dependent existence, that it does not exist under certain conditions, but under these conditions disappears and becomes impossible. Of course it is not necessary to detail the steps in this discovery. It is sufficient to point out that it is made as all other discoveries are made. I learn that there has got to be a certain kind of organism in order to have consciousness, just as I learn that there must be eyes in order to see, or moisture in order to have things wet. There is nothing unique regarding this discovery about consciousness. We make it by observation, experiment, and inference, just as we make other discoveries.

If consciousness begins to exist not only at some point in the individual's life, but also at different points in his life, and is, thus, an interrupted existence, it appears to be quite impossible to regard it as a possession of the individual, something in him possibly, situated in his head perhaps, and affected by outer or other things. An individual may be affected, and, as a result, be conscious; but that this result should come about by operations upon his consciousness which, admittedly, does not yet exist, would seem to be a most untenable position. The notion that an individual becomes conscious because he already has a consciousness subject to operations upon it, appears to involve the existence of consciousness prior to these operations and independent of them, possibly independent of the individual himself. No satisfactory evidence for such an existence has been produced.

I find myself in hearty agreement with many recent discussions of consciousness, especially with that of Professor James, which aim to take consciousness out of the realm of terms and put it in the realm of relations. But there are some points of disagreement which I should like to note. These recent views aim to define consciousness as, in some way, a function within experience whereby experience itself becomes differentiated into the objective and the subjective, into the physical and the psychical, into the objects of the outer world and the events of a personal biography. That such a differentiation arises in the course of experience is, I suppose, beyond question. But I have been unable to discover that the differentiation throws light on the nature of consciousness. The differentiation simply divides the field of consciousness into two parts, but does not isolate a separate field in which alone consciousness is found. Physical objects just as much as personal histories may be objects in consciousness. Both are known; and to know the physical world does not convert it into autobiography. The element of experience which in one connection figures as a thing, appears to me never to figure in another as an idea; and no matter in what direction it figures, it is an element of which we are conscious so long as it remains an element of experience. The differentiation in question thus appears simply to reveal between our objects one of the distinctions of which we are conscious.[1] Furthermore, the term "experience" which occurs so frequently in recent discussions, appears to me so shot through with the implications of consciousness, that it obscures the problem at issue. Objects, when in consciousness, may be regarded as elements of experience, but this experience, like consciousness, has discoverable conditions of existence and can hardly be regarded as the fabric out of which it is itself composed.

The conclusions I should like to draw from the preceding considerations are more negative than positive. That is, I should lay greater stress on what consciousness does not appear to be than on my positively characterizing, as a continuum, that type of connection which it constitutes between objects. The facts at our command do not warrant us in concluding that consciousness is a kind of receptacle, situated where you will, into which things somehow get in the form of ideas or mental states. Things, or a part of them, may be in consciousness, but they are in it as things are in space. From such a parallel we are to find the clue to the interpretation of the preposition *in*. We have no right to conclude that consciousness constitutes a series of existences parallel to other existences, no right to conclude that the objects in consciousness are ideas of things outside, and no right to conclude that the objects in consciousness are *states* of consciousness. But we do, apparently, have abundant right to conclude that, when consciousness exists, a world hitherto unknown has become known. This does not mean that the world hitherto unknown has been transformed into ideas, but that this world has been illuminated, as it were, by consciousness, that it has been connected up in a new way. The fact that we should be able to

[1] In other words, it appears to me impossible to define consciousness by means of the distinction between "the physical" and "the psychical."

discover the conditions of such a connection is very strong evidence for the position I have taken, for this fact discloses the very simple truth that the conditions under which a world becomes known are, themselves, conditions which form a part of the events of that world. For clarifying this general position and to emphasize the fact that consciousness is only a form of connection of objects, a relation between them, I find the conception of a continuum useful and suggestive. It is useful because it correlates consciousness with facts of a similar general nature. It is suggestive because a study of the nature of continuity may lead to an important understanding of the principles of connection which unite the things of the world.

OF WHAT SORT IS COGNITIVE EXPERIENCE?*

PROFESSOR DEWEY's recent article[1] has definitely contributed to a clearer understanding of what the term "real" means to many advocates of immediate empiricism and pragmatism. The real is simply *that* which is experienced and *as* it is experienced. It would seem that there could be little further misunderstanding on that point. The challenge to the pragmatist to tell what he means by reality appears, thus, to have been met successfully. If it were necessary to lend external authority to Professor Dewey's exposition, one might cite the ancient statement of Aristotle that reality is whatever can be the subject of investigation. From such a definition of reality it is evident that reals may differ from one another in any way in which they are found to differ; and that, consequently, there may be "true" reals and "false" reals if warrant can be found for such a distinction among the things which may be investigated.

There is no need of an elaborate proof to show that this definition, in spite of—rather, just because of—its simplicity and obviousness, is the only fruitful definition of reality. The history of thought is in evidence. To the metaphysician it is a real blessing, for it frees him from the trivial question whether there is anything real at all, and turns him to the more fruitful and important question, What is the nature of the real, When is it most fittingly and appropriately defined?

Now, it is just that question which seems to cause confusion and dilemma. And it is here that further clarification is needed. For the natural and obvious answer to the question, When is reality most fittingly and appropriately defined, seems to be

* In the *Journal of Philosophy, Psychology and Scientific Methods,* Vol. II (1905), pp. 573-576.

[1] "The Postulate of Immediate Empiricism," *Journal of Philosophy, Psychology and Scientific Methods,* Vol. II (1905), p. 393.

this: When it is *truly* defined. That this answer is the cause of the greater part of current controversies about pragmatism is obvious enough. It seems worth while, therefore, to say something about it, and elicit, possibly, further discussion from Professor Dewey and others.

The dilemma in question is apparent. If reality as true is but one sort of reality or one sort of experience, how can it possibly be affirmed that the nature of reality is most fittingly defined, when we have that sort, when, that is, reality is experienced as true? The answer occasionally given that it is thus most fittingly defined because defined in a way which most usefully meets the needs which raise the demand for definition, seems to many minds to be unsatisfactory. The reasons for dissatisfaction vary much, from quaking fear for the possible loss of an absolute to a genuine conviction that the whole knowing experience is a transcendent kind of experience, related to all other kinds in a way in which they are not related to it. I willingly leave the absolutist to his fears, but would say something in favour of the transcendence of knowledge.

As what I have to say has been definitely shaped in its formulation by Professor Dewey's article, I use some of his expressions to bring out the point I would raise for discussion:

> In each case [says Professor Dewey] the nub of the question is, *what sort of experience* is meant or indicated: a concrete and determinate experience, varying, when it varies, in specific real elements, and agreeing, when it agrees, in specific real elements, so that we have a contrast, not between *a* Reality, and various approximations to, or phenomenal representations of, Reality, but between different reals of experience. And the reader is begged to bear in mind that from this standpoint, when "an experience" or "some sort of experience" is referred to, "some thing" or "some sort of thing" is always meant.
>
> Now, this statement that things are what they are experienced to be is usually translated into the statement that things (or, ultimately, Reality, Being) *are* only and just what they are *known* to be, or that things are, or Reality *is*, what it is for a conscious knower—whether the knower be conceived primarily as a perceiver or as a thinker being a further and secondary question. This is the root-paralogism of all idealisms, whether subjective or objective, psychological or epistemological. By our postulate, things are what they are experienced to be; and, unless knowing is the sole and only genuine mode of experiencing, it is falla-

cious to say that Reality is just and exclusively what it is or would be to an all-competent all-knower; or even that it *is*, relatively and piecemeal, what it is to a finite and partial knower. Or, put more positively, knowing is one mode of experiencing, and the primary philosophic demand (from the standpoint of immediatism) is to find out *what* sort of an experience knowing is—or, concretely how things are experienced when they are experienced *as* known things.

Again, Professor Dewey says in a footnote, "The adequacy of any particular account [of the truth-experience] is not a matter to be settled by general reasoning, but by finding out what sort of an experience the truth-experience *actually* is." I have italicized the word "actually."

Now, my difficulty in getting a clear understanding of these and similar statements gets sharply pointed in the question: In what sort of experience do I find out what sort of experience is, and is *actually* or otherwise? Is the answer to that question this: In the sort of experience you are having at the time? If so, I find out what sort of an experience a moral experience is by having it, and what sort a cognitive experience is by having it. But how shall I distinguish a moral experience from one that is cognitive? By having, I suppose the answer would run, a new experience in which the two are experienced as different.

Such an answer—and let it be kept in mind that I am not burdening anybody with such an answer, but am using it as one which seems to be implied in the statement under consideration—deserves to be pushed to its full limit in order to get a clear view of the sort of experience which it indicates. So pushed it appears to me to be this: If I am to find out what the different sorts of experience are, how they are related to one another, how they are distinguished, what sorts of objects constitute them, what has been their history, what their promise is, which of them may be called true, and which false, I must have an experience in which what I desire to find out is to some extent, at least, experienced. But this desired experience, which would contain within it all the possible riches of science and philosophy, is just the sort of experience which is generally called a cognitive experience. If, therefore, the suggested answer is the correct one, it appears to me clear that in cognitive experience all other sorts of experience may exist without alteration; for, otherwise, how could we find out what sort they are? How could they be identified as the concrete, particular sorts of experience indicated? In other words, in the cognitive sort of experience all other sorts appear to be transcended. The nub of the *question*, to use Professor Dewey's words once more, is, undoubtedly, what sort of experience is meant or indicated. But it would appear that this question can be *answered* only in a cognitive experience!

As I have said, I burden no one with the answer which appears inevitably to lead to this conclusion. Yet I willingly take the burden myself. While I do not like the word "experience" as an ultimate term in metaphysics, I can find little objection to it when it is used as equivalent to "some thing" or "some sort of thing," when "thing" may be, apparently, any term or any relation. Thus using the word, I can readily assent to such expressions as this: There are many sorts of experience of which the cognitive sort is only one and one which can be confused with the others only to the detriment of all. But I must now add that the cognitive experience is of such a "sort" that it enables us to tell what the others *actually* are when we ask the question about *their* sort. This question may not be asked and may not be answered. In that case no one sort of experience is identified or distinguished. And what sort of an experience would that be if not precisely what we should mean by an unconscious experience?[2]

I do not know whether those philosophers who bear by choice or by imputation the name of pragmatists deny, as a rule, the transcendence of the cognitive experience as here defined. When it is denied, I see no alternative but to assert that in the cognitive experience all other experiences become altered. But if we must have cognitive experience in order to have science and philosophy, and cognitive experience alters things, why, then, it appears to me that science and philosophy will be hugged to the bosom of the absolute idealist as his legitimate offspring!

In the endeavour to escape from the barren consequences

[2] That, I may remark, is why I dislike the word "experience." "Unconscious experience" looks so like a contradiction.

of the position that *all* experience is in its nature cognitive and cognitive only, or in other words, that all *things* are "states of consciousness," there appears danger of running to the opposite extreme. That is why, as it seems to me, the revolt against absolutism fails to convince many who are by no means absolutists. We attempt to give an account of experience which will commend itself to thought. How can we succeed if we raise the suspicion that any account of experience for thought must necessarily be, not only partial and inadequate, but radically different from what experience is? Surely here is a point where discussion can not fail to be important and profitable.

THE PROBLEM OF CONSCIOUSNESS*

THE remarkable philosophical development which began with Descartes and Locke and culminated in Hegel, and which has had various revivals and restatements since, appears to have been controlled by a few basal conceptions. One might even claim that a single conception, namely, the conception of the mind with its related conception of consciousness, has given to the whole movement its significant character and its typical problems. That mind or consciousness should have been made the central fact for the philosophical interpretation of the world stands out as one of the striking achievements of modern thinking. Around this central fact have grown up systems of idealism possessing remarkable ingenuity and thoroughness. Yet there are many indications today that these systems, once so generally fascinating, are losing their interest. Among the most striking illustrations of this is the remarkable diminution in the influence of the Kantian philosophy during the past decade. To the average university student today, that philosophy appears not simply unconvincing, but decidedly on the wrong track. It represents to him the philosophical expression of the eighteenth-century glorification of reason rather than a serious inquiry conformable in principle to the present status of our general knowledge. The great German systems are not now read with the eagerness with which many of us were once familiar. There are also indications of radical opposition which has put idealism on the defensive. Pragmatism and radical empiricism, although owning a certain kinship with the great modern systems, are disturbing factors which put many traditional convictions in peril. Natural science, increasing the scope and depth of its interests, and the theory of evolution, in its attempt at recovering a genuinely cosmic point

*In *Studies in Philosophy and Psychology: The Garman Commemorative Volume*. Boston, Houghton Mifflin, 1906, pp. 137-166.

of view, have tended to displace the mind from its central position in the interpretation of the world. There are, thus, not only clear evidences of a transition in philosophy—our age has long been characterized as one of transition—but the motives and the direction of the transition are gaining clearness.

The situation has its distinct logical interest, for transitions naturally indicate a change in controlling ideas. Thinking is guided by convictions instinctively or traditionally acquired which seldom come to the surface for critical scrutiny until the systems they carry have attained a high degree of logical perfection. When, however, the system has passed beyond the period of enthusiastic construction and become familiar, its hidden assumptions tend to appear as problems. Astronomy and geometry present classic illustrations of this movement of thought in science. The progress of philosophy follows the same principle and appears to be giving present illustration of it. I propose in this paper to examine certain features of this illustration and to indicate, if possible, some of the directions which this transition is taking. I desire to do this, however, under the restrictions imposed by a consideration of the problem of consciousness.

This restriction has, as I have already suggested, its motive in the central position which the traditional conception of consciousness has had in modern philosophy. It will be my aim, first, to show how this traditional conception has been logically responsible for the characteristic doctrines of modern idealism; secondly, to indicate some of the natural difficulties which these doctrines present; and, thirdly, to suggest a modified conception of consciousness and some of the problems to which it appears to lead.

I

The conception of consciousness which has controlled the major portion of modern philosophy, reaching over even into the thought of such men as Huxley and Spencer, was pretty definitely fixed by Descartes, Locke, and Kant. In Locke, however, it appears to have received its simplest formulation and to have afforded the first clear and definite statement of the fundamental principles which have characterized the idealistic development through Hegel and since. These principles are the following: (1) the only objects of knowledge are ideas; (2) all ideas are acquired; and (3) knowledge is a synthesis of ideas. It is apparent at once that we have here the germs of the idealistic doctrines of phenomenalism, of experience, and of rationally deduced, synthesizing categories. These were the doctrines which the subsequent development was interested in perfecting. The three propositions appear also to have been certain limiting conditions under which the philosophy of individual thinkers took specific directions. They controlled Berkeley, for instance, in his analysis of the meaning of existence when applied to the objects of knowledge, and in his interpretation of the conceptions of the external world, of substance, and of causation. Hume was driven to skepticism because he could interpret only in terms of the customary grouping of ideas that type of knowledge which purported to be valid beyond the senses and memory. Kant, it would appear, expended his skill in answering the question, How, under the conditions stated, can the understanding be said to have an object at all? and exhibited in the answer what he regarded as the essential synthetic conditions of objects of experience in general. With still deeper logical insight, Hegel saw in the structure of the "idea" itself a fertile and active principle capable of generating a succession of related experiences. But the whole remarkable development moved within the limits determined by the principles of Locke.

While attempts were occasionally made, notably by Kant, to furnish evidence for the validity of Locke's principles, they have usually been presented as self-evident truths, apparent to trained philosophical reflection at least. Yet it is clear that they rest, and did rest with Locke, on an initial conception of the mind and consciousness without which their validity is far from apparent. The mind, that is, was conceived as an original capacity or receptacle, endowed with certain constitutional powers and needing the operation of some alien or resident factor to arouse it to activity. It was the end-term of a relation, the other term of which might be the external world, another mind, the divine being, or some unknown source of excitation. The important end-term was the mind. The other end-term tended constantly to sink into unimportance and mystery, dwindling on the way into the Kantian *Ding an sich*, until, indeed, as in the post-Kantian philosophy, the source of excitation was brought within the mind itself and assigned to the mind's essential instability. This basal conception of the mind as an original end-term was expressed in various forms and different words, but in them all are discoverable the essential originality, isolation, independence, and exclusiveness of that plastic and impressionable thing which through experience of some sort comes to possess consciousness and knowledge, or to be itself the consciousness of a world.

One sees now very clearly what history has so abundantly illustrated; namely, that the outcome of such an original and controlling conception of the mind and consciousness is pretty definitely determined in its general outlines by the logic of the situation. Strip the mind so conceived of every determinate character, and the concept of it yields, as Hume showed, absolutely nothing. It is then a wholly useless conception. Its value can be preserved only by assigning to it in increasing measure the character which may ultimately give to the whole of experience and the world their essential features. Of this latter method, Kant and his successors are the beautiful illustrations.

The logical influence of the end-term conception of the mind on modern philosophy becomes more evident as one examines with greater minuteness some of its major doctrines. The doctrine of ideas, or states of consciousness, is a natural deduction from it. Locke's statement of the situation is typical: "It is evident that the mind knows not things immediately, but only by the intervention of the ideas it has of them." This statement is clearly evident if the mind is a plastic capacity modified by some sort of operation. States of consciousness naturally appear as distinctly mental facts constituting some sort of an intervening group of existences. Sensations and ideas find their place in the mind alone. They can not be in the physical world nor have physical characteristics. Being made up wholly of the mind or consciousness, they must obey exclusively mental laws. Their enumeration, classification, and combinations afford psychology characteristic problems. As ideas are the only objects of knowledge, knowledge itself must be explained through either the association or the synthesis of ideas. This doctrine of ideas or mental states or states of consciousness has been worked out with characteristic skill and zeal in much of modern epistemology and psychology. Every student of these subjects has become familiar with the details and problems of the movement. Note, for instance, the multiplication of ideas and the distinction between substantive and transitive states involving the recognition of such feelings as of "and" and "if," the controversy over the question whether states of consciousness are spaceless and timeless, the association controversy, the puzzling question how one state can know another state, and the doctrine of successive representation. I do not ask what real progress has been made or what satisfactory solutions reached. I wish here solely to connect the whole movement with the end-term conception of the mind as the logical outgrowth of that conception. While this connection gives the movement motive and definition, it can not, of course, give it truth or validity, for these desired merits depend on the truth and validity of the specific notion of the mind which controls the details, the problems, and the solutions.

The doctrine that knowledge is a synthesis of ideas is a natural derivative from the same conception. The general conditions of the synthesis were conceived by Locke in a very simple way. Ideas, he thought, were originally produced in the mind in an isolated and disconnected manner because of the isolation and disconnection of the avenues of sense. The mind was consequently passive in the first reception of ideas, but as soon as it had received them, it became active, and combined and related its ideas in various ways. Here we find the important beginnings of the doctrine of synthesis, involving its two significant features, namely, an original confusion and a subsequent order, and its essential problem, namely, How is the passage from confusion to order effected? The history of the doctrine is a familiar story. But it is important to note how some of its most revolutionary features have been motived with a kind of logical necessity. Take, for example, the Kantian doctrine of space and time. This might readily be deduced from Locke's position. Since our only objects are ideas and these appear first in confusion, their subsequent spatial and temporal order must be an arrangement in a space and a time which are first in the mind. And in general, if there are any universal and necessary types of arrangement or order arising out of the original confusion, these types must indicate the fixed mental conditions under which the progress from confusion to order is effected. Their deduction becomes then a pretty problem for the ingenious. Again, thus, there is forced upon one who would analytically examine the progress of modern idealism with the view of discovering its logical motive, the realization that this motive lies originally in the end-term conception of the mind, in the notion of consciousness as a receptivity.

This conception appears not only to have motived the major doctrines of modern idealism, it appears also to have controlled in large measure the various problems which arise when the attempt is made to put the deliverances of the idealistic philosophy and psychology into some intelligible relation with the deliverances of physical science. This is notably the case in the problems of the relation of mind to body and of the efficiency of consciousness. For the thorough and absolute idealist these problems may not exist in any vital or disturbing manner. But for the less thorough, for those who have not yet quite succeeded in attaining a satisfactory deduction of the course and laws of nature from the cognitive syntheses of experience, these problems have been serious. Others have made them the points of departure for a subsequent idealistic philosophy. But why should such problems exist at all? Natural science may indeed afford some occasion for their existence, and certainly has done so in its emphasis on the principle of the conservation of energy. But it seems to me that science, unaided by the dominant notions of the philosophical movement under consideration, could not have raised these problems in the form with which we are familiar. So long as the mind is conceived as an end-term we may speculate concerning its relation to the other end-term; and so long as consciousness is the mind's possession we may inquire about its relation to the body and its physical efficiency. On this basis automatism, interaction, and parallelism are formally statable problems. Without any appeal to physical science, the logical preference for parallelism is apparent. For if consciousness constitutes an intervening group or order of existences, if ideas or states of mind, with their exclusively mental relations and laws, comprise its whole content, then anything, such as the body, beyond consciousness is forever beyond. No relation, least of all that of efficiency, can be constituted between such disparate existences. If we hold to these existences, the most we can claim is that they are concomitant or parallel.

The foregoing considerations have warranted, I think, the thesis of the first part of this paper: namely, that the conception of the mind as an end-term of a relation, the notion of consciousness as a receptivity modified somehow into a synthesis of its own states, has motived and controlled the development of modern idealism and the characteristic philosophical problems related to that development. I have cited, to be sure, a limited number of instances and treated these briefly. Both the number of instances and the treatment could be extended, but I have not been able to discover that such extension would do anything else than add to the claims of the thesis. It appears to me, therefore, that the attempt to assault the logical structure of idealism is futile. Such a procedure begets not understanding and appreciation, but only fruitless controversy. If philosophy is to advance in any other direction than a still greater logical perfection—if that indeed is possible—of the structure, the basal conception of consciousness must first be altered.

II

Theories are, however, to be estimated, not only by their logical perfection, but by their believability. The latter excellence is indeed the more to be desired, for a believable theory may patiently wait for its successful logical systematization, while one not believable is always at a discount no matter how perfect its structure. The existence of positivism, to say nothing of the excessively controversial atmosphere of modern philosophy, is proof enough that the completest philosophical product of modern times is not generally credible. The taunt that Hume threw at Berkeley—that the latter's philosophy admitted of no refutation and produced no conviction—has been frequently repeated with wider application. Its significance is typical, and warrants the inquiry why the whole philosophy of ideas, in spite of its logical beauty, has so often produced no conviction. A ready answer might be found in the suggestion that its controlling conception has been repeatedly subject to suspicion. Until quite recently, however, this suspicion has received little really positive formulation. It is worth while, therefore, to examine some of the general causes of doubt.

First among these might be noted the fact that modern idealism, when clearly envisaged in its completest forms, appears to be markedly artificial, to have what we might call a too predominantly literary character. It is like a work of art, affecting the beholder æsthetically, enthralling his contemplation, rather than like a work of science, convincing on account of the familiarity and homeliness of its terms and its procedure. Besides this it forces upon one a view of things which is not an extension and refinement of his natural, instinctive view, but a radical transformation of it. It begets the sense of illusion, a kind of Platonic wonder. Then, too, it requires a resoluteness of will and a vigorous control of the emotions to hold one up to it with an orderly, every-day acceptance. In eating and drinking, in marrying and giving in marriage, in being born and in dying, in begetting offspring and rearing them, in loving and hating, in wars and tumults, in plague, pestilence, and famine, humanity is very prone to lapse into the crudest forms of realism. There is, undoubtedly something preposterous in the notion that one can attain to anything like a complete insight into the nature of reality by a scrutiny of the processes of knowledge, while actual living is such a totally different affair.

The artificiality with which idealism is chargeable appear on examination to lie in the logical constraint which its controlling conception exercises. What ideas are and what the mind essentially is are questions to be answered by it *a prior* and transcendentally. Huxley tells us, for instance, that sensations "have no attributes in common with those we ascrib to matter; they are, in the strictest sense of the words, immaterial entities." And what Huxley says of sensations has been repeatedly said of ideas and states of consciousness in general. They are spaceless and timeless, obeying only immaterial or mental laws. To think in this way concerning the objects we directly perceive is clearly to think under the constraint of assumptions, but not under the constraint of the objects we examine. Ideas *ought* to be immaterial on the idealistic basis. But is this anything more than a statement of what logical consistency demands on this particular basis? Psychology after psychology has told us that we know what mental states are much better than we can define them, and then proceeded to enumerate a lot of things we can put into our pockets or throw out of the window, or take into our stomachs, or shut our eyes and ears to. No wonder that honesty has at last compelled the admission that such things are in space and in time, are weighed and measured, obey the laws of gravitation and motion, so that they begin to look perilously like physical and material things after all. Even Berkeley would admit as much, and yet he could claim that he had dealt materialism its finishing stroke! And Kant, to preserve the doctrine of ideas, *must* make space and time and the laws of nature synthetic principles of the mind! Surely here is the refinement of artificiality. The characteristics of the things we perceive suffer no change by being alternately called material and immaterial. They do not alter their weight or their color or their distances from each other. In themselves they exhibit no striking preference for metaphysical terminology. A preference is imported from an assumption, and that assumption does not throw any light whatever on the character or history of the things we perceive. The statement, therefore, that we perceive states of consciousness rather than physical objects appears to be pretty much of a merely verbal affair.

If we can have no genuine and ultimate contrast between states of consciousness and things which are not states of consciousness, if our only contrasts can be between completeness and incompleteness, or between internal and external meanings of ideas, wherein lies the propriety of the philosophy of ideas? What gives it distinctive features to set it off by contrast from other philosophies? These are current questions and await an answer. By asking them with perfect clearness and insistence, pragmatism has put idealism entirely on the defensive. The historical answer would appear to be that the distinctive feature of idealism lies in its initial assumption. But if it is only assumptions that make differences in philosophical systems, the dispute about the relative merits of rival assumptions must seem, even to the combatants in their calm and reflective moments, very strained and artificial.

Locke, we know, facilitated his own thinking by his doctrine that all ideas are acquired, and thus furnished the motive for the subsequent idealistic doctrines of experience. Since all ideas are acquired by the mind, we may, says Locke, conceive the mind to be originally empty, devoid of ideas. Let the mind now be capable of receiving impressions, and let some impressing agency affect it, then immediately the mind will have ideas after the old analogy of the wax impressed by the seal. Much of modern psychology has travelled the same road. But what warrant is there for conceiving the mind to be such a receptive plasticity? An empty mind, a consciousness-producing receptacle, turns out to be anything we arbitrarily and artificially choose to make it. We can give it any powers or potencies we desire, and no one can reasonably say us nay. Yet it may be claimed that while the mind may be an assumption, we may not be arbitrary in determining its character, for that, like the character of any hypothesis, must be determined in accordance with the facts of experience. The mind, consequently, can have only that character which the constitution of experience makes necessary. But even so, nothing can prevent our supposing as the correlative of mind the physical world of Newton, as Locke did, or other minds, as the panpsychist does, or conceiving the mind as an absolute self-representative system, as other idealists do. And so far it would appear that all the facts of experience are accounted for to the satisfaction of him who entertains any one of these suppositions. Yet we can hardly claim that these three suppositions are simultaneously true. Suppose that there is a mind, and its nature may be such as experience leads us to conclude, but that does not warrant us in supposing that there is a mind in order to account for the facts of experience. Fruitful hypotheses from experience are not made after that fashion.

Undoubtedly, if the term "mind" has any meaning, that meaning must be determined by a study of ascertainable facts. But just as undoubtedly that study must begin with the facts as they are given, untransformed by any assumption. And what I desire to maintain is that these facts, in their ascertainable character, can not be essentially and metaphysically characterized as "ideas" without appeal to assumptions which deliberately attempt to carry us back of the facts to which appeal is made. When this is done, all progress is blocked. Thought then wanders aimlessly in a circle. One can not reach the mind by claiming that all objects are ideas and then trying to establish this claim by insisting that from the nature of mind ideas can be its only objects. It is precisely the suspicion that this is just what idealism does, that tends again to make it appear artificial and incredible.

A critical examination of the attempted definitions of the physical and the psychical, of the body-mind problem, and of the problem of the efficiency of consciousness, as these problems have been stated and discussed from the idealistic point of view, would only multiply the instances where the philosophy of ideas begets the sense of artificiality and incredibility. These instances and those already discussed arise within idealism itself. There are exterior sources of doubt which also should be noted.

Among these the contrast which the content of natural science presents to idealistic philosophy has been repeatedly pointed out. No doubt idealistic philosophers may feel little difficulty in harmonizing natural science with their systems. Their claims are not the point at issue. The fact is that natural science has steadily tended to decrease the importance of man and his philosophizing about the world. I do not speak of natural science turned dogmatic and become as final a metaphysics as any idealism ever claimed to be. Such a metaphysics could be, at best, only a rival, and a rival carrying his own big burden of doubt. I speak rather of that sense of a vast and enfolding nature which science in its steady, progressive achievements constantly deepens within us, begetting, in spite of most signal successes, a feeling of intellectual impotence and humility. Under its spell we seem to be of the earth, anchored to it, with our metaphysical excursions only imaginary voyages. If we embark for conquests, our spoils of victory are not of the metaphysical kind. The mind and heart may cry out for philosophies, but nature replies only with what we call scientific knowledge. This contrast between the desired and the attained puts the desired ever within the sphere of hope, never within that of achievement. Thus we are warned that all philosophies must be aspiring and tentative only. No one at all attentive to the spirit of our age can fail to appreciate how deeply rooted this feeling has become. Long ago there arose protestantism in religion, and now there arises protestantism in thought. All this may, however, indicate a return of philosophy to sanity, but it indicates assuredly a source of suspicion of those philosophies which seek to explain the world primarily from the initial fact that man happens to be conscious of a small part of it.

Not only does natural science thus raise doubts of idealism, but also, and more significantly perhaps, does the fact that evolution has been slowly and steadily altering our fundamental ways of looking at the world. It has made it less natural for us to think of the mind and consciousness after the manner of Locke and Kant. We have been led rather to think of it as a thing with a history, an event the causes of which we might some day discover. In evolution there is no mind as an end-term whose relations eventuate in consciousness. There are rather processes of various sorts undergoing continual reorganization until, at last, they become conscious and understand the conditions out of which they grew, learn their own history and genesis, and thus awake to the conviction that consciousness is not something original, but derived. This conception of a natural evolution of the mind and consciousness has not been worked out as thoroughly as the idealistic conception, but, grasped even in dim outlines, it must render the older conception suspicious. What becomes of the vast synthetic machinery of the mind, if the mind itself has been dethroned? Can the question, "How does the mind know the world?" have significance when you are asking the question,

"How does the world evolve to consciousness of itself?" To answer, "The world grows to consciousness of itself because fundamentally a mind is, or minds are, evolving a world to know," can carry little conviction to the attentive reader of Darwin and Spencer. The more clearly the concepts of evolution are understood, the more impossible the traditional idealistic approach to philosophy appears to be.

Observe, too, in what a different position evolution places the body. It makes it no longer some strange phenomenon of mind, a kind of garment with which the soul covers the nakedness of its immateriality. It makes it rather the mind's essential basis and support, a thing wherein the mind can appear. More correctly stated, the mind is the body's perfected operation and achievement, as Aristotle taught us long ago. The question, therefore, whether mind is efficient would appear meaningless to the evolutionist. He would find it difficult to take the problem of interaction seriously. For to him it is quite evident that conscious bodies are more efficient than those that are not. His evidence rests on no speculation as to the relation of mind to body, but on the fact that greater organization means both greater efficiency and a new type of existence. Here he keeps close company with our ordinary kinds of knowledge. No one doubts that beings become more efficient by becoming conscious, any more than one doubts that a live man is more efficient than a dead one. No one doubts it, not because he merely wants to believe it, or because he can not doubt it, but because the greater efficiency of conscious beings is matter of common knowledge and ordinary proof. How artificial and strained the evolutionary line of thought thus makes a much debated problem appear!

I do not mean to imply that consciousness and its relation to the body present no problems for the evolutionist. He must admit that the peculiarities of conscious activity give to the study of its conditions peculiar interest. That a being when he becomes conscious can think of things very remote, both in time and space, from his organism is a very unique and baffling kind of fact. But I would imply that, in dealing with it, the evolutionist will not be likely to find himself on the road which leads to the philosophy of ideas. When he does that, he has already despaired of his problem. Huxley, we may remember, reluctantly admitted that if he had to, he could embrace idealism, but also insisted that he would not be compelled to that embrace.

Evolution is modifying also our conception of what "ideas" themselves are, and this modification is distinctly in the direction of setting aside the notion that they constitute an order of existence in a region distinct and isolated from the rest of the world. For if consciousness is the outgrowth of reorganization, what one is immediately conscious of would appear to be only the results of this reorganization. Still further, if we suppose that the history of this process can be continuously traced, there remains no motive for supposing that somewhere an entirely and essentially new order of existences has intervened. Evolution may not be true and its assumptions may be unwarranted, but they exist none the less, and point distinctly to a new order of philosophical problems. Their existence is a natural menace to the claims of idealism.

There are, thus, within idealism and without, reasons which tend to make that philosophy appear artificial and unbelievable, and these reasons have today assumed such great proportions that they can no longer be dismissed by the idealist in the easy fashion which too often is his wont. He can no longer simply bid the doubter study Kant and Hegel once again. He can no longer discharge with telling effect the reproaches of materialism and naturalism. For we have attained a new respect for matter and a new affection for nature. We seem to have entered into a new world, where, indeed, we may not see very clearly, but where there is light enough at least to show that no extraordinary wild beasts are waiting to devour us. We may have lost much, but surely there must be a fair prospect from the hills we see.

III

The need of reconstruction in philosophy has thus been felt in many quarters. However varied the attempts to meet the need may appear, they have in general regarded the problem of consciousness as fundamental and initial to any satisfactory reconstruction. The necessity of such a point of view may be seriously questioned. An enlightened naturalism might see in the fact of consciousness no problem of a peculiar or fundamental kind. It might be claimed that when we become conscious we become able measurably to understand the world in which we live and to discover the natural conditions on which our becoming conscious depends, but that the discovery of these conditions presents the same sort of problem which the discovery of the conditions of any other event presents. If it should be objected that this procedure involves the assumption of the reality and validity of knowledge, and thus an epistemology, the naturalist might readily assent. He would probably claim, however, that the attempt to discover anything whatsoever, even the validity of knowledge, for instance, makes the same assumption. He would doubtless point to all existing epistemologies in confirmation of his contention. Yet even so, there is at least an opportunistic reason why the philosopher should assign special importance to the problem of consciousness. That problem has been the central and controlling problem of modern idealism. Our philosophy has become so disturbed and disorganized by it, that we can not hope to find our way about with confidence and freedom until the problem has been reckoned with. We can hardly dismiss idealism cavalierly as a great mistake. The field of consciousness, however small it may be, remains the point of departure for every inquiry and the point of arrival for every solution. This fact, which idealism has put beyond all haughty disregard of it, furnishes a reason much more than opportunistic for a special interest in the problem of consciousness. There would seem, therefore, to be both propriety and justification for the continued importance of that problem.

The recent attempts at reconstruction to which I have referred show a general agreement in their conception of consciousness. Instead of conceiving it as an end-term of a relation, they have conceived it as a relation itself. If this change is to mean anything more than a merely logical contrast with the starting-point of idealism, or a new assumption the conclusions from which are to be deduced, it is important that the sense in which consciousness is conceived as a relation should be made clear. To this end we may make an examination of the conscious situation itself from such points of view as may prove suggestive. It is perhaps the difference in points of view rather than in the real nature of the results reached that accounts for much of current misunderstanding. I desire, therefore, to lay special emphasis on the point of view adopted in this paper, namely, the point of view of our reflective conscious inquiry. No situation can be more familiar to us or less equivocal than that in which we deliberately engage in some sort of inquiry, seek to solve some problem, or put questions to the objects and events of life in the hope of getting the answers we call knowledge. The situation is, in short, that of our conscious inquiry into whatever we may be conscious of.

It has been claimed that it is impossible to examine such a situation. While such a claim appears to me to be not only incapable of justification but also absurd, a brief consideration of it may aid the purposes of definition. The claim in question asserts that from the temporal or flowing character of consciousness we can never be conscious of a situation at the same time in which the situation exists, but are conscious of it only in representation. Stated in terms of introspection, we introspect only situations that have passed; in terms of states of consciousness, one state can never be its own object, but the object only of a succeeding state. I was about to say with reference to this claim what has been often said; namely, that if it were true we then could never introspect anything or be conscious of anything. It is more important, however, to note that the truth of the claim is a matter about which it may not be profitable to dispute, for we want to know whether consciousness has just that flowing, successive character which gives to the claim all the force it has. Surely, if that question can not be settled, the claim is at best only gratuitous or presumptive. If the question can be settled, however, I am perplexed in trying to understand what an affirmative answer really means; for so far as I am aware, every affirmative answer has really presupposed the successive character of consciousness. The presupposition may have some doctrine of time back of it. If so, the question is pertinent, Have we consciousness of time? Again, the alternative answers appear either to throw no light upon the question at issue, or simply to continue controversy. I would emphasize also the fact that the doctrine of successive consciousness is bound up with the end-term conception of the mind and the doctrine of mental states.

The dispute, however, may, as I have suggested, aid the purposes of definition. Whatever we may conclude the nature of consciousness to be, we start our investigations from a point that can be commanded. Our conclusions are derived from that commanding point; they are explications and elucidations of it. We may admit that it is possible that our conclusions may completely revolutionize our point of departure, but it is important that we should always see just how that revolution is effected. So long as we can not do that, we are still in the realm of tentative guesses. I feel constrained, therefore, to abide by the limitation I have imposed. Problems appear only in situations immediately within our grasp. No matter what causes may have generated them, they must first be problems for inquiry before their causes can be discovered.

The same considerations warrant, I think, the rejection of the genetic point of view for the primary consideration of consciousness. Consciousness may, no doubt, have had an evolution, it may begin to be, and the conditions of its genesis may be discoverable. But clearly that discovery will be made by starting from some present situation which must first be defined if the discovery is to be estimated properly. Again, there may well be lower grades of consciousness which are prior to the grade where problems exist, and out of which problems emerge; but such grades are inferred in order to answer existing problems which must first have been stated. In short, a metaphysics of consciousness, an inquiry into its nature as an existing concrete situation, appears to be fundamental to any fertile theory.

Theories of perceptions are not directly a help in such an inquiry. They have, indeed, been more productive of confusion than of enlightenment, on account of their connection with the doctrines discussed in the second part of this paper. Yet the present status of the theory of perception has an indirect bearing which should be noted. The theory appears to have attained the character of a natural science, and as such has the same general philosophical bearings as any other natural science. This means, of course, that the theory does not exist to its own prejudice. It exists rather in its own right. By that I mean that the facts in terms of which the theory is formulated do not undergo any transformation in their nature on account of the theory, although they may undergo refinement and extension. The psychologist discovers what the conditions of seeing or hearing are, precisely after the manner in which the chemist discovers the conditions under which certain combinations occur. In each case we start with definite, relatable facts which remain just those facts and no others throughout the inquiry. No other presuppositions are made besides the existence of the facts in the manner in which they are found to exist before the theory is framed. The theory of perception as a theory of natural science does not interpose a percept between a mind and a stimulus. It simply takes the stimulus and asks what machinery is involved in perceiving it. There is no mystery about the stimulus. It is always something that can be produced in definite, concrete form. The act of perception is equally definite and concrete. Given the definite stimulus and the definite act, the theory simply asks for the machinery which connects them. When thus conceived, the theory of perception can throw no direct light on the nature of consciousness. It may illumine the question indirectly by showing that in order to exist, the theory of perception does not need to distinguish between what we are conscious of and what not. It takes its departure, therefore, from just the sort of initial situation which a theory of consciousness should attempt to define. To that situation we should now turn.

In general, the situation of conscious inquiry exhibits a great variety of things, grouped in various ways and having manifold relations to one another. A book may be on a table, a bunch of flowers may be in a vase, a stroke of a bell may follow a previous stroke, a pain may be in the head. The whole situation seems resolvable into things related somehow to one another. Some general types of relation stand out more prominently than others. Conspicuous among these are the spatial and temporal relations. On account of their character it is impossible for one to be on a distant elevation without going there. These relations hold the things together, constitute such bonds between them, that any alteration which space and time permit must involve a certain amount of change both in space and time. Thus we may bring materials together from far and near and in the course of time erect them into a building. But even before the materials are collected and reared they may suggest the future building or many incidents of their own history. This fact reveals another conspicuous relation which holds the things together in quite a different manner from the spatial and temporal. One thing may be a certain measurable distance from another thing, but it may *mean* that other thing without encompassing the distance. And I wish to emphasize the fact that this relation of meaning which is so prominent among the things is just as much *a relation between them* as is space or time. It is the ice which means that it will cool the water, just as much as it is the ice which does cool the water when put into it. The water which means that it will quench thirst is the water which does quench thirst when swallowed. I take a powder to dispel the pain in the head, not only because pain and powder are incompatible in juxtaposition, but incompatible also in their meanings.

We should note, moreover, that the relations of meaning are capable of remarkable systematization, synthesis, condensation, and unification, and that this takes place apparently without any corresponding change in the other relations which subsist. The meanings of the solar system may be condensed in a book, but not the solar system as a thing in space. Here, I suppose, we find the motive, so prominent in philosophy, for making meanings immaterial. For the syntheses in the meaning relation are as different from those in the spatial and temporal relations as the immaterial and the material could well be conceived to be. In spite of the burden of perplexity which these terms have had to carry, they have done too good service to be wholly discarded. So I venture to formulate the facts I have noted as follows: The situation under examination exhibits a variety of things in a variety of relations, but some of the relations make possible a material synthesis of the things, while one of the relations makes possible an immaterial synthesis.

The situation has been described as conscious. Without now

departing from the situation itself, or seeking a position prior to it or beyond it, I should like to suggest that it is by virtue of the possibility of the immaterial synthesis alone that the situation is so described. The distinction between consciousness and not-consciousness would thus be brought within the situation itself, and be capable of verification and examination by any one interested. Such a view is at least largely consonant with common sense and science. For under their guidance we are wont to think of a world without consciousness in it as a world devoid of meaning. Add consciousness to that world and then meaning is added, but nothing else. But it is often claimed that in adding consciousness, we also add at least the so-called secondary qualities and pains and pleasures. I can not examine this contention here with the thoroughness it merits, but I may observe that it is still in the realm of doubt and difficulty. In addition it is to be noted that the secondary qualities, and pains and pleasures also, are capable of the contrasted syntheses I have emphasized. Still further, when we ask for the proof that secondary qualities and the like are due to consciousness, the proof is always stated, not in terms of consciousness, but in terms of a physiological organism which is one of the things in the conscious situation. These facts make it extremely difficult for me to assent to the statement that consciousness is in any way responsible for the specific characters of the things in the conscious situation. In the absence of logically coherent proof that it is, I incline to the more natural view.

Such phrases as "conscious of" and "conscious that" have often been taken to indicate that consciousness is not simply the kind of relation I have indicated, but that it has in addition the property of "awareness," which gives to things a peculiar and immediate kind of presence. I am not sure but that we find ourselves here in a verbal difficulty, for what is it "to be aware" of anything? If we can not make the "awareness" responsible for the thing's qualities or for its spatial and temporal relations, what is then left to constitute that peculiar presence? Indeed, it seems to me, on analysis of the situation, that just this character of "awareness" turns out to be the manifold and irresistible meaning connections which the things in the conscious situation have. These connections hold the things in such a network of immaterial groupings that their presence is quite other than merely spatial, temporal, or specifically qualitative. It is to be noted also that the "awareness" diminishes in its evident character just in proportion as the linkage of meanings becomes deranged. I do not find at present, therefore, convincing facts to indicate that "awareness" involves an additional characterization of consciousness.

Such is the initial conception of consciousness which I wish to suggest. It appears to be a relation between things which makes a synthesis of meanings possible, a relation markedly distinct from other relations between the same things which make possible other sorts of syntheses. That the conception may not be misrepresented, I would call attention again to the distinct limitations under which it has been formulated. No attempt has been made here to discover the conditions under which consciousness exists or to show why it has its specific character. My sole attempt has been to examine the situation where all our problems arise in the hope of discovering in it an initial conception of consciousness the further development of which might be fruitful. I am of the opinion that such an attempt is fundamental to all further inquiry, and affords the point of departure for an investigation of genetic conditions. Naturally, the conception is not itself a solvent for philosophical problems, but is rather a creator of them. I should like, therefore, in conclusion, briefly to indicate some of the problems which it suggests.

The description which I have given of the conscious situation accords, I suppose, with an idealistic description of experience when experience is taken in its immediate and evident character. After Kant, no one can claim any novelty or originality in pointing out a synthesis in space and time or a synthesis in the "understanding." It is important, however, that these syntheses should not be construed after the Kantian fashion or on the basis of idealistic assumptions. They should in no sense be tainted with "subjectivity." They should not be regarded as syntheses of "phenomena." Yet the idealistic attempt to "deduce" them presents, in its essence, a problem to engage attention. In other words, if we may describe the conscious situation as a grouping of things in different syntheses, the question whether these syntheses are co-ordinate or subordinate to one another, or involve a general, unifying synthesis, is a natural one to ask. But prior to asking it, the situation presents the general problem of groups, relations, and syntheses, their kinds, their classification, and their most general definition. The science of mathematics has already been so productive in this direction that we may confidently look for still greater aid from it. If all things exist in relations, we may naturally regard the relational formula as expressing the simplest and most general type of existence. It would appear that this formula, if it is to be general, should express a relation of some sort between two variables, and thus be of the general form xRy. This formula applied to any situation would mean that R expresses the way x and y vary in relation to each other, but not the fact of variation in x and y. It is thus apparent that R will always express a law and be a principle of uniformity and necessity, while x and y will express facts which are a source of change and variety. If we are dealing with the causal relation, for instance, R will express the fact of uniformity and necessary connection, while x and y will express the fact of efficiency. The general problem of "deduction" would thus involve the discovery of an R of such a type that, as x and y vary, their variations will result in an order of R's. But it is to be noted that the fact of variation in x and y could not by this means be "deduced." Their original variation is essential to the deduction.

It is at least superficially apparent that these considerations apply to space, time, and consciousness as relations between things. Each of these relations conforms to the general type indicated by the formula. The relation space, when defined, expresses certain laws and necessary connections which, no matter how the things in space may vary, are always in force; and it is, of course, true that the things vary in many ways in independence of this relation. The same general considerations apply to time. They appear to apply also to consciousness. If consciousness is defined as the relation of meaning, then the fact of meaning gives rise to certain necessary connections which it is the business of logic to formulate; but the things related in consciousness will vary independently of that fact. And this seems true. Call the things in consciousness by whatever names we please, they appear to vary independently of the existence of consciousness. Otherwise, logic should suffice for all the materials of knowledge. Thus it would seem that if consciousness alone ceased to exist, things might still be connected in all their other relations. This would undoubtedly be the case unless the existence of consciousness were so bound up with the existence of all other relations that its disappearance necessarily involved theirs. In this case consciousness would appear to be the type of relation required for a deduction of an order of relations. Yet even so we should still have independent variables as necessary constituents of this basal relation. Consciousness is, however, apparently not of this fundamental type. Its intermittent existence seems to forbid it. Of course its intermittent existence is not a fact in the conscious situation; but of course, also, there are changes in things in other relations, which changes do not take place in the conscious situation itself. We are forced, therefore, to distinguish between permanent, or relatively permanent, and intermittent relations. "Deduction" would naturally proceed from the more permanent relations. The problem thus presented may be impossible to solve, but one is tempted not to dismiss it without serious examination.

Intermittent relations themselves present a variety of problems of peculiar interest. I shall mention only one of them, and this one on account of its intimate connection with the general problem of consciousness. Many intermittent relations—and some of the permanent ones too—are, so to speak, centred. Some group or some one of the things connected in them, is of such a character that its variations determine in some way the scope of the relations. Such centres wherever found, present problems of special difficulty. The body, or a part of it, or a systematization of its parts, is such a centre in the relation of consciousness. I need not detail the problems which arise from this fact. Their solution, however, can be facilitated, I think, in proportion as we devote attention to the study of similar centres in other relations. It is not unlikely that they all have common features. If these were once discovered, the task of ascertaining their specific features could be more readily outlined. The hope also may be entertained that a study of such centres and of the general fact of relations would yield a body of knowledge of wider applicability than the very narrow domain within which philosophers are very prone to allow themselves to be restricted.

I have defined consciousness as the relation of meaning between things and suggested that "awareness" may be but another term for meaning. Yet it is apparent that a specific characterization of the relation consciousness which would helpfully distinguish it from all other relations must be much more than a matter of names. For while the general characterization of consciousness as a relation may be a fruitful means toward philosophical reconstruction, its specific characterization must be thoroughly worked out, if the relational theory of consciousness is to approach completeness. To assign consciousness to the intermittent and centred types of relation is a step in that direction, but this road, thoroughly travelled, may leave regions of investigation still untouched. The personal and self-reflective character of consciousness, its privacy, its continuity, and other characters which have often been enumerated as its essential features, should be shown to be various aspects of its specific character or deductions from it, or to be connected with other more general features of the type. The specific characterization of space in terms of such axioms as that of free mobility has done much for those departments of knowledge the objects of which involve the spare relation. We need corresponding characterizations of time and consciousness for similar successes.

Another group of problems is connected with a study of the types of synthesis which are effected in the conscious relation. Indeed, some of the problems cited in the preceding paragraphs may belong to this group. But I refer here more especially to those syntheses which give us related or contrasted bodies of knowledge. The results of such an examination would appear to involve a developed doctrine of categories, providing us with their enumeration, their relations, and the methods and genesis of their formation. The bearing of such a doctrine on logic and metaphysics would doubtless be far-reaching. Evolution as a category of wide application has familiarized us with the conception of a reality in constant process of transformation and reorganization. The place of consciousness in such a process and the conditions of its genesis there afford inquiries of endless interest and fascination. Indeed, if the world evolves to consciousness, we should have in consciousness itself the most immediate and significant instance of evolution, revealing what that process is in its most intimate and essential features.

PERCEPTION AND EPISTEMOLOGY*

"WHAT perception is," says John Locke, "every one will know better by reflecting on what he does himself, when he sees, hears, feels, etc., or thinks, than by any discourse of mine. Whoever reflects on what passes in his own mind can not miss it. And if he does not reflect, all the words in the world can not make him have any notion of it. This is certain, that whatever alterations are made in the body, if they reach not the mind; whatever impressions are made on the outward parts, if they are not taken notice of within, there is no perception. Fire may burn our bodies with no other effect than it does a billet, unless the motion be continued to the brain, and there the sense of heat, or idea of pain, be produced in the mind; wherein consists actual perception."[1]

Psychologists since Locke have often thought of perception more narrowly, but his words still serve to point out the different attitudes towards the fact that to know our world we must perceive and reflect upon it, which have been conspicuous in modern inquiries into the subject. They suggest that perception is a process which we may examine by considering what we do when we see or hear, and that it is a content, a result, which we may, consequently, consider as such, and about the nature and relations of which we may inquire. It is with these two attitudes towards perception that this paper is primarily concerned, so far as the problem of knowledge is affected by them.

* In *Essays Philosophical and Psychological: in Honor of William James* by his colleagues at Columbia University, N. Y., Longmans, Green, 1908, pp. 137-166.

[1] *Essay concerning Human Understanding,* edited by A. C. Fraser. Vol. I, p. 183.

I

Inquiry into what we do when we see involves us naturally in researches into those physical and physiological processes which Democritus seems to have been the first to formulate with any great amount of completeness. We are led to recognize sources of stimulation, media for the transmission of the stimulus, organs for its reception, and reactions of the individual possessing the organs. In a particular case, as in that of seeing, we try to isolate a particular process and discover how it is related to other similar processes. In short, we inquire into the mechanism of perception. We deal with factors, processes, and quantities supposed to be known or ascertainable. Stimulus, medium, and organ, for instance, are distinguished as identifiable factors in one continuous sphere of investigation. Any doubt about their existence, their character, or their mode of operation tends to vitiate and obscure our understanding of the mechanism we are trying to discover. Further, our procedure is not speculative, but experimental. So far as possible we measure the stimulus, the rate of its transmission, and its effect. We do what can be repeated by others, because to others our method is intelligible and the means of repetition are at their command. Should we engage in mere suppositions, admit that the stimulus, for instance, were not something given with which we can experiment, but something assumed to account for certain facts, our laboratories might well be closed, and the mechanism of perception left for anyone to conceive according to his preferences or whims. But it is precisely such admissions which we do not make. We may admit that other points of view may lead to a revision of the ultimate significance of our results, but we never willingly admit that the method and the factors of our investigation are not intelligible, clear, and unambiguous.

Still further, we are quite unwilling to set any arbitrary limit to the extent to which inquiries of this nature may be successfully pursued. Whatever limits we discover we set down to our ignorance, to our lack of appropriate instruments, to our failures, but not to any restraints due to the method we employ or to the nature of the factors with which we deal. We may characterize certain results of perception as illusions, but such a characterization does not deter us from inquiring into their mechanism in precisely the same way as we inquire into the mechanism of those results we call normal or real. We may even ask, as Locke suggests, what we do when we think, and admit that the only bar to our discovery of the mechanism of thought is a temporary ignorance which at any moment may be removed. In general, then, perception as a process defined broadly in terms of Locke's general definition of it is a process open to experimental inquiry in an intelligible and unambiguous manner, an inquiry which can be repeated, checked, and verified by anyone who takes the pains to do so. The result is a concrete body of knowledge steadily increasing in extent and definiteness, and gradually accumulating solid information about the world in which we live. No one naturally fails to grasp its aim, its method, or its import. No one finds confusion in it unless he departs from the point of view from which it is instituted and proceeds to estimate it according to standards and criteria other than those which are employed in building it up.

Similar observations may be made about the results reached when we take the other attitude towards perception; when, that is, we regard it as a content or product. Naturally we are now no longer concerned with the process or mechanism by which the content is attained, but solely with the facts which are the outcome of that process. When we see, certain things are done, but something also is seen. That which we see we now call *a* perception, and in general we may use the term "perceptions" to denote whatever may be the objects of our regard. Now these perceptions we may enumerate. We may classify them. We may analyze them into such elements as we may be able to discover. We may find out how these elements are related to one another, how they may be combined, how they modify one another. About the combinations we may make similar inquiries. In short, we may institute a wide range of investigations into the things we perceive without departing from the point of view which takes these things simply as the objects of our regard, and without asking how we perceive them. Such inquiries may be as free from speculation and mere assumptions as those we make into the mechanism of perception as a process. They may be equally as experimental. They may be kept true to their point of departure and yield concrete bodies of knowledge of great value. The results attained are accessible to anyone who cares to review them. The methods and experiments by which they are attained can be repeated, they can be checked and verified at any point desired. We find no ambiguity or confusion in the knowledge they afford us so long as we do not depart from the point of view from which these particular inquiries are instituted.

When we speak of those bodies of knowledge which result when we regard perception solely as a content or product, we are apt to think primarily of analytic and descriptive psychology. But it is clear that they may not be so restricted. They comprise, in fact, by far the greater part of what we know. The astronomer, the biologist, the chemist, the historian, the student of literature—to mention only a few instances—are all engaged in increasing our knowledge of what our perceptions are and how they are related to one another. Their studies are not prefaced by an examination of how we perceive. They take their material as so much given stuff, and then proceed to tell us what, when so taken, they discover it to be. If they are invited first to examine the mechanism of perception, they regard the invitation as impertinent and irrelevant. They have found such an examination to be unnecessary, and so believe that they can rightfully neglect it. Even when their attention is called to the fact that the processes by which we perceive have important bearings on what we perceive, they find that their observations can be controlled by well-known methods, by putting them, for instance, in the context which theories of probability, based on a number of observations, afford. They can thus make their observations approach any degree of theoretical accuracy desired.

We should, doubtless, count among the bodies of knowledge which result when perception is regarded as a product more than history and the greater part of natural science. For, naturally, we may make these bodies of knowledge themselves objects of investigation, asking after their general constitution, the manner of their building up, and the grounds which lead us to view them with confidence. These are problems with which logic is concerned. How far they constitute the full extent and nature of logical theory may be left for the present purpose undecided. But it is clear that a logic which would deal with them successfully would be a very comprehensive science. When we should know how different bodies of knowledge differ, how far these differences are due to material, to method, and to aim, when we should know how these bodies of knowledge are built up from what we perceive, and with what degree of confidence they may be entertained, we should then have largely satisfied the demands which our interest in logic occasions. Such a logic, like the bodies of knowledge it reviewed, would be experimental, it would itself be capable of review by anyone interested without involving the reviewer in ambiguous assumptions. It would simply say to him, Such and such is the case with these bodies of knowledge; examine them for yourself and you will find it so or be able to indicate where inaccuracy exists. It is quite inconceivable that such a logic could afford matter for debate rather than for investigation. It would hardly be called by the names of those who worked at it, or be the possession of a "school" or a "philosophy." It would constitute a body of common knowledge which investigators could enlarge and thereby enlarge their own reputations. In proportion as it kept clear its title to common knowledge, admitting review and repetition of experiments at all points, it would be free from ambiguity and confusion.

It seems clear, further, that the point of view under consideration could yield a metaphysics which, like history, the sciences, and logic, could claim to be experimental and constitute a body of common knowledge. For it may well be that the things which we perceive, when taken in as comprehensive totals as we can grasp, present certain general features of character and connection which we tend to disregard or overlook when the same things are taken less comprehensively and completely. Such characters and connections have been historical themes of metaphysics. When looked for in the world of concrete perceptions they may not constitute all that historical metaphysics has been pleased to investigate, but the experimental restriction can not obscure the magnitude or importance of the body of knowledge which might result. For, most assuredly, if there are general types of existence among the things we perceive and general types of connection, the clear definition of their characters and modes of operation could not fail to be of importance, or to afford problems of ceaseless and varied interest. A metaphysics of the kind suggested would admit of natural growth from generation to generation, because it would be knowledge of the kind that pursues a common road and that can be repeatedly checked and reviewed.

Bodies of knowledge of the kind described by no means constitute the sole results of our inquiries. We seek to supplement them by hypotheses, theories, and philosophical speculations, but we find our vision of the world grows clearer thereby only as these supplementations are genuinely such. The moment they lead us to deprive the results of careful research of their natural character and purport, these results become ambiguous and misleading. We no longer remain clear as to the information they intend to convey. When, for example, Huxley tells us that "a sensation is the equivalent in terms of consciousness for a mode of motion of the matter of the sensorium," and that the assumption of the existence of matter is a "pure piece of metaphysical speculation,"[2] our thoughts on the subject of sensation become confused instead of clear. It seems unjust to his careful investigation to conclude that a sensation is a certain kind of equivalent for something the existence of which is a pure piece of metaphysical speculation. Indeed, if such is to be the outcome of our study of sensation, that study is hardly worth while. It does not clarify the thing it intends to clarify. It obscures it and makes it unintelligible. Thus it is that speculation only confuses experimental knowledge when, by depriving our results of their evident import, it fails genuinely to enlarge or supplement them in the direction in which they naturally point.

Again, it is only by being such genuine enlargements or supplementations that speculation can be controlled and pre-

[2] *Hume: with Helps to the Study of Berkeley.* New York, D. Appleton & Co. p. 317.

served from mere idiosyncrasy. As pragmatism has now abundantly taught us, with fresh insistence on a piece of wisdom long familiar, speculations which can own no checks or make no differences in the world with which we directly deal are matters which it is idle to seek to verify. We may accept them, not because they give us information about our world continuous and homogeneous with what we naturally acquire, but because of their inherent interest or their consonance with our moods.

Whether, therefore, we regard perception as a process the mechanism of which we are to discover, or as a product comprising the realm of what we perceive, it is evident that we may sketch out extensive bodies of knowledge consistently and unambiguously pursued from these two points of view. Even if the points of view differ, the resulting bodies of knowledge are of the same general character. They are what I have called experimental. And by that I have meant that the elements, the terms, the relations, the connections, the qualities, the quantities—or whatever terms we may choose by which to designate the various things we study—can all be identified by anyone who wishes to identify them, and that whatever is said about these things can be tested by anyone who will refer to the things in question. The bodies of knowledge are not mere possibilities which we may some day realize, but they are actual bodies of knowledge already existing in various stages of progress. What I would particularly emphasize about them is their experimental character and the fact that they are accepted by the vast majority of people at their face value, as measurably accomplishing the thing they set out to do.

That they are so accepted will, probably, be generally admitted. When we are told that under specified conditions objects excite certain disturbances in the medium between them and our eyes, and that our eyes are affected by these disturbances in various ways, that retina and nerve are thereby stimulated, and that consequently we see, we tend to believe what we are told. When we are told that the medium is the ether, we may have difficulty in comprehending just what the ether is, but we tend to believe that there is such a thing or something like it which we might understand better with increased knowledge. We tend to believe these things just as we tend to believe the historian when he tells us that the Pilgrims landed in 1620 A. D. Indeed, we naturally regard statements about the ether, about the processes and results of perception, and statements about the Pilgrims, as statements of the same general kind purporting to inform us about the conditions and happenings in the world in which we live. Similarly, we incline to accept the statements of the sciences for just what they purport to be: that there is such a substance as oxygen and that it combines with other substances in certain ways; that these substances may be atomic in structure or of a structure more complex; that living beings vary in certain ways and preserve an amount of continuity in their succession; that the natural history of the world is, in large measure, a genuine account of what has happened. In short, whatever knowledge is of the experimental kind we take its deliverances as probably correct information about the things with which it deals. This habit of mind is by no means incompatible with the liberal recognition that we know but little and that the little we know is doubtless subject to revision. But we naturally hold tenaciously to that little until the need of revision has become apparent. The revised knowledge is, however, the same in kind as that which it supersedes.

II

Whether we regard perception as a process or as a content, concrete bodies of knowledge result purporting to give us approximately correct information about the world in which we live. Yet it has been repeatedly insisted that just because these two attitudes towards perception exist, information about our world can not ultimately be taken at its face value and with its natural import. For, it is urged, if we mean by perception as a content that which we immediately perceive, it is evident that, in the last analysis, perception is given to us only as a content. We may, of course, still speak of examining into the processes of perception and even of experimenting upon them, but it should be evident that these processes, so far as we directly attack them, are themselves perceptions, they are what we immediately perceive, they are contents. How, then, can we be justified in regarding them as the real processes which precede contents and result in perceptions? On the other hand, if we cut the contents wholly off from their supposed processes, how can we be justified in longer believing that they, with the bodies of knowledge built directly upon them, afford us reliable information about our world? Are we not confronted here with the problem of knowledge in its most serious and fundamental form, and confronted with it in a manner requiring a procedure and point of view in marked contrast with the procedure and points of view which have given us our bodies of positive knowledge? Do we not need a theory which may free us from a situation which, otherwise, must remain ambiguous and paradoxical? We have in these questions one way of stating the central problem of modern epistemology.

More attention has been paid to the soundness of the solutions which have been offered of this problem than has been paid to their success in modifying positive knowledge and in giving us increased reliable information about our world. If, however, we do not raise the question of their validity, but ask rather concerning their importance for the bodies of knowledge which are steadily built up in the ways indicated in the early paragraphs of this paper, we are confronted with the fact that they have not modified these bodies of knowledge in any essential particular, nor supplemented them in any continuous and homogeneous manner. Their efficacy has exhibited itself primarily in modifying our personal estimate of the significance of what we know. Some illustrations of this result may reinforce the general statement.

Professor Karl Pearson's characterization of the concepts of science as conceptual shorthand has, as is evident from his *Grammar of Science,* an epistemological basis. There may be no atoms and no ether. Indeed, he conceives their existence to be relatively an unimportant matter. The important matter is whether they, as conceptual shorthand, help us to resume the routine of our perceptions. But it is clear, none the less, that scientists attempt to discover the constitution of the ether, the weight of atoms, their structure, and their relations to one another. I say they attempt to *discover* these things, they do not attempt simply to *conceive* them. The acceptance or rejection of Professor Pearson's epistemology does not appear to affect their methods of research or the formulation of their results. He may lead us to believe that an epistemological estimate of the value of science is a very important matter, but it seems to be important not because it makes for a better or a more accurate science, not because it increases our success in using the results of research in industry and the arts, but because it tends to modify our personal estimates of the ultimate significance of knowledge. The *Grammar of Science* contributes, undoubtedly, to the methods and results of science, but its epistemology contributes not to their enlargement, but to their spiritual evaluation. It leads us to reflect on the importance of the proper estimate of science for social progress and citizenship.

As a second illustration, I take the following paragraph from Professor H. Poincaré's *Value of Science*:

> Does the harmony the human intelligence thinks it discovers in nature exist outside of this intelligence? No, beyond doubt, a reality completely independent of the mind which conceives it, sees or feels it, is an impossibility. A world as exterior as that, even if it existed, would for us be forever inaccessible. But what we call objective reality is, in the last analysis, what is common to many thinking beings, and could be common to all; this common part, we shall see, can only be the harmony expressed by mathematical laws. It is this harmony then which is the sole objective reality, the only truth we can attain; and when I add that the universal harmony of the world is the source of all beauty, it will be understood what price we should attach to the slow and difficult progress which little by little enables us to know it better.[3]

Even if these words contain the proper estimate of the value of science, even if it is true that the only genuine objective reality is a harmony which does not exist outside of the intelligence which discovers it and is yet common to many thinking beings, we find thereby no new ways to enlarge or correct our positive knowledge about the world. We may be freed, as Professor Poincaré suggests, from a certain fear of scientific truth which might otherwise oppress us. We may have our spiritual vision broadened. But the progress of sci-

[3] *Popular Science Monthly,* Vol. LXIX, p. 196.

ence does not seem to be affected by such services except in so far as they help to remove our prejudices or make us enthusiastic.

If we turn to the writings of those who are more exclusively epistemologists, the same general conclusions will be forced upon us. How repeatedly we have been told that epistemology does not disturb the ordinary processes of knowledge! How naturally philosophers have been led to commend it for its effects on character! "If, therefore," says Berkeley, "we consider the difference there is betwixt natural philosophers and other men, with regard to their knowledge of the phenomena, we shall find it consists, not in an exacter knowledge of the efficient cause that produces them—for that can be no other than the *will of a spirit*—but only in a greater largeness of comprehension, whereby analogies, harmonies, and agreements are discovered in the works of nature, and the particular effects explained, that is, reduced to general rules." Again he says: "From what has been premised, no reason can be drawn why the history of nature should not still be studied, and observations and experiments made; which, that they are of use to mankind, and enable us to draw any general conclusions, is not the result of any immutable habitudes or relations between things themselves, but only of God's goodness and kindness to men in the administration of the world."[4] Illustrations from certain contemporaneous philosophers might also be cited to indicate that in their opinion the great aim of philosophical inquiry into the foundations of knowledge is not to rectify or homogeneously to supplement the results of positive knowledge, but to afford us a spiritual estimate of these results. By considering epistemological speculations we are led to reflect on our relations to the absolute.

Considerations like the above point to the conclusion that the service which epistemology renders is not logical, but moral and spiritual. It affords us, to use the expression with which Professor Santayana describes religion, "another world to live in," a world where it may indeed be good to dwell now and then, but which is so different and remote from the world where perception is a fact and a process for investiga-

[4] *Works,* Fraser's edition, 1901, Vol. I, pp. 315, 317.

tion that the problem of perception receives thereby no genuine solution. In terms of that other world we may describe perception in ways endeared to epistemology, but when we seek information about what we perceive and how we perceive it, we return to the world of positive knowledge. Should we ask if this information is correct, we should find no answer in that other world. It would appear, therefore, that the problem of the relation between the content and the process of perception is not clarified by epistemology. Possibly it is a problem which does not involve the question of the nature and validity of knowledge at all, for it may well be that the relation between content and process is not a cognitive relation.

In spite of what appears to be its logical irrelevancy for all bodies of positive knowledge, epistemology, it may be urged, can hardly be dismissed for that reason. The processes of knowledge, studied as empirically and experimentally as you please, may occasion problems the solution of which may force us to recognize that there is a region of philosophical truth different from what positive knowledge reveals and beyond it, a region that forms indeed a supplement to that disclosed by science, but a supplement to be reached by other methods. That other world to live in may not at all be damaged by the recognition of it as another world; it may, rather, thereby receive added importance. If we are actually forced by the peculiarities of experience to frame a theory in the light of which we may scrutinize the truth of the bodies of knowledge we build up directly from the facts of life, we ought, no doubt, to submit to such pressure and do the best we can in the way of such a theory. Furthermore, it may appear arbitrary and high-handed to claim that epistemology itself is not built up directly from the facts of life, or that it is without experimental warrant. The facts of experience justify it, one may claim, and make it necessary. If its development leads us radically to revise our estimate of the results of positive knowledge, and to find in them a significance deeper than what they obviously disclose, is it not irrelevant to reply that epistemology does not alter the methods of positive knowledge or enlarge the content of history and the sciences in any continuous and homogeneous manner? The realist may clamour for the recognition of the fact that all philosophy can do is to tell us in the most comprehensive way what we have found our world really to be, but the idealist can always retort that he has found our world to be precisely that which his own idealistic epistemology has disclosed. The clamour and retort do not, however, advance our knowledge.

Yet I believe that the student who is interested in recording the results of modern intellectual inquiry is warranted in upholding the conclusion on which this paper has, thus far, insisted. We build up directly from considering the processes of perception, and also the results of those processes, vast bodies of knowledge without seeking any epistemological warrant for our procedure. We may build up an epistemology also, finding our warrant for so doing in matters which the bodies of knowledge referred to designedly and systematically neglect, and be led thereby to scrutinize the truth of our positive knowledge from the vantage ground whither epistemology has carried us. But if we ask what actual service this scrutiny performs, we seem compelled to answer that the service is not logical, but moral and spiritual. It does not modify knowledge. It modifies character. It does not give us new or increased information about our world whereby that world may be more effectively controlled. It gives us rather considerations the contemplation of which is more or less satisfying to the spirit.

III

Such a situation is provoking. It has given rise to noteworthy systems of metaphysics which may serve to explain why the bodies of positive knowledge and epistemology have so little mutual relevance, and appear, nevertheless, to be natural and inevitable intellectual products. But the question I would raise here does not primarily concern these systems. It concerns rather the initial step which carries us to them. I should like to ask whether, as a matter of fact, the difficulties to which the theory of perception gives rise demand an epistemological solution. In other words, does the fact that the processes of perception result in contents which alone we can be said to perceive necessitate the question of the validity of what we know? Can the problem of perception be intelligibly defined as a problem of cognition? It has been quite generally assumed that we must ultimately define it as such a problem even if by so doing we become unintelligible, concluding that the content of perception is subjective because it is other than and subsequent to an objective process which produces it, and then concluding that we must question or reconstruct the objectivity of the process because the only means by which we know it is the content. It is that assumption which gives point to the question whether we perceive things as they really are and which makes the claim that knowledge should be taken at its face value as a natural product appear so violent to many minds. Until this assumption is reckoned with we can hope for little clear appreciation of differences of opinion. I propose a general examination of it here in the hope that I may at least suggest that its claims are far from final.

"Fire may burn our bodies with no other effect than it does a billet, unless the motion be continued to the brain, and there the sense of heat, or idea of pain, be produced in the mind; wherein consists actual perception." From the truth of this statement few would naturally dissent. It contains, however, a formulation of the relation between the mechanism and the result of perception which is ambiguously sustained by the facts. It is evident that unless the motion be continued to the brain we do not perceive the burn. But it is not evident *in the same way* that the sense of heat or idea of pain is produced there in the mind by the continuation of that motion. As has been repeatedly maintained, we can follow that continuation of motion pretty far and the farther we follow it the more we grow convinced that we should not, could we follow it completely, ever come upon the sense of heat or the idea of pain. We are reasonably convinced that without sense-organs, nerves, and brain, we should never perceive the world as we do perceive it, but the more completely we understand organs, nerves, and brain, the less we think of ever discovering in them that world of varied objects and events. Now this fact has led, as it led with Locke, to the assumption that, therefore, the world which we perceive can not be continuous and homogeneous with the process by which we perceive it. That world must be of a nature quite different, a world of "ideas," of "states of consciousness," a mental world, in short, the relation of which to the world in which the process occurs we must now speculate about and construct an epistemology to explain.

The disparity, however, between the world which we perceive and the world where the processes of perception occur, tends to vanish on close examination. When once perception as a content is styled "idea," many minds, under the logical restraint of such ambiguous propositions as "the idea of weight is not heavy" and "the idea of length is not long," have violently robbed "ideas" of the qualities they rightfully possess. What we perceive may be styled "ideas," but the name ought not to obscure the fact that some of these "ideas" are actually red and green, others sweet and sour, others noisy, others too heavy to be lifted, others of measurable length. Were they not such, it is clear we should never speak of such qualities or seek to discover their causes. Epistemologists have struggled over the question of the relation of mind to matter, and idealists have insisted that matter is, after all, mental, but the obvious fact is that "states of consciousness" when made to include all that we perceive, do, some of them at least, possess the qualities which have been invariably ascribed to matter. Epistemology has done much to obscure this fundamental fact. Berkeley asks: "What do we perceive besides our own ideas or sensations? and is it not plainly repugnant that any one of these, or any combination of them, should exist unperceived?"[5] Clearly it is plainly repugnant and a manifest contradiction to suppose that perceptions are not perceptions, but is matter thereby destroyed? Is not what we perceive red? Is it not a deafening noise? Of those two things we perceive, is not one longer than the other? Has not what we perceive momentum and weight? Is it not, then, plainly repugnant to conclude that the contents of the mind are, all of them, immaterial?

Even, then, if we assume that the world we perceive is not continuous with the process by which we perceive it, it is a

[5] *Works,* Vol. I, p. 259.

world not so very unlike the world in which the process takes place. It may be made only of the stuff of consciousness, but then consciousness is the kind of stuff that may be condensed into a lump of sugar with which to sweeten coffee. Nor can we hope to obscure the fact by insisting that "states of consciousness" are at best "representations" of other things, which other things have the qualities in question. For, however that may be, the "representations" have also the same qualities and obey the same laws. The world which we perceive turns out thus to be of the same general kind as the world in which the processes of perception occur. Even if the two worlds are numerically distinct, they are essentially alike. The problem of their relation to each other is not a problem of the relation between two natures radically different and heterogeneous.

From these considerations certain conclusions appear to me to be obvious. If the processes of perception about which physiology and psychology inform us are the processes by means of which we perceive our world, then, if the perceived world is not continuous with those processes, it is none the less homogeneous with the world where they occur, and might contain them if they are ever given "in representation." If the processes belong to a world entirely physical, the "representations" belong to a world at least partly physical. In other words, if there is a physical world external to consciousness, there is also a physical world within consciousness. The physical things we perceive may not be the physical things which cause our perceptions, they may be only representations or reduplications of them, but they are physical things none the less. There has never been discovered in "consciousness" any activity or power by virtue of which a physical thing even if reduplicated must lose its physical character or the general homogeneity of the world be disrupted. If, however, the processes about which physiology and psychology inform us are not the processes by which we perceive our world, the question of reduplication and representation is meaningless. We need no longer be perplexed over the problem of the homogeneity and continuity of the perceived world with the processes which give rise to it, for the problem then no longer exists.

The conclusions stated in the preceding paragraph can not, however, fail to modify our attitude towards the problem of such continuity. To suppose that physiology and psychology give us no reliable information is preposterous. Yet the fact remains that the perceived world can not be located at any point in the perceptive process forming therewith a continuous series of events. Must we therefore conclude that there are two worlds, one representing the other, both essentially homogeneous, and yet presenting a problem of continuity and relationship which we can never bring within the domain of positive knowledge, but of which we must always give only a speculative solution? This conclusion has become less easy with the recognition that the perceived world is essentially like the world of processes, is the kind of a world which might contain them and does contain them continuous with the rest of itself if the processes are ever given in representation. A world, a representative world, which can thus so faithfully copy, even in part, another world which is somehow its cause, would appear to contain within itself all the elements necessary to show how process and result are related to each other, at least "in representation." And if "in representation," then surely the need of duplicated worlds has disappeared so far as any positive result for knowledge is concerned, for process and result would, in that event, be given in a manner wherein their relation to each other could be defined. It would appear artificial and strained, therefore, if we were to continue to suppose that the problem of the relation between process and result is ultimately of an epistemological character. It appears rather as a problem of reorganization and rearrangement, of new relations in one continuous world, not the problem of the reduplication of a world forever excluded from the place where it is known.

In general, then, the problem of the continuity and homogeneity of the perceived world with the processes which give rise to it appears to be a problem lying wholly within the domain of positive knowledge. We may proceed to solve it without first securing epistemological warrant for so doing. If we fail, the reason can hardly be that we lack the proper epistemology from the vantage ground of which our procedure may be philosophically scrutinized and corrected. For, again, the processes of perception are such as we discover them to be, or they are not. If they are not, there is no problem of continuity and homogeneity. If they are, that problem, from the nature of the case, does not involve the question of the validity of our knowledge of the processes or of the world resulting from them, but only the question of the sort of connection which exists between the processes and the resulting world. That connection is not cognitive, because the results of perception are not the knowledge of its processes; the thing seen is not the knowledge of the mechanism of vision.

The same result might be reached by considering the problem of perception directly and in detail. There are many cases in which we make a distinction between what we perceive and what really exists, cases, that is, where we seem forced to distinguish between appearance and reality, and ask whether we perceive reality as it is. Every one is familiar with such cases. Who sees reality correctly, the colour-blind observer or the one not colour-blind? Now it is interesting to observe that when we attempt to answer such a question we really restate it so that it loses all its epistemological character. For what we seek to discover is not whether the colour-blind see reality as it is, but why they make the colour discriminations they do. If we succeed in our discovery, we have learned that reality is so constituted that, given certain conditions, certain results are the outcome. We need no epistemology to estimate the truth of our discovery. Again: we perceive the stroke of the distant woodsman's axe and its sound in succession. How, then, can we be said to perceive reality correctly, since stroke and sound are in reality simultaneous? But the difficulty thus presented is gratuitous. For most assuredly did we perceive stroke and sound simultaneously, the constitution of things would have to be different from what we have discovered it to be; light and sound would then travel at the same rate. The so-called spatial and temporal discrepancies in perception turn out on examination to be, not matters of cognitive importance putting the validity of perception in peril, but definite and ascertainable factors in the constitution of the world.

The question, whether we perceive the world as it really is, turns out thus to be an ambiguous question. If it means, is a perceived world the same as an unperceived world, the answer is, naturally, in the negative. If it means, have we discovered how we perceive the world, our answer will disclose whether we have or not. But if it is claimed that from the nature of the case we can never tell whether the discovery has been made, it is quite idle to speculate about the matter. It would appear, therefore, that whatever problems a theory of perception may involve, they are not problems of epistemology, but of natural science and positive knowledge. No matter what difficulties these problems present, they furnish no warrant for the assumption that they necessitate an epistemology which shall estimate the truth of those bodies of knowledge we build up directly from considering how we perceive and what we perceive. They necessitate only problems of definition and positive relationship. In the words of Jevons: "We can not suppose, and there is no reason to suppose, that by the constitution of the mind we are obliged to think of things differently from the manner in which they are."[6]

[6] *Lessons in Logic,* p. 11.

CONSCIOUSNESS, THE SENSE ORGANS, AND THE NERVOUS SYSTEM*

IN ARTICLES already published[1] I have suggested that if we directly question reflective experience as to what consciousness is, we get the answer that it can not be identified with the objects of that experience, but is to be identified with a relation between them, and that this relation is the relation of meaning or implication, in short, the logical relation. In other words, I have taken the fact of meaning to be the fact of consciousness, and urged, consequently, that consciousness is just the existence of logical relations. If all the rest of experience existed, but these relations did not exist, I am of the opinion that we should not be warranted in describing such a situation as one in which there is consciousness of anything. These conclusions were based on a direct analysis of reflective experience without considering the relation of the organism which is said to be conscious to its surroundings. It is natural, however, to expect that such a consideration would have important bearings on these conclusions. For if we are entitled to believe that consciousness is a result of the interaction between the organism and its surroundings, the ways in which this interaction is effected should not be irrelevant to the conclusions reached by the analytic study.

It is pertinent to ask, therefore, How is that interaction between the organism and its surroundings effected which results in conscious experience? The answer is old and obvious.

* In the *Journal of Philosophy, Psychology & Scientific Methods,* Vol. VI (1909), pp. 449-455. This article is a revision of a paper read before the meeting of the American Philosophical Association, at Baltimore, in December, 1908, as a contribution to the discussion of idealism and realism.

[1] "The Nature of Consciousness," the *Journal of Philosophy,* Vol. II, p. 119, and "The Problem of Consciousness" in *Studies in Philosophy and Psychology*: The Garman Commemorative Volume, p. 137. See also "Consciousness and Meaning," in *The Psychological Review,* Vol. XV, p. 397.

It is effected by means of the sense organs and the nervous system.[2] By these means what the organism in interaction with its surroundings undergoes, is made into a conscious experience.[3] I desire, therefore, to emphasize certain well-known facts about the structure and functions of the sense organs and the nervous system, and to point out that they lead to conclusions in suggestive conformity with those drawn by other means.

A superficial examination of the sense organs and the nervous system reveals a striking difference in structure and function which becomes more striking the more thorough the examination is made. Thus the sense organs appear to be constructed and differentiated in relation to specific differences in the stimuli which may affect them, while the nervous system appears to be constructed and unified in relation to co-ordinated activity by the organism. While the sense organs put

[2] I limit the consideration here to the human organism for the sake of clearness in the general exposition.

[3] Lest there may appear in this statement a forgetfulness of the question, How can such interaction produce consciousness? I beg to refer the reader to the following words of Dr. Adolf Meyer: "We admit that we do *not* know *why* certain combinations of molecules of definite kind form a constellation which implies with necessity the phenomena of electricity. It is a fact which we accept as a fact of experience. Those who are trained to make the dualistic division between mental experiences or occurrences and physical ones, merely *assume* that they can understand *why* such constellations of certain metallic stuffs as the above mentioned, go with the phenomena of magnetism, others with the phenomena of electricity, etc.; and they refuse to see that the biological events of the order of mentation are no doubt in a similar way dependent on sufficient organization and constellation of an organism and that the coexistence of these constellations with their manifestations is a fact we have to accept as merely *one instance* of the general problem of the qualitative differentiation of the universe. The question why mind is mind, and just what it is, can be as little answered as what gold is, and why it is and why it should be so. Consequently, the impossibility of getting an answer to the puzzle—what makes mind mind, and what the relation is between the underlying physical constellations and the 'result'—is only part of the problem why the world is organized as it is. Our inability to answer that does not imply that we are any worse off in regard to mind than with other facts of quality which we accept without puzzle, satisfied if we can determine the *conditions* of their occurrence; and it does not follow that for this reason, mind must be something quite different from the rest of experience, provided that we realize that it presupposes sufficient organization and opportunities of work." *Psychological Bulletin,* Vol. VI, p. 177. The reader is referred to the article from which these words are taken for a discussion of consciousness analogous to the present study.

the organism in diversified interaction with its surroundings, the nervous system prevents this diversification from resulting in disintegrated and isolated reactions. It is thus apparent that the nervous system secures to the organism individuality and unity of life in spite of very great diversity of stimuli and environment. We have in these considerations, I believe, the means of stating the relational view of consciousness in biological terms. An organism so situated that it should be in differentiated interaction with the specific differences in the world about it, but which should, none the less, react in a unified and co-ordinated manner no matter how it might be stimulated, might well be defined as a conscious organism. Its consciousness would be a relational system integrating and unifying its differentiated interaction with its surroundings. Furthermore, its consciousness would naturally be marked by many of the characteristics usually attributed to consciousness. It would, for instance, be what we call individual and personal, and, being unified, it would present features often ascribed to a self or a mind. Different organisms could readily be conceived as exhibiting those varieties and even abnormalities of experience with which we are familiar and which appear to be due to individual differences in structure or circumstances. On some of the basal features of this general view I wish now to be more explicit.

That the specific structure of a given sense organ disappears in its corresponding sensory nerve is a fact frequently commented upon. The eye is an optical apparatus, but not so the optic nerve. While the sensory nerves may be specifically habituated to the activities of their corresponding organs, they none the less present a similarity of structure and function in marked contrast with the diversification of the organs themselves. We seem, therefore, forbidden to attempt to account for the differentiation of the organs without assuming a corresponding differentiation in the stimuli which affect them, and forbidden also to assign to the sensory nerves the particular functions which the organs themselves fulfill: It is the eye, not the optic nerve or its cortical center, which sees; it is the ear, not the auditory nerve, which hears. Thus the general lack of structural continuity between the sense organs and their nerves points, it seems to me, on the one hand, to the fact that the organism is related in specifically different ways to specific differences in its surroundings and, on the other hand, to a radical difference in function between the organs and their nerves. The organs possessing structural differences of specific character are, properly, specifically sensory, while the nerves, just because they lack these structural differences, are not.

Turning our attention to the organs exclusively, I repeat the observation that they point to specific differences in the surrounding world. In other words, it would appear that there are specific differences in the surrounding world with which the organism would not be in interaction unless there were organs by means of which this interaction is brought about. Or, if I may speak in what is often regarded as the objectionable language of teleology, the organs exist for the purpose of realizing interactions which, otherwise, would not be realized. Eyes would be useless unless there were something to see. Accordingly we may not account for vision by pointing to the structure and functions of the eye alone. The structure is adaptive and the function interactive. Seeing would thus appear to be, not a process set up exclusively in the organism itself, but an interaction or relation between the organism and its surroundings effected by means of the eye. It is not a reaction solely, but an interaction as well.[4] Sensation in general, it appears to me, should be similarly described.

If we identify sensations with the specific kinds of interaction which may be brought about by specific organs, sensations appear to be robbed of much of the mystery with which they have often been clothed. They may not, with Locke, be described as an order of existences intervening between a supposed mind and a supposed world. They need no mysterious process of projection in order that they may appear to constitute an outer world without really doing so. It is natural to them to be objective. It is natural that we should not find them in the brain—or perhaps I should say it is natural that we should find only a brain when we examine a brain—and

[4] Compare the article by Professor Dewey on "The Reflex Arc Concept in Psychology" in *The Psychological Review*, Vol. III, p. 357.

that we should find them constituting in large measure the objects of the world in which we live. They would appear to be natural events of the same general status with all other natural events. They are not knowledge any more than an eclipse of the moon is knowledge. They are, like such an eclipse, objects to be studied, the antecedents and consequents of which it is the business of knowledge to discover.[5] Since, therefore, the structure and functions of the sense organs provide for a variety of interactions between the organism and its surroundings, they appear to me to account thereby for the sensory content of experience without the addition of any faculty or power of sensibility, simple apprehension, or awareness. The bare existence of the interactions thus constituted appears to be the fact of sensation.

In the light of these considerations the distinction between primary and secondary qualities may indeed be regarded as sound, but also as requiring restatement. The restatement should be made, not in terms of epistemology, but in terms of causation. In order, that is, that certain specific differences in the world may have their specific effects there must be some means provided for their specific causality to operate. Without such means, the differences might well exist, but lack their appropriate efficacy. Such means may well be the sense organs or structures analogous to them. For instance, a landscape may in itself have all the variety of its objects and their relative positions which we ordinarily ascribe to it, but this variety may fail to affect the sensitive plate in a camera as a variety of objects in relative positions unless a lens is interposed. Thus we approach the primary qualities of things as we rob things more and more of their specific differences. Secondary qualities are those which require the intervention of some special structure if their appropriate causality is to be effective. This view preserves the important distinction between primary and secondary qualities, but by explaining the distinction in terms of causation removes it from the perplexities of epistemology.

[5] Compare the article by Dr. Bush on "Knowledge and Perception," in the *Journal of Philosophy*, Vol. VI, p. 393; and compare also my own article, "Perception and Epistemology," in *Essays Philosophical and Psychological: in Honor of William James*, p. 137.

Furthermore, if this interpretation of the distinction is correct, sense organs or similar structures may be necessary to make the secondary qualities effective according to their specific characters, and yet not force us to conclude that the existence of these qualities is subjective.

So far, then, as the sensory content of experience is concerned, the view here outlined suggests that that content is amply provided for by the existence of specific means for rendering the differences in the world effective according to their specific characters. In order, therefore, that what we are wont to call sense qualities may exist, consciousness would appear to be unnecessary. Such things as colours and sounds could operate according to their own nature anywhere within the sphere of their influence provided only there existed the appropriate means for making such operation effective. And what on this view appears true of colours and sounds appears to me to be true also of all varieties of sense qualities.

Important, therefore, as the existence of sense organs may be for the richness and variety of our conscious life, sense qualities do not appear of themselves to constitute that life. Did our sense organs exist in isolation and remain only disconnected media for specific causation, the world might possess all the variety we ascribe to sensation, but contain no more consciousness than exists in a camera when the sensitive plate is exposed. But they exist neither in isolation nor disconnection. We possess them in number and they are connected by a most intricate mechanism, the mechanism of the nervous system.

When we turn to examine this mechanism, we are impressed by the fact, already noted, that it does not possess the specific structural differences characteristic of the sense organs. It would, therefore, appear to play no part in the production of sense qualities. To be sure we distinguish between sensory and motor nerves, but the distinction seems to be based on differences in terminal endings or in the direction of what we call the nerve current rather than on any radical difference in function. The service which the nervous system, as a whole, and the brain in particular, fulfills, seems to be that of connected and co-ordinated reaction. By means of this mechanism the organism is enabled to react as a whole and in a co-ordinated manner to any stimulus no matter by what organ that stimulus is received and no matter what may be its specific quality. A given stimulus produces, thus, not only its appropriate sense quality, but also induces, on the part of the organism, a reaction which is not confined solely to the sense organ affected, but which involves in some measure the entire organism itself. In other words, the organism with its sense organs and its nervous system provides a centre for the connected interplay and co-ordination of the varied differences in the world without allowing these differences to lose their specific characters. In such a statement we have, I venture to believe, a biological expression of the nature of consciousness. Its similarity to the analytic expression made at the beginning of this paper is, I think, apparent. For an organism so situated that differences in stimuli should, none the less, produce in it co-ordinated and unified reactions would be an organism in which the reception of stimuli would involve adaptive and even prospective adjustments. In other words, sense qualities would become indexes of a variety of possible reactions and thus be connected in the relation of implication.

The nervous system is, moreover, not only a mechanism for connection and reaction, but it is also a mechanism with an activity in a measure independent of the activity of the sense organs. For the nervous system is also a connection and co-ordination of nerve centres culminating in the brain. Stimuli produce not only adjustments external to the organism, but also internal systematization of connection. Thus the organism as a centre for the connected interplay and co-ordination of the varied differences in the world is such a centre in conjunction with a highly specialized and integrated life of its own. It is thus able to preserve, in spite of changing stimulation and environment, an individual stability. It thereby conserves its own past and draws upon it in its own reactions. It has, consequently, a peculiar efficacy of its own which is not to be explained solely in terms of the stimuli affecting it, and which presents those features of spontaneity and initiative so characteristic of conscious beings. To set a limit to the system of intricate natural connections which may be effected as a result of the equipment of the organism in relation to its environment is impossible. The richness of the life thus engendered baffles the imagination. It seems as if nature in producing highly organized beings achieves her completest syntheses. To call them minds appears but to give them another name. We thus approach something like the conception of Aristotle, that mind is not simply the thing which knows nature, but is, perhaps, nature's completest realization. The consonance of this view with the theory of evolution and with the relational theory of consciousness attained by an analytic study of reflective experience is so apparent that no detailed exposition of it seems necessary.

The brevity of the exposition of the nature of consciousness here presented has given it, I hope, clearness and precision which greater detail might have obscured. I should like, however, in conclusion, to emphasize again one of the considerations of the preceding paragraph. It is customary with philosophers to speak of the flux of things and to point out that the flux takes an order only because there arise within it certain factors of sufficient relative stability to provide for repetition and sequence under the control of such connections as may exist among the elements of the flux itself. Now the stability given to the organism by the nervous system is manifestly different from what it would otherwise have. It is a stability by means of which the flux of sensation takes an order. In spite of the variety of sensation the nervous system changes slowly and, with its changes, undergoes at the same time increasing internal co-ordination. The order, therefore, which sensations take in consequence would appear to be subjected to this movement of internal co-ordination. There thus exists amid the flux of sensation a factor which is not only relatively stable, but which has a stability of such a kind that the movement of internal co-ordination is relatively independent of the external movement of the flux. Thus we might say that so much of the flux of sensation is ordered as the internal movement of co-ordination will allow. This ordering would, consequently, be selective and progressive. One is thus tempted to conclude that in the direction of such considerations as these lies the natural explanation not only of consciousness in general, but also of its more specific forms of memory and imagination.

THE PROBLEM OF TIME IN MODERN PHILOSOPHY*

As is well known, Kant connected space with the external sense and time with the internal sense. In so doing he was giving an obvious expression of a point of view which had become or was becoming habitual with many philosophers. From that point of view the mind was not regarded as the product of conditions which antedated its own existence. In that case time could not readily be connected with the internal sense. The mind was regarded rather as the knower of a world which either passed before it or could be taken up into itself through synthetic processes. For purposes of record, knowledge of the world in any specific instance could be thought of as an event, and the synthesis as actually performed by an individual mind could be thought of as an occurrence in the history of that mind. But judged metaphysically, the world known or synthetized was apparently implied as a datum logically given in its entirety before knowledge of it or synthesis of it could take place. A contrast between the temporal and the timeless was, thereby, defined. Any time span could mean only an amount of knowledge or of synthesis of a whole which, as a whole, is timeless.

Illustrations of this general point of view and its metaphysical results are many. Take, for instance, these statements from Bradley's *Appearance and Reality*: "What is impossible is to construct absolute life in detail, to have the specific experience in which it consists," and yet "we can form the general idea of an absolute experience in which phenomenal distinctions are merged, a whole become immediate at a higher

* In the *Journal of Philosophy, Psychology and Scientific Methods,* Vol. VII (1910), pp. 410-416. Contributed to the discussion of the problem of time in its relation to present tendencies in philosophy, at the meeting of the American Philosophical Association, at New Haven, December 27-29, 1909.

stage without losing any of its richness."[1] Or take this from Royce's *The World and the Individual*: "Now, in time, I seek, as if it were far beyond me, that goal of my Selfhood, that complete expression of my will, which in God, and for God, my whole life at once possesses."[2] Such statements appear to be intelligible only if we regard the mind's relation to reality as a sort of temporal approach to a timeless whole. As the expanding circles in a pool find their limits in the pool's extent, which, even as they expand, is itself fixed, so my experience or my mind, as it enlarges, finds its limits in an absolute experience or an absolute mind which, even now, while my enlargement proceeds, undergoes itself no expansion.

This conception of the mind's relation to reality has, in one form or another, motived the greater part of modern philosophy, set its problems, and provided their solutions. In so doing its achievements and successes have been noteworthy. Their present philosophical value has, however, become a matter of serious doubt largely because it is becoming less habitual among philosophers to think of the mind's relation to reality after the manner of this suspected philosophy. Many, today, can think of the mind as reality's knower only with difficulty. They can recognize that men have so thought of it and that some still so think. But they can not think that way for themselves and at the same time cherish the belief that they are thinking adequately, sanely, and truthfully.

Let it be supposed that whatever those facts may be that we denominate "mind" or "experience," they constitute with the rest of facts no distinction between knower and known, they form no widening circle in a shoreless pool, they form no incomplete will whose completeness they none the less imply; or let it be supposed that what we call knowledge is not a time span's grasp of a reality which that span would envisage as a whole—then the philosophy of the absolute, its motive, its problems, and its solutions appear strange and artificial. To put the matter in positive terms—let knowledge be conceived to be a natural event like a storm or an earthquake, then the only problems of knowledge as knowledge which we can

[1] *Op. cit.,* p. 160.
[2] *Op. cit.,* Vol. II, p. 150.

have are those that are involved in its definition and in seeking its natural antecedents and its natural consequences. There can be no more of a problem of the relation of knowledge to reality than there can be of the relation of a storm to reality; but there can be problems of what knowledge is and what precedes and follows it just as there can be problems of what an earthquake is and what precedes and follows it. Such problems will hardly carry us to the absorption of time in eternity or lead us to conceive, however inadequately, of a whole become immediate at a higher stage without losing any of its richness.

The oppositions which current studies in philosophy present, I take, therefore, to be radical and far-reaching. Controversies are no longer about methods and results, but about initial facts and points of departure. But points of departure can not be set down as merely arbitrary and unmotived assumptions. Nor can they be justly regarded as convenient hypotheses whose claim to acceptance or recognition resides in the facility with which they can be used. They are rather to be regarded as simplifications of those more general conceptions which the significant achievements of knowledge lead us to entertain. What we call our view of the world is by no means simply the outcome of our philosophy: it is equally the picture of things which we naturally form as a result of the significant deliverances of knowledge in the concrete. It is necessary, therefore, to place points of view in that more general setting of which they are simplifications.

What then is the general setting which motives the assumptions of that philosophy which can regard experience as a time span within a timeless whole? The question may be answered by an examination of the philosophies themselves. The examination would, I think, reveal that the general setting is that afforded by Newtonian physics and the astronomical achievements of such men as Copernicus and Laplace. Upon the background furnished by such a setting is reflected such diverse things as Kant's *Kritik der Reinen Vernunft* and Addison's hymn, "The Spacious Firmament on High." Indeed that background constituted the general and controlling world view for several centuries. Men viewed the world as through a telescope, and philosophy took its departure from such a view simplified and reduced to terms of a mind and its object. As the eye at the telescope watched for some portion of the heavens to swing within its field of vision, so the mind watched for reality to appear within the limits of experience.

How little other sciences besides astronomy and physics contributed to shape the general view of the world in most men's minds is seen as late as 1872 in the reception accorded Emil du Bois-Reymond's sensational address at Leipzig, "Ueber die Grenzen des Naturerkennens." The copy I have of that address is of the seventh edition of 1891, and by that time it had been translated into English, French, Italian, and Servian! It is well known that that address elevated astronomy to the ideal of knowledge and that it pictured the limits of knowledge attainable by even a finite mind in terms of a mind to which, in the words of d'Alembert, "the whole world would be one single fact and one great truth."

Now such a general view of the world appears to be one where space conceptions dominate time conceptions. It is the world "as all there," so to speak, which has captured the imagination: a world as a totality which may admit certain internal changes in the relations of its elements to one another, but which, as a whole, is forever and permanently "there" "where." Such a view makes my present experience, my time span, a given *presence* of the whole, a given "hereness" of it. Such a view makes it natural for Kant to affirm, "that, in order to know that there is something permanent, which corresponds to the conception of substance, and thus to prove the objective reality of the conception, we must have the perception of that which is in *space*, in other words, the perception of matter; *for only space has in it anything permanent,* whereas time, and therefore all that exists in the inner sense, is in perpetual flux."[3]

In short, then, I take it, that the philosophy of the eternal and the absolute is a philosophy which flourishes where the picture men naturally form of the world is an astronomical or spatial picture. There is the world; here is the mind. There is the outward; here is the inward. There is the external meaning of ideas; here is their internal meaning. There is the

[3] Watson's *Selections,* p. 127.

object; here is the subject. There is all possible experience; here is my actual and incomplete experience. "There" and "here" is the basal contrast; and as "here" is "now," time is genuine, but it is never "there," for if it were, all would be "here" and "now."

The picture of the world which the notable achievements of knowledge lead us to form today is the picture of a world in the making, an incomplete and unfinished world, a world which has had a past and will have a future. It is almost needless to say that this picture is formed under the controlling influence of biological and evolutionary conceptions. It is the picture of the world as a thing with a history. And this history discloses not the possible successive arrangements or relations of the elements of one vast whole which is always there, but, if we may speak of a whole at all, it discloses that whole as itself changing and growing, as a thing which could never be grasped by any mind as one single fact and one great truth. The possibility of permanence in the world is not space, as with Kant, but time, for we can say of things that the place which knew them knows them no more. Only that is permanent which *lasts*, but space held much which it holds no longer. Thus time tends to become as dominant and controlling a factor in our thinking as space was formerly. It is Darwin's picture which tends to replace that of Newton.

A warning should doubtless be sounded lest philosophers, with their imaginations fired by the more recent vision, should forget that there is the spacious firmament on high, lest they should exalt the world's ceaseless flux, but neglect its stable factors. Yet, even so, it needs little wit to see that the newer vision means a radical transformation of philosophy. Most radical, I think, is the transformation likely to be wrought in our conception of thought and its relation to the rest of things. It seems to me very difficult for one to believe that consciousness is an event in the world's history and still hope to understand that event, still hope to throw light on the relation of thought to the rest of things, if he follows the traditional lines of modern epistemology and psychology. How can one longer deal with the old antitheses between the ego and the non-ego, subject and object, the mind and the world, thought and reality, ideas and things, the internal and the external, if one is genuinely convinced that sense organs, a nervous system, and exciting stimuli must first be *produced* before thinking can occur? I am well aware of the obvious rejoinder at this point, namely, that we can know nothing about sense organs and the rest except as they are given in our experience. But the rejoinder most successfully misses the point. For what is to be our attitude of the insistent lesson of our experience of things if that experience itself is a happening? How can I take the necessity I am under of experiencing things in order to have knowledge of them as the fundamental fact in my philosophy, if the knowledge I thus acquire reveals my experience of things as an event in their history? There are many who can not. Those who can not, believe that whatever problems consciousness, knowledge, and experience present, they must be handled from a point of view radically different from that which has quite generally prevailed since the time of Locke. The eye at the telescope serves them no longer as a figure.

The historical point of view is significant not only as a new point of departure, but also because it tends to discredit many of those problems of philosophy that have often been regarded as persistent. From among them I select for illustration the problem, How can experience give us knowledge of reality? Now, if experience is an event which happens to nature in the course of her history, if it is an event in her life, so to speak, how can we define a distinction between reality and experience which would give us an important and vital philosophical problem? In other words, does the event we call experience point to anything besides its antecedents and its consequences? Is there anything in the situation which should lead us to suppose that besides a reference to its antecedents and its consequences, experience has also another reference, to something which is neither an antecedent nor a consequence, but something which we may regard as the reality which experience represents or which somehow appears in experience? I venture still another form of the same question. If the pointings of experience are temporal, to the past and to the future, but not spatial, to an outside or an other, or to something at right angles with itself, what philosophical problem of reality as opposed to experience can we scare into being? Surely such questions make such a problem look queer and artificial. Again, if we can discover no genuine antithesis between reality and experience, there remains no compulsion to conclude that what precedes and follows experience is itself also experience or at best a picture painted only in the colours of experience. For experience discloses the history and connections of its own facts. To ask, therefore, whether these facts actually had this history or do have these connections, is simply to ask in general form such questions as these: Did the cave bear live before man? or Does the Atlantic Ocean lie between Europe and America? In brief, experience is a natural event; it is not a representation of nature.

If experience provokes no problem of reality as opposed to itself, it would appear that metaphysics discovers its own problems not in epistemology, but in those bodies of specific knowledge which result from our study of the nature and behaviour of definite things. Its procedure becomes experimental, inductive, and objective. As I have elsewhere discussed the general aspects of this view, I content myself here with a single illustration.[4] A metaphysician may ask, Is chance real? But what does he mean by "real"? That little word has made his question interesting, but it has not made it a metaphysical question. If it had, he must first discover what it is to be real. But how can he make that discovery, if every fact, every event, every distinction, every connection, every relation—everything, in short—which he wishes to investigate brutally forces upon him the problem of its own reality? If, however, the word "real" provokes no metaphysical contrast, the metaphysician will ask, What is chance? When is it found? How does it operate? But he must first have chance to investigate before he can investigate it. And if he has chance as a problem, he will never have a metaphysical problem of its reality. For, I repeat, the moment we are convinced that experience creates no philosophical distinction between itself and reality, the adjective "real" takes a modest position among all other

[4] *Metaphysics.* Columbia University Press, 1908.

adjectives; it ceases to be the metaphysical adjective *par excellence.*

I have, in the foregoing, indicated what appears to me to be a fundamental contrast in current philosophical controversies, and attempted to put that contrast in its general setting and to suggest some of its possibilities. If I have made myself clear, I think it must be apparent that time itself, in the light of what has been said, does not present a unique problem. It may present difficult and intricate problems, but it does not present a problem which can be regarded philosophically as different in kind from any other problem whatsoever. It may, however, be made to present specious problems like the problem of the specious present, but these tend to disappear, I am convinced, when time is taken as a given subject of inquiry and not as a mystery to be explained. If experience is a natural event with antecedents and consequences, it is itself a time affair, a thing with a past and a future. If, further, consciousness and knowledge are bound up with experience, I find no more difficulty in admitting consciousness and knowledge of time than I have in admitting consciousness and knowledge of anything else. Things are all in the same boat when it comes to that. But I do find a problem in so defining consciousness that provision may be made for the fact that things sail into it and out again without any break in the continuity of their being. To affirm that the definition must be such as to provide also for the occurrence of consciousness itself as a temporal event, may seem to some like affirming a paradox, but it appears to me to be an affirmation based upon the conviction that the bodies of knowledge we build up from our study of things are knowledge of the kind of world in which we live. These bodies of knowledge may be enlarged, or improved, or greatly changed, but it appears to me to be unsound to suppose that they can be enlarged or improved or changed by thinking that they necessarily involve a metaphysical distinction between time and eternity or between appearance and reality. Furthermore, a metaphysics which can be regarded as true no matter what truths the special sciences contain, appears to me to be interesting, but inadequate.

CONSCIOUSNESS AND OBJECT*

FROM Professor Thilly's article[1] I take the following extract: "Starting out with a naturalistic metaphysics, these philosophers naturally end with a naturalistic metaphysics: consciousness is an epiphenomenon, inhering in the objects. The object figuring in a conscious perceptual situation differs from the object out of it in the possession of consciousness. The nervous system, in Woodbridge's view, connects the sensations in a relation of implication; consciousness as a relation of implication appears as a kind of unnecessary adjunct; why it appears no one knows; the connections are not conditioned by its existence; its existence is conditioned by them. Consciousness looks on; there is nothing else left for it to do" (p. 429). There are two propositions in this extract on which I wish to comment in the hope of making clear the sense in which they appear to me to be sound. They are (1) "The object figuring in a conscious perceptual situation differs from the object out of it in the possession of consciousness"; and (2) "Consciousness looks on; there is nothing else left for it to do."

I

The first proposition appears to me to be self-evident if it means anything. I suppose that the only assignable difference between an object and consciousness of it is consciousness. The proposition means nothing, if there is no difference to assign. But if the proposition is intelligible, if we do distinguish between an object and consciousness of it, it would seem that this distinction is what it purports to be. If so, it does not appear to be debatable whether the distinction in question is the distinc-

* In the *Philosophical Review*, Vol. XXI (1912), pp. 633-640.

[1] "The Relation of Consciousness and Object in Sense-Perception," *Philosophical Review*, Vol. XXI (1912), p. 415.

tion consciousness. We face, rather, a question of fact. Do we or do we not distinguish between an object and consciousness of it? If we do, we ought to be able to tell what the distinction is. If we do not, we ought not to discuss the question, in spite of our wonder that it should, nevertheless, be asked.

For my own part, I do not doubt that we can and do distinguish an object from our consciousness of it. I am conscious of the words I am now writing, but my consciousness is something different from the written words. And as for the reader, I suppose that he is conscious of the printed page before him, and that he does not identify his consciousness with the printed page itself. What, then, I would ask, is the difference between the printed page and his consciousness of it, if it is not the difference of his consciousness? Just what the difference is specifically, I have elsewhere tried to define. I may not have succeeded in stating accurately what the difference specifically is, but that is just now immaterial. At present, I am interested only in an attitude toward a question of fact. I am insisting that, for my part, I take it for granted that we make a certain distinction and that it is no other than just the distinction we make. The first proposition, thus understood, appears to me to be self-evident and not debatable. We may debate only the question whether we make the distinction.

Taking it for granted that the only difference between an object and consciousness of it is the difference of consciousness, I should like to emphasize two considerations which have been important in my own study of the problem of consciousness. These considerations appear to me to be so obvious that I can do little more than state them.

1. The distinction between an object and consciousness can be defined only in a situation where that distinction exists. Of course there may be many objects of which I am not conscious. The difference between them and my consciousness of them does not exist. Yet it would appear that the demand is often made of those who claim to distinguish between objects and our consciousness of them, to define that distinction before they have discovered it. Of course, I may attempt to tell what objects are like when I am not conscious of them, but this attempt is not the same as that instituted in the interest of

telling how they and my consciousness of them would differ if I had it. The former attempt may be impossible without the latter, but the two attempts are different. So I repeat, the distinction in question can be defined only where it exists, but not where it does not exist.

2. If, now, the distinction is defined, it is, as I have already said, just that distinction and no other. If I do distinguish between objects and consciousness, the objects are not the consciousness. Their characteristics, behaviour, and laws, if they are distinguished from consciousness, are not consciousness. Furthermore, their characteristics, behaviour, and laws are not determined by consciousness, except in so far as I discover them so to be determined. They are otherwise determined in so far as I discover that to be the case. If, for instance, I discover that the reason why the colour-blind do not discriminate between certain colours[2] is the structure of their eyes, and if I do not identify their eyes with their consciousness, I may not properly claim that the reason is their consciousness. If, in general, I discover that what objects are as distinguished from consciousness of them is due to certain features of their own or to certain relations to one another, or, if you will, to "the interaction between the real world and the organism," I ought not at the same time to conclude that it is due to consciousness. What they are as distinguished from consciousness, —that they are as so distinguished.

These points have been fundamental in my own studies. I am aware that it may be claimed that I am avoiding the real issue. For, one may say, the issue is not whether objects as distinguished from consciousness are what they are so distinguished to be, but whether as so distinguished they can also exist apart from consciousness. This issue, as the discussions of it have shown, has led not only to different conclusions regarding it, but also to fundamentally different conceptions of the way it should be defined. To a reviewer of the discussion it is apparent that the participants are arguing to cross pur-

[2] It seems to me to be improper to say, as Professor Thilly and others do, of the colour-blind man who does not discriminate red, that "his sensory content will be blue or yellow." It looks too much like saying that the sensory content of beings, without eyes will be black, or of beings without ears, will be silence.

poses, that although they employ the same terms, they do not employ them with the same meanings, and that, as yet, they can form no common platform for the discussion. I do not discuss the issue here, but simply state that as I understand it, it appears to be disposed of by the two considerations I have already emphasized. I may, however, comment on this statement.

Objects as distinguished from consciousness do not exist apart from consciousness in the situation where the distinction between them and consciousness exists. A fish in the water, although different and distinguished from the water, does not at the same time exist out of the water. So also with objects in consciousness: while in it, although they are different from it, they are not also out of it. There would appear to be nothing debatable here, but the situation constitutes a difficulty in some minds because while a fish may leap out of the water and be still a fish, who can possibly follow in consciousness the disappearance of objects out of it? No one, apparently, unless it be some of the anti-intellectualists. For my own part, I do not attempt such a flight. I seek no other road to a knowledge of objects than that which my consciousness affords.

But I am interested in knowing what the objects of which I am conscious are, what their history has been, and what I may reasonably expect from them. In pursuing this interest, I am led to conclude that my consciousness once began in a world composed of the very type of objects, with their connections, behaviour, and laws, which I discover the objects of which I am conscious to be. I discover that my thinking is concerned with much that I can not possibly call thinking. In our stock phrase, my ideas are woefully dependent on my experience, and my experience has had a history which I can trace back approximately to its birth. I find it, therefore, quite impossible to believe that whenever there are objects of the type I discover mine to be, there also is consciousness. Of course, if one defines an object as always "of consciousness," there is no room for dispute. But if one does not so define it, if one defines it in terms of discovered characteristics, behaviour, and laws which are different from a discovered consciousness, I must believe that I live in a world where consciousness, so far as I can distinguish it, exists only now and then. Consequently when I speak about that world apart from consciousness, I speak about the world I have discovered minus the consciousness I have discovered.

As I said, I am not discussing the issue. I am rather trying to define it as I see it. Since we do talk about objects apart from consciousness, I have been interested in trying to find an intelligible basis for our conversation. I find it necessary, first to distinguish consciousness from objects,[3] secondly, to define what that distinction is; and, thirdly, to subtract the consciousness thus distinguished and defined. The result is the objects less the consciousness. "Ah! But you are still conscious of them," the philosophy which stops here may cry. But the philosophy which goes on from here will ask, "Is your consciousness of them the reason why objects are as they are and behave as they do?" To any one who answers, he can not tell, the reply may be made, "When you need to name a reason why objects are as they are and behave as they do, do you name your consciousness?" If one starts out with a naturalistic metaphysics, he will naturally, unless he falls by the way, end in a naturalistic metaphysics.

II

"Consciousness looks on; there is nothing else left for it to do." This appears to be a conclusion from what I have said above and from what I have said elsewhere, but I should like to alter it, because, in its present form, I can not subscribe to it. I should say that consciousness does not look on, not because it does something else, but because there is nothing for consciousness to do. It doesn't even look. Yet we may not say that it is impotent, unless, in denying that it is potent, we refer it, after the manner of formal logicians, to the class "non-potent." Then we may say that consciousness belongs to the class of things that do nothing, not because it is impotent, but because the "do nothing" class contains other members be-

[3] Professor Thilly says: "To decide what consciousness adds to the status of the unperceived object, we must have some notion of what is meant by the unperceived object." But surely we must also have some notion of what is meant by consciousness.

sides the "impotent" and it is among these other members that consciousness is to be found. This formal statement is worth notice, because from the assertion that consciousness does nothing, the conclusion is so frequently drawn that it must be, therefore, a passive spectator of objects, and from the assertion that it is not a phenomenon, the conclusion is drawn that it is an epiphenomenon. And these conclusions are used to end an argument or refute a statement.

Now the claim that no efficiency belongs to consciousness directly, that, in other words, consciousness *does* nothing, is by no means new, but has been made again and again by many inquirers. It may be admitted that the claim is still in dispute, and, so far, one who believes that consciousness does something may urge his belief as against a theory which claims the contrary. But I take it that the recent theories of consciousness which Professor Thilly has under review are not primarily significant for claiming that consciousness does nothing, but rather for attempting to make that claim contribute to a better understanding of the nature of consciousness itself. They have recognized that the discovery that consciousness is not to be defined in terms of efficiency, is not a conclusion in which to rest, or a discovery which at once falsifies their analysis, but a discovery which should be followed up and which provokes further inquiry. And following up this inquiry, they have been led to conclude that one of the basal misconceptions in nearly all modern theories of consciousness has been the unanalyzed assumption that consciousness belongs to the class of existences of which efficiency is predicable. They have felt that so long as consciousness is assumed to be a thing which can interact with other things, that affects other things, and is affected by them, that it would do something if it could, or could if it would, so long it remains a thing which analysis steadily pushes out of nature, and of which even the existence may be seriously questioned. They have all felt, however, that consciousness is something natural, that it is something of which it can not be truthfully said that it is an "unnecessary adjunct." They have tried not to let this conviction carry them back again into the habit of assuming that consciousness is a term among other terms, or a thing interacting with other things. They have tried to define it in terms of other categories than those which have led to confusion and an unconvincing philosophy.

I am not claiming that they have as yet succeeded, but I do claim that their attempt is fundamental to any appreciation or criticism of their point of view. With others, I have held that consciousness is not a term, but a relation. I am aware that such a contention needs a good deal of clarification, but I am also aware that an attempt to work out a theory of sensation, perception, and thinking under the general supposition that consciousness is a relation, is not greatly affected by criticisms directed at its details from the point of view that consciousness is a term. It would be quite sufficient to show that consciousness is a term and not a relation. It is not convincing to criticize what in a relational theory of consciousness is said about perception, or about the relation between the organism and its environment as if *in that theory* consciousness were still functioning as a term. Consequently, to discover that consciousness has nothing to do under a theory which starts with that conviction as a datum is not to have seen that theory's end, but only to have glimpsed its beginning.

To put the matter a little more concretely, Professor Thilly appears to represent the theory as if it proceeded as follows: Consciousness is a by-product of the interaction between organism and environment; therefore, it is a harmless looker-on, it does nothing. It would have been more consonant with the spirit of the theory to have said: Consciousness does nothing, but it is by virtue of the interaction between organism and environment that all we do is done; how, then, must consciousness be construed if its natural place and significance are to be defined? The attempt to answer that question has not led those who are making it to any suspicion that to be conscious is to be something wholly superfluous in this world. It is leading them to discover in the fact that the conscious situation is mediated problems of vital interest and importance. The efficiency which others impute to consciousness they discover to belong to the being who is conscious; and they find no contradiction in affirming that there belongs to conscious beings an efficiency which unconscious beings do not possess.

It should be apparent, I think, that the particular problem with which Professor Thilly deals, namely, "The Relation of Consciousness and Object in Sense-perception," will take on a different look when approached from the point of view of a relational theory of consciousness than it does when approached from the point of view of a term theory. If these expressions "term" and "relation" are too objectionable, or, in this context, too obscure, it may be said that the inquiry in question will not appear the same to one who is looking for something which consciousness does and to another who, convinced that it does nothing, is asking, "What then is its nature?" In other words, I should say, as I suggested in the first part of this paper, that the question, what difference, if any, consciousness makes in objects, is not a question to be asked today without first defining the conception of consciousness employed in the question. If consciousness interacts with its objects, I do not see how the question can be answered. If consciousness is mediated, the exhibition of the manner of this mediation disposes of the question at once; the question is irrelevant.

I have written these comments, not in answer to Professor Thilly's argument, but with the desire of emphasizing two particular problems: (1) What difference, if any, is there between consciousness and objects in terms of which consciousness may be defined? and, (2) Since our life so manifestly appears to be an interaction between organism and environment, and not an interaction between consciousness and objects, how is consciousness to be construed as something mediated in that interaction? These problems seem to me to be important, not as reminiscent of the past of philosophy, but as suggestive of its future.

THE DECEPTION OF THE SENSES*

IN CURRENT controversies it is often assumed that the deception of the senses affords an *experimentum crucis* to test the validity of different theories of knowledge. This assumption appears to me to be unwarranted, and I offer, therefore, the following comments in support and illustration of this contention. The first section expresses in general form what I have to say. The other sections are little more than restatements and are added in the interest of varied illustrations rather than as sections in a progressive argument. Altogether they constitute a defense of two positions: (1) that the deception of the senses is significant not for cognition, but for action; and (2) that speculative theories of knowledge are, and are from the nature of the case, independent of any empirical evidence to be derived from the fact that the senses deceive.[1]

I

If the deception of the senses is taken to be a fact, then we must obviously keep that fact genuine and unequivocal throughout our inquiry. We can not profitably admit the fact, use it as evidence for a theory of knowledge, and then use this theory to discredit the fact or to alter the character which

* In the *Journal of Philosophy, Psychology and Scientific Methods,* Vol. X (1913), pp. 5-15.

[1] I am aware that arguments are drawn from other facts of perception, such as dreams, hallucinations, after-images, etc., to reinforce the evidence which the deception of the senses is supposed to afford. These facts have not been overlooked, but they are not here considered. I have found nothing in them as yet which modifies in any important way the position here taken. I wish to remark also that the abnormal is often given weight altogether disproportionate to our knowledge of it. The things we know less about should not set a standard for construing the things about which we know more. When we have discovered, for instance, *why* we dream any *specific* dream, with as much clearness and certainty as now marks our discovery of *why* the straight stick appears bent, then we can use dreams as unambiguously in evidence for such positions as they may support.

it had as evidence. For we have not used the deception of the senses as a *supposed* fact which a *reductio ad absurdum* might overthrow; we have used it as an *evidential* fact which loses its evidential character the moment it is discredited or altered. In other words, if a theory of knowledge is to be proved or disproved by the deception of the senses, that theory can not determine the nature or character of the facts of that deception. Yet there are arguments offered to our consideration which appear like attempts to disprove one theory of knowledge and to prove a contrary theory by appealing to the deception of the senses, and then, on the basis of the theory thus proven, apparently proceed to explain that the deception is not genuine, that it is only a quasi deception, that the difficulties connected with it consequently vanish. Such arguments are not convincing. If the deception of the senses is to be an evidential fact, it must be a genuine fact *and genuine in the same way*, both in the theory which it disproves and in the theory which it proves.

A common illustration may be used to put this consideration in concrete form. If my eyes deceive me because I see as bent a stick which is really straight, I may conclude that I do not see the stick as it really is; but I ought not to go on and say that the stick as it really is is, strictly, neither straight nor bent, that, as it *really* is, it is something quite different. If I see as bent a stick which is really straight, I must conclude that I do not see the stick as it really is, *if I mean by "really," "straight";* for, assuredly, if I see it bent, I do not see it straight. I may also hold that the stick *as it really is* is, strictly, neither straight nor bent, but my reason for so holding can not possibly be the fact that I see as bent a stick which is really straight. It must be a totally different reason. In general terms, once more, I can not pass from an empirical distinction which is taken to be precisely what it appears to be to a speculative distinction which is totally different. I can not use one distinction between appearance and reality as evidence of or in illustration of a totally different distinction between appearance and reality. If the stick is really neither straight nor bent, then its appearance as bent is not the appearance of a stick which is really straight.

Consequently it seems evident, if the deception of the senses is to have any evidential force, that the senses must deceive us in the way and in the respect they do deceive us. If I hold, for instance, that my senses deceive me because through them things appear to me to be distorted, then that is the way in which they do deceive me. But if this is so, then the things must be the undistorted originals which appear through my senses to be distorted. Otherwise it means nothing to say that they appear to me to be distorted. Thus if my eyes deceive me because through them a straight stick appears bent, then it must be a straight stick which so appears. Otherwise what would it mean to say that I see a straight stick bent? If the stick is not straight how could my vision of it be a distorted vision? It seems clear, therefore, that, if the senses deceive me, the things in respect to which they deceive me must be themselves of the character in regard to which I am deceived. The distinction between appearance and reality, therefore, in so far as it is defined in terms of the deception of the senses, implies that the character of appearance and the character of reality are comparable and commensurable in the same terms.

In what, however, does the deception of the senses consist? It evidently does not consist in any distortion of reality if by that we mean that reality appears to us in ways in which it ought not to appear. The way in which things appear to us is the natural result of discoverable conditions. Reasons are found for it and these reasons exclude the possibility of another way of appearing. We can not say, therefore, that the senses deceive us because they represent to us things in a way in which they ought not to represent them. That is, there is no deception *in* the way things appear to us, *in* the appearances. The appearances deceive us, not by being what they should not be, but by leading us to do what we should not do —to think that reality is what it is not or to use things as if they were not what they are.

Since the senses do not of themselves reveal to us why things appear to us as they do, and since things appear different under different conditions, it is natural that we should be led into error so long as we are ignorant of the reasons why things so appear. But it is evident that we should not be led into error *if we did not react to things as they appear to us*. There is thus no cognitive character whatever in the appearance of things to us, and consequently no cognitive adequacy or inadequacy in what we see, hear, touch, smell, or taste. The senses are then not deceitful, although *we* may be deceived by them just as we may be deceived by the absolute candour of a statement. Not only are the senses not deceitful, but they would be so if by their means things did not appear to us as they do, provided, of course, that the conditions under which things appear remain unchanged. Naturally we can not entertain the supposition here implied, because we are so well assured that if things appeared to us different from what they now do, the conditions of their appearance would be different from what they now are. Yet we may imagine into what hopeless confusion of action we should be plunged if things always appeared the same while the conditions of their appearance constantly changed.

It seems evident, therefore, that the appearances of things are in no sense cognitive, but that cognition arises only as we react to these appearances. The deception of the senses is significant, then, not for cognition, but for action. To see a straight stick bent is not to see erroneously. Such a sight could never lead us into error if we never reacted to it as if we were seeing a bent stick. A fisherman's spear does not err, for the fish does not appear to it. The fisherman may err, not because the fish appears to him, but because he does not allow for the water. Thus it is the reacting to appearances which leads to knowledge, and furthermore, this reacting must be of a specific kind. It must be what we call conscious reacting and this type of reacting has never been successfully reduced to the fact of appearance itself.

These considerations seem to me to be quite sufficient to warrant the conclusion that the deception of the senses is a trivial matter in any theory of knowledge. But the distinction between appearance and reality may not be a trivial matter in the theories of knowledge which I have called speculative. If I read these theories aright, I discover that they do not begin with the distinction between appearance and reality, but conclude with it. They do not appeal to straight sticks which look bent as evidence. It is only by inadvertence that they seem to rely on such facts of experience, and they frequently profess to discard such reliance altogether. Their procedure is quite different. They ask you to consider not what you mean when you say that a stick which is really straight looks bent—for they are, I take it, quite willing to admit that you mean then something for action and not for cognition—but they ask what you mean when you say that a stick or any other supposedly isolable fact of experience is *real.* In other words they ask, What is it *to be real?* And they insist that no fact of experience can measure up to the standard set by the answer to that question. They then conclude that the facts of experience are appearance and not reality.

Such speculative theories exist. It is their procedure, standing as it does in such marked contrast to experimental procedure, that makes them impressive and challenges attention. They do not claim that the facts of experience are not strictly reality, on the ground that the senses deceive, because the deception of the senses is itself a fact of experience, to be characterized as appearance as much as any other fact. They ask of it as of all others, Can it be consistently construed in terms of what it is to be real? And they answer, No. If such is their procedure then it is evident that the other position I urge in this paper is sound, namely, that speculative theories of knowledge are, and are from the nature of the case, independent of any empirical evidence to be derived from the fact that the senses deceive.[2]

II

There is an argument which runs somewhat as follows: If the senses deceive us, then we do not perceive things as they are; we perceive something else, their appearances, representations or images of them; now, since the things can not be the representations, nor the representations the things, there are two regions of existence, things and representations, reality and appearance, which, from the nature of the case, can not

[2] The difficulty I find with these theories lies, as I have pointed out elsewhere, not in the consistency of their procedure, but in their credibility. See "The Problem of Consciousness" in *Studies in Philosophy and Psychology*: The Garman Commemorative Volume. Boston, Houghton Mifflin, 1906, pp. 137-166.

be bridged by perception; we need, therefore, a theory of knowledge which will give us some insight into this distinction between appearance and reality, and show how knowledge is possible in view of it.

But what is the initial antithesis between appearance and reality? Is it between a bent stick and a straight stick, the former being appearance and the latter reality? If so, what is there to make clearer and what demand is there here for a theory of knowledge? If we want to know why the stick is straight, is not the answer because it conforms to the definition of a straight stick, is what a straight stick is, and does what a straight stick does even to appearing sometimes bent? If we want to know why it appears bent and not straight, is not the answer water? Is not the case now disposed of? It is water which makes the straight stick appear bent, *but not the eyes.* The senses deceive us because, not revealing the causes why things appear as they do, we are led astray. The moment we discover that it is water which makes the stick appear bent, we can allow for the refraction and be satisfied. But this is not a matter of epistemology, but of action, of stimulus and response. If, however, the antithesis between appearance and reality is not the initial antithesis between the bent stick and the straight stick generalized, but a totally different antithesis, we must be told what it is. And clearly, whatever it is, it can have nothing to do with the deception of the senses, for no specific case of that deception falls under it.

But, it may be asked, how can we escape the conclusion that we perceive not things, but only their appearances? The problem is not how may the conclusion be escaped, but whether it has any meaning for a theory of knowledge. It is too generally taken for granted that we know what it means—that there are things and there are appearances of them, that the things and their appearances are different, and that *this is a knowledge or a representative difference.* It is too uncritically assumed that the bent stick is the means of knowing the straight stick, or that the former is a representation of the latter.

Now there seems to be no evidence for this assumption. Seeing the stick bent is not a means of knowing that it is straight, nor is the stick seen bent a representation of the straight stick. It is not the first, evidently, for it is absurd to say that we know a stick is straight by seeing it bent—that we know that reality is reality by perceiving that it is appearance. It is not the second, evidently, for the bent stick does not represent the straight stick cognitively, is not a substitute for it, is not something different from it, is not a picture of it. If there is representation in the case, it is of the fact that a stick which looks bent in one set of conditions may look straight in another set. One has only to thrust his walking stick into the water to be assured that what he now sees is not a picture, a copy, "idea," or representation of his stick, because he knows he is looking at his stick and not a picture of it. Consequently we again approach the conclusion that the deception of the senses has nothing to do with a theory of knowledge, since it has nothing to do with knowledge or representation. Consequently, also, we are under no obligation to escape the conclusion that we perceive not things, but only their appearances, and under no obligation to subscribe to it. The difficulties attending the attempt to escape or to subscribe are artificial difficulties. They are not *real* difficulties, but only *apparent* ones.

It has already been pointed out that the senses deceive us, not because of any defect in the senses or in the appearances of things to us, but because of a defect in action. Briefly the stick seen bent may lead us to act as if it were seen straight. In no intelligible sense can we claim that the stick ought to be seen straight if our senses are not to deceive us. How, we may ask, ought a straight stick in the water to appear if it is really a straight stick? Ought it to appear straight or bent? If it appeared straight, it is clear enough that our senses would then deceive us by letting the stick appear as it ought not to appear. But that is not the way in which they deceive us. They let things appear as they ought to appear and that fact is no small item in our happiness. Again; if we never acted, if we did nothing in response to the appearance of things to us, we should never be deceived by our senses. It is evident, therefore, that we are deceived not because the appearances of things are not cognitively or representatively adequate—there being no cognition or representation involved—but because the appearance of things to us is not alone sufficient to enable us to react effectively. If it were, not only would the senses never deceive us, but we should have no use for consciousness or knowledge.

III

Yet it may be urged again that in spite of all that has been said we have, none the less, appearances or images on our hands and these are not the things which appear or of which we have images. "It is evident the mind knows not things immediately, but only by the intervention of the ideas it has of them." Any one who denies this is refuted by the evidence of the deception of the senses. Thus that deception does imply an epistemology. To overlook the implication is to assume a theory of knowledge without making the assumption explicit.

This seems to be only a restatement of positions already considered; and what has been already said applies to it. Let us admit that there are any number of appearances or images or ideas, the evidence goes to show that they are not cognitive or cognitively representative. They are stimuli to thinking and doing—to action—and it is not in having them, but in reacting to them, that knowledge comes into play. They are not the means by which we know, they are items with which our knowing deals. Our knowledge, so far as they are concerned, consists, not of them, but of propositions about them. The appearance of a straight stick bent in the water is not knowledge at all. Knowledge exists only when we are able to say that the straight stick appears bent because of the water. We should, doubtless, not say this if we did not see the stick bent, but only because the fact for which we are seeking a cause would not then be an object of our inquiry. Moreover, we make the inquiry because we are radically convinced that appearances are what they ought to be, and that, consequently, if we err, the cause of our erring is not due to any defect in them, but to our own ignorance.

It may be urged, however, that such considerations are inadequate and really avoid the issue. They may be adequate so long as we don't make the distinction itself between appearance and reality an object of inquiry. We may admit, that is, that appearance is not knowledge and has as a stimulus to action no cognitive significance. But we can, notwithstanding, ask, what is the reality which appears? The moment we ask that question we come upon a case of knowledge for which the distinction between appearance and reality is crucial. Indeed we come *only then* upon a theory of knowledge in the strict and philosophical senses. A theory of knowledge in the philosophical sense is something different from a theory of knowledge in a logical, scientific, or pragmatic sense.

If this is so, we have certainly made an important advance in our analysis of problems. It is a step forward to recognize that a philosophical theory of knowledge is something quite different from a logical, scientific, or pragmatic theory. It is a step out of ambiguity into clearness. There are those who would say that, while this may be so, it is a step not worth while, for it is a step in the direction of frivolity and visionary speculation. But what they say can have force only if philosophy turns out to be frivolous and visionary. Certainly philosophy ought not to be discredited at the start. We may leave the question of its value untouched and still insist that the deception of the senses has no bearing upon a theory of knowledge which is professedly not empirical. In such a theory we are dealing with a unique kind of knowledge which we may call theoretical or speculative, but which is not the kind of knowledge with which action, science, and affairs are concerned. It is difficult to see, therefore, how the deception of the senses, which is a matter of action, science, and affairs, can have any bearing upon a philosophical theory of knowledge as it has just now been defined.

In other words, our contention now takes this shape: Granted that the distinction between appearance and reality, as just that distinction and no other, is a distinction which now raises the problem of the knowledge of reality as reality in distinction from the knowledge of appearance as appearance—granted this, we may still insist that the distinction as thus construed is not, whatever else it may be, the distinction between appearance and reality involved in the deception of the senses. It is another and a different distinction, and, at present, we need not be at all concerned with just what it is. In support of this contention all that has been already said might be repeated. In what follows, it is repeated, but in a different form in the interest of clearness and reinforcement.

IV

It is a variation on the theme of the deception of the senses to point out the fact that the same thing may appear in contradictory fashion to different observers at the same time and to the same observer at different times. This fact may raise the question, What then is the thing?[3] It can not very well be all of its contradictory appearances combined *and it can not very well be any one of them exclusively*. When we take them one by one, *each has as much right to be the thing as any other*. This is so undeniably true that writers who suspect that it is denied are filled with amazement.

But to what is its truth relevant? As simply true all by itself there is little in it to stimulate thought. The truth must be put into a context in order to move on. If, for instance, some one now goes on to say: Since the truth is as you have admitted, then "things" have no *originally objective* existence as set over against us; they are not ready-made things-in-themselves which affect us and with which we deal; they are *objective* in the Kantian sense, let us say; they are the objective of their varied appearances. Here certainly we have a theory of knowledge. Now we may readily admit that what such a theory says about the objectivity of things—that they are not things-in-themselves—is true, but we can not admit that the reason for its truth is the reason that has been here assigned, namely, that a thing can not be all of its appearances combined or any one of them exclusively. It will be the different reason—and more in accord with the Kantian philosophy—that appearance has nothing to do with knowledge. We should claim with him that *the* theory of knowledge is not an empirical theory based on observing the variations and sequences of phenomena.

[3] I do not think it does raise the question legitimately, because if we do not know what "the same thing is" which "appears different," we can not identify the fact we are investigating. Our question is not, What is the thing? but Why does it appear different?

To appeal to experience is to invite experience to declare itself on the matter appealed to, and here experience declares emphatically that while a thing can not be all of its appearances combined or any one of them exclusively—simply because it never is—*it is every one of them in every instance which can be defined.* Was it not admitted that the same thing appears different to different observers at the same time, and to the same observers at different times? Was it not admitted that this is a plain fact of experience? Was it not also admitted that to identify the thing with all of its appearances at once or with any one of them exclusively is a plain impossibility? But how can these admissions have any force if the thing is not always what it appears to be when and to whatever observer? If a straight stick which appears bent is not a straight stick which appears bent, what is it?

But some one may say, You have passed from "appears" to "is" without any warrant whatever; you can not affirm—and you have admitted that you can not—that the stick which *appears* bent *is* bent. In reply we urge again that the transition from "appears" to "is" in cases like this is not a cognitive transition. But we may again vary the reply. Some sticks *appear* bent which *are* bent. Some *appear* bent which *are not* bent. In the first case we may say that the sticks are what they appear to be, but in the second we may not say this. But why? Because it is false. But it is false *not because there is any error in the appearance,* for the sticks appear precisely as they *must* appear, *if the conditions of their appearance are genuinely what we take them to be and if they are straight.* Otherwise there is no meaning in saying that straight sticks appear bent. The difference between our two cases is, therefore, a difference which does not imply any error in the appearance or any ambiguity in the reality. The difference is of a totally different sort. In other words if we leave out action—thinking or doing—we have no distinction between appearance and reality in these cases and we must reduce our second case to a simple tautology: a straight stick appearing bent is precisely a straight stick appearing bent—or a straight stick in the water is precisely a straight stick in the water—and the stick is thus precisely what it appears to be. *To just such tautologies, knowledge, when it is attained, reduces the distinction (for action) between appearance and reality.*

V

In conclusion I wish to point out an assumption which is often made in discussions about appearance and reality, and which, to my mind, is the principal thing which may lead some readers to think that what I have said is not only unconvincing, but irrelevant. I shall approach it by using a specific instance, not the stick this time, which I abandon with regret, but the circle.[4]

A circle appears different to different observers differently situated. It may appear, to use a common mode of expressing it, as any one of a series of appearances varying from a line through ellipses of varying diameters until the circle appears again as a line. These appearances may be graphically pictured to any desired number. Now let us suppose that ten observers are given in different situations, then it is evident that the circle will appear ten times conformably to the ten situations. But over and above this evident fact *it is assumed that there will then be ten different shapes which are existentially separate and distinct from one another, and of which each is existentially separate and distinct from the circle itself.* That is, if the circle appears to one observer as a flat ellipse, then it is assumed that the *appearance* is itself a flat ellipse.[5] What these shapes are in their essence, where put them, what to do with them when they are put there, how explain their relations and connections with one another and with the circle —here are problems to tax all our ingenuity, and problems on which no experiment or no fact of experience can throw

[4] I have stuck to the stick because it is handy. It should be evident, however, that other current examples would have done just as well; the whistle, the sound of which *must* be heard later than its puff of steam is seen, the vanished star which *must* still appear in the sky, etc. The star had peculiar claims for its use instead of the stick, because some writers seem to have overlooked the fact that it would be very difficult for a vanished star to appear *as a vanished star.*

[5] Perhaps I ought to have stuck to the stick and said that it is assumed, if a straight stick appears bent, that the appearance is itself a bent stick! Let me add also that, following the illustration of the text, we have now two geometrical figures instead of one. Yet it is to be observed that the properties of the second figure, *although it is an ellipse,* are *demonstrably* the same as the properties of the first figure, *although it is a circle.*

any light. To affirm that if a circle appears elliptical, then its elliptical appearance is an ellipse, is not to state a fact, it is to make an assumption which condenses whole volumes of speculative philosophy and psychology into a single sentence.

It is not my intention to discuss here the merits of this assumption, but rather to call renewed attention to it. I have stated it crudely because more refined statements of it tend, in my opinion, to obscure rather than clarify it. We gain nothing by calling these shapes "images," "mental processes," "sensations," "ideas," etc. We undoubtedly affirm that things appear in various ways and, so affirming, call attention to an interesting and analyzable fact. But to convert this fact into an assumption of an order of existences which are "mental" or "psychical" and which, none the less, have qualities, intensities, space and time characters, and also laws of succession and coherence, is to make an assumption which is not self-evident, but which demands the most careful scrutiny and the most unequivocal evidence.

THE BELIEF IN SENSATIONS*

In few of our sciences is the contrast between theory and practice so pronounced as in psychology. Its methods are, for the most part, as direct and as easy of comprehension as the methods of other sciences. They are, in general, the same methods. There is as little difficulty in following intelligently an experiment on the time of perception, or on the delicacy of sensory discrimination, or on memory, as there is in following an experiment on the velocity of sound or on the expansion of gases. But there is extraordinary difficulty in finding in the standard works on psychology clear conceptions of the subject-matter of the science or clear definitions of its most elementary terms.

"Sensation," "perception," "consciousness," "mind," "state of consciousness," "mental process," are terms currently employed to indicate the specific character of the material with which the science deals, but there are no generally accepted definitions of them among psychologists and there is much confusion in attempts to state what they mean. For example, what difference, if any, is there between "tone" and the "sensation of tone," between "red" and the "sensation of red"? If there is a difference, the difference does not prevent the assertion that sensations have specific qualities, nor the enumeration of these qualities in terms of such distinctions as those of tone and colour. Why, for instance, should sensations of colour be qualitatively defined in terms of the spectrum or in terms of any of the numerous diagrams which may contain every possible colour, if colour and the sensation of colour are different? If, however, they are not different, just what does their identification mean? Must we seriously conclude that

* In the *Journal of Philosophy, Psychology and Scientific Methods,* Vol. X (1913), pp. 599-608. Read at the tenth meeting of the American Philosophical Association at Princeton, December 27-29, 1910.

colours are sensations? Are noises and tones sensations? Is pain a sensation? The answers to these questions are neither uniform nor unambiguous, and yet the assertion is repeatedly made, in some form or other, that sensations are the "first things in the way of consciousness," that they are the "elements of mind."

Similar confusion is evident when we look for some clear and generally accepted definition of "consciousness" and "mind." Is it proper to distinguish consciousness from what we are conscious of? If it is, how can we affirm that consciousness is a complex of elements such as "sensations" or "mental processes" and at the same time define these elements in terms of the things we are conscious of? But if "consciousness" and "what we are conscious of" are to be identified, what can such an identification possibly mean? Does anybody really believe that a "complex" of the elements of a consciousness thus identified with its object could ever be the memory of an event or the knowledge of a world?

Furthermore, while we perceive, remember, imagine, think, reason, and act in a world which our best efforts can not distinguish from the world of physics, chemistry, and biology, psychology has so pictured its world—the mental world—that its relation to the world of general scientific interest becomes a problem which is often fundamental to the understanding of the scope and aims of psychology itself. The problem thus raised has afforded much discussion of the relation of mind and body, but it has received no solution. To say that the mental world and the physical world are "parallel," that they are two aspects of the same world, that they are indications of two different points of view, that the one is the world of all observers, while the other is the world of one observer—to say these things is not to solve the problem, but to comfort oneself and possibly others by that illusion of progress which often attends the restatement of a difficulty. Although it is repeatedly asserted that "psychological parallelism" is the working hypothesis of psychology, I have not been able to discover any achievement of psychology which depends on that hypothesis or which that hypothesis serves in any degree to clarify or explain. Indeed, it seems as if all theories of the relation of mind to body are entirely irrelevant to the methods and results of psychology.

Some writers of psychological books still think it important to devote at least one chapter to a discussion of what "science" and "law" are in general, and to a vindication of psychology as a science which deals with laws. Chemists and physicists, however, do not generally begin their work with such epistemological introductions and are usually unconscious of any need of vindicating their methods or aims. Only bigotry could deny psychology the status of a science, so that this concern about "psychology as a science" must probably be set down more as a lingering reminiscence of the days when controversy was keen than as an indication of confused thinking. Yet the discussions of "introspection" as the peculiar method of psychology often cause doubts whether an introspective psychology is worth serious consideration. These discussions raise again the old questions which no one has successfully answered: How can a conscious process know itself? How can a succession of thoughts know itself as a succession? How can states of mind be observed if they are only remembered? How is identification by memory possible if no state of mind was ever conscious of itself? If it is true that "no subjective state, while present, is its own object," but "its object is always something else"[1] is it not fair to ask if it is sensible to talk about "subjective states" at all? What are they? Who in the history of mankind has ever identified one, finding somewhere in his conscious life a "state" which was "not its own object," but "whose object was always something else"? The question is not asked with the purpose of suggesting that there may be "states" which are "their own objects." It is asked solely with the purpose of indicating that the conception of such states is inherently unintelligible.

In striking contrast to all this confusion and ambiguity stand the performances and achievements of psychologists. Although their science is one of the youngest of sciences, if we have in mind the modern status, its record in the matter of practical success must be regarded as gratifying and encouraging. Psychology has profoundly affected our educa-

[1] William James, *Principles of Psychology,* Vol. I, p. 190.

tional theory and practice. It has influenced medical science and therapeutics in a manner which, on the whole, has been helpful and sound. It has enlarged the outlook of physiology and given fresh impetus to the comparative study of behaviour.[2] It bids fair to provide us with means of securing valuable estimates of human ability and capacity. In view of these successes, it would be absurd to claim that the theoretical confusion, which has been pointed out, is a necessary accompaniment of the science, something which must be put up with, but which is of little importance since practice goes on triumphantly in spite of it. Such an attitude is an indication of philosophical weariness, but not of matured wisdom. The moral for psychologists, if we must draw a moral for them, is obviously to give up the pretense that psychology is a science of consciousness, and then to redefine their science in terms of the material they actually study, the methods they actually use, and the results they actually attain. The theoretical confusion in psychology has not been pointed out here, however, with the intention of drawing any moral, but rather to introduce the consideration of a preconception which appears to have been at the bottom of that confusion and which seems to have been fatal to the attempts which psychology has made to tell what consciousness is.

It may be extravagant to single out one preconception in psychological theory and make it responsible for all the confusion. Yet there appears to be one which must bear the greater share of responsibility. To pursue it through all its windings and show just how it has motived this and that ambiguous statement or conception, would be a wearisome task. Economy of effort may be served by examining it directly and showing how the abandonment of it works in the direction of clearness and simplicity. This preconception consists of the

[2] This word will frequently occur in these pages. As the sequel will show, "behaviour," but not "consciousness," seems to me to be the thing which the psychologist does, as a matter of fact, investigate. To my own mind the psychologists who have used the concept of behaviour rigidly have passed at once from theoretical confusion to theoretical clearness. Compare E. L. Thorndike, *Animal Intelligence,* Ch. I.

I take this opportunity to refer, also, to the articles by Professor John Watson in the *Psychological Review,* Vol. XX (1913), p. 158, and in the *Journal of Philosophy,* Vol. X (1913), p. 421.

very current belief that there are such things as "sensations" which form a kind of elementary component of a stream of consciousness or of a mind.

The statement that belief in the existence of sensations is a preconception and the suggestion that the belief is unsound should not be set down at once as wild. To be sure, James, speaking for many an active worker in psychology, has said: "That we have *cogitations* of some sort is the *inconcussum* in a world most of whose other facts have at some time tottered in the breath of philosophic doubt. All people unhesitatingly believe that they feel themselves thinking, and that they distinguish the mental state as an inward activity or passion from all the objects with which it may cognitively deal. *I regard this belief as the most fundamental of all the postulates of psychology,* and shall discard all curious inquiries about its certainty as too metaphysical for the scope of this book."[3] Yes: but did he not follow this confession of faith by considering "a question of nomenclature" and finding no satisfactory term to "designate all states of consciousness merely as such, and apart from their particular quality or cognitive function"? Most evidently, then, "the most fundamental of all the postulates of psychology" had not impressed itself upon current speech nor produced as yet an appropriate expression of itself. In twenty years we are no better off. And the reason is this: while all people believe that they cogitate, very few people, if any, are able to distinguish their mental states as inward activities or passions from all the objects with which those mental states may cognitively deal. As a matter of fact, very few people believe that there are "states of consciousness as such," and consequently very few have felt the need of a term to designate them.

It may be said, however, that most people believe that they have "sensations." Yet it is very doubtful if the sensations in which people generally believe are the elementary components of mind in which psychologists often believe. For the term "sensation" is decidedly ambiguous especially in its psychological usage. The word "sense" may be used as a verb to denote a uniform operation which may be directed toward

[3] *Principles of Psychology,* Vol. I, p. 185.

different materials. Thus one may "sense a sound," or "sense a colour," or "sense a pain." Such usage is not common, but it seems to indicate that the term "sensation" may be regarded as a general term for the operation of sensing. Sensations would then be "sensings," the performance of the same operation more than once or in different directions. They would not be marked by qualitative distinctions from one another since they are just so many instances of the same operation. We may "shoot" in various directions and at various games, but our "shots" as "shootings" are all alike. No serious objection need be raised to the term "sensation" in the manner here indicated, as a general term to cover such operations as seeing, hearing, or, in general, sensing. So used, it is not marked by disastrous ambiguity.

But the term may be used to denote the material which is the object of the operation. Thus the colour which is seen or "sensed" may be termed a "sensation," and we may recognize a great variety of sensations differing in quality in a manner corresponding to the different qualities of the things sensed. Here the term begins to be seriously ambiguous. For it is one thing to affirm that "blue sensed" is a sensation, but quite a different thing to affirm that blue as blue is a sensation. We may speak of the things we have shot as our "shots" if we are mindful why we so designate them, but it would be improper to affirm that a partridge is a shot. It is, however, just this sort of impropriety of which much psychology has been guilty. It has treated the things we sense as if their qualitative characters were themselves sensations, some kind of mental operation or process, and supposed, consequently, that an analysis of the qualities, intensities, extensities, etc., of the things we sense was an analysis of consciousness itself.

Now one does not ordinarily or readily believe that his consciousness or his mind is made up of colours, sounds, tastes, smells, and the like. Indeed, most well-trained and scientifically minded persons experience a shock if they are told that consciousness is so constituted. They may be willing to admit that they are conscious only when they see or hear or perform some similar operation, but they find consciousness unrecognizable when told that it is made up of what they see or hear, or that such things are the elements of mind, the first things in the way of consciousness. The psychologist may be justified in using the term sensation to denote the objects of sense as well as the operation, but he is under the serious obligation of showing by what right he regards the distinctively qualitative characters of these objects as sensations, mental elements, mental factors, mental functions, or mental processes; by what right he regards as conscious or mental anything whatsoever which is characteristic of the object.

It is at this point that the basal preconception which has vitiated so much psychological theory becomes most evident. It may be stated in several ways. For example, it is assumed that the immediate data of consciousness—let them be called sensations, perceptions, thoughts, ideas—are somehow products or effects of the stimuli which excite the sense organs or the organism. Or we say it is assumed that the effect produced in the nervous system by a stimulus causes, or is somehow attended by, a fact which does not belong to the chain of facts which connects the stimulus and the organism, but which is a fact of a different order, a mental fact, a sensation. Or we say that it is assumed that the mechanism which is involved in the operations of consciousness somehow transforms, or is attended by, the transformation of the external stimuli to conscious activity into an internal world of conscious phenomena or states of mind. The simplest statement may, however, be taken from Locke's *Essay concerning Human Understanding*:

> Our senses, conversant about particular sensible objects, do convey into the mind several distinct perceptions of things, according to those various ways wherein those objects do affect them. And thus we come by those *ideas* we have of *yellow, white, heat, cold, soft, hard, bitter, sweet,* and all those which we call sensible qualities; which, when I say the senses convey into the mind, I mean, they from external objects convey into the mind what produces there those perceptions.[4]

This is the belief in sensations, in a kind of thing which is neither the stimulus nor the effect it produces through the sense organs on the nervous system, but which is believed to be a mental equivalent of that effect; and these effects are supposed

[4] Book II, Ch. I, p. 3.

to be either the immediate objects of consciousness or the elements of which consciousness or the mind is a system.

The remarkable thing, to my mind, about this belief is that there is so little good evidence for it. There is a general admission that it is not natural. We are repeatedly told that by far the greater number of us naturally believe that the immediate objects of consciousness are the very same objects which are the stimulus to thought, and that we need instruction by philosophy, psychology, and physiology in order to discover our mistake. We are also told that the natural belief in this matter represents the general attitude of positive science. Such admissions make it important that the evidence for the belief should be exceptionally strong. It is, however, exceptionally weak.

There is, for example, the evidence derived from the so-called relativity of sensation. Locke's instance of the water which is warm to one hand, but cold to the other is typical and frequently cited. The water itself, it is urged, can not be both warm and cold at the same time. The difference lies in our sensations. In other words, the fact that water is cold to one hand and warm to the other is taken as evidence that we do not sense the heat of the water, but only its effects in us, the sensations it produces. But the relativity cited is evidence only of the fact that the water is warmer than one hand and colder than the other. Every case of the relativity of sensations can, I think, be dismissed in a similar manner. They all indicate the relativity of things to one another, but not the relativity of things to the mind or to our sensations of them.[5] Even the straight stick bent in a pool and the man who can not tell red from green lose their supposed metaphysical importance in the face of the fact that things vary in varying conditions quite irrespective of any appeal to states of mind. It is the difference between the refractive powers of water and air that bends the seen stick and it is a retinal, not a mental, consideration which makes the discrimination of colours impossible. I have even found it urged that the variation of colour in different lights or under different conditions of colour

[5] Compare the article by W. P. Montague, "A Neglected Point in Hume's Philosophy," *Philosophical Review,* Vol. XIV, p. 30.

contrast proves that colours are sensations for the astonishing reason that if a rose were really red it ought to be seen red in the dark! Again; seeing things double has been used to prove that we have sensations, while all it proves is that we have two eyes. Moving the eye and so seeing the landscape move is cited as a good reason for concluding that we do not see the landscape, since the landscape surely does not move. But how can any landscape maintain an immovable relation to a moving eye, and how can an eye move except in relation to its surroundings? No, I repeat, the relativity of sensations witnesses to the relativity of things, but not to the existence of sensations as the component elements of consciousness.

There is also the type of evidence drawn from a consideration of such experiences as dreams and illusions. It is urged that here, at any rate, we have instances where on its qualitative side experience can be only mental. A dream as a dream or an illusion as an illusion must be of the very stuff of consciousness. Let them be. But one may still ask, How does that in any way prove that "sensations" exist and are the constitutive elements of mind? Whatever may be the causes of dreams and illusions and of whatever stuff they may be made, they exist apparently only because the sensory mechanism is inoperative or out of order. Our dreams vanish when we wake and the greatest obstacle in the way of having illusions is an unclogged sensory mechanism. It is difficult, therefore, to see how they can witness to the existence of sensations. Furthermore, it is too readily assumed by many that if one thinks he sees something which he really does not see, he must, none the less, see something like it; and that if one dreams of going to his boyhood's home, he is having an experience similar to what he would have if he went there. When we dream of colours, do we see colours? When we have illusions of sound, do we hear sounds? Such questions have not yet been finally answered, but they must first be answered before we can give much evidential value to dreams and illusions. In our present state of knowledge dreams prove, when we have them, that we are dreaming of things, but not sensing them; and illusions prove that we are making mistakes, but not that we are having sensations.

Then there are such experiences as pain. I stick a pin into my brother's leg. He reacts in various ways, winces, cries out, but no scrutiny of mine can reveal distinctly to me the pain he feels. Yet he does feel pain, and any doubt I may have on the subject is sufficiently dispelled by sticking the pin into myself. And if so, how about my brother's tastes and smells, his feelings of roughness and smoothness? And if I infer these also, where am I to stop, short of concluding that he has an inner life of consciousness made up of existences like the existence of pain, real sensations of varying qualities?

But does this inaccessibility of pain to external observation prove in any way that pain is a sensation, a mental element, or state of consciousness? Does the fact that I can not sense my brother's pain, but must infer it, prove anything else than that my pain-sensing machinery is limited to my own pains? The pin may be a stimulus to both our organisms at once, but the pain is in my brother's leg, not mine, nor in the pin. We may both see the pin, hear the pin, touch the pin, taste, and even smell the pin, but neither of us sees, hears, touches, tastes, or smells the pain. If his pain were blue, I could see it; if loud, I could hear it; if sweet, I could taste it; and so on; but since it is none of these, I naturally can not sense it in these ways. And since my pain-sensing machinery is limited to my own pains, I never can sense his. But were this machinery not so limited, were it distance-sensing like my eyes, why, then, I could feel his pains as readily as I can see his face. Surely pain is not proved to be a sensation, a mental thing, by the fact that my own pains are all the pains I have. Having thus no evidential value in its own domain, it has none elsewhere.

The case of pain recalls the fact that believers in the existence of sensations as the elements of mind usually claim that sensations are accessible only to introspection. When, for example, the processes of vision are experimentally followed, the effect produced in the organism is some form of movement or behaviour, but not a colour. And what is true of vision appears true generally. Stimulate an organism and follow the stimulus experimentally through all the mechanism involved, and the only discovered effect is a reaction, a type of behaviour, but never a sensation. But, it is claimed, the sensations are discovered to introspection and we are bound, accordingly, to infer them or eject them whenever the situation warrants it. But the plain fact is that introspection does not disclose the existence of sensations, but only the existence of the things sensed. In one's own experience scrutinized and reflected on by one's self, colour, for example, is never discovered in any respect as an elementary component of one's consciousness, as a mental thing; it is discovered as a stimulus to thought and behaviour, but not as a stimulus to the production of a colour sensation. Indeed the whole evidence of introspection makes for the non-existence of sensations. That it can be supposed to reveal to us what is experimentally undiscoverable is evidence solely of philosophical confusion. The appeal to introspection is, in reality, an appeal to the most direct, simple, and naïve conceptions of things. If, therefore, one is to test the belief in sensations by one's own direct and immediate experience, then the belief is doomed. And surely if sensations as the first things in the way of consciousness, as the constituent elements of mind, are discoverable neither by external observation nor by inward reflection, there is no good reason to believe in their existence and there is no conceivable service which this supposed existence can render. They form the subject-matter of no intelligible science whatever.

The belief in sensations has been questioned here in the interest of freeing the conception of consciousness from certain misconceptions and primarily the misconception that consciousness is definable in terms of the qualities of which we are conscious. But the position here taken should be construed as primarily negative, and not as warranting the affirmation of what it may appear to imply. For instance, when we deny that the things we perceive are in the mind, we are supposed to affirm that they are out of the mind. When we deny that we perceive internal objects, we are supposed to affirm that we perceive external objects. When we deny that sensations are effects somehow produced in the mind by stimuli affecting the organism, we are supposed to affirm that the mind somehow runs out of the organism and gets hold of the object, or surrounds it, or pervades it. Such suppositions may be naturally suggested by the denials, but they are not here intended. What is intended is simply that consciousness should not be thought of in a certain way. Freed from the notion that sensations are the primary objects of consciousness, we may proceed to the inquiry into what the objects of consciousness as a matter of fact are.

TANGLING COGNITION*

"CONSIDER what a tangle cognition would be, if, in order to cognize anything, we had to cognize also the relation of our own cognitive experience to it!" This sentence, quoted from Mr. C. A. Strong's article on "The Missing Link in Epistemology,"[1] is devastating. It reduces to unintelligibility much that is written about knowing and knowledge, for it makes clear at a glance that the relation—if we will speak of a "relation" in this context—between cognitive experience and what is thereby cognized, is simply cognition itself. The sentence suggests others correspondingly framed. Consider what a tangle seeing would be, if, in order to see anything, we had also to see the relation of our visual experience to the thing seen! Consider what a tangle motion would be, if, in order for a body to move over a given track, it had also to move over the relation of its motion to the track! Or consider Achilles and the tortoise! Reflection on such and similar variations of the sentence tends to make one suspicious of the problem of the relation of cognitive experience to what is thereby cognized.

But, it may be urged, the relation of experience to what is experienced is precisely what the problem of knowledge is, even if we do not experience that relation, for our experience reveals itself as the means of knowing something else, and, therefore, sets the problem of its relation to that something else. For example—to use one of many examples—our visual experience of a railroad track is that its rails converge, but we know that they do not converge. Were it not for such examples as this, knowledge would not be a problem at all. But the multitude of examples of this kind which the advance of knowledge has disclosed and which seem to be the more im-

* In the *Journal of Philosophy*, Vol. XXIX (1932), pp. 688-690.

[1] *Journal of Philosophy*, Vol. XXIX (1932), p. 677.

posing the more they involve expert knowledge for their statement, force the problem upon us. To revolt against it is not to solve it. It is only to ignore it. The problem stays even with those who refuse to recognize it. Seeing is a means of knowing, but that which is known is not that which is seen. Some sort of epistemological or ontological dualism is affirmed to be unavoidable, so long as seeing and knowing, experience and what is experienced, are contrasted as they so evidently are.

Those who are concerned about the problem of knowledge so stated, object to being told that cognition is experience as much as seeing and the rest, and that consequently the problem of knowledge ought not to be stated in the way they state it. And they do not like to be told that the inevitable dualism on which they insist, is only a restatement of their problem and not a solution of it. Mr. Strong's sentence impresses me as a fortunate way of telling them both these things at once. Since the dualism is only a restatement of the problem, the consequence is that cognition becomes only a tangle which could be untangled only by cognizing something which is never cognized. Mr. Strong's phrasing is fortunate because it avoids the pitfalls of such expressions as "thoughts and things" or "ideas and objects" and emphasizes the fact that cognition is an act and not a discovered or supposed relation within or without the field in which it occurs, nor a relation between two fields. Consequently, whatever dualism is implied by or involved in the occurrence of cognition, is neither epistemological nor ontological, but something which characterizes the behaviour of the field in which cognition occurs. For my part, I have failed to find any fact or argument which, when analyzed, warrants the contention that the behaviour of this field is altered by the natural or artificial means of discovering what that behaviour is. The behaviour may be dualistic. The rails which do not converge are the rails which are seen to converge. That is the way they behave and because they behave that way we invent microscopes and telescopes which would be useless if the rails did not so behave. The convergence of parallels is a principle by means of which the world is explored. I can not transform this principle into an argument which puts parallels in the system of the world and convergence in our experience. My seeing the rails is not what makes them converge. If it were, then they ought not to converge when photographed. Whatever dualism is here involved is an operation of nature and an operation by means of which the dualism in it is discovered. To put the parallels in one realm of being and the convergence in another is to define a situation in which a photograph could never be taken. Shall we ask the camera to photograph not only its object, but also the relation between that object and its photographing? If not, why ask something similar of a thinking man? It seems to me to be inevitable that a being blessed with the ability to see a world in which cameras, microscopes, and telescopes behave as they do, would see the principle of the convergence of parallels illustrated wherever he looked. His seeing would not be an impairment of his knowing, but an increase of its power.

I have already said that dualists object to being told that cognition is itself experience. In general I think they are justified, because the appeal to cognitive experience so often leads to the doctrine that the system of the world is a construct of that experience. It is not difficult for dualists, by analyzing this doctrine, to confront it with the fact that it derives its force and intelligibility from the dualistic position itself. The construct to be available either theoretically or practically can not be wayward or willful, and this makes an appeal to its availability inept as a guarantee of its soundness. But emphasizing cognition as experience may have the effect of pointing out that the dualist's procedure involves some command of the terms of his dualism. The system of the world and our experience are at least subjects of discourse. This fact brings us again to Mr. Strong's sentence. Thinking about the system and the experience goes on. The attempt to deduce the thinking from either the system or the experience is futile, unless it is first read into the one or the other. It is obviously not a discovered relation between the two. The results of our thinking can not be an explanation of it. Or, if we take them as such, we ought not to deceive ourselves about what we have done. We have then defined explanation as an analysis of what we know and left the knowing precisely what it was before the analysis was made, precisely what it is, for example, to a physicist who never troubles himself about the problem of knowledge. He explains the operations of his subject-matter and not his cognitive relation to it. Current literature shows how much unintelligible nonsense can be written when the latter is attempted. The attempt to examine our cognitive relation to our subject-matter has not increased our knowledge. It is only analysis of our subject-matter that does that. Cognition is experience in such a sense, but this sense does not imply or involve a dualism of any other sort than is implied or involved by the fact that verbs as well as nouns are necessary for intelligible discourse—there is no knowledge without knowing.

Increase of knowledge, as Bacon said, is increase of power —increase of the possibilities of acting. I ask, therefore, if it is not wiser to take this dynamic fact as having a significance for the system of the world, than, by neglecting it, to turn cognition into a tangle?

THE PROBLEM OF CONSCIOUSNESS AGAIN*

RECENT rereadings of William James have vividly recalled to me the early days of the *Journal of Philosophy* when the "problem of consciousness" was exciting and James challenged the debaters of it with the question, "Does Consciousness Exist?" In retrospect, the controversy wears for me a different look than it had at the time of its activity. Then it seemed that all that we mortals mean when we use the word "soul" was at stake. Now it seems that we were tricked, allowing ourselves to be influenced more by forms of speech than by what we were talking about. What is *consciousness*? What is it *to be conscious*? These two questions might have been more generally suspected to be identical, if we had not been so much obsessed by the disjunction: consciousness must be either a *stuff* or a *function*. James's challenge brought some calm to many of us in spite of the fact that it made "consciousness" a *function* of the *stuff* of "experience." We could stop worrying about "consciousness" in the old way and start worrying about "experience" in a new way; so helpful is language to philosophers! Behaviourists could march on with "language patterns" as a banner and Gestalters could come along with a German word for decoration. All of us, however, in spite of controversies, still seem to be more or less awake to an environment of earth and sky and find ourselves vitally interested in common sense, society, religion, art, and science. After all, nothing much seems to have happened. Whatever *consciousness* is, we seem still *to be conscious*.

Perhaps the debate about consciousness is a typical case of philosophical absent-mindedness, like looking for one's spectacles to find them on one's nose. Obviously the instruments of vision are not found without their exercise nor the motion

* In the *Journal of Philosophy*, Vol. XXXIII (1936), pp. 561-568.

of bodies detected without their moving. Are such elementary instances of being, so evident, accessible, and inescapable, problems to be solved? A growing plant may find a problem of finding moisture, but in solving that, does it find a problem of its own growth? Even in that strange submicroscopic world which the scientifically inspired tell us about, there may be uncertainty managed by probability, but if so, the management itself can hardly be a problem in that world; it is rather something characteristic of that world. What nature does, she does, and may raise problems in the doing of it, but can her doing what she does be itself a problem? When I ask a question like that, two lines of Matthew Arnold's verses on "Morality" occur to me. He puts a similar question to nature and finds her vaguely reminiscent of a time when there was anxiety about herself:

> 'Twas when the heavenly house I trod
> And lay upon the breast of God.

Philosophers may obscure by their language the desire of their hearts to solve the problem of creation, but they should, for their soul's health, remember the fate of the Titans who tried to scale heaven. It is a perilous business in which they are engaged. They may be "Intelligence in Chains," as Æschylus pictured Prometheus, but they are bound both in fact and in morals. They are bound by the forces of the world in which they live and they are bound not to forget it even if a vulture gnaws at their vitals. They may defy God or bless his name; creating a world is not their business. They may be forced to admit, as they often confess that they are, that nature is created since there is no evidence that she creates herself; she reveals no reason why she *should* do what she does, she reveals only that there is competence to do what is done.

I think that it is a fair conclusion to draw from considerations like these that the problem of consciousness is at least equivocal. It may be what Professor Bush, before the days of logical positivism, called an artificial problem, one, that is, that arises from the manner of its statement rather than from the exigencies of subject-matter. How, for example, can we be conscious of the past since the past is no longer present for us to be conscious of it? If today we still invoke memory as a solution, we might do well to reread Bergson's *Matière et mémoire*. Or the problem may be real enough, if we let our being conscious be itself explanatory of nature's processes. Then Bergson may be recommended again along with James on habit and Hering's little book on memory. These suggested readings do not imply the acceptance or recommendation of individual philosophies. They imply rather an appeal to modern writers who happily combine the sense of exploration and analysis with a genius for generalization. If it is characteristic of living matter to grow with respect to what has happened to it heretofore, then there would seem to be less a problem of memory than of forgetfulness. Diversification and restriction of memories would begin to look like the diversity and restriction of lives generally. Then one might be tempted to ask, Why stop at living matter; does not nature remember? Who then would let just a word associated with human faculty trouble him?

Taking the problem of consciousness to be of the latter sort, a real and not an artificial problem, it seems clear enough to us today as it was clear enough to the ancients, that being conscious, if it requires further specification, is seeing, hearing, tasting, smelling, feeling; thinking about what we see, hear, taste, smell, and feel; and expressing the result in language of some sort. That is what being conscious is, and no philosopher has ever delivered anything more, be he ancient, mediaeval, or modern. Even Descartes, excited over *cogito ergo sum*, had to find an object for *cogito* if he was to get on with a discourse on method. Thinking about a surrounding world in which we find ourselves alive, awake, active, planning, and telling ourselves and others about it—that is what it is to be conscious. And this is quite literally a principle, a beginning and not an end, a start and not a finish. Idealists and realists alike insist on it and are both, so far, incontrovertible. Abolish being conscious and there is nothing to talk about. Being conscious is the source of common sense, society, religion, art, and science. Santayana has well named them the phases of human progress. Since being conscious is the admitted source of all our problems and of their solution—a genuine principle

—in what sense can it itself be a problem; in what sense, *then,* if the problem is not the problem of creation; in what sense, if the question is *not*, Why *should* consciousness, in the sense of being conscious, exist at all?

If, then, we are not titanically engaged in first creating a world in which consciousness *might* exist and be fruitful, but humanly employed in exploring a world in which it *does* exist, what is it that *generates* a problem of consciousness? The italicized word in the question suggests the answer. The problem of consciousness, when being conscious is made that problem, is a problem of genesis. Were no genetic considerations involved, it is difficult for me to see how a situation like that which being conscious presents, would be a problem at all. Did we, for example, see permanently and all around us, I wonder what clues we could find for suggesting that vision was in any sense a problem. But we see now and then and under conditions which force themselves on our attention. Vision is generated and being conscious is generated; and we naturally ask how. The answer involves the attempt to transform a situation in which consciousness does not exist into one in which it does. In spite of Berkeley's contention, not yet refuted, that such an attempt involves a *petitio principii* somewhere, his contention is rarely convincing enough to stop argument about the matter. Even with him it did not stop it. Even with him spirit with spirit had somehow to meet first; and although what we call nature might be the order of God's own perceptions, we still needed eyes to behold it and touch to help us find the significance of spatial distinctions; we still *became* conscious of God's own world. We sensed it and reflected on it, not always, but now and then; we talked about it and often fell into confusions of speech. Being conscious was like a light that comes and goes, leaving the question of its antecedents open even if the attempt to illuminate them involved the assumed continued presence of that light. Even if only a conscious being can distinguish between being conscious and not being conscious, he has the distinction on his doorstep like a foundling, must take the child in and attend to it.

I find no other problem of consciousness than the genetic

one and this I really do not find; it is found for me, lying on my doorstep as suggested. The death of others makes me expect my own and a dead body seems to be as clear an example of what not being conscious is as one can cite. Of course, without being conscious myself, I do not think of the dead; and I can not imagine them being conscious in any other way than I am. I picture them as observed and possibly observing, as still living somewhere and somehow, thus proving Berkeley right, but, like Berkeley, too, I know that they are not evidence of what I picture. As evidence, they are evidence of not being conscious, not of what it is to be conscious. But can they or anything like them define the antecedents of consciousness? Can they do it without ceasing to be perceived or thought about? Such a question seems to make the foundling on the doorstep lose all parentage whatever. Can we *by being conscious* define *what it is not to be conscious*, and then conclude that we have found the antecedents of consciousness? And yet, *being conscious* lays a genetic problem at our door.

The predicament we meet in trying to solve it, although it may seem peculiarly acute when consciousness is concerned, is inherent in genetic problems generally. The antecedents of an event are not disclosed as such until the event happens. Not until America was discovered were the antecedents of that discovery definable. Not until eggs are hatched are they definable as antecedents of chickens. I know of no genetic problem where the rule does not hold, that antecedents are discovered after the event; alleged cases to the contrary yield to the rule if the analysis is thorough. Clearly I should have no ancestors if I had never been born. Without me my ancestors could neither be nor be conceived. Of course it may be claimed that a rule like this is relative only to *our* search for origins. We must start that search with the event or circumstance the origin of which we seek, but having found that origin we are then entitled to reverse the process and go from origin to product, if we are to depict the processes of nature. Having found that chickens come from eggs, we imitate nature and employ eggs to produce chickens; having found the origin of eclipses, we anticipate nature and predict their occurrence to a nicety; having found the "periodic law" of chemistry, we admit the existence in nature of elements as yet undiscovered. Let all this be so; but one should, I think, pause at this point and reflect. We are now affirming that, because we are conscious, our method of discovery goes from product to origin, but we are entitled to reverse the order of this going for nature and affirm that nature goes from origin to product. The order of ideas is the reverse of the order of things. The "mind" waits for eventualities in order to determine what their antecedents were, but nature so operates that her past performances determine what are to be antecedents. The mind's order aims at knowledge, control, and use; nature's order does not *aim* at all, it only produces.

This result ought, I think, to clarify the problem of consciousness. Clearly it ought to if the genesis of being conscious is admitted to be an event in nature's order. It is not an event in its own order which I have ventured to call the order of the mind. Here being conscious is a principle, a beginning and not an end, a start and not a finish. The discoveries of nature and nature's order are among the issues of that principle, are attainments from that beginning, are, in a way, a finish from that start. For these discoveries by the mind, the mind claims pre-eminence over its own operations. To them is imputed the position of being antecedents to being conscious.

In other words, by being conscious we are led to think of a world in which we become conscious and that our becoming conscious is timed, as it were, as an event in that world. If we are to conclude that in the discovery of the genesis of that event we proceed from it to its antecedents while in that world the procedure is the reverse, then we must, it would seem, assign to consciousness the ability to recover its antecedents and to nature the ability to produce that recovery by generating conscious beings. This looks very much like saying that nature, in producing conscious beings, can and does produce consciousness of herself. If the order of nature does generate the order of the mind, what else can one say? One may here remember Hegel; but is there any good reason why Hegel should not be right on one or two points at least? If by means of ideas generated in us by our experience we are able to delineate the world in which that experience is generated, what has that world done if it has not rendered itself accessible in terms appropriate to it? Does it not now look a little absurd to say that nature by producing conscious beings renders herself inaccessible or accessible only on condition that we somehow solve first the problem of her accessibility? Does consciousness exist for the sake of making that problem the crucial problem of philosophy?

The conclusion I now reach is this: validating the ability of conscious beings to discover the genesis of their being conscious as an event in the order of nature, forces us to regard the order of nature as itself an historical process of which "being conscious" is the most effective example. The "problem of consciousness" ceases at once to be an epistemological problem of any sort. Being conscious may generate problems of knowledge such as what one must know in order to double a square correctly; what one must know in order to compass a given distance in a given time; what one must know in order to govern a state well, live a good life, or paint a picture which will delight the beholder of it; or by what circumstances or conditions do we find ourselves controlled when we solve such evident problems of knowledge and communicate with one another or decently order our reflections. But "being conscious" does not now generate a problem of its own cognitive validity because now such a problem no longer exists.

Put a little differently: if nature produces the conditions under which she becomes accessible to knowledge, the conditions of accessibility are not themselves of cognitive significance. Theories of perception become what Aristotle hinted they are, theories of what is perceived and not the validation of perception itself. A star seen in the sky does not now influence us to suppose that it is, for purposes of knowledge, a symbol of a star which we do not and can not see at all. It is seen where it is in relation to other stars that are seen, and the company of heaven bring the accessibility of their own history along with them. Knowledge might convince us that we could never reach that star even if we could travel forever, but in what sense that conviction raises a problem of the cognitive validity or invalidity of perception, I do not see. Seeing and hearing are not knowledge of what is seen or heard, but the natural existence of sights and sounds. Berkeley ought to have stuck to that even if he got no farther. Knowledge of them is not a fancied perception of what they would be if they were not seen or heard. Knowledge of them is like optics and acoustics, if an example of knowledge is here desired. Those sciences are about sights and sounds, but divorced from sights and sounds they are knowledge of nothing at all; nor are sights and sounds knowledge of anything at all. To be sure optics may be taught the blind and acoustics the deaf, but the teaching must ultimately be done by those who can see and hear. Without the production by nature of accessibility to sights and sounds optics and acoustics could neither be nor be conceived. These sciences—and any other science, for that matter—are not the discovery of substitutes for sights and sounds of a kind which, if we could only perceive—that is, see or hear—them, would entitle us to say that we perceive nature as she really is. Knowledge is the elaboration of perception and not its undoing. It is something which can be taught, communicated, and exchanged; and it is these characteristics of it which are the keys with which to unlock the door into its chamber of secrets. He that knows nature has penetrated beyond eye and ear, but without them his penetration would not go very far.

To be free of the habit of turning perception—being conscious—into a problem of knowledge is to be well-nigh free of the problem of consciousness altogether. The fact that conscious beings have had a history, since it is itself a delivery of consciousness, may stimulate us to find out what that history has been just as the star seen in the sky stimulates us to try and find out its history. There may be thus an historical problem, but it is now a natural-history problem. It is the problem of exhibiting the ways nature has followed and the means she has used in generating conscious beings. This exhibition, like others of a similar sort, will be also an exhibition of nature's history and nature's character. Unless I yield to the insistence that consciousness must supervene on natural processes or that ideas must overlay things with an impenetrable veil, I discover no problem of consciousness except this one of natural history. To admit that consciousness, in the sense of being conscious, is a natural event adequate for the recovery of history, is at least to suggest that the disjunction "stuff or function" is perilously misleading. As a stuff, consciousness has been made to look like a superstition; as the function of some sort of stuff, I doubt if it fares any better. For consciousness is seeing, hearing, and the rest, and seeing and hearing —and the rest appropriately—are sights seen and sounds heard, and in what sense these are functions of anything is hard for me to discover. They are materials of knowledge.

In the light of the analysis here proposed, the problem of consciousness is not single, but multiple, not *a* problem, but *many* problems; and these are the historical problems of that accessibility of nature which is effected in being conscious. One of them may be a problem of knowledge. This, however, can not now be a problem of a cognitive relation between "being conscious" and "not being conscious." It is rather the problem of discovering and analyzing the factors which control the elaboration of what we are conscious of into systematic and communicable expositions of it, for it is these expositions which are now knowledge. But knowledge in this sense is, in its basic character, never free from the fact that whatever may control its development, nature, with which it is concerned, is an historical matter, a productive enterprise, fixed, determined, necessary, or absolute only in terms of the discovered controls of its genetic procedure. Otherwise it is fluid and contingent. An historical process is dynamic. Its exhibitions may be subject to control, keeping some sort of balance among themselves, as Heraclitus seems to have suspected long ago; but it is not the balance that keeps them coming on. Here may be a problem indeed, but it is final and not initial. To be conscious and to have knowledge we do not have to wait upon its solution. Much desired as its solution may be, it is very doubtful that its possession would make the slightest difference to the problem of consciousness.

ADDRESSES

THE ENTERPRISE OF LEARNING*

"I CAN NOT but be raised to this persuasion, that this third period of time will far surpass that of the Greek and Roman learning: only if men will know their own strength and their own weakness both; and take, one from the other, light of invention, and not fire of contradiction; and esteem of the inquisition of truth as of an enterprise, and not as of a quality or ornament."[1] The words have the marks of age upon them, but three centuries have not weakened their power to provoke reflection. Is learning an enterprise or an ornament? Are schools busy in advancing it or in conserving a quality? Questions like these carry us at once into the thick of educational problems. Yet such questions are not apt to be profitably answered unless they are asked with some lively appreciation of the function and significance of intelligence in human life. For there is the life of reason and there is the life of instinct and emotion. To consult the former with eyes too much fascinated by the allurements of the latter is to turn the pursuit of learning into a discipline in irrationality; to make it fortify a prejudice instead of illuminate an action, or support an hypothesis instead of clarify an ideal.

Since we have intelligence not that we may act or be happy, but that our acts may be intelligent and our happiness rational, to pursue learning as a motive to action or as a means to happiness is unreasonable. Consequently, the contention that education should equip the young for life, or for service, or for citizenship, or that it should develop character, or make men of them, or promote their efficiency—a contention sound enough certainly when uttered without a context—should be viewed with caution. Education's basal function is to make

* In the *Amherst Graduates' Quarterly*, Vol. I (1911), pp. 1-12.

[1] Francis Bacon, *The Advancement of Learning,* Clarendon Press Edition, p. 252.

men wise, to promote their intelligence. It is an enterprise. It is not a quality or an ornament. It is not one of the aids of living generally, but a discipline in a particular kind of life. Character, manhood, efficiency, culture, able citizenship, sound bodies—all these excellencies education undoubtedly supports, but it supports them, as philosophers say, not essentially, but accidentally. They are its by-products. They may be the things ultimately esteemed as worth while, like the farmer's price for his wheat. The principles of finance are not, however, the principles of agriculture. The farmer must cultivate his field if the crop is to be of value. So youth must cultivate the mind if the market for intelligent manhood is to be supplied.

All this is, perhaps, elementary and obvious. Yet it is infrequently practiced with conviction and enthusiasm. Our institutions of learning rarely have an eye single to their proper function. I do not speak of the students particularly, because it is to be expected that youth should be irrational. A college of boys who knew not the enticements of sport and society, and were devoid of any other interest than the curriculum, would not be a healthy place whither to send other boys. But the great interest of boys in these things puts no obligation upon the college to be interested in them greatly. Yet we hear fully as much about student interests as we do about study, and often more. We are told that young men may be educated on the campus as well as in the classroom; for was not Waterloo won, on good authority, on the fields of Eton and Rugby? The college paper should be recognized as a course in rhetoric; for does it not teach students to write? Youth gets much more than knowledge out of a college course; then why should instructors hold themselves aloof from that much more, or insist that proficiency in learning should form the sole basis for the reward of degrees? Let the student attain a fair percentage; for it is not character better than marks? Yes, character is far better than marks, but not in a college, just as it is far better than the ability to swim, but not when you are in the water.

It is, however, principally upon the faculty that the burdens of esteeming the inquisition of truth as other than the primary enterprise of their existence fall. Their leisure is precious, but, instead of devoting a part of it sacredly to the pursuit of learning, they are often compelled to devote the whole of it to irrational undertakings, to the machinery of administering a complex of activities, or to the supervision and promotion of student interests. The ablest of them are too frequently tired men whose sole consolation is that of duty faithfully done, but who seldom taste the sweets of the mind. Their subtle temptation is to believe that they have done well if their students turn out to be fellows of character and call them friends, even if they themselves have long neglected the enterprise of learning. And the devoted teacher has much popular support in his intellectual inadequacies.

Now these things are mentioned here not for the purpose of bringing again an oft-repeated arraignment against our colleges, or to subject them to abuse or carping criticism. For, abuse them as we like, they are the saving institutions of society. They are abundantly worth while as they are. Yet, like Bacon, we would be raised to a persuasion. Having gone to school to Greek and Roman learning for centuries, we should like to surpass it by far, excelling its products, which we have often done, and rivalling its spirit, which we have never done. We should like to see in the college the home of ideas, the abode of the intellectual life, the place where youth is stimulated to grasp the world as a man should who is possessed not only of a moral, a social, a political, a religious nature, but also and emphatically of a mind. We should like to see it pursuing knowledge, not with the purpose of incidentally imparting sound information about history, literature, and the progress of science and philosophy, but for the purpose of turning such information into a powerful stimulus to intellectual conquests and creative activity. We should like to see it promoting the life of reason as over against the life of instinct and emotion, or, more adequately expressed, devoted to bringing the life of instinct and emotion within the illuminating sphere of the life of reason, making young people essentially intelligent and accidentally good, so that there may be a fair chance that their goodness will be rational goodness and not merely instinctive and emotional goodness.

The way in which such a result may be forwarded and sustained is obvious. The college should give its attention resolutely and passionately to the things of the mind. As a college, it should be unconscious of athletics, society, and "student interests," but intensely conscious of the needs of the intellectual life. No; it is not because the way is obscure that it is difficult to transform our colleges into genuine institutions of learning; it is the lack of the desire to do so, and it is the lack of faith in the desirability of doing so. There are a great many people who do not want the college to be a place where the inquisition of truth is an enterprise. They prefer that it should be a place where learning is made an ornament or a quality, where the young are prepared for the life of convention or success, and not disciplined in the life of reason. There are, too, a great many people who do not believe that it is desirable to treat college students as if they were principally and fundamentally minds. They are afraid of such treatment, afraid that it will lead to disaster, corrupt the morals of the young, and destroy their religion. It is the number and influence of such people which constitute the difficulties. Now these people have a right to be heard and a right to make and support institutions which are not institutions of learning. That right is not here denied or questioned. It is, once more, with a persuasion that this paper deals, a persuasion to which its author has been raised by the study of history and philosophy—the persuasion that the only genuine progress is rational progress, and that consequently the inquisition of truth should be esteemed as an enterprise, the loftiest and most characteristic in which rational beings can be engaged. He frankly believes in the intellectual life as a better life for man than any other. He holds to the conviction that it is far more important to make young people intelligent, rationally alert and inquisitive, blessed with a buoyant and trained imagination, than it is to make them efficient or to make them good; for he has learned that without discipline in rationality they may be made industrious and trustworthy animals, but wholly lack those intimations which impel men onward with the vision of their existence progressively enlarged, transformed, and beautified. He is assured that the world suffers more from ignorance and folly than it does from vice and crime. He is persuaded that just in the measure in which we succeed in bringing our desires and emotions, our instincts and impulses, the fundamentally irrational springs of all our actions, up into the light of reflective and prospective intelligence—in that measure we succeed in progressively making this world a better place in which to live.

The persuasion of Francis Bacon was uttered with a fine enthusiasm. Conceiving of the inquisition of truth as of an enterprise, the characteristically human adventure to be undertaken in the spirit of discovery and conquest, he had one of the world's great visions of human society transformed through science, industry, and the arts from a life of undisciplined passion into a life of disciplined and progressive happiness. Greater men had lived before him; greater men have lived since; but few have equalled him in the clearness of his vision or in the charm and enthusiasm of his words. Contrast with the quoted few with which this paper began these from Sir William Ramsay:

> I venture to think that, in spite of the remarkable progress of science and its applications, there never was a time when missionary effort was more needed. Although most people have some knowledge of the results of scientific inquiry, few, very few, have entered into its spirit. We all live in hope that the world will grow better as the years roll on. Are we taking steps to secure the improvement of the race? I plead for recognition of the fact that progress in science does not only consist in accumulating information which may be put to practical use, but in developing a spirit of prevision, in taking thought for the morrow; in attempting to forecast the future, not by vague surmise, but by orderly marshaling of facts, and by deducing from them their logical outcome; and chiefly in endeavoring to control conditions which may be utilized for the lasting good of our people. We must cultivate a belief in the "application of trained intelligence to all forms of national activity."[2]

There is here no lack of confidence in learning as an enterprise, but the buoyant note of hopefulness is absent. One might say: Three hundred years should have accomplished more, affording us the happy privilege of recalling Bacon's words as a prophecy fulfilled rather than as a vision so largely only

[2] Address of the president of the British Association for the Advancement of Science, *Science,* September 8, 1911, p. 291.

vision still; finding it a thing accepted and enthusiastically supported rather than a thing in which few seriously believe. How have we profited if, still cherishing an ancient vision, our words have the ring of despair?

The historian is doubtless competent to expose for our view the dominant characteristics of modern civilization in order that we may appreciate how little intellectual progress we have really made. He can point out that never, since the time of the ancient Greeks, has there been a people who, as a people, accepted without question the ideals of intelligence. He can show how modern culture has been the domestication of classical culture, how western Europe did not possess the scientific spirit as a native endowment, but borrowed it or acquired it from antiquity. He can tell us how in our educational policy we have sought inspiration and guidance from the achievements of Greek and Roman learning, but have never made habitually our own the natural sources from which the Greeks drew for themselves, or the rational spirit which kindled their imagination. While giving the highest praise to modern scientists for their achievements, he will still insist that "few, very few, have entered into the spirit of science." In short, he can clearly indicate that modern civilization has never been characteristically and habitually a rational civilization. It has been marked by no clear perception of human progress. It has blundered along through revolution and compromise, through partisanship and accommodation, through a kind of chaotic empiricism and a firm reliance on Providence to avert the results of stupidity. It has believed that its destiny was a thing the gods cared for, and, when it recovered for itself a philosophy of development, it converted the fact that nature is productive into a theological proposition, and drew comfort from the fact that evolution goes on. It has experimented much, but reflected little.

Still further, the historian can, doubtless, do much to satisfy our curiosity about the causes of these characteristic tendencies in modern civilization. He can point to the complications due to the growth of nationalities; to the estrangements between the life of the people and the policies of their governments; to the mixture of temperaments; to the kind of problems modern men have been called upon to face, noting that "during this period of evolution" men have been called upon to go out and possess the world in the interest of their material enterprises, with their armies and institutions, and their accidental patriotism. They have been called upon to facilitate transportation and to exploit the hidden places of the earth. Their individuality has been personal and isolated rather than social and communal. They have not been called upon to rationalize their lives with the consciousness of human solidarity. Whenever they have had leisure to attempt this important task, they have been bewildered by their material successes, their comforts, and their wealth: the conveniences of modern life have mastered them, so that their highest conception of human joy is prosperity. Their type may be caricatured in the man who cannot pursue happiness without the stenographer and the telegraph. The diagnosis could be extended, and the strangely contradictory symptoms of the modern disease detailed. Some trace of malice and unfairness is admitted in this hasty sketch, but, I take it, our virtues are in no need of commendation. They are prosperously apparent. Nor are our vices so excessive that no balance can be struck to afford some consolation for a troubled conscience. Emphatic phrases of characterization have been used for the sake of securing contrast, to indicate how far our civilization, admitting its excellencies, has fallen short of a rational civilization, although there have not lacked men who have seen the greater opportunity—seen it, too, three hundred years ago.

Much might have been different, we may venture to say, if modern philosophy had been consistently a rational philosophy; if it had steadfastly viewed mind as a natural activity intervening in the stream of impulses and habits to awaken the creative desire to transform existence in the light of possibilities disclosed, and only secondarily and as an aid thereto seeking the past and present constitution of things; or if it had believingly found the source of human inspiration and outlook in the exercise of progressive and sustained rational vision instead of in the constitution of matter, or the natural history of the human animal, or in epistemology. Yet modern philosophers have largely neglected the consideration of the mind as a natural activity exercised in the interest of the rational expansion and control of human impulses and the forces of nature. They have generally preferred to consider it the norm and touchstone of reality, expecting to find in its supposed contents and operations a deeper insight into the structure of things than they could attain by the direct study of nature's performances. They have, consequently, done very little to advance learning and very little to further the cause of a rational education. For men naturally turn to philosophy for some quickening comprehension of their activities. If, so turning, they are told that theories of perception and of the way the mind acquires knowledge point out the road to salvation, or that the essence of all philosophy is at last this—that the world of our experience is the only real world, or that the outcome of our intellectual striving is the confession of ignorance—they do not return with confidence strengthened in the inquisition of truth as the supreme human enterprise. It is not surprising that they should esteem it as an ornament or a quality, or that they should come to insist that education should be practical and provide young people with the kind of knowledge they will find useful in their future undertakings. Surely, if the outcome of philosophy is a trivial proposition or the admission of intellectual impotence, it would seem far better to cultivate and refine our instincts and emotions than to subject them to a rational discipline by the progressive cultivation of the life of reason.

Happily, current philosophy, once more outstripping the times, is steering a different course. It no longer regards the study of mental processes as the solvent or despair of human problems. It is vigorously insisting that the romanticism and subjectivism of modern systems is a travesty of nature. It refuses to regard the mind as a kind of essence distilled for the purpose of affording in its own nature a criterion of all reality. It thinks of the mind, not as a substance, but as an activity, as the "spirit of prevision" which leads man to anticipate his future and to control the discovered forces of nature for the realization of his desires, making thus its great function the discovery, not of what is real, but of what is attainable.

He who, first aroused by the quickening touch of creative

fingers, looked forth upon the world with a mind behind his eyes saw, not the constitution of things, but a prospect. His first questions were not, Why does yonder sun shine self-poised aloft, or yonder rivers flow along their course? He asked rather after the morrow and what lies beyond the enclosing trees. Henceforth paradise discontented him. He felt equipped for an enterprise. He would attain an ampler existence than he discovered his to be. Forth he went, not to live in accordance with nature, but to subdue it. At every step there was borne in upon him the realization that his anticipations must be disciplined, not through any increment to his instincts and emotions, but through a progressive insight into their import, their tendencies, and their efficacy, and through a progressive conquest of natural forces. Put in words less figurative, we should say that philosophy is now beginning hopefully to recognize that the primary function of the mind is imagination. Thc dawn of intelligence in the world indicated, not, first of all, that some one had become aware of its processes, but that some one was taking thought of the future. It indicated that these processes would be learned because there had first been born the intent to use them. In a cosmic sense it meant that conceptions of the future, ideals attractive and worth while, had now become factors in the world to change and transform it, and that the discipline of the imagination had become imperative.

Since it is intelligence, therefore, that opens a career for man by causing him to leap ahead of his present existence in anticipation of the changes he may effect by his own power, it would seem to be the first step in irrationality for him to convert the study of nature into a quest for some justification that he has a career at all, forgetting that such study should carry him to greater heights. To be sure, he has to learn that matter does not equally support all his enterprises, that it has its rigid laws to which he must conform or perish. This experience may lead him into the superstition that matter itself intends a career for him, carries his secret hidden within it, and being the stuff of which he is made, must also be the norm of his destiny. He may then sink his existence to the depth of a propitiation of nature's forces. Yet intelligence was designed, if we may dare say it, for a different purpose: that he might conqueringly rise above matter and attain the divine, not by discovering the origin and first intent of things, but by reaching forward to make his visions real.

If intelligence is such, there is little need to insist that for intelligent beings the training of the mind is not only the most important training, but also a discipline in the kind of life which should be most characteristic of them. We may train men's manners and their bodies, but, if we do not train their minds, they are "rational animals" to no purpose. And what needs repeated insistence from age to age, in every civilization, however efficient, comfortable, and prosperous, is that the training of the mind is, for rational animals, far more important than the training of their bodies or their manners. For the latter training is easy by comparison. All the forces of matter side with it. The instincts, impulses, and emotions, which need clarification in the light of the ideals intelligence can anticipate, find our bodies and our manners easy material to mould and fix, until we value the ornaments and qualities of our existence above its rational enterprise. Intelligence was not given to man to be hidden away, like the talent in the napkin, in fear lest it might be soiled by the increment its exercise would earn from a material world. No multiplication of the five of the body or the two of manners could compensate for that loss.

Surely, "there never was a time when missionary effort was more needed"; and surely, too, if philosophy is reaching out once more to be a genuine ally of progress, that need spells opportunity likewise. The growing dissatisfaction with the kind of life our youth lead in college, the increasing suspicion that healthy bodies and acceptable manners do not make rational men, call for the esteeming of the inquisition of truth as an enterprise, and may evoke once more Bacon's hopeful persuasion. Only, let our colleges be genuine institutions of learning, fostering the inquisition of truth, and training the young in the habits which fortify and discipline the spirit of prevision. Only let them pursue knowledge, not for the primary purpose of imparting true and useful information, or of affording some proof and justification of instinctive beliefs, but for the more exalted purpose of keeping the imagination awake and creative, and thus holding the mind true to its natural office of enlarging the future that the present may be redeemed. Only let them believe that the life of reason is unquestionably the best life for man. "If reason is divine in comparison with human nature, then the life of reason is divine in comparison with human life. They are not right who say that men should think of human things and mortals of mortal things. For a man should, as far as in him lies, aim at immortality and do everything with a view to living in the light of the highest that is in him. For, although that is small in size, in power and honour it far excels all the rest."[3]

[3] Aristotle, "Ethica Nicomachea," 1177b, 30 f. *εἰ δὴ θεῖον ὁ νοῦς πρὸς τὸν ἄνθρωπον, καὶ ὁ κατὰ τοῦτον βίος θεῖος πρὸς τὸν ἀνθρώπινον βίον. οὐ χρὴ δὲ κατὰ τοὺς παραινοῦντας ἀνθρώπινα φρονεῖν ἄνθρωπον ὄντα οὐδὲ θνητὰ τὸν θνητόν, ἀλλ' ἐφ' ὅσον ἐνδέχεται ἀθανατίζειν καὶ πάντα ποιεῖν πρὸς τὸ ζῆν κατὰ τὸ κράτιστον τῶν ἐν αὐτῷ. εἰ γὰρ καὶ τῷ ὄγκῳ μικρόν ἐστι, δυνάμει καὶ τιμιότητι πολὺ μᾶλλον πάντων ὑπερέχει.*

THE DISCOVERY OF THE MIND*

"MEN are strangers to that with which they are continually familiar." Heraclitus, the Dark, used these words apparently to express his opinion that, while men have minds, they are not ordinarily aware of it. His opinion seems to have been the result of his observation. He saw men speak and act as if mind were a stranger to them, the sort of thing at which dogs bark. Since the barking of dogs is his figure, it is apparent that his words are not the dispassionate statement of his observation. Looked at, however, in the light of the many centuries which have followed them, they may be cited as the simple record of a fact, the fact, namely, that the mind needs repeatedly to be discovered. It is continually there, from the beginning to the end—as Heraclitus says, using Homer's word for a tale fully told—it is continuously there, but it must be found.

History might be written in terms of its finding, marking its discovery and loss as the crises of civilization. For such a history the case of Heraclitus himself would be typical. With each new discovery to be recorded one would find an enthusiasm like his possessing the discoverer, the consciousness of insight and of having beheld a great vision, the sense of a new and unlimited power, the laying hold of a new confidence. One would find, on the part of those who had not made the discovery, incredulity, the insight suspected, the vision described as visionary, the power denounced as impotence, and the confidence held to be misplaced. All of which goes to show that the discovery of the mind is a characteristic human experience.

Heraclitus is, perhaps, too remote a figure to touch us of

* In the *Columbia University Quarterly,* Vol. XV (1912), pp. 1-10. Address delivered at the opening exercises of the one hundred and fifty-ninth academic year, September 25, 1912.

today very intimately. So I repeat a common observation of historians that the discovery of the mind on a large scale was one of the striking events that marked the beginning of modern times. Our historians would, perhaps, be more acute if they said that times are modern when the discovery is made. The finding of the mind is not something incident to an artificial period of time. It is the one event which makes it possible to regard the past as antiquity, the sum of things accomplished, to view the present as opportunity, and to see the future fluid. It is not a characteristic of modernity, but its essence.

Open the books of men like Roger Bacon, Galileo, Francis Bacon, Descartes, Hobbes, Grotius, Newton, and a host of others, and while one finds striking evidence of advances in knowledge along old and established lines, one finds also the consciousness of a new age at its morning. One finds the spirit of inquiry exalted above any admiration of what has been already done. One finds an uncontrollable desire to go on and to progress. One finds an unbounded confidence in the possibility of improving the life of man and of lifting him to the heights. One finds visions of a transformed society without vice, without crime, without idiocy or disease, without poverty or want. One finds these things because those who express them have discovered the mind. They are conscious of the discovery. It is that consciousness which has fired their imaginations and kindled a new insight and a new faith. For how is it that such men as these commend their hopes to others? By their attainments, by their positions, by their inventions, by their wisdom, by their authority? Not at all; but because the mind is discoverable, and to discover it is to share with them the thing that has awakened them.

Let the contrasting picture be unlined. Let us forget, on this occasion, the incredulity which they met and the opposition they aroused. Let us not remember that words spoken in the interest of human progress were heard as the cry of revolution. Because it is on the discovery that our emphasis would fall. What, then, is that discovery? It may be expressed by saying: it is the discovery that the world, although it is moved by its own forces and according to its own laws, is yet controllable just in proportion as it is understood. By itself, it is solid and unyielding; penetrated by the mind, it is fluid and convertible. By itself, it is man's master; through his mind, it is his servant. Expressions of the discovery vary. Heraclitus, taking his figure from the sea, says: "One thing is wisdom, to understand how all things are steered through all things." Bacon puts it bluntly: "Knowledge is power." And our own Emerson, with a prophet's voice, exclaims:

> Every jet of chaos which threatens to exterminate you is convertible by intellect into wholesome force. Fate is unpenetrated causes. The water drowns ship and sailor like a grain of dust. But learn to swim, trim your bark, and the wave which drowned it will be cloven by it and carry it like its own foam, a plume and a power. The cold is inconsiderate of persons, tingles your blood, freezes a man like a dew-drop. But learn to skate, and the ice will give you a graceful, sweet, and poetic motion. The cold will brace your limbs and brain to genius, and make you foremost men of time. Cold and sea will train an imperial Saxon race, which nature can not bear to lose, and after cooping it up in yonder England for a thousand years, gives a hundred Englands, a hundred Mexicos. All the bloods it shall absorb and domineer: and more than Mexicos, the secrets of water and steam, the spasms of electricity, the ductility of metals, the chariot of the air, the ruddered balloon are awaiting you.

That is all very familiar, continually familiar. It is proclaimed as a discovery to men who are strangers to it.

Schools exist, I suppose, because the mind has been discovered. Their obvious purpose is to keep us acquainted with the mind and to promote the intelligent penetration of things. This purpose is often obscured, and there is little doubt that the word "school" itself has facilitated the obscuration. It is a foreign word, which is one disadvantage; and it is a metaphor, which is a second disadvantage. Long ago a Greek observed that it is in leisure moments, when men are free from the stress of affairs and have time to think, that the mind is discovered. The observation caught the fancy. "To enjoy leisure" came to mean "to go to school." It was a happy conceit, we may say, and indicated much nobility in its author, since he could think of leisure as time which intelligence may claim. But the serpent is always in the garden. The perilous suggestion lies coiled in the metaphor—"to go to school is to enjoy leisure."

You can write the history of education, its reforms, its reactions, its revolutions, and its progress, in terms of that transfer of emphasis. Our thinking on scholastic matters has been controlled too much by a metaphor. The coupling of intelligence and leisure, although we may recognize it as a happy conceit in the man who made it first, gives a poor pair of categories in terms of which to discuss the business of the mind. It renders our propositions ambiguous and controversial, rather than simply true or false. It arouses an initial suspicion regarding what lies back of our programs. Our vision is not single with one eye on culture, refinement, manners, and a rich familiarity with nice things, and the other eye on intelligence, discipline, control, and creative curiosity. If, for instance, I express my conviction that education should be liberal, there will be those who approve and there will be those who dissent, while I shall probably be found working, not with those who approve, but with those who dissent, incurring thus the enmity of my friends and the friendship of my enemies. If I affirm that it is the great business of man to live his life to the full, but to live it to the full with intelligence, I shall, doubtless, win applause even if I am credited with stating the obvious impressively. But if I go on to propose to teach young men how to till the soil successfully and young women how to cook and sew admirably, there will be many who will ask first, not is it worth while in the interest of intelligent living, but is it education? Do you intend to give them the bachelor's degree? I may reply that degrees were not in mind, but I shall be warned to be very careful.

Naturally, when I say these things, I do not wish to be misunderstood in regard to the intent with which I say them. I am not proposing to discuss educational programs or to take sides in the controversies besetting them. I am proposing something different, namely, the recognition of an emphasis. If it is true that the discovery of the mind is our reason for being here, for taking up again the complicated work of an institution like this, and also the reason why educational programs are things of importance for us; then I am insisting that that discovery should be the source of our programs and the criterion by which they should be judged. No tradition, however sanctified by a beautiful and suggestive metaphor, can be sacred to us if in any way it weakens our important task. Are we making intelligence prevail? Are we invading with the spirit of inquiry every department of life? Are we letting no chance slip to bring under the control of reason the least as well as the greatest undertakings of men? Of such a type are the questions which those who believe that the mind has been discovered will ask first; and they will insist that their labors be judged by the standards such questions suggest and by no others.

There appeared recently in one of our daily papers an editorial entitled "New Ideas of a University." It sees in the rapid expansion of our universities, as shown in the increasing number of courses undertaken and of new degrees offered, a response to a genuine demand on the part of large numbers of our people. It believes that this expansion is "bringing light into dark places," but that it is also "ousting older and more deeply thought-out ideas of education." How "the older idea of a university" is consequently affected may be seen by considering the diminishing proportion of the degree of bachelor of arts among all degrees now conferred. It finds that "the strength of the courses in which first degrees are granted in law, medicine, engineering, agriculture, and household science is a sign that the future typical university of America is not likely to bear much resemblance to Oxford and Cambridge." It affirms that what many people want is "a college where the buildings exemplify the latest advance in sanitation, and the laboratories are within six months of the latest discovery in applied science." It declares that "it is only in a new country that dietetics, the fine arts, the art industries, music, and physical training, can be made to lie in the lap of one university"; and it finds "consolation" in the "belief that the students who follow these new courses will go into those subjects anyway, and that it is better for the community that they should be half educated in them than wholly ignorant." It closes with this warning:

If universities and men who should know better allow themselves to reckon elementary and cursory training in the application of scientific or artistic principles on the same level of honor with exhaustive and exact knowledge, they are doing wrong to the country. It may be that for a time we may have to see through a glass darkly; but if they declare that the imperfect vision is just as good as the perfect they are sapping standards. In education the idea of the best is the touchstone of all sound judgment.

This editorial is typical of many recent utterances on education. It reflects a current searching of the heart and a genuine questioning of methods and results. Its statements of fact may remain unchallenged, but what of its emphasis? If the future typical university of America is not likely to bear much resemblance to Oxford and Cambridge, is that, considered in the light of history and of present needs, a misfortune or a blessing? Is it the end of an argument or the beginning of one? Why, I ask, if it is better for the community that certain of our people should be half educated in certain subjects than wholly ignorant, why should that fact be a consolation for attempting to educate them? Why is it not a command and an obligation? Does the expansion of our universities mean that we are in grave danger of wronging the country by allowing ourselves to reckon elementary and cursory training in the application of scientific or artistic principles on the same level of honour with exhaustive and exact knowledge; that we are seeing through a glass darkly; that we are sapping standards? Or does that expansion mean that we are raising standards in every walk of life we touch, seeing more clearly, and widening the sweep of exhaustive and exact knowledge?

If the mind has been discovered it is time that people stopped looking to the past for standards and to the present for consolation. They should look to the past for experience, for guidance, for instruction, not that they may restore the past, be like it, ape its achievements or its culture, but that they may entertain their own visions with a chastened enthusiasm and press on to make them real. No one who has discovered the mind can take his standards from an alien time. More than the past ever held awaits him.

It is possible, therefore, to see in an increasing number of intelligent farmers something else than a decreasing number of promising philologists. Or, to put the matter in general terms, it is possible to see in the expansion of our universities something else than a menace to culture. In strictness of speech—or, one might say, metaphysically—there can be no new idea of a university which is not a wrong idea. For there is something Platonic and eternal about that idea, a changeless essence which may shine through many changing things. The only sense in which it can be called new is the sense in which we indicate that some one has seen it for the first time in his own experience. There may be new courses, new methods, and new degrees, and these may displace older and long established institutions, but there can be no new university. The accidents are old or new, the substance, never; for the idea of the university is the idea of the organized discovery of the mind.

The university is, therefore, not simply a place where a number of people are engaged in teaching and being taught a number of subjects of greater or less importance. It is much more than a collection of different schools brought together under one administration for purposes of economy or size. It is much more than a haphazard arrangement of different courses leading to different degrees and framed to meet demands of the moment, or to illustrate passing fashions, or to compete with rivals. To see no more is to see with myopic vision. To be sensible of no more is to be insensible to opportunity. The university is always at the beginning of a greater career when it finds a region which intelligence can invade and master, for that means progress in organizing the mind's discovery. It looks with a jealous eye on every educational enterprise and every attempt to advance learning which seek an independent existence.

A generation ago there was not a university in the land that paid any significant attention to the art of teaching as a subject worthy of special inquiry and of a special technic. There were training classes for teachers connected with local high schools and normal schools scattered here and there. But there is a vast difference between setting up a normal school, however excellent, by itself or in connection with the schools it serves, and setting up such a school in a university. In the one case you leave it isolated and disconnected, in the other you bind up its destinies with the career of productive scholarship. There is a vast difference, and the same sort of difference, between setting up a law school even in the heart of a great city, under the shadow of courts of law and in sound of the strife of men, and setting it up in a university. In the one case you link it with its necessities merely, the contingencies it has to meet. In the other you link it with progressive ideas in economics, politics, sociology, ethics, and the scientific investigation of human institutions. And you quicken the life of the university, too, by demanding that it respond to questions which must be settled now. There is a vast difference, as has been abundantly demonstrated, between setting up a medical school in a hospital and setting it up, hospital and all, in a university. There is a vast difference between setting up a college of liberal study in some beautiful country place where cloister and landscape, friendship and study, invoke *alma mater*, the nestling divinity whose charm makes "old" the dearest of adjectives, and setting up such a college in a university, where the many things in which it is possible to substitute knowledge for ignorance, intelligence for stupidity, reason for irrationality, find a place and demand that culture be more than an ornament, that it be rather a power to quicken, beautify, and ennoble the things men have to do. He who has seen these differences steadily and seen them in the light of the mind's discovery will not think of the university as a place from which a glory is passing away.

These things are said here deliberately and unblushingly for purposes of enthusiasm, to enhance the belief that the university is in idea and shall be increasingly in practice, the most important of human institutions. It sets faith in the controlling power of the mind in contrast with faith in any other power. It insists that a technic of curiosity, criticism, and control is superior to every other kind of technic, because it is applicable to every undertaking. It demands, since there is always an intelligent and rational way of doing what needs doing, that that way be found and followed, not only in mathematics and philosophy, in literature and science, in industry and the arts, but also in public life, in business, in politics, in society, in morals, and in religion. The proposition that we must think one way in the cloister, but must live and behave a different way in the market, is to it intolerable. The notion that we are the products of our ancestry, it supplements with the notion that we are the ancestors of posterity, making us thus indebted to the past, but obliged to the future. It aims to be the place to which men can look for judgments which are disinterested and therefore just. It is content only as it sees ignorance, prejudice, passion, partizanship, superstition, and privilege progressively giving place to the life of reason. If the prospect tends to make enthusiasm spontaneous, that which has been accomplished may make it sane. For the discovery of the mind is annually turning more and more of the world's wealth into lines of beneficient research; it is spreading education and enlightenment; it is making clear that only in its interest dare human life be held cheap; it is adding a deepening sense of the responsibility for vice to the personal obligation to be virtuous; it is subduing enemies as the armies and navies of the world have never subdued them; it is making daily clearer the truth that the rational conquest of the whole of nature means the happiness of men. Yes: these things have been said for purposes of enthusiasm, to see in the expansion of the university a prospect of goods to be won and not a prospect of goods to be lost; and to set faith in the mind squarely in opposition to every philosophy of life which disparages intelligence and feeds our inherited romantic fascination for the mysterious, the obscure, and the vague.

History may be written in many different ways and our philosophies of life are individually characterized by the type of history we prefer. The rise and fall of states, the conflicts between nations, the political upheavals of the peoples of the earth, may possess the imagination, so that history becomes political and military. We then count the decisive battles of the world, and scan the types of political organization, seeing in man a political animal with a political destiny, one hand grasping the sword and in the other withdrawn behind the shelter of steel a scroll half unrolled on which is written the law and constitution of a state. Or the character of coast lines, the drift of currents and prevailing winds, the number and courses of rivers, the productivity of soils, the presence of mineral stores in the earth, the varieties of climate—such may be the things on which we seize, and then we shall see civilization under the control of economic needs and economic laws, and find the gold of Arabia more significant than the Battle of Marathon. Or we may see in the political and economic animal more of the noun than of the adjective. An animal he is and like all animals a product of variation, struggle, selection, and heredity, one species in a vast evolution of life, subject to one cosmic law which he illustrates in every adjective by which he is described: biped, because the variation into hands outran the two additional feet of his ancestors; social and political, because a variation in the direction of interdependent living turned out to be advantageous; and rational, because the development of his nervous system holds his responses to stimuli in check so that when he does act, he acts as a creature who has had experience and profited by it. His future will illustrate the same law as his past and continue his career as an evolution. We may give to this conception a romantic colour, veiling providence in our terminology or deifying evolution into a creative energy more profoundly real than any of its manifestations and more satisfying to the spirit of man than any of its accomplishments. These things we may do, and, reading history in the terms they set, find profit in the reading. But we may also read history in terms of the discovery of the mind. We may see man rising from the ground, startled by the first dim intimation that the things and forces about him are convertible and controllable. Curiosity excites him, but he is subdued by an untrained imagination. The things that frighten him, he tries to frighten in return. The things that bless him, he blesses. He would scare the earth's shadow from the moon and sacrifice his dearest to a propitious sky. It avails not. But the little things teach him and discipline his imagination. He has kicked the stone that bruised him only to be bruised again. So he converts the stone into a weapon and begins the subjugation of the world, singing a song of triumph by the way. Such is his history in epitome—a blunder, a conversion, a conquest, and a song. That sequence he will repeat in greater things. He will repeat it yet and rejoice where he now despairs, converting the chaos of his social, political, industrial, and emotional life into wholesome force. He will sing again. But the discovery of the mind comes first, and then, the song.

PLACES AND MEN*

IT IS because we reflect that our living becomes a life. Since we do not count the passing days as a mere succession of isolated events, but weave them into something other than an aggregate, into a kind of unity which we can think of as present and enduring through all changes, colouring them with the reflections of a personality which is not itself one of the incidents it owns—since we do this, we are led to make that distinction between soul and body, between a man and his place, between ourselves and the world, which is the pivotal distinction of human life. Thereby we demonstrate our spirituality. For a span of time which must be construed biographically, and not simply as a body's duration and incidents through a term of years, has surpassed the matter to which it clings, and evoked that new interest which we call spiritual. Thus it is that in all the crises of life the soul and not the body sets the terms in which those crises receive their most characteristically human expression. Thus it is that death is sad, for it involves the soul's departure. No longer will that span of time, those daily incidents, those engaging enterprises, all that made the man's work, be unified into his personality or filled with his spirit. The matter of his body remains, but the place that knew *him* shall know him no more.

We sometimes say that a man's place can not be filled, but that may only express our conviction that his successors will not equal him. It does not indicate that places have a memory. It does not endow them with any concern for the life which vivified them. Places are heartless. They count no man indispensable. They receive his successor without prejudice, regret, or expectation. Strip the world of personality, the body of its soul, and it is an indifferent, a careless world that remains.

* In the *Columbia University Quarterly*, Vol. XIV (1912), pp. 113-119. Address delivered at the Commemorative Service held in St. Paul's Chapel on Sunday, December 10, 1911.

A prolonged absence from his work will bring to any man an acute sense of his local unimportance. Can affairs go on without him? Must not everything be stayed, expectantly awaiting his co-operation? Then he realizes that while a few may count on his return and defer matters for his advice and assistance, he has been proved to be unnecessary. The world can get on without him. The students will come and go. His friends will perform their tasks. The issues of the day will be settled. Some compensation may be extracted from the reflection that the work is greater than himself. He may try to lighten the ignominy he feels by telling himself that it was a high privilege to have been engaged in great concerns that will outlast him; yet it is the feeling of ignominy he is trying to lighten and for which he is seeking a substitute. It is a privilege to be busied with labour that shall not fail when we are gone, but it is not a privilege to be idle or to have been busy. If under such circumstances the heartlessness of places is felt acutely, how much more acutely is it felt when one thinks of the permanent absence from his work, of the time when in grim truth the place that knew him shall know him no more.

The contrast between a man and his place may sound the depths of human despair. Yet it also evokes a spiritual enterprise. Men everywhere have their sacred places, not only where the bush burned and was not consumed, or where the ladder stretched from earth to heaven, or where divinity was glimpsed with startled eyes, but also where other men have moved and worked. Florence has been called a dead city. She knows no more the illustrious men who made her great centuries ago. But it is not the dead city which the traveller goes to see, but the sanctified city. Measured by our current standards, the place on the Arno is not progressive. Its houses are not comfortable. Its streets are not clean. Its people are not prosperous. Yet the traveller lingers there because he is dwelling in a spiritual city, the home of the illustrious. No ghost walks there. Yet should the visitor meet Michelangelo upon the crumbling walls or Dante on his threshold, he would not start and find it strange. Florence knows them no more, but her heartlessness, her lack of memory, count for nothing since men ever since have sanctified her into an eternal city. We call it her influence, but she has none while she lacks souls to create a civilization and still a world. Spirituality is not a power which can work from behind, pushing on and controlling by its own momentum. It lives through its recovery by other spirits. Without that it is impotent and dead. There could be no Florence to stir men's minds now, quicken their imaginations, fire their creative zeal, had not men turned Florence into a sacred place, stretching their living personalities to possess her and call her their own.

And this place—let us risk the contrast—this place where the hammer still rings, but not at the work of repair to arrest decay; this hill not yet fully crowned with its citadel of learning; these buildings which point, not backward to a past accomplished, but forward, fuller of promise than of retrospect; this city throbbing with life, teeming with multitudes whose eyes, however bewildered, see visions, whose wills, however blindly, stir with unmeasured power, and whose minds, however irrationally, construe the past as a failure—this place, does it know only the lust of the eye and the pride of life? Is it materialized, taunting the souls of men with the pitiless words, "the place that knew him shall know him no more"?

I do not ask the question to provoke an answer, to give voice to discontent or eulogy. I ask it to suggest once more the contrast I have made my theme, the contrast between places and men, between the remorselessness of matter and the spiritualizing enterprise of personality. And I have used my chance illustration to make that contrast vivid by putting side by side a place that is dead, yet sacred, and a place that is living, so full of energy and the dreams of conquest, that to step aside from its business and pause, even for one brief hour, to call to mind the times accomplished, and the dead men that live no longer, may seem but the perfunctory recognition of a pious duty.

To remember our dead—you know the scene of Maeterlinck's *Blue Bird*, the frightened children in the graveyard waiting the hour when the graves will open and the ghosts appear, the expected hour struck, and then under a new and beautiful light a garden of living flowers and the boy's words, "There are no dead"—to remember our dead is to be numbered among the living. We are not met together here to see ghosts, to behold the men we honour pass by in solemn procession while their deeds are called to mind. We are not tourists reading inscriptions on memorial tablets. We are the place's continuing soul. The spirit of the University is not an idol to be worshipped occasionally, to be called upon to justify our deeds, or to be made a substitute for rational enthusiasm. We may personify it, calling it *alma mater*, we may embody it in forms of art, sing of it, voice it in boisterous shout, we may hallow it so that nooks and corners are shrines and trees whispering oracles, but this is all the operation of a living spirit, the enlargement of personality to include every fragment of the place and every detail of its history. If the remnants of the past can become so sacred that travellers from the ends of the earth will visit ruins to find them quickened into life by that occasional act of piety, who would venture to estimate the power of a living place with a memory still unbroken, the possibilities of vision and achievement, the opportunities for enduring friendship, that mighty solidarity of a continuing group of men engaged in the highest human undertaking, the conquest of matter by the spirit of man?

To remember all those who during their lifetime advanced the honour of the University is thus much more than to remember the past. It is that undoubtedly. It is a summons to piety, to visit sacred places, to rejoice in good works done, to take holy pride in ancestry. But it is more. It is to be conscious of the spirit of the University, self-conscious, if you will. It is not to look upon Columbia as some external thing which men have honoured, to which they still sacrifice their lives, or give their gifts of money and enthusiasm. It is to look upon Columbia as the personality continuously vivifying these grounds and halls, replying to that taunt of matter, "the place that knew him shall know him no more," with the boast of the spirit, "the place that knew him shall have known him through all our years to come."

Places and men—the contrast may carry us beyond any local and incidental illustration of it. What is this division of body and soul, of matter and spirit when naturally construed, when taken as a thing to be considered rationally? Or, to put the question in another form, imputing design to nature as men are wont to do when they speak of her, for what purpose is memory denied to places and imagination given to men? Shall we say, That men may for a brief season find their way about in a strange world, discover the chemistry and physics of their bodies, learn the animal affinities of their passions, discover that their hopes are born in superstition and their religion in the fear of matter; and that so enlightened, they should live a literally-minded existence, sobered at last by a steady and unenthusiastic contemplation of their origin? Or shall we rather say, The purpose was sublime? It was that nature would keep herself inflexible, true to unchanging laws and yet work an astounding miracle. Touched by imagination she would become plastic, material for art and industry, capable even of transforming a stone into a god. Matter may have produced imagination, but we may say it did so at its cost. After that it could still obey what we call its laws and be the subject of physical science; but it had to submit to a process of idealization. The rising sun would still illustrate the principles of celestial mechanics, but it would shine on places where men would welcome it with ceremony. Buildings would rise subject to gravitation, but would embody an idea and symbolize an enterprise. Men would die, but ancestors would be worshipped. Places where imagination dwelt would become sacred and the men, who during their lifetime advanced the honour of those places, would be remembered.

Now all this, I would affirm, is not simply matter for pleasing speculation. It is not idle fancy. It is natural history, the simple truth about places and men. It may be turned into superstition. Because men idealize the stars, they may incorrectly look to the stars to settle the destinies of men. Because they worship the dead, they may irrationally except the dead to interfere in nature in their behalf. But it is only the stupid and the literally-minded who can not distinguish between the natural function of the imagination and the imputing of physical causality to the operation of the spirit, or who would insist that because the operation of the spirit has no physical causality, the natural function of the imagination ought not to be exercised, or if exercised, is trivial and misleading.

If there is a place where stupidity and literal-mindedness ought not to dwell, it is in a university like this with its history and its situation. Surely the place is propitious. It has been splendidly endowed by nature, by the accidents of civilization, by the lives and bounty of men. And surely the enterprise to which it is committed is human. It is a place for imagination and for piety. And it is pre-eminently a place for these things because of its devotion to science. This I would emphasize. I would emphasize it because devotion to science is so often thought to be incompatible with the idealizing tendency of the imagination. The serious, laboured, renunciatory effort to maintain a steady and true perception of external things, to master the mechanism of nature and of history and of art, destroys many an illusion. Yet it would be a pity if it destroyed imagination as well. To be sure we want to be sane, we want to avoid cant, hypocrisy, and sentimentality. We want to take ourselves to witness and say that we have

> Loved no darkness,
> Sophisticated no truth,
> Nursed no delusion,
> Allow'd no fear![1]

But I can not call it sanity to take the knowledge that matter is heartless, or that mechanism is careless of results, or that the fittest survive and the dead are dust, as the organon for the enthusiasm of men. So to take that knowledge, is to deny to man a thing of which he is capable, the thing that turns his life into an epic. And, believe me, there is an epic in this universe of ours as surely as there is an evolution. A sound philosophy, sensible of the contrast between places and men, will confidently behold the larger vision and "look to science for its view of the facts and to the lives of men on earth for its ideals."[2]

We are met, therefore, to perform a pious duty, and we are met also to quicken and deepen the sense of piety within ourselves; to remember the past without affectation, to worship the dead without superstition, and to rejoice that the place knows and has known men.

[1] Matthew Arnold, "Empedocles on Etna."
[2] G. Santayana, *Three Philosophical Poets,* p. 5.

THE PRACTICE OF PHILOSOPHY*

WE ARE often told to be philosophical or to take things philosophically. It is supposed that we rarely are this or do this. Indeed, I suspect that each of us would hesitate to profess that he was a philosopher or that he took things as a philosopher ought to take them. We may heartily admit that to be this or to do this is an excellent thing, but we hesitate to exhibit ourselves as examples of this excellence, because we are a little afraid of the effect which the exhibition will produce in those who are bidden to observe a rarity. The confession is too naked.

I have sometimes found myself in this predicament when among strangers who, as conversation became general, have expressed curiosity about my business or profession—on a journey, for example, when the incidents of travel bring people together who have not met before. For a while, I can hide behind the anonymous title of Mister, as my fellow strangers do, exhausting the weather, prohibition, and the general follies of mankind. If, however, the conversation grows sprightly or a little intimate, curiosity is born in us. We want to discover who each of us is, what road in life we individually travel. On such occasions, I find that men are quite willing to confess that they are doctors or lawyers or engineers or clergymen or business men or artists, and so on through the generally recognized occupations or professions. But I hesitate to confess that I am a philosopher and still more that I am a professor of philosophy. I have experimented with the confession, but have not been sure about the effect it produces. There is always surprise. As to the rest of it, I am left wondering whether it is disbelief or amusement or a sense of deep waters. A shyness

* In the *Institute Magazine,* Vol. III (1931), pp. 8-22. The second Davies Lecture in Philosophy, delivered before the Institute of Arts and Sciences, March 2, 1931.

seems to settle upon my fellow strangers who, before the confession, were anything but shy. If it is not a sense of deep waters, it is, evidently, a sense of strange currents or uncertain winds which makes further conversational sailing hazardous with a philosopher on board. It may be a compliment to be called a philosopher by others, but to own up to being one actually, is quite a different matter. Between "You are a philosopher" and "I am a philosopher" there is much more than a change of pronouns. There is a decided change of atmosphere.

There are, perhaps, fair, if not good, reasons for this. From lectures I have heard before this Institute and from books I have read, it is clear that much is expected from philosophy and from philosophers, much more than is expected from ordinary men. Plato, you may remember—and everybody says that Plato was a philosopher although he seems not to have said so himself—you may remember that Plato made Socrates say that we should never have good government until philosophers became our governors or our governors became philosophers. Imagine what the Senate would be like if either of these things happened! I have had, however, to point out to my classes that the young men to whom Socrates said these hopeful or hopeless words greeted them with laughter. These young men had seen philosophers and were quite sure they would not do. Socrates changed their minds, however, by telling them that he did not mean the fellows they knew; he meant genuine philosophers. The young men would be glad to have the genuine, but not the existing philosophers. And it has to be admitted that existing philosophers such as you and I could name would not do much better than the Senate. Mankind, generally, has sided with those young men of old and I and my colleagues are still waiting for political recognition! We must admit, if we are honest, that we are human, rather than genuine, and as much in need of philosophy as anybody else. And philosophy may be said to be something which the governed need more than their governors, the people more than the Senate. A nation of genuine philosophers might not need a governor at all.

Another circumstance is worth noting in this connection.

We frequently hear it said or read it in books that philosophy is expected to decide all the ultimate questions raised by science and faith. The expression "the philosophy of" is familiar —the philosophy of art, of politics, of science, of morals, of religion, of education. The expression implies that unless we have the philosophy of these various matters, we do not have them as they ought to be. One may be religious, for example, but one really ought to have a philosophy of religion to be sure about it. Or one may be a teacher and a good teacher, but one ought really to have a philosophy of education, if one is to teach the right subjects in the right way and for the right end. Schools are often thought to be in a bad way if there is not a philosophy in them which shapes their courses of study and defines their purposes. This is a popular idea. We see new schools and new philosophies springing up about us. Now, when it is said that philosophy should give us all this expected assurance and solidity, it is clear that it can do so only through the mouths of philosophers. And this means quite definitely through my mouth, or Professor Dewey's, or Professor Whitehead's, or Mr. Bertrand Russell's, or Mr. Walter Lippmann's, or, perhaps, Professor Eddington's, or Sir James Jeans', or Professor Einstein's. All the members of this distinguished company are in the habit, now and then, of telling others what is right and proper in certain respects. But we are all human beings, men of like passions with the rest of men. We were once crying babies, and although we may have modified the method of complaining with the world, we are still infants in knowledge when one thinks of the vast store of knowledge which must needs be ours if we are to utter those final words which are expected of philosophy. We may write confidently and speak confidently, but we dare not profess that we are those genuine philosophers who never provoke laughter or distrust.

What I have said has not been said to disparage philosophy or to bring contempt on philosophers. It has been said, rather, to disparage a certain attitude towards philosophy. I think it is idle to suppose that there is a particular group of men, called philosophers, who have that superior ability and knowledge which philosophy is supposed to give them. There are, of course, men of superior ability and knowledge in all the walks of life and they ought to be better leaders to follow than others, but no man is competent to settle for others those ultimate problems of life and mind which are settled only by living. I think it is also idle to suppose that there is a body of knowledge called philosophy which, when acquired, will make all the dark places in the world clear and bright. Further, I think such a supposition is dangerous. It is dangerous because it fosters the habit of letting life wait until philosophers and philosophy have had their say. That makes life wait too long. We have the untimely habit of dying before we hear those final words. In saying all this, however, I do not want to be misunderstood. Philosophers and philosophy have wisdom to impart. It is not, however, their own wisdom. It is that wisdom which the centuries during which man has lived in the world and thought about it, have been trying to make more habitual than it is in the minds and hearts of mankind. There is nothing secret about this wisdom and nothing abstruse about it. It is not difficult to understand although it needs attention to practise it. It is not something for a select few to possess in order that they may tell the rest of us where to get on and where to get off. It is something for everybody to possess. It is not something to live by; it is a way or habit of living. It is a thoroughly practical matter. It has long been, so far as its expression in words is concerned, a human possession. We do not have to wait for its discovery. But the possession of it in words is worthless unless it is also possessed in practice.

There are, to be sure, theoretical philosophies and many of them. From time to time, great minds, and little minds too, impressed by the strange wonder of the world in which we live, attempt to make some comprehensive account of it all. They are impatient with partial and fragmentary pictures of it. They want to see it as a whole. So they make systems of the world and we are in the habit of calling these systems philosophy. Some of them are among the most impressive creations of the mind of man. One has only to recall great names like Plato, Aristotle, St. Thomas, Spinoza, Hegel. It is decidedly worth while to become acquainted with such minds. One could greatly lengthen that brief list, including many a thoughtful mind whose speculations have enlarged our vision and elevated our imagination. They can save us from pettiness and widen our sympathies. But there is need of an antecedent philosophy to learn from them profitably, the kind of philosophy which the word "philosophy" implies, the practice of that wisdom which the experience of the ages has been trying to teach us. Without it, systems of philosophy are apt to be bewildering, to confuse rather than enlighten. Their appeal is to the disciplined mind. So it is the practice of philosophy which needs cultivation first. If we are not to be swept off our feet by every theoretical wind that blows, old winds and new, if we would live well and not hastily or experimentally, it is of first importance that we take note of that wisdom which the experience of mankind recommends.

Philosophy, as you know, is a Greek word. I can not believe that it is only an interesting accident that this word has found a place in almost all the languages of the civilized world without undergoing translation. People have liked it when they have caught its meaning. It gets over into daily speech and will not let itself be monopolized by some to the exclusion of others. When we translate it, we speak of the love of wisdom and recognize that it is apt and worthy to speak that way. Wisdom is a thing to be loved, to have and to hold. Plato went so far as to say that if we saw wisdom with our eyes as we see beauty, it would, like beauty, fill us with a longing to possess it. But I leave the praise of it to others. I would speak about the loving of it—not about the theories of philosophers, but about the practice of philosophy; not about a philosophy of life, but about philosophical living. There are principles of it which can be cultivated and which make less easy the practice of being a fool.

Let me begin with the principle which the Greeks, who coined the word "philosophy," laid down as fundamental to everything else. They had a story to tell about their Seven Wise Men, whom they delighted to honour as bright examples of wisdom. These men, so we are told, once made a pilgrimage to the oracle at Delphi. Now it was the custom of pilgrims to commemorate their visit to that shrine by making a gift of the best they had to give, a kind of offering of first fruits, as it were. These men offered the first fruits of wisdom, and the first of them was the maxim: "Know thyself." Self-knowledge is the first principle of the practice of philosophy.

The best definition of self-knowledge I have come upon is the one made by Santayana. He says it is to know one's own mind or to discriminate clearly what one means and loves. I should like to illustrate this by the old story of our first parents, Adam and Eve. One can learn something from one's parents, and the older, perhaps, the better. You will remember that only one thing was originally required of our first parents, namely, obedience. They were given a beautiful garden to live in where an abundance of food and drink was provided and where there was no need of artificial clothing or shelter. They were not ashamed. But they were told not to eat the fruit of a certain tree in the garden under the penalty of death. They did not know what death was because they had not experienced it. A serpent visited them. He told them that he thought they would not surely die, at least not right away, if they ate of the tree. Something else would happen; they would become like gods, knowing good and evil. Our first parents were innocent and inexperienced, but they had seen the Lord and so had some idea of what the serpent was talking about. They had heard what the Lord had to say, and now they heard what the serpent had to say. Eve looked at the tree and saw that it was good to look at and that the fruit was to be desired to make one wise. So she ate of the fruit and gave some of it to Adam.

They did not die at once. Indeed they lived much longer than we do now-a-days—Adam, nine hundred and thirty years. But they became frightened and hid themselves when they heard the Lord coming. They told him that they hid because they were naked. He knew that this could not possibly be true unless they told themselves so; so he asked: "Have you eaten of the tree?" Then Adam's excuse was the woman and Eve's excuse was the serpent. They did not know their own minds. They did not clearly discriminate what they meant and what they loved. If they had, instead of being frightened, they could have said: "We ate of it to become like thee." That was apparently why they ate of it. The story says: "When the woman saw that the tree was good for food, and that it was pleasant to the eyes, and a tree to be desired to make one wise, she took of the fruit thereof, and did eat, and gave also unto her husband with her; and he did eat." Those, clearly, are excellent reasons for eating fruit even when told not to. But our first parents did not give those reasons to the Lord. Adam's excuse was the woman, and Eve's the serpent. Our first parents fell, not because they disobeyed, but because, having disobeyed, they did not know their own minds.

I hesitate to enlarge on so simple and so profound a story. It is obvious enough that a woman is a poor excuse for what a man does, and a serpent is a poor excuse for what a woman does. It is needless for us to ask whether the events recorded in the story happened a long time ago. The like of them happens every day in the week. The story is evidently true in that realm of ideas which throws light on human life. The fall of man is a recurring event. We may take the story of the Garden of Eden as a tale to tell us one thing that is the matter with us. Then we should read it in its current setting. We are frequently advised by serpents that experience rather than obedience is the best teacher, advised, that is, by those who, like the serpent was said to be, are subtle. I have no doubt that this advice is sound, but I think it is also serpentine. For experience is no teacher at all unless its lessons are obeyed, unless we are quite sure in our own minds that it is teaching rather than experience that we want. Now the practice of philosophy in this matter of self-knowledge would foster the habit of being clear in one's own mind just which it is one wants when trying something out—experience or teaching. Do we want to *have* something or *learn* something? That is a question which searches our minds pretty thoroughly. It can readily be reduced to particulars.

What, then, do we want? Love, or what can be learned from love? Do we want marriage, or what can be learned from marriage? Do we want to be divorced, or what can be learned from divorce? War, or its lessons? Peace, or what peace can teach? A college experience, or what can be learned from a college experience? Riches with what they can buy, or the lessons of riches? Pleasure, or the instruction it can give? Where shall I stop? I must stop somewhere, but I add: Religion, or what it teaches? To live forever, or the lessons of immortality? There is nothing which escapes the searching question. It forces upon us a scrutiny of our choices. Philosophy does not tell us which of the alternations we ought to choose. It puts the question, but leaves the decision to us. Only it would have us clear in our minds what the decision is which we make. The Lord told our first parents not to eat. The serpent advised them that experience is the best teacher. We like to blame them for listening to the serpent instead of to the Lord, just as Adam blamed the woman and Eve, the serpent. The trouble was, however, that they did not know whether they ate because the tree was pleasant to the eyes or because it was to be desired to make one wise. They were confused and made excuses. I often wonder what would have happened if they had known their own minds and had truthfully told the Lord why they ate. I often wonder what would happen today, in the home, in society, in schools and colleges, in the nation and in our relations to other nations, if we really knew our own minds and should truthfully tell ourselves, at least, what we really want in leading so abundantly the experimental life, in "living dangerously," as we sometimes say. Is it experience, or the lessons of experience?

I have said that philosophy in the practice of it does not tell us which we ought to choose. And certainly it does not suggest that we always ought to choose one rather than the other. It has no objection to having a good time. But it has something to say on the matter of choosing. Here it makes its great distinction between wisdom and folly. Here it does not hesitate to say that he who in the choice pays no attention to the lessons of experience is a fool. Let his experience be what it may, he is still a fool. Wisdom is born out of attention to the lessons and grows as that attention grows. Just having one experience after another, no matter how rich and full they may be, philosophy says is the best illustration of a foolish and wasted life. Goethe wrote his great "Faust" to illustrate it. But he who chooses experience in the light of its lessons is on the way to wisdom. He needs and has no other guide, but he can go far. This strikes me as a most fortunate circumstance. We do not have to wait for some philosopher or for some revelation to tell us what to do. We can begin to find out without their help. And when we begin, we find at our disposal the great storehouse of the experience of mankind. The great lessons of that experience are written so large that one must close one's eyes not to see them. One must make excuses for one's ignorance. The practice of philosophy has the power to free men and women from the need of a mentor to hold their hands or lead them about.

There was a second maxim—there were only two—which the wise men enshrined at Delphi, the second of the first fruits of wisdom: "Nothing in excess." It sounds like a practical maxim, one that has to do with conduct. It is that and, as such, recommends temperance and moderation in whatever one does. But it is also an intellectual maxim and, as such, recommends steadiness of outlook on the world. So we may put down steadiness of mind as the second principle in the practice of philosophy, self-knowledge being the first. The two do not go well apart from each other. They are supplemental. The first is a direction inward and the second a direction outward. They define, thus, an attitude towards the self, on the one hand, and towards the world, on the other. They combine to give unity to the practice of philosophy. To have a steady mind is to keep one's balance or not lose one's mental equilibrium when confronted with what the world seems to be when it is explored and contemplated. I might illustrate this by a story, but I admire that story of our first parents so much that I would leave it without a rival. I could, for example, use the story of Job, for that thundering voice from the cloud: "Where wast thou when I laid the foundations of the earth?" was certainly a challenge to Job to have a steady mind.

I begin, however, with a quotation from a letter which a friend, interested in philosophy, recently wrote from the desert of Arizona. Here is the quotation: "After a heavy rain, which comes about twice a year, all sorts of beautiful wild flowers spring up in the sands and rocks, primroses, verbenas, and lilies. They have been latent in the desert all the time, and only need the life-giving rain to make them blossom." These words bring a delightful picture before the imagination. I do not quote them for that reason, however, although the delightful picture is worth sharing. I quote them to illustrate steadiness of mind. Desert and flowers and rain may be taken as symbols of many things. We have only to put other words in their places to get a variety of illustrations. Would one have a steady mind in a desert if one saw the desert only and not also the possibilities of flowers after rain? The illustration is poetical and I always hate to mar what is poetry by trying to reduce it to some general principle, stated barely and robbed of its appeal to the imagination. When a thing is seen poetically, a general principle rarely looks lovely. Yet I must say, in the interest of developing my theme, that there are many possible pictures of the world and that the practice of philosophy would counsel a steady mind and not a forgetful mind when looking at them. This principle also is in need of some reduction to particulars.

There are many people today, as there have been in times past, who, like artists, are busy painting pictures for us to look at, pictures of the universe, of Europe, of America, of Russia, of India, of the Great War, of education, of marriage, of love, of religion, of sex. They are painted in all sorts of colours and with the evident intention of making a particular impression on those that look at them. There is need of great steadiness of mind in wandering through that art gallery. The emotional experience can readily be blinding. There is need of the cultivated habit of seeing what is on the canvas and what possibilities are left out—the desert *and* the flowers or the flowers *and* the desert. This means much more than seeing both sides of a question, for desert and flowers are not two sides of any question. A desert is a desert and a flower is a flower. The world contains them both as quite genuine in themselves apart from contrast. The one is not one side of something of which the other is the other side. Steadiness of mind sees, not disjunctions but conjunctions, not "either, or" but "both, and." If one paints the world as a desert, he has left out the flowers, and if he paints it as a flower, he has left out the desert. The same is true of Russia and sex. Both are desert and flower. This is important if there is not to be too much of something or other. I fear that I am getting seduced by poetry, for I was about to say that what is needed, is neither desert nor flower, but rain. Perhaps I ought not to have quoted from that letter, for after desert and flowers and rain have been said, it seems that the essential thing about steadiness of mind has been said. But let us forget desert and flowers and rain—only please don't quite forget them. I want to say something about adjectives and about the universe.

Adjectives can be great disturbers of steadiness of mind. I sometimes wonder if the grammarian who invented the name for them was not conscious of this, for an "adjective" is something which is thrown at something else. Of course all adjectives do not impress one as being hurled at the things or people to which they may be attached, but there are certain of them which, from time to time, are so thrown about that people seem to be either merrily engaged in catching them or warily engaged in dodging them. Different times have their different favourites. There is just now, for example, the adjective "American." It is thrown at people and things promiscuously both by ourselves and foreigners. There seems to be interest in it pretty much all over the world. Foreigners come here to tell us what it means and write books in which we and their compatriots can read about it. Some of us are engaged in confirming by our own actions and books what these foreigners say and others of us try to set them right by telling them what we ourselves think the adjective means. There seems to be a widespread notion that whatever it means, it is always one hundred per cent. It is a theme for many lectures instead of for a part of one. But this is an institute of arts and sciences. Here it is pertinent to ask if it is a mark of wisdom either in ourselves or foreigners to throw the adjective "American" as it is so currently thrown, with a scope mounting to one hundred per cent, at art, literature, culture, philosophy, manners, morals, money, and murders? Does it promote steadiness of mind in us when we look at ourselves and our world neighbours, or in them when they look at us and themselves? Is not most of it nonsense and triviality? And a kind of nonsense and triviality of which no people on the face of the earth is anywhere near a one hundred per cent illustration? For our part, it is natural and human to let the heart glow with pride when an American distinguishes himself in any walk of life. It becomes us to love our land as others love theirs. But it seems at times as if a great part of the world and many of our own members were turning an adjective which we love and honour into a missile to make us dizzy. There is plenty of room here for the practice of steadiness of mind.

Once started with adjectives which are used like missiles to shake our judgment and not as words to qualify what we mean, where shall we stop? Freudian, conditional, psycho-analytic, Victorian, mid-Victorian, Bolshevik, revolutionary, reactionary, conservative, Puritan, ascetic, liberal, modern, materialistic, sexual, democratic—all such are challenges to have a steady mind. They are fighting and frightening adjectives. They rarely qualify in any helpful way what we do. They tend to make people either timid or reckless. There is something both silly and pathetic in seeing in the natural affection between children and parents an Oedipus complex and in looking upon self-restraint and discipline as an ascetic practice which robs life of its buoyancy. Steadiness of mind would let the fighting and the frightening adjectives go by and self-knowledge would make it clear whether an adjective was used to steady or to frighten or to unnerve.

Now I turn to the universe. It is news. Journalists have discovered it. We are no longer surprised on reading in the morning paper a dispatch from Europe or California that the picture of the universe has been retouched. Eddington, Jeans, Einstein, DeSitter, Millikan, Heisenberg, Michelson, and Morley are names that make news and the portraits of these men appear in the papers. Vast distances, light-years, the galactic system, gravitation, cosmic rays, the velocity of light, the structure of the atom, with such colours as these, the pictures of heaven and earth are painted. Every effort seems to be made to make us cosmically conscious, to make us conscious of the world in which we live, in terms of physics and astronomy. The universe around us and even the table at which we write or eat our breakfast are described in terms of ions, electrons, rays, quantums, mass, and so on, terms we do not ordinarily use in describing New York City. It is an extraordinary description. It calls for great steadiness of mind. The picture of the universe is a very imposing picture and in looking at imposing pictures there is danger of being imposed upon. The seat of that danger is not in the picture, but in ourselves, in letting ourselves be so impressed by the picture that we forget what is not there, or, remembering the excluded things, turn the picture to the wall as not worth looking at. Neither of these actions is a sign of wisdom. A mind that cultivates the habit of steadiness would gladly welcome these pictures and try to understand them, but it would never be so deluded or so frightened that it would suppose that they change the face of nature or the character of human life in any essential respect. They are pictures of the world in which we live, but not at all pictures of our living in it. They create no conflict between science and life. They enable man, they do not belittle him. To say this, to affirm that there is no conflict between science and life, is not to express a hope or a faith, not to offer a comfort to troubled souls. It is to express a fact.

The universe is a pretty large thing, much larger than the United States of America. There is no doubt in my mind—and I do not see how there can be any doubt in anybody's mind—that it contains atoms or something very much like them. The evidence for that is good. The universe contains much more. It contains people, for example. Now what people do is just as interesting and just as important as what atoms do. For the people it is far more important, for, when we think of people, the burning question about the atom is What will people do with it when they find it? The atom will not and can not tell them. It may reveal to them a new world of possibilities, but it will never tell them what to do with that world. The actions of people as people are not the actions of atoms. You have only to read a book about atoms to discover that this is so. You will not find that the actions of the atoms are described as going to church or to school or to congress. But that is just the way the actions of people are described. Describe people in terms of the atom and we learn absolutely nothing about going to church, school, or congress. Describe the atom in terms of these goings and we learn absolutely nothing about it. This is not theory or faith or comfort. It is just fact. We may wish that we had a theory to explain why this is just so, but if we suppose that we must have a theory first before we can recognize that it is so and act on the recognition of it, it would be a blessing for us to hear a voice thundering from the clouds: "Where wast thou when I laid the foundations of the earth?" That might help to steady our minds.

Theories of life and the world which are called philosophical, are one thing; the love of wisdom, which is called philosophy, is a different thing. The theories call for much knowledge. The love calls for practice and the answer to this call does not have to wait until the knowledge is acquired and the theories have had their say. No theory is required in order to practise knowing one's own mind or to practise steadiness of outlook on the world. These, the first fruits of wisdom, may be eaten by every Adam and every Eve without disobedience or shame and without the fear of losing paradise.

THE PREFACE TO MORALS*

THERE is on page nine of Walter Lippmann's *A Preface to Morals* a sentence which as *the* preface to morals has no rival whatever. After portraying the modern man who has ceased to believe without ceasing to be credulous, hanging as it were between heaven and earth, and at rest nowhere, Mr. Lippmann has this to say of him: "There is no theory of the meaning and value of events which he is compelled to accept, but he is none the less compelled to accept the events."

That sentence interrupted my reading of the book. It lost its context. It made me forget the modern man and made me think of every man. It took on the character of an oracle, the authoritative utterance of a god of whom pilgrims had asked a revelation to end their perplexities: "There is no theory of the meaning and value of events which you are compelled to accept, but you are none the less compelled to accept the events." Thus personally addressed, this oracle did not prompt me to question its truth; it prompted me to follow its lead. I became so occupied with this that it seemed that I was not reading a book peculiarly relevant to the modern situation, but that I was reading about a great episode in which every man plays his part in response to that oracle as his cue. We are compelled to accept events. There is no doubt of that. They are what they are and they operate as they do. We deal with them as best we can. They clamour for attention. To get out of the way of one is to get in the way of another. There is no escape from them while life lasts, and we often wonder if there is escape from them when life is over. They make of living a mixture of good and evil, happiness and misery. We assign to them degrees of importance as they affect our well-being. Yet our fate seems to be in their hands, for it is by events we are mastered in the end. Yes,

* In the *Yale Review,* Vol. XX (1931), pp. 691-704.

we are compelled to accept events, but among their number is to be counted the oracle itself as an eventual issue of trying to think the matter through.

I am sensible of some trouble with the verb "compel." Obviously we are not compelled to accept events without doing something about them. We do or can go to a doctor when we are ill or to the experienced when we need guidance. We are not helpless in the hands of events, but our freedom here is, in the end, no more than the acceptance of one set of events as against another. We are helped only by being in their hands, and this is where the compulsion resides. Again, beliefs are sometimes said to be compelling and forced upon us against our will. Theories of the meaning and value of events have been, and are, held with unshaken and perhaps unshakable confidence by many who find them irresistible. Indeed, it may be said that some such theory, even if inarticulately expressed, every man is compelled to have. The moment he begins to justify himself, either to himself or others, he is set on its way. These facts need not be doubted. They would convict the oracle of error and prove it to be no oracle at all were it true that the compulsion here did not vary in its character, its motivations, and its results. Fear, desire, shame, hope, the pressure of authority and tradition, the conventions of society and the intellectual temper of associates may compel acceptance when acceptance would otherwise be denied. Every man—certainly I myself—can confess that he has sometimes accepted a theory because he was afraid of what would be said of him if he did not, and sometimes because he was afraid that a glory might leave the earth. Some faith to cling to may often be a poignant necessity in one's life, but the character of the faith is determined by the character of the necessity. Faiths born of exuberance and the fullness of life are born in that way. Circumstances may compel and the character of their compulsion determine the character of the theory accepted. And this is abundantly confirmed when we examine the results of these compulsions, the theories which spring up as a consequence of them. They are all equally acceptable if we disregard the circumstances which produced them. They become rivals for acceptance when these circumstances are taken into account. If among them all there were one which of itself compelled and forced the intellect to assent, so that by it the meaning and value of events were made unmistakably clear, it might be read even by him who runs. Such a theory may be desired, but it is not possessed in human experience.

The oracle is, then, to be read in the light of this experience. We are compelled to accept the fall of the apple, but we are not compelled to accept the theory of gravitation. We are compelled to accept the rising and setting of the sun, but we are not compelled to accept either the Ptolemaic or Copernican astronomy. We are compelled to accept the events made evident by scientific research, but we are not compelled to accept a theory of these events. Experience and history are the proof of all this. And the same contrast between facts and events on the one hand and theories and interpretations on the other, confronts us when we pass from such impersonal illustrations to those more personal. Sex we must accept, but no theory of it; a soul in each of us, but no theory of it; the moral differences and conflicts in human society, but no theory of them; the religious beliefs and practices the world over, but no theory of them. All such facts and events define in clear and unmistakable terms the kind of circumstances under which we have to lead our intimate and personal lives. We can not escape them and still live. But when it comes to dealing with them in terms of a theory of their significance and value which is as clear and unmistakable as they are, then history and experience have none to offer. They give us the oracle instead. And it may now be seen that the oracle is no respecter of theories. It recognizes no distinction between the scientific, the moral, and the religious. It embraces them all and casts suspicion on the habit of mind which fosters the belief that the adjectives "scientific," "moral," and "religious" make a mighty difference in the matter of acceptability.

Suppose, I find myself asking, there were a theory of the meaning and value of events which we were compelled to accept, what would be the consequence? Questions contrary to fact are difficult to answer. This one, however, is somewhat relieved by the circumstance that adoption of any theory of meaning and value has consequences which can be examined. Once adopted, the theory does compel. There are many such theories, each with its company of adherents. They may have much in common. They may often be tolerant of one another, but at the last, each has its exclusive particularity, without which it would lose its character. Here it demands all or nothing. Here it is stubborn and imparts its stubbornness to those who hold it. They obey, not because they choose, but because they must. They are compelled to accept. Such is the effect of a compelling theory. At the extremity, there is no choice under it. There is a choice only between it and some other. I have been told, but I do not know whether it is true, that under the theory that events are all for God's glory, candidates for the Christian ministry were sometimes asked as a crucial test of their faith if they would be willing to be damned for the glory of God. It was a crucial test, for with a negative answer faith in the theory vanished. An affirmative answer in a particular case might be eased by the egotistic expectation that God would not demand a sacrifice so extreme, but there were the damned to witness to God's glory.

The ultimate consequences of a compelling theory are thus hazardous for the theory itself. They demand the virtue of consistency, but they provoke the prudential question of transferring that virtue to another allegiance. This is the story of human experience. Choices tend at last to ultimate breaking-points. It is a familiar story. I often wonder at the way we play with it, finding delight in its representation in literature and on the stage. We dramatize it, bringing laughter to our lips and tears to our eyes over the fate of imaginary creatures caught in the entanglement of their own choices. The broken promise, the broken vow, the broken faith, which are comic or tragic enough as realities in the day's work, become themes for an ideal sublimation to enchant us in our moments of leisure. Art comes to rival nature in our enthusiasms so that we sometimes give greater honour to him who paints life well than to him who lives it well. Although the business of life is living—the compelled acceptance of events and the dealing with these for better or worse—we love commentaries on it, philosophies of it, and even agonized renderings of it. We know what living is—birth, food, sleep, work, joy, sorrow, love, death, yet we want to be shown what it is. Its natural opposite is death, but our favourite opposites are art, literature, science, morals, and religion. And not content with dramatizing our own lives, we dramatize the universe and tell stories of its entanglement in its fate.

I must not, however, forget the oracle and be diverted from it by letting a picture of our idiosyncrasy possess my imagination. Picture and oracle may be put side by side and the question asked whether the picture could be drawn if the oracle were not sound. If there were a theory of the meaning and value of events which we were compelled to accept, would there be any interest whatever in the picture or any excitement about it? Would there be any interest even in the theory? It is, doubtless, better to be certain than perplexed in a perplexing world, but in a world of certainty, there would be nothing to be perplexed about. If there were a theory of the meaning and value of events which we were compelled to accept, it seems certain that there would go out of life the elements which give it the meaning and value which it evidently possesses without any theory at all to support them.

The absence of such a theory seems, therefore, to be a matter of some importance. I confess that I grow more and more astonished at those who seem to find in the oracle the last word in despair and fondly suppose that we should be much better off if the oracle were not true. I must believe that they have not sounded the matter to the bottom. There is a popular literature of disillusionment and defeat. There is much publication of the devastating effect of modern science and modern criticism on man's moral and religious life. Old illusions are now gone, and there are no new illusions to take their place.

> Achilles ponders in his tent.
> The kings of modern thought are dumb.
> Silent they are, but not content,
> And wait to see the future come.

All this may describe a mood. We may, with Mr. Krutch, label it "the modern temper," when we forget the many who do not share it and who may yet claim to be intelligent and modern and to have emancipated minds. But a show of hands in a matter of this kind is not proper. Dispute about a label is unprofitable. It is, however, pertinent to ask whether the oracle is the last word in disillusionment and despair or the first word in sanity and wisdom. Is it the end of the philosophy of life or the beginning of it?

Taking it as a beginning one may discover in it a very precise definition of what morality is. A precise definition is never discovered by comparing the shifting laws, customs, rules of conduct, or religions which diversify mankind into alien groups the world over. These are what they are, instruments of administration and control or of edification and spirituality. They are brought to bear on the moral situation in the interest of regulating or sanctifying it. But the moral situation is there first. The verbal kinship between the words "morals" and "morality," or the fact that a logician may see in the latter the abstract of the former, ought not to be allowed to obscure a very concrete and a very evident distinction in the facts to which these words are relevant. To be obliged to accept events, to work with them and adjust them in order to live well, and to do this without being compelled to accept a theory of their meaning and value, is something very real and very concrete, and something very different from having shifting opinions and beliefs, or living up to a code or worshipping a god. It is this compulsion which makes men make morals and which makes them religious. It is not the other way around, as if this compulsion were the product of legislative authority or priestly craft. Human history can not be adequately read in that fashion, for it is the initial compulsion to morality in us all that gives the king and priest their power. To get the distinction between morals and morality, the situation defined by the use of power and the situation defined by the oracle should be put side by side. There is then no mistaking the difference. Morality is then self-revealed.

In view of this revelation it is very far from a just and realistic picture of human beings to see in them ultimately the victims of caprice, folly, or illusion, desperately trying to decide whether they ought to be Puritans or libertines, ascetics or hedonists, rigorists or opportunists, theists or atheists, whether they should keep the commandments or break them, and being unable to decide with any confidence beyond their own biased, wilful, or egotistic assurance of it. This is not enough. Nor is that nobler attitude enough which sensitive and sympathetic, yet robust withal, stands like a rock stoically four-square to all the winds that blow, hearing above the tumult the whisper of Marcus Aurelius, "You can end it when you will." There is not enough until there is clear recognition that without the oracle human life would not be a moral event at all. Then we strike bottom. Then we may confidently put over against the picture of our defeatists and our stoics, the picture of that soul in Plato's *Republic* who, having spent a thousand years in heaven where everything was decided for him, made a wreck of his next life on earth. Human life in its own terms, without any supplementation or explanation, is a moral event in the universe. All the evidence at our command goes to support this without a shadow of doubt. No theory of it, no speculation about it, no cosmology which the wit of man has ever framed, has altered by one jot this its basal character. It persists in being precisely what it is. We may not like it, we may rebel against it, we may wish it otherwise, we may make theories to justify or explain it, but all this is renewed evidence of its basal character. If we come into the world for any purpose which can be clearly defined, that purpose is that we should illustrate a moral life. If we come into the world for no purpose at all, we illustrate such a life none the less. It was such before we began to think about it, and it remains such when our thinking is through. The oracle *is* the preface to morals. It defines a beginning and not an end.

The acceptance of the oracle as the preface to morals is not a confession of intellectual defeat. It is, rather, the recognition of intellectual freedom and moral power. It involves a habit of mind which can be cultivated, one which, on the negative side, does not look first to a solution of cosmic problems for a solution of human problems, and, on the positive side, looks at the possibilities of human life as affording a good, if not the best, indication of what the cosmos is like.

The practice of framing some system of things, in which man and everything else have their ordered and appointed places, is very ancient and very human. The story of the world is an interesting and fascinating story. The attempt to write it ought not to be set down as wholly futile, for history and experience prove that it is not. It is pertinent to ask, however, how far the solution of human problems is, as a matter of fact, dependent on the solution of cosmic problems. It is all the more pertinent in view of the current promulgation of the opinion that our morals must be all at sea because an inherited system, a cosmology, which made the earth and man the centre of things, has been so progressively shattered since the days of Copernicus.

It can be a healthy exercise for any man with a tendency towards cosmology to review a typical day of his life, from the time he gets up in the morning to the time he goes to bed at night, asking himself how much the solution of cosmic problems has had to do with the solution of the human problems he has met in that one day. Let him review his actions from the most trivial to the most important, neglecting neither the claims of his body nor the propinquity of his neighbour. Let him not neglect the claims of his soul. Let him be saint or sinner, but let him be thorough. Let him search diligently for every instance of which he can truthfully say: "Here my conduct was motivated by the claims of a cosmology which I or others have framed." It is a healthy and an illuminating exercise. That he will admit some such instances is fairly certain, but it is equally certain that they will be few. And it is likely that the more he examines these few, the more clearly he will see that cosmological problems are important for human problems only because human problems are important first. Just because there can be loss of faith and that loss is perilous, just because there can be enfeebling disillusionment, blank despair, excessive exuberance, and cruel bigotry, the moralist needs repeatedly to advise us how little an antecedent cosmology has to do with the concrete business of human living. He renders us no service by pointing out that the cosmologies which science makes leave us hopeless, and the cosmologies which religion makes are illusions.

Indeed, if he is profoundly conscious of that intellectual freedom and moral power which the oracle uncovers, he may profitably pass from human life to life at large. He will insist that every system of things, to be worth the paper it is written on, must make room for living beings since they with all their peculiarities are just as much and just as fully events in the cosmos as the flashing of electricity or the concentration of the hydrogen ion. He will call the natural historian to his aid. Unrolling before us the amazing panorama of life, he will drive home the most obvious of all cosmological facts, namely, this: since the cosmos is equally responsible for everything it produces, none of its products is less a product than any other, and every one of them throws some light on what the cosmos is. With a mixture of malice, irony, and wisdom, he will put to cosmologists such naïve questions as this: Is a mosquito's bite or a bird's song cosmically any more futile, trivial, or meaningless than the polarization of light? Old Xenophanes is credited with saying: "If oxen and lions had hands and could paint, oxen would paint gods like oxen, and lions like lions." The remark has been considered profound. Its profundity is marred by the fact that neither oxen nor lions have hands and neither of them paint. They lack this ministration to their lives and yet live like oxen and lions. They, like the lilies of the field, may have a moral lesson to teach man, the lesson of life at large, the lesson of possibility. In the matter of cosmologies, the choice is not between a scientific cosmology and a religious cosmology, but between no cosmology at all and one which allows life to have precisely the significance and value which it has as a matter of fact.

The light that human living throws upon the cosmos is as good a light as we have. We can not better it. It is part of the cosmos and the cosmos is, obviously, competent to produce it. It can be exceptional or miraculous only when projected against a background which requires it to be exceptional or miraculous. It is natural when nature is conceived to include it. It is supernatural when it and nature are conceived to be ultimately and unintelligibly antithetical. This alternative appears to me to be unescapable. If we do not take human life as a natural event in precisely the same way as we take any other event as natural, then we are forced to deal with it in other terms than the terms of nature. This fact needs more deliberate attention than it often receives. In a good deal of current thinking suggestions of the supernatural are taboo, in spite of the fact that it is just this kind of thinking which involves a distinction between what is and what is not nature.

To insist that life is only accidental to natural processes and that these pursue their inevitable way entirely irrelevant to the fact that they none the less support life, is definitely to exclude life from the realm of nature. To those who take this view, there is a realm which is nature and a realm which is not nature. Into the latter, they contend, go man's thoughts, his literature, his poetry, his morals, and his religion. Since he thinks and writes, and dreams and worries and prays, it ought not to surprise anybody that when he turns cosmologist, he invents a scheme of things which finds no place or date in nature's space and time. If between him and nature there is only separation and indifference, it is not likely that he will look to nature for light on his own separate capacity or on the things which to him are anything but indifferent. If, as against nature, his life is a dream, he can find no possible advantage in being awake.

I do not propose to question this divorce between nature and life, nor to examine the arguments which support it. I am willing to let it stand, for it is by letting it stand that the importance and significance of its implications are disclosed. The moment the processes of nature are defined to be wholly antithetical to the quality and character of life, the distinction between the natural and the supernatural is factually made. If from the point of view of nature, life is without significance and value, no consideration of nature can lend it value and significance. Life deals with these in wholly different terms. It may be true, as William James somewhere suggested, that "we do not cry because we are sorry, but are sorry because we cry," but then the value and significance of sorrow in human life will never be discovered by the study of physiology. Sorrow will do as it does and find expression in language which can not possibly describe the lachrymose glands. It seems to me, consequently, to be anything but surprising that scientists should often be religious or that physicians should sometimes go to church. Nature can not be left wholly free from the language of the emotions without leaving that language relevant to something which is not nature. And the language of the emotions is a good part of the language of men.

But "nature" is a slippery term. In spite of our efforts to restrict it to that field of inquiry which demands the language of quantity and number only, it returns to mock us, as I myself now illustrate by saying that we fall *naturally* into personification. We habitually speak of nature as "she" instead of as "it," owning a mother who does nothing in vain although she follows lines of least resistance. It is difficult indeed so to describe her or conceive her that she becomes wholly alien in character to our character. Neither this difficulty nor the natural habit, however, is any proof that there is not something to be called "nature" which is wholly impersonal and which can be discovered by those methods and expressed in that language which are neither the methods nor the language we employ when dealing with life as a mixture of good and evil, of success and defeat. Yet both are proof of something none the less. They prove, and it seems to me that they prove conclusively, that a wholly impersonal language is not adequate to what the scheme of things is. What can be said in such a language is very far from all that can be said. Indeed it often seems as if nothing said in that impersonal language is wholly intelligible until it is translated into another. We must learn, for example, that $2 + 2 = 4$. But what does that expression mean as something numerical only? I confess that I have spent weary hours and read dreary books in an effort to find out. Yet a child two years old can be led to some suspicion that in two more years it will be four. By operating within the framework which the arithmetical expression describes, the child finds memory, significance, and a prophecy. A language in itself impotent has been translated into a language of promise and power. Here is a type of event we are compelled to accept. The more I consider it, the more it impresses me as the only kind of event in the scheme of things wherein significance and value are found. It is not limited to human experience. It is not limited to things that live. It seems to be found everywhere. The impersonal language of an impersonal nature describes nothing that happens. It describes only the framework or frameworks within which something may or can happen, and it is only as something happens that significance and value can be at all.

This matter may be put in a different way. Our experience and our inquiries are ample proof that the language of quantity and number alone, a language, that is, which deliberately eliminates from its vocabulary terms like "seeking," "finding," "joy," "sorrow," "triumph," "defeat," "purpose," "design," "prophecy," "power," is a language inadequate to the facts and uses of existence. It does not and can not express to the full what existence is. The recognition of this does not impugn the validity or the power of that language. It does, however, make other languages legitimate. There are facts of existence which can be expressed only in such terms as the languages of poetry, art, morals, and religion employ. It is difficult to see how these languages could be if there were nothing in existence to support them. And it is also difficult to see how they could have the character and exactness of the language of quantity and number, and then remain unspoiled. That character would ruin them as effectively as their character ruins it. So far as we seek to get existence properly expressed, we find that our seeking is rewarded only by the use of more languages than one. This also is an event we are compelled to accept, and its acceptance is our most precious possession. In times like ours, or like what ours are said to be, times of unhappy moral perplexity, what is needed is not some new theory of the meaning and value of events which will banish perplexity for a season, but a renewed contemplation of what existence is like. It is the simple and the obvious that needs emphasis, not the complicated and the obscure. And the obvious here calls for a sane and liberal cultivation of the languages of life, a cultivation which recognizes that the purposes these languages serve can never be expressed in a language that says only $2 + 2 = 4$.

Recently I made a pilgrimage to two shrines, Mont Saint Michel and Chartres. It is true that I did not go like the pilgrims of old, on naked or sandalled feet, with a burden on my back and a staff in my hand. I went in luxury, a luxury at which they would have marvelled and which they would have despised, seeing in me an affront to their devotion instead of an illustration of it. Yet I went as a pilgrim. My purpose was devout even if my approach was luxurious. Ever since my reading of the book by Henry Adams, Mont Saint Michel and Chartres have been shrines in my imagination. I had not seen them before. I had read of them and talked of them, and I had been led to believe that if I went there something would happen to me. Henry Adams had invested them with a quality which I had found elsewhere, as in the moving ruins of Tintern Abbey, but had never found with quite that mastering effect which he had led me to believe was to be felt in their presence. At Chartres everything that needs forgiveness seems to be forgiven, and at Mont Saint Michel everything that is difficult seems to find a triumph in its difficulty. Both were built by men, but by men possessed by what they built, men who were but instruments in the hands of forces that mastered them. Under the spell of these shrines, it seemed as if man had never produced them by his art, in an effort to embody his imagination in a structure, but as if nature had produced them, using man for her subtle purposes, as she uses soil and moisture and sunlight, to diversify existence with illustrations of her power.

BIBLIOGRAPHY

BIBLIOGRAPHY

OF ARTICLES AND BOOKS BY FREDERICK J. E. WOODBRIDGE

1894

*THE ARGUMENT FROM DESIGN AS AFFECTED BY THE THEORY OF EVOLUTION. In *Papers, Addresses, and Discussions at the Sixteenth Church Congress in the United States.* New York, Thomas Whittaker, 1894. pp. 193-197.

1896

THE PLACE OF PLEASURE IN A SYSTEM OF ETHICS. *International Journal of Philosophy,* Vol. VII (1896), pp. 475-486.

1901

THE DEPARTMENT OF PHILOSOPHY AT COLUMBIA. *Columbia University Quarterly,* Vol. III (1901), pp. 143-150.

THE DOMINANT CONCEPTION OF THE EARLIEST GREEK PHILOSOPHY. *Philosophical Review,* Vol. X (1901), pp. 359-374.

1902

*WHAT IS PERSONALITY? In *Papers, Addresses, and Discussions at the Twenty-first Church Congress in the United States.* New York, Thomas Whittaker, 1902. pp. 125-130.

1903

THE PHILOSOPHY OF HOBBES IN EXTRACTS AND NOTES COLLECTED FROM HIS WRITINGS. Minneapolis, H. W. Wilson, 1903. xxxvi, 379 pp.

*THE PROBLEM OF METAPHYSICS. *Philosophical Review,* Vol. XII (1903), pp. 367-385.

1904

*THE FIELD OF LOGIC. Proceedings of *St. Louis Congress of Arts and Science,* 1904. Boston, Houghton Mifflin, 1907. Vol. I, pp. 313-330. Also *Science, ns,* Vol. XX (1904), pp. 587-600.

* Appears in this volume.

Herbert Spencer. *Review of Reviews,* Vol. XXIX (1904), pp. 2, 67-70.

Jonathan Edwards. *Philosophical Review,* Vol. XIII (1904), pp. 393-408.

*Review of H. Heath Bawden, *Meaning of the Psychical from the Point of View of the Functional Psychology. Journal of Philosophy, Psychology, and Scientific Methods,* Vol. I (1904), pp. 386-387.

Review of Sir Leslie Stephen, *Hobbes. Journal of Philosophy, Psychology, and Scientific Methods,* Vol. I (1904), pp. 636-641.

1905

*The Nature of Consciousness. *Journal of Philosophy, Psychology, and Scientific Methods,* Vol. II (1905), pp. 119-125.

*Of What Sort Is Cognitive Experience? *Journal of Philosophy, Psychology, and Scientific Methods,* Vol. II (1905), pp. 573-576.

Review of George Santayana, *Reason in Common Sense* and *Reason in Society. New York Evening Post,* July 1, 1905.

1906

*The Problem of Consciousness. In *Studies in Philosophy and Psychology: the Charles E. Garman Commemorative Volume.* Boston, Houghton Mifflin, 1906. pp. 139-166.

Review of George A. Hight, *Unity of Will. New York Evening Post,* June 23, 1906.

Review of George Santayana, *Reason in Science. New York Evening Post,* March 10, 1906.

Review of T. B. Strong (ed.), *Lectures on the Method of Science. Journal of Philosophy, Psychology, and Scientific Methods,* Vol. III (1906), pp. 692-695.

1907

*Naturalism and Humanism. *Hibbert Journal,* Vol. VI (1907), pp. 1-17.

Pragmatism and Education. *Educational Review,* Vol. XXXIV (1907), pp. 227-240.

Review of Alexander T. Ormand, *Concepts of Philosophy. Nation,* Vol. 84 (1907), pp. 108-109.

Review of Simon S. Laurie, *Synthetica: Being Meditations Epistemological and Ontological. Nation,* Vol. 84 (1907), pp. 390-401.

* Appears in this volume.

1908

CONSCIOUSNESS AND MEANING. *Psychological Review,* Vol. XV (1908), pp. 397-398.

*METAPHYSICS. A lecture delivered at Columbia University in the series on Science, Philosophy and Art, March 18, 1908. New York, Columbia University Press, 1908. 26 pp.

*PERCEPTION AND EPISTEMOLOGY. *Essays Philosophical and Psychological in Honor of William James.* New York, Longmans Green, 1908. pp. 137-166.

Review of Borden P. Bowne, *Personalism. Nation,* Vol. 86 (1908), pp. 559-560.

Review of Josiah Royce, *The Philosophy of Loyalty. Nation,* Vol. 87 (1908), pp. 17-18.

Review of Leonard T. Hobhouse, *Morals in Evolution. Political Science Quarterly,* Vol. XXIII (1908), pp. 741-745.

Review of Walter B. Pillsbury, *Attention. Nation,* Vol. 86 (1908), pp. 406-407.

Review of William S. Lilly, *Modernism. Nation,* Vol. 87 (1908), pp. 16-17.

1909

*CONSCIOUSNESS, THE SENSE ORGANS, AND THE NERVOUS SYSTEM. *Journal of Philosophy, Psychology, and Scientific Methods,* Vol. VI (1909), pp. 449-455.

Review of Lorenzo M. Billia, *Has the Psychological Laboratory Proved Helpful? Journal of Philosophy, Psychology, and Scientific Methods,* Vol. VI (1909), pp. 438-440.

1910

*THE PROBLEM OF TIME IN MODERN PHILOSOPHY. *Journal of Philosophy, Psychology, and Scientific Methods,* Vol. VII (1910), pp. 410-416.

THE STUDY OF PHILOSOPHY. *Columbia University Quarterly,* Vol. XIII (1910), pp. 39-45.

1911

EMPIRICISM. Article in *A Cyclopedia of Education*, Vol. II (1911), pp. 442-444.

* Appears in this volume.

ETHICS AND EDUCATION. Article in *A Cyclopedia of Education*, Vol. II (1911), pp. 500-509.

THE ENTERPRISE OF LEARNING. *Amherst Graduates' Quarterly*, Vol. I (1911), pp. 12-21. Reprinted in *Columbia University Quarterly*, Vol. XIV (1912), pp. 249-256.

*NATURAL TELEOLOGY. In *Essays in Modern Theology and Related Subjects: the Charles A. Briggs Commemorative Volume*, New York, Scribners, 1911. pp. 307-326.

Review of O. Habert, *La Religion de la Grèce antique. American Journal of Theology*, Vol. XV (1911), p. 330.

Speech at Dr. Butler's Dinner in celebration of the tenth year of Dr. Butler's service in the Presidency of the University and of the twenty-first since his election as first Dean of the Faculty of Philosophy. *Columbia University Quarterly*, Vol. XIII (1911), *June Supplement*, p. 29.

1912

*CONSCIOUSNESS AND OBJECT. *Philosophical Review*, Vol. XXI (1912), pp. 633-640.

*THE DISCOVERY OF THE MIND. *Columbia University Quarterly*, Vol. XV (1912), pp. 1-10.

*THE ENTERPRISE OF LEARNING. *Amherst Graduates' Quarterly*, Vol. I (1912), pp. 12-21. Also *Columbia University Quarterly*, Vol. XIV (1912), pp. 249-259.

*EVOLUTION. *Philosophical Review*, Vol. XXI (1912), pp. 137-151.

JOHN LOCKE. Article in *A Cyclopedia of Education*, Vol. IV (1912), pp. 58-59.

PHILOSOPHY. In *Greek Literature*. New York, Columbia University Press, 1912. pp. 209-228.

*PLACES AND MEN. *Columbia University Quarterly*, Vol. XIV (1912), pp. 113-119.

SEVENTY-FIVE YEARS OF ALPHA DELTA PHI IN AMHERST COLLEGE. In *An Account of the Celebration on the 75th Anniversary of the Establishment of the Amherst Chapter of Alpha Delta Phi, February, 1912*. pp. 27-32.

1913

*THE BELIEF IN SENSATIONS. *Journal of Philosophy, Psychology, and Scientific Methods*, Vol. X (1913), pp. 599-608.

DAVID HUME. Article in *Encyclopedia of Religion and Ethics*, Vol. VI (1913), pp. 867-870.

* Appears in this volume.

*THE DECEPTION OF THE SENSES. *Journal of Philosophy, Psychology, and Scientific Methods,* Vol. X (1913), pp. 5-15.

THE MORAL ASPECTS OF PRAGMATISM. *Church Congress Journal,* 1913, pp. 200-205.

THOMAS HOBBES. Article in *Encyclopedia of Religion and Ethics,* Vol. VI (1913), pp. 728-731.

1914

FAITH AND PRAGMATISM. *Chronicle,* Vol. XIV (1914), pp. 319-323.

1915

THE UNIVERSITY AND THE PUBLIC. *Educational Review,* Vol. XLIX (1915), pp. 109-125.

1916

THE PURPOSE OF HISTORY. New York, Columbia University Press, 1916. vii, 89 pp.

1917

COMMENT ON PROFESSOR BROWN'S "MATTER AND ENERGY." *Journal of Philosophy, Psychology, and Scientific Methods,* Vol. XIV (1917), pp. 373-379.

THE IMPORTANCE OF PHILOSOPHY. *Columbia University Quarterly,* Vol. XIX (1917), pp. 367-383.

*STRUCTURE. *Journal of Philosophy, Psychology, and Scientific Methods,* Vol. XIV (1917), pp. 680-688.

1918

BERKELEY'S REALISM. In *Studies in the History of Ideas,* Vol. I. New York, Columbia University Press, 1918. pp. 188-215.

CARRYING ON. *Columbia Alumni News,* Vol. X (1918), pp. 287-289.

THE FUTURE PLACE OF THE HUMANITIES IN EDUCATION. *Journal of Proceedings and Addresses of the Association of American Universities,* 1918. pp. 97-100.

THE "ISSUES OF THE WAR" COURSE IN THE S.A.T.C. SCHEDULE. *Columbia Alumni News,* Vol. X (1918), pp. 217-219.

THE ORGANIZATION AND INTERNATIONAL RELATIONSHIP OF UNIVERSITIES AND COLLEGES. *Journal of Proceedings and Addresses of the Association of American Universities,* 1918. pp. 46-47.

* Appears in this volume.

1919

PLURALISM. Article in *Encyclopedia of Religion and Ethics,* Vol. X (1919), pp. 66-70.

1920

HERBERT SPENCER. *New York Evening Post,* April 27, 1920.

THE SOCIAL ENVIRONMENT OF THE GRADUATE STUDENT. *Journal of Proceedings and Addresses of the Association of American Universities,* 1920. pp. 71-78.

1921

AFTER THIRTY-FIVE YEARS. *Atlantic Monthly,* Vol. 127 (1921), pp. 721-731.

AMHERST IN EDUCATION. *Amherst Graduates' Quarterly,* Vol. X (1921), pp. 253-263.

ARMISTICE DAY ADDRESS. *Fortnightly Bulletin* of the Institute of Arts and Sciences, Columbia University, Vol. IX, No. 4, 1921.

*MIND DISCERNED. *Journal of Philosophy,* Vol. XVIII (1921), pp. 337-347.

Review of *The Letters of William James. Yale Review,* Vol. XI (1921), pp. 182-187.

THE SUPPLY OF ADEQUATELY TRAINED UNIVERSITY TEACHERS. In *Educational Problems in College and University.* University of Michigan Press, 1921. pp. 159-174.

1923

ANNUAL REPORT OF THE DEAN OF THE FACULTIES OF POLITICAL SCIENCE, PHILOSOPHY AND PURE SCIENCE. *Columbia University Bulletin of Information,* 24th series, No. 6, 1923, 10 pp.; 25th series, No. 7, 1924, 7 pp.; 26th series, No. 6, 1925, 12 pp.; 27th series, No. 6, 1926, 12 pp.; 28th series, No. 6, 1927, 22 pp.; 29th series, No. 8, 1928, 12 pp.

1924

EDUCATION AND LEARNING. *Minnesota Alumni Weekly,* Vol. XXIV (1924), pp. 179-191.

HOW TO MAINTAIN STANDARDS WITHOUT EXCESSIVE STANDARDIZATION. *School and Society,* Vol. XX (1924), pp. 767-773.

* Appears in this volume.

*MENTAL DEVELOPMENT. *Journal of Philosophy,* Vol. XXI (1924), pp. 449-456.

Review of Alfred W. Martin, *A Philosophy of Life and Its Spiritual Values. Journal of Philosophy,* Vol. XXI (1924), pp. 27-28.

Review of Angus S. Woodburne, *Psychological Tests of Mental Abilities. Journal of Philosophy,* Vol. XXI (1924), p. 364.

Review of C. F. Russell, *Religion and Natural Law. Journal of Philosophy,* Vol. XXI (1924), p. 448.

Review of Charles H. Haskins, *The Rise of Universities. Journal of Philosophy,* Vol. XXI (1924), p. 28.

Review of François d'Hautefeuille, *Le Privilege de l'intelligence. Journal of Philosophy,* Vol. XXI (1924), pp. 139-140.

Review of George Santayana, *The Unknowable. Journal of Philosophy,* Vol. XXI (1924), pp. 55-56.

Review of M. Laurent Dugas, *Le Philosophe Théodule Ribot. Journal of Philosophy,* Vol. XXI (1924), p. 336.

1925

*BEHAVIOR. *Journal of Philosophy,* Vol. XXII (1925), pp. 402-411.

1926

*CREATION. *Atlantic Monthly,* Vol. 137 (1926), No. 3, pp. 335-342.

THE REALM OF MIND. New York, Columbia University Press, 1926. 141 pp.

Review of George Santayana, *Dialogues in Limbo. Atlantic Monthly,* Vol. 137 (1926), *Atlantic's Bookshelf,* p. 12.

1927

ADDRESS AT NEWBOLD MEMORIAL MEETING. In *Proceedings of a Meeting Held at the University of Pennsylvania on December 1, 1926, in Memory of William Romaine Newbold.* Baltimore, Waverly Press, 1927.

THE OLDS ADMINISTRATION, 1923-1927. *Amherst Graduates' Quarterly,* Vol. XVI (1927), pp. 249-257.

1928

CONTINENT AND ISLAND. *Revista de estudios hispánicos,* Tomo I (1928), pp. 235-240.

* Appears in this volume.

PHILOSOPHY AND MODERN LIFE. In *The Creative Intelligence and Modern Life*, University of Colorado Press, 1928. pp. 35-67.

*SUBSTANCE. *Journal of Philosophy,* Vol. XXV (1928), pp. 685-691.

1929

CONTRASTS IN EDUCATION. Three lectures given under the provisions of the Julius and Rosa Sachs Endowment Fund. Bureau of Publications, Teachers College, Columbia University, 1929. 50 pp.

*THE PROMISE OF PRAGMATISM. *Journal of Philosophy,* Vol. XXVI (1929), pp. 541-552.

SOME IMPLICATIONS OF LOCKE'S PROCEDURE. In *Essays in Honor of John Dewey*, New York, Henry Holt, 1929. pp. 414-425.

THE SON OF APOLLO. Boston, Houghton Mifflin, 1929. 272 pp.

1930

Address to the *Ninety-eighth Convention of Alpha Delta Phi*, Portland, Maine, January 1, 1930. 6 pp.

A COMMENT ON COLLEGE ADMINISTRATION. *American Philosophical Society Proceedings,* Vol. LXIX (1930), pp. 281-294.

*CONFESSIONS. In *Contemporary American Philosophy,* Vol. II. New York, Macmillan, 1930. pp. 415-438.

* EXPERIENCE AND DIALECTIC. *Journal of Philosophy,* Vol. XXVII (1930), pp. 264-271.

HAPPILY FOUNDED. *Columbia University Quarterly,* Vol. XXII (1930), pp. 118-130.

HERBERT GARDINER LORD. 1849-1930. *Columbia University Quarterly,* Vol. XXII (1930), pp. 222-225.

[THOMAS] HOBBES, SELECTIONS. Edited, with an Introduction by F. J. E. Woodbridge. New York, Scribners, 1930. xxx, 418 pp.

WHAT IS EXPECTED OF A COLLEGE? *Amherst Graduates' Quarterly,* Vol. XIX (1930), pp. 78-87.

1931

*IMPLICATIONS OF THE GENETIC METHOD. *Proceedings of the Seventh International Congress of Philosophy,* 1931. pp. 65-69.

*THE NATURE OF MAN. *Columbia University Quarterly,* Vol. XXIII (1931), pp. 402-419; also, *American Scholar,* Vol. I (1932), pp. 81-96.

*THE PRACTICE OF PHILOSOPHY. *The Institute Magazine* (Columbia University), Vol. III (1931), pp. 8-22.

* **Appears in this volume.**

*The Preface to Morals. *Yale Review,* Vol. XX (1931), pp. 691-704.

1932

Spinoza. *Columbia University Quarterly,* Vol. XXV (1932), pp. 107-119.

*Tangling Cognition. *Journal of Philosophy,* Vol. XXIX (1932), pp. 688-690.

1933

The Social and Educational Significance of the Growth in Numbers of the Graduate School. *Journal of Proceedings and Addresses of the Association of American Universities,* 1933. pp. 100-110.

1934

*The Universe of Light. *Journal of Philosophy,* Vol. XXXI (1934), pp. 15-21.

1935

*An Approach to the Theory of Nature. *Howison Memorial Lecture for 1935.* Given at the University of California, Berkeley, California, February 8, 1935.

Locke's Essay. In *Studies in the History of Ideas,* Vol. III. New York, Columbia University Press, 1935. pp. 243-251.

1936

*The Problem of Consciousness Again. *Journal of Philosophy,* Vol. XXXIII (1936), pp. 561-568.

* Appears in this volume.

INDEX

INDEX